Studies in Global Justice

STUDIES IN GLOBAL JUSTICE

VOLUME 14

Aims and Scope

In today's world, national borders seem irrelevant when it comes to international crime and terrorism. Likewise, human rights, poverty, inequality, democracy, development, trade, bioethics, hunger, war and peace are all issues of global rather than national justice. The fact that mass demonstrations are organized whenever the world's governments and politicians gather to discuss such major international issues is testimony to a widespread appeal for justice around the world.

Discussions of global justice are not limited to the fields of political philosophy and political theory. In fact, research concerning global justice quite often requires an interdisciplinary approach. It involves aspects of ethics, law, human rights, international relations, sociology, economics, public health, and ecology. Springer's new series *Studies in Global Justice* up that interdisciplinary perspective. The series brings together outstanding monographs and anthologies that deal with both basic normative theorizing and its institutional applications. The volumes in the series discuss such aspects of global justice as the scope of social justice, the moral significance of borders, global inequality and poverty, the justification and content of human rights, the aims and methods of development, global environmental justice, global bioethics, the global institutional order and the justice of intervention and war.

Volumes in this series will prove of great relevance to researchers, educators and students, as well as politicians, policy-makers and government officials.

More information about this series at http://www.springer.com/series/6958

Helmut P. Gaisbauer • Gottfried Schweiger
Clemens Sedmak
Editors

Ethical Issues in Poverty Alleviation

Springer

Editors
Helmut P. Gaisbauer
Centre for Ethics and Poverty Research
University of Salzburg
Salzburg, Austria

Gottfried Schweiger
Centre for Ethics and Poverty Research
University of Salzburg
Salzburg, Austria

Clemens Sedmak
Centre for Ethics and Poverty Research
University of Salzburg
Salzburg, Austria

This publication was supported by Academics Stand Against Poverty (ASAP) Austria

ISSN 1871-0409 ISSN 1871-1456 (electronic)
Studies in Global Justice
ISBN 978-3-319-41428-7 ISBN 978-3-319-41430-0 (eBook)
DOI 10.1007/978-3-319-41430-0

Library of Congress Control Number: 2016953345

Printed on acid-free paper

This Springer imprint is published by Springer Nature
The registered company is Springer International Publishing AG Switzerland

Contents

About the Editors and Contributors

Editors

Helmut P. Gaisbauer is Senior Scientist at the Centre for Ethics and Poverty Research, University of Salzburg. Recent publications include (with Gottfried Schweiger and Clemens Sedmak) *Philosophical Explorations of Justice and Taxation*. Dordrecht: Springer 2015; (with Clemens Sedmak) "Neglected Futures. Considering Overlooked Poverty in Europe"; and in the special issue of the *European Journal of Futures Research*, "The Future of Europe", 2014, 2–8.

Gottfried Schweiger is Senior Scientist at the Centre for Ethics and Poverty Research, University of Salzburg, and there the Principal Investigator of the research project "Social Justice and Child Poverty", funded by the Austrian Science Fund (FWF). Recent publications include (with Gunter Graf) "The Subjective Experience of Poverty", in *Northern European Journal of Philosophy* 15 (2) 2015, 148–67, and (with Gunter Graf) *A Philosophical Examination of Social Justice and Child Poverty*. Basingstoke: Palgrave Macmillan 2015.

Clemens Sedmak is FD Maurice Professor of Moral and Social Theology, King's College, London, and Associate Director of the Centre for Ethics and Poverty Research, University of Salzburg. Recent publications include (edited by Elisabeth Kapferer and Andreas Koch) *Strengthening Intangible Infrastructures*. Newcastle upon Tyne: Cambridge Scholars Publishing 2014, and Sustainability: Ethical Perspectives, in C. Weidinger et al. (eds.): *Sustainable Entrepreneurship, CSR, Sustainability, Ethics & Governance*. Berlin-Heidelberg: Springer 2014, 51–65.

Contributors

Txetxu Ausín is Tenured Scientist at the Institute of Philosophy of the Spanish National Research Council in Madrid.

Tendayi Bloom is a Global Justice Program, MacMillan Center, Yale University, New Haven, CT, USA.

Maria del Mar Cabezas is Postdoc at the Centre for Ethics and Poverty Research, University of Salzburg.

Monique Deveaux is Professor and Canada Research Chair in Ethics and Global Social Change, University of Guelph.

Gunter Graf is Postdoc at the international research centre for social and ethical questions and also works at the Centre for Ethics and Poverty Research, University of Salzburg.

Elizabeth Kahn is SNSF Ambizione Fellow at the Faculty of Law, University of Basel, and also JSD Candidate at Columbia Law School.

Elisabeth Kapferer is Centre for Ethics and Poverty Research, University of Salzburg, Salzburg, Austria.

Max Kelly is Senior Lecturer in International and Community Development at Deakin University.

Christian Neuhäuser Institut für Philosophie und Politikwissenschaft, Dortmund, Germany

Joy Paton is an Honorary Associate in the Department of Political Economy, University of Sydney and Senior Research Associate in the School of Social Sciences and Psychology at Western Sydney University.

Thomas Pogge is Leitner Professor of Philosophy and International Affairs as well as the founding Director of the Global Justice Program, Yale University.

Elena Pribytkova is Postdoc at the Faculty of Law, University of Basel, and also JD candidate at Columbia Law School.

Jahel Queralt works as a Postdoc at the Ethics Centre of the University of Zurich.

David Rodríguez-Arias is Ramón y Cajal Research Fellow at the Philosophy I Department of the University of Granada.

Rosana Triviño is Lecturer at the Philosophy of Law Department of the University of A Coruña.

Elisabeth Valiente-Riedl is Deputy Director of the Master of Human Rights and Democratisation, University of Sydney.

Chapter 1
Ethical Issues in Poverty Alleviation: Agents, Institutions and Policies

Helmut P. Gaisbauer, Gottfried Schweiger, and Clemens Sedmak

Abstract In this chapter we introduce the topics of this volume. We start by distinguishing and discussing three issues that are of importance for an ethical reflection on poverty alleviation: the definitions of poverty and poverty alleviation, the normative background theories of poverty alleviation and the identification of the agents and institutions of poverty alleviation. After discussing these we will go on to present a brief overview of the chapters in this volume.

Keywords Poverty • Poverty alleviation • Human rights • Justice • Institutions

1.1 Introduction

In today's world, poverty is one of the most pressing social problems, and it is one that has gained significant and increasing attention from philosophers over the last years. Whilst most of them agree that global poverty is morally wrong and unjust we can find large disagreement on how we should solve this problem and how we should distribute the associated tasks and burdens of poverty eradication. This volume aims to contribute to this literature by focusing on philosophical, and more precisely on ethical issues concerning the conceptualization, design and implementation of poverty alleviation measures from the local to the global level. In this introduction we want to explore three issues that are closely connected with such an ethical exploration of poverty alleviation: the definitions of poverty and poverty alleviation, the normative background theories of poverty alleviation and the identification of the agents and institutions of poverty alleviation. We think every attempt to ethically reflect on poverty alleviation and every attempt to provide ethical guidance for the practice of poverty alleviation has in some way or another to deal with

H.P. Gaisbauer (✉) • G. Schweiger • C. Sedmak
Centre for Ethics and Poverty Research, University of Salzburg,
Mönchsberg 2a, 5020 Salzburg, Austria
e-mail: helmut.gaisbauer@sbg.ac.at; gottfried.schweiger@sbg.ac.at;
clemens.sedmak@sbg.ac.at

H.P. Gaisbauer et al. (eds.), *Ethical Issues in Poverty Alleviation*, Studies in Global Justice 14, DOI 10.1007/978-3-319-41430-0_1

these three issues. As we will see they are not completely separate but are interconnected. Hence, they provide a good starting point for this book.

1.2 Defining Poverty and Poverty Alleviation: Issues of Multidimensionality, Complexity and Ethics

The first issue is that of defining poverty and poverty alleviation. Unfortunately there is no consensus on both questions, but it is clear that they are somehow connected, in a way that every concept of poverty alleviation includes a concept of poverty but not the other way around.

Hence we will begin with the question of what poverty is. In poverty research the distinction between absolute and relative concepts of poverty is sometimes used. Absolute poverty assumes capturing a minimum standard, while relative poverty is measured against the welfare or income level of a particular social context like a particular state. There has been some dispute among poverty researchers about this distinction and which approach is best suited to capture poverty (Sen 1983; Townsend 1985). One absolute concept that is often used in debates about global poverty is the measure of the World Bank, maybe most famously the poverty line of 1.25$ per day (World Bank 2011; see for a critique: Pogge 2009). Using this poverty line around 1.2 billion people were living in severe poverty in 2011. The main idea behind such absolute poverty lines is to capture the minimum income that is necessary to survive. But also other poverty measures have been developed, that go beyond the measurement of income and try to capture the multidimensionality of poverty. For example Sabina Alkire of the Oxford Poverty and Human Development Initiative has developed a Multidimensional Poverty Index (MPI), based on the capability approach, which covers the three dimensions of health, education and standard of living (Alkire 2008). This poverty measures produces different results, like on the one hand in the Democratic Republic of Congo around 87 % of the population lives of less than 1.25$ a day with around 75 % of the population being poor according to the MPI. In Chad on the other hand only 35 % have less than 1.25$ a day but the MPI counts 87 % as poor. Two different examples of so-called relative poverty measures would be the relative income poverty threshold and the concept of material deprivation that are both used by the official statistics office of the European Union (Guio et al. 2012). Relative income poverty describes a person who has less than 60 % of the equalized median income of the country in which he or she resides. And a person is severely materially deprived according to that indicator if he cannot afford four out of nine goods or services, which are deemed necessary for a decent living. As of today these nine goods and services are defined by people who cannot afford to (1) pay their rent or utility bills; (2) keep their home adequately warm; (3) face unexpected expenses; (4) eat meat, fish or a protein equivalent every second day; (5) enjoy a week's holiday away from home once a year; (6) have a car; (7) have a washing machine; (8) have a color TV; or (9) have a telephone. Currently about 48.7 million people in the European Union are severely materially deprived according to this measure, and about 84.1 million live in relative income poverty.

What does that have to do with the ethical issues in poverty alleviation? We think that at least three points are important to make. Firstly, it is necessary to define and measure poverty in order to know what poverty alleviation is in the first place. If we confine poverty to income poverty like the 1.25$ a day line of the World Bank, then the most effective, maybe the only possible, measure of poverty alleviation would be to raise the daily income of these people. This would be effective regardless if that income raise comes from state benefits, development aid or labor. If one agrees that poverty is not only about income but a multidimensional phenomenon that also has something to do with health, housing, education or participation then poverty alleviation would also be more complex. An increase in income will affect some of these areas but not all. A child who has no opportunity to go to school or is not allowed to go because she is a girl would still be poor – at least in that dimension – even if the income of her parents rises. Secondly, and closely connected to the first point, the ethical issues do not begin with poverty alleviation and how the poor should be helped and who should do it. The ethical issues are present in the definition and measurement of poverty itself. There is no neutral poverty definition, which does not rest on certain assumptions about what a decent minimum or a good life or a just society is. Every poverty measure tries to capture something that is of the utmost importance for a decent human life, whether it focuses merely on biological survival, material well-being or social inclusion. This means that the ethical questions begin here. What should be deemed part of such a decent life? How can we define what a human being needs to live a life of a minimum standard? What role should choice and autonomy play in our measures of poverty? Thirdly, also within this distinction of absolute and relative poverty, ethical issues are present. Sometimes it seems that absolute poverty, especially if it is used to identify the bottom billion, the most deprived people in this world, is by definition morally worse than relative poverty. Although we do not want to disagree with such a statement, it says something about the entanglement of ethical judgements and poverty research and poverty alleviation. If one form of poverty is morally worse or more unjust than another this certainly affects how we should design poverty alleviation and what kinds of poverty we should target with higher priority. But there is also another issue present in the distinction between absolute and relative poverty, namely the differentiation between sufficiency and inequality. Both are terms that are very important in ethical debates about justice and morality.

So what is then poverty alleviation? Broadly speaking it is every effort to alleviate the effects of poverty or to help people to escape poverty. Obviously this can be done in many different ways and there is no agreement within poverty research which ways work best. At least three aspects need to be considered in any poverty alleviation measure. (a) What is the target group? The answer to this question is closely tied to the conception of poverty that is used. If only income poverty is deemed relevant, then those who live above the income threshold but are deprived in other areas will not be targeted by poverty alleviation measures. Other restrictions – or decisions that need to be made – are relevant as well: what about illegal migrants? Does the state also provide for these or can and should it restrict its poverty alleviation measures to the regular citizens? It is also an important difference whether poverty alleviation aims to prioritize those who are worst off or if it aims at those who are not so far below the threshold and hence can be helped most effectively to escape poverty. (b) What are the intended effects? Poverty alleviation measures can have multiple intended effects. The aim can be just to push those below above the income threshold regardless of how that is achieved. Or the main goal may not be to increase income but to help them to find employment and to become independent from state money. Poverty alleviation measures that are based on a multidimensional understanding of deprivation will have to acknowledge that it is very difficult to tackle all deprivation simultaneously. Should education, employment, housing or health be prioritized and supported? (c) What is known about the side-effects? Every poverty alleviation measure affects many dimensions of a single life, the local community and if it is a large scale measure maybe even the global community. A good example is the increase in productivity and hence consumption of poor people that affect the environment and may add to ongoing climate changes. On a smaller scale it is possible that well intentioned humanitarian actions of poverty alleviation have a negative impact in the long run. The provision of second-hand clothes for free can destroy local clothing industries.

As one can see in all these three aspects of poverty alleviation we encounter ethical issues that need to be addressed. Under circumstances of scarcity very difficult questions of trade-offs and prioritizing have to be answered. These are present at all levels where poverty alleviation takes place or is supported. An individual in the rich west can only give a certain amount of money but has more than enough options about what to give it for: the beggar on the streets in his neighborhood, the NGO that supports street children in Romania or UNICEF that supports children in a refugee camp in Somalia. All those poor people are obviously in need. Similar decisions have to be made by the state in regard to poverty within its own borders and in regard to global poverty. Compared to what the western states invest in local poverty alleviation within their countries the sum they give for global poverty alleviation is tiny but is that unjust?

1.3 Normative Background Theories of Poverty Alleviation: Human Rights, (Global) Justice, and Humanitarian Aid

Having said that every conceptualization of poverty and poverty alleviation brings forward normative questions of ethics, it becomes clear that we face the task of identifying a normative background theory that guides the analyzation and criticism of poverty as well as poverty alleviation measures. Philosophy has many possibilities to offer in that respect and we cannot hope to discuss or even name all of them. Also the chapters in this book give only a limited and incomplete picture of the philosophical discussions that have unfolded around poverty over recent years. We chose to focus on three concepts – one might also call them approaches: human rights, (global) justice and humanitarian aid.

Human rights, and especially those human rights which are covered in the UN Declaration and in other official documents like the Declaration of the Rights of the Child or the European Social Charter, are far from uncontroversial and their main normative point of reference, human dignity, is also in dispute (Boersema 2011). We cannot tackle these fundamental questions here but only try to flesh out the relationship between poverty alleviation and human rights and what the human rights agenda has to offer in terms of a normative and not merely political background theory. The first important point is that many scholars argue that poverty, at least in its most severe forms, is a violation of human rights and that it should be alleviated for that reason. The human rights agenda is obviously broader than the problem of poverty but to tie poverty and human rights together has significant normative force. Human rights are universal and must not be violated under any circumstances and – at least as many scholar argue – they are binding for each and every individual as well as institutions and states. No one is allowed to violate the human rights of another person and if poverty is such a violation the claims of the poor to being helped and supported are very strong. Thomas Pogge is one of the most prominent philosophers who have argued in this direction (Pogge 2008). He aims to show that global poverty is a human rights violation because it is based on a violation of the negative duties of rich countries not to harm others. Trade agreements and other international institutions are all set-up and work in the favor of rich countries while they produce and sustain global poverty, especially in the poorer countries. Poverty alleviation is hence not a demand of charity or benevolence. The second important point is that since the human rights agenda also has a close relation to legal and political agreements and institutions it is believed by many of its advocates to have a greater chance of actually changing the situation of the global poor for the better if it can be showed that there is a human rights argument for poverty alleviation. Poverty alleviation is not only – as some argue maybe not even primarily – an obligation of individuals and also not of the particular state in which the poor reside but global institutions and the actions of rich countries also have to change (see for example O'Neill 2001).

Theories of global justice can have close ties to theories of human rights and can argue that the demands of justice have a significant overlap with human rights. Pogge for example argues in this manner. Also Martha Nussbaum, maybe the most prominent advocate of a philosophical capability approach as a partial theory of (global) justice, understands her approach as a human rights approach (Nussbaum 2011). In her view global poverty is a violation of human rights because it denies the poor the opportunity to achieve those capabilities which every human is entitled to as a matter of universal human dignity. In general every theory of (global) justice has to answer three questions: what is the currency of justice – for example resources, capabilities or opportunities –, what is the principle of justice that guides the distribution of the currency, and, finally, who is responsible for this distribution to happen. If these three questions are settled – and there are nearly countless alternative ways to do so discussed in philosophy – one can ask whether or not, and to what extent, poverty is a violation of justice and what that means for demands of redistribution or other obligations of justice that different agents of justice have (see for example Brock and Moellendorf 2005; Pogge and Moellendorf 2008). We can only highlight two pairs of alternatives: resources vs. capabilities (see for example Kelleher 2015) and equality vs. sufficiency (see for example Casal 2007). The first pair refers to the question about the currency of justice. On the one hand resourcists like John Rawls argue that what matters for justice is how much of a certain resource or good a person has. This can be income, wealth or food, clothes or housing. Resources have at least two advantages: they are countable and allow an easy comparison between people and they are distributable directly. Also in poverty research most approaches focus on the resources poor people have and ethical theories of poverty alleviation that employ a resourcist approach to justice can argue for redistribution of resources that are deemed to be distributed unjustly. On the other hand the capability approach criticizes resources approaches and argues that what ultimately matters are capabilities, meaning freedoms to do something or to be someone valuable. Resources are only a means to an end. In the case of poverty this means that only such forms of poverty are unjust, which lead to a deprivation in important dimensions regardless how much income that person possesses. Hence, the goal of such poverty alleviation is not to redistribute resources but capabilities. The differentiation between equality and sufficiency refers to the principle of justice. That also has a bearing on poverty alleviation. Egalitarians will often view poverty alleviation as only a first step towards justice as long as inequalities in relevant resources or capabilities still exist. Most poverty alleviation measures today are not egalitarian in that sense and they do not aim to bring the poor to the same level as all others and to equalize resources or capabilities. Rather, they aim to alleviate the hardship of poverty, for example, by raising the income level of the poor or by providing them with food and shelter while they more or less leave untouched the income and food and housing of the richer and more well-off. For sufficientarian approaches to (global) justice, which claim that justice is done if everyone has enough and not if everyone has the same, non-equalizing poverty alleviation efforts might be the just thing to do. But one thing is common for all theories of (global) justice, that they view duties of justice as mandatory and binding. Not for all theories of (global) justice is poverty a violation of justice but as soon as it is deemed as such, poverty alleviation is no longer something that can be ignored.

The third normative background theory that might be employed is that of humanitarian action or charity (Langlois 2008). Those theorists argue that there is no duty of justice towards the poor to help them and that neither richer individuals nor states or global institutions are obliged as a matter of justice to alleviate poverty. Still they argue that it would be good to help the poor. Two important points should be made here: firstly, it is possible to differentiate between different groups of poor people. For some scholars who are particularists – for example David Miller (2007) – important differences exist between duties we have towards fellow citizens and towards foreign people living in other countries. Such an approach argues that because of the particular relationship that citizens have – a shared identity, interest in the common good etc. – duties of justice exist between them while such duties do not exist on a global and international level. For poverty alleviation this has interesting and important consequences. Particularists can bring forward important and strong arguments for why poverty alleviation within a state is a matter of justice and why the set-up of a functioning welfare state is necessary but they will deny that international development aid or other duties towards the global poor exist for the same reason or can claim the same normative force. Secondly, charity often only refers to individuals or institutions – for example companies etc. – to give to the poor but they seldom call for a change of rules and institutions themselves. Furthermore charity, as we have said, is not a duty of morality or justice, it is something that should be done but the poor have no claim or right to be helped. That also influences the relationship between those who give and those who receive.

Human rights, theories of (global) justice and approaches to humanitarian aid based on moral duties are just three examples of normative background theories to poverty alleviation. They also can have significant overlap.

1.4 Agents and Institutions of Poverty Alleviation: From the Individual to the Global Level

The third issue that we want to explore in this introduction is the necessary task of identifying the agents and institutions of poverty alleviation. We have already touched upon that issue because it is present in many normative background theories right from the beginning, like for example Pogge's critique of the unjust global trade system. We want to discuss here four different types of agents and also four different ways of attributing responsibilities to them. In this we will follow Iris Marion Young's suggestions.

In most philosophical approaches to poverty alleviation the relevant agents are identified on the institutional level, with either global institutions or states as the most prevalent choices. Global institutions are relevant because it is obvious that global poverty is not a domestic problem: it is at least co-produced by the global economic and political system. And even if poverty were not the result of an unjust global system of rules and institutions its extent and severity points into the direction that the poor states alone are not able to solve their problems and to alleviate poverty sufficiently. The 48 least developed countries in the world with a population of nearly one billion have a combined GDP which is only a quarter of the GDP of Germany with its 80 million inhabitants (870$ billion compared to 3,7$ trillions). Without external help there is little chance that poverty in these countries can be reduced and alleviated (Arda 2014). Illicit financial flows from developing countries to tax havens and to richer countries are also an increasing problem, one which costs hundreds of billions each year and exceeds development aid at large (Reuter 2012). Under such circumstances it seems the right choice to target the global order and institutions like the World Bank, the World Trade Organization, the International Monetary Fund or the UN as those who should deliver poverty alleviation. Only such big institutions seem able to implement changes that can turn whole countries around and lift billions of people out of poverty. The efforts made by those organizations have been heavily criticized for producing and sustaining poverty and also many of those critics agree that they need to change in order to alleviate poverty most effectively (Babb 2009; Güven 2012). From an ethical perspective it is also important to note that assumptions about cosmopolitanism and global justice are underlying such calls for change in the global order (for example Crocker 2008).

Nevertheless the global order and its institutions and organizations are not the only relevant agents of poverty alleviation. Also the state, in which the poor reside, has some obligations. If one looks at poverty in affluent countries this is without question. The welfare states in North America, Europe or Australia are actually alleviating poverty – more or less successfully, one has to add – and they use significant funding to do so. There are important differences between the welfare systems in developed countries and also between the ideologies behind them, but in most countries there is some agreement that people in poverty deserve at least some assistance and protection (Alesina and Glaeser 2006). Many theories of (social) justice demand poverty alleviation in order to achieve justice. For example Elizabeth Anderson's approach, which demands a sufficient distribution of certain capabilities with the goal to allow every member of society to become an equally respected citizen, can be interpreted in a way that it is incompatible with at least most forms of poverty and that the state has an obligation to intervene (Anderson 1999). Most ethical approaches to poverty alleviation are not much concerned with poverty in affluent societies though (two exceptions are Neuhäuser and Müller 2011; Schweiger 2013), but focus on global poverty in developing states, which are characterized by having lesser abilities for poverty alleviation and which most often do not have a functioning social protection system. Under such circumstances two points can be raised: firstly, such states will depend on some assistance from other countries or international institutions and this rests on at least some ethical assumptions that such responsibilities to assist exist and can be justified. Secondly, as some scholars have also argued, developing countries have some obligations to alleviate poverty as much as possible and to try to overcome their state of underdevelopment and to build systems of social protection. Another important point for both affluent and poor states is that all actions of poverty alleviation raise ethical issues in themselves. It is well studied that poverty is closely connected to shame and that the public institutions can also be a source of that shame (Walker 2014). It is one demand of ethics that poverty alleviation carried out by the state is done in a way that is not shameful but respectful, and does not add insult to injury.

We have seen that most agent-centered approaches, such as that of Thomas Pogge, focus on powerful agents and on institutions either on the national or international level (in questions of global poverty). This focus neglects the contribution of the poor themselves to overcoming their poverty. They are conceptualized mainly as beneficiaries with very limited power, or none at all, to contribute to poverty alleviation and the realization of justice. Monique Deveaux uses the concept of agents of justice for all who can and should have an active role in the process of fighting injustice (Deveaux 2015). This is further supported by insights provided by participatory approaches to poverty and pro-poor initiatives, as well as research on ways to empower the poor by taking them seriously (Drydyk 2013). Conceptualizing the poor as agents of justice is empowering; it acknowledges that they still have the capacity to alter their lives and that they are not completely dominated. Furthermore, such a view entails that there is a responsibility on the side of other agents of justice to provide poor people with the means and resources they need to make choices and to become active agents. Such an approach that takes the poor themselves seriously as agents of poverty alleviation will also reflect on the role they play – or in reality, that they are not allowed to play – in poverty research and the planning and implementation in poverty alleviation. We might find here forms of epistemic injustices (Fricker 2007), which undermine the credibility of the poor as agents of knowledge as well and which treat them as if they were unknowing and helpless children.

Iris Young has famously distinguished between two different ways of attributing responsibilities for alleviating injustices, of which poverty is certainly one (Young 2011). There is the liability model, which can be roughly described by means of two components. It (a) connects responsibility with directly causing harmful outcomes and (b) assigns responsibilities only to agents who perform the action in question voluntarily and with adequate knowledge of the situation. The liability model is the dominant one in legal reasoning, and it can also be considered the standard account of moral responsibility found in ethical theory. In this model, it is clear that responsibilities are assigned to concrete agents. Difficulties arise, however, when we are confronted with structural injustices, where the causal relationships of causing harms are often diffuse. This is clearly the case with (global) poverty where there is much in dispute about how it is produced and sustained. For such problems, Young introduces a second account of responsibilities: the social connection model. Young introduces four different grounds, which are relevant for balancing and weighing responsibilities: power, privilege, interest and collective ability. They are related to the social position of an agent and can be used to identify the kinds and degrees of responsibilities different agents – individual and collective ones – have in order to confront structural injustices.

One can see how the differentiation of agents and Young's model of attributing responsibilities can work together. It is necessary to identify the relevant agents and since there are many possibilities it is also necessary to argue for why a particular agent is responsible while another one is not. Think of the example of global poverty in an underdeveloped country. Although most people will agree that something should be done to alleviate poverty, fight hunger and child mortality it is less clear who should do what and on what grounds. Both the liability and the social connection model can be employed to analyze such a situation and they can both be connected to other insights we have about poverty alleviation. This will produce a differentiated and maybe even conflicting picture of the responsible agents.

1.5 Overview of the Book

As has become more evident now, this book is a normative philosophical one on poverty alleviation. The chapters that are brought together show some overlap but also significant differences in how they approach this topic and how they engage with the three tasks set out before. Some simply assume an existing concept of poverty and poverty alleviation without reflecting on it, others question the standard understandings of poverty. Some chapters focus on the normative background theory that is best suited to criticize poverty and to design poverty alleviation, others focus on the agents and institutions which should be attributed with the tasks of poverty alleviation. We have organized the chapters in this book along four areas of concern, which we have identified, although we admit that we do not aim for completeness.

The first one is the relation between (human) rights and poverty alleviation. There is a widely shared agreement that at least severe poverty is a violation of (human) rights and that a rights-based approach to poverty alleviation has some political and normative force. What is less clear is what kind of rights exactly are violated by poverty, what follows from the rights claims of poor people and how the rights of the poor can be effectively protected. This is closely related to questions regarding more inclusive social protection rights, which are established in most welfare states but missing or ineffectively granted in developing countries. Hence, many chapters in this volume touch upon the issue of rights poor people have (or should have) and how the effective implementation of these rights can help them to move out of poverty. In the first section, we have clustered three chapters on human rights that deal with such rights on a very general level. It opens with Thomas Pogge's chapter that argues why and how "we" as citizens of the developed world are violating the human rights of the world's poor and what follows from that in terms of our moral responsibility towards the poor. Elena Pribytkova then deals with the issue that the right to a decent social minimum is often not accepted as a genuine human right, even though it is part of the convention. Her chapter thus demonstrates why we should accept a human right to a decent social minimum, and that doing so sheds light on the human rights violation of severe poverty. The third chapter in this section, contributed by Gunter Graf and Mar Cabezas, shows that the capability approach can be used as a normative grounding of the human rights of children and how their rights are violated by poverty. The main aim is to explore how such a concept of the human rights of children can be used to establish priorities in poverty alleviation for children living in severe poverty.

The second area of concern this book wants to explore is the connection between development and poverty alleviation. In the context of global poverty, the development agenda has the most prominent place when it comes to poverty alleviation. Currently discussions are going on about the post-2015 development goals of the United Nations and how we should appreciate and shape a new understanding of development that can ultimately have success, in particular in regard to the worst-off. There are different agents involved in development (international institutions, states, communities, NGOs, individuals), whose roles and obligations have to be scrutinized. The chapters in this section focus on such particular agents and their interactions: the chapter by Jahel Queralt Lange is concerned with the obligations of beneficiary countries of development aid and how their efforts to raise domestic taxes affect the obligations of donor countries. She argues for moving away from a donor-centric view that suggests that beneficiary countries are only passive objects and for acknowledging that poor and underdeveloped countries also have to establish tax justice within their borders, meaning that they contribute to their own development and become more independent from outside development support. The second chapter by Elisabeth Valiente-Riedl and Joy Paton then deals with a specific group of countries in need of development aid that are often not in the focus of philosophers' attention: the small island development states. Based on the capability approach, their case study of Papua New Guinea shows the limitations of orthodox development tools, which threaten existing capability derived from culturally specific institutional arrangements. They argue for a different approach to global development, which acknowledges such country-specific differences. The third chapter by Max Kelly also focuses on an ethical issue that is often overlooked in debates about development: the role of animals and their welfare in development processes. Hence the three chapters in this section on development shed light on issues that have not gained sufficient attention from philosophers, but show that ethical tensions are deeply rooted in the design and implementation of development and poverty alleviation efforts. Finally, the fourth chapter by Gottfried Schweiger provides a critical commentary on the Sustainable Development Goals (SDGs), which will play a key role in global poverty reduction in the next 15 years.

Thirdly, poverty alleviation is not only an issue in poorer or developing countries but is also needed within welfare states. With this section, our book moves from the level of global poverty to poverty within affluent countries that are also less dependent on outside support when dealing with poor people within their borders. The economic crisis has also hit many welfare states and increased the problems of poverty and unemployment in certain states, especially in Southern Europe. All chapters in this section are written within the European context. The chapter by Christian Neuhäuser is concerned with our understanding of poverty within welfare states. He argues that such poverty is also a violation of human dignity and thus deserves to be alleviated. Welfare states have a moral obligation to reduce relative poverty to a minimum if they want to be decent. This implies the need to alter unjust background structures that force people into poverty in the first place. While Neuhäuser mainly deals with poverty as it is represented in the common statistics and political discussions about welfare states, the crisis has also intensified other forms of poverty that are often overlooked. Besides income poverty, we also find severe forms of social exclusion and deprivation within welfare states, such as people living on the streets, panhandlers or undocumented migrants with no, or just very limited, access to social care and protection. The chapter by Helmut P. Gaisbauer and Elisabeth Kapferer complements the argument of Neuhäuser's chapter by focusing on the overlooked poor outside the welfare system and argues that such forms of excluded – and often severe – poverty constitute still another form of violation of human dignity. Reflecting on shame and privacy as crucial dimensions in the experience of poverty the authors reveal paradoxes of (in-)visibilities that generate different challenges to poverty alleviation measures that have to be reflected and analyzed thoroughly. The third chapter in this section is then a case study of Spain, a country that is suffering severely from the on-going economic crisis, focusing on the country's health care. The determination of health by poverty is well-studied and access to health care is one crucial issue here. As many theorists claim, poverty is a violation of a well-justified right to health (care). Rosana Triviño, David Rodríguez-Arias and Txetxu Ausín explore the ethical shortcomings of austerity measures in the health care system that affect the poor and their exercise of a right to health care. They also explore the individual reaction of health care professionals under such non-ideal circumstances. Based on ethical grounds, they argue that physicians are righteously acting against the law when they treat illegal migrants who are now excluded from the health care system. Such individual compensations of failures of the welfare state are still only an option of last resort.

Finally, we identified the topic of obligations of individuals in regard to global poverty. Individuals living in affluent countries, but who are not in high positions of power or exceptionally well-off, obviously have limited possibilities. For this reason many philosophers, also those pursuing an agent-centered approach, focus on agents that can effectively change the situation and most discussions about poverty alleviation are held on an institutional level and examine the roles of agents such as countries or global institutions like the UN, World Bank or the Monetary Fund. The chapters in this section also take agent-centered approaches, but focus on individuals. Beth Kahn explores the obligation of individuals in affluent countries to take political actions that effectively implement measures of poverty alleviation and regulate the actions of agents who cause poverty. Rejecting utilitarian ideas of an effective altruist approach Kahn instead argues for the recognition of multiple *pro-tanto* duties, including political duties that require that individuals act responsively so as to form a collective, willing and able to establish just governing institutions that effectively prevent foreseeable and avoidable poverty. Monique Deveaux then advocates in her chapter a shift from a resourcist approach to global poverty and the redistributive paradigm closely associated with it to a more relational understanding of poverty. Such conception of poverty allows for taking into account one often neglected but crucial agent in poverty reduction efforts: poor-led social and political movements. By the same token it allows addressing structural inequalities, social exclusion, and relations of subordination and disempowerment as central to the experience of poverty.The third and fourth chapter in this section are equally specific in regard to the agent they have in mind: Tendayi Bloom takes the example of irregular migrants to show how the non-recognition of some persons who do not have any form of citizenship or citizen-like relationship with the State where they live gives rise to a form of intractable hidden poverty impairing access even to basic human rights. Her chapter then goes on to explore how academia can play a special role in addressing this human rights violation. Clemens Sedmak focuses in a more general approach on the university and its members and their duties and possibilities to tackle poverty. While there is increasing attention given to the social responsibility of universities and their members (students, professors, administration) and how they can contribute to the common good, the idea that they should realize something like a "preferential option for the poor" has not been fleshed out in detail.

The chapters in this book thus cover a broad range of ethical issues that are involved in poverty alleviation. The aim of the editors is not to present a thorough overview of the topic but rather to shed light on a limited list of selected topics of interest, some of them rarely treated (e.g. child poverty, animals or the role of academics). All chapters aim to add some value to the existing literature, either by exploring new issues or by exploring them from a different perspective. Thus, the book's overarching aim is to broaden and deepen the discussion around poverty alleviation. Many chapters point to further general questions of global and social justice, but they are not the main concern. As with most collections of essays, this book has the strength of bringing together different approaches and normative frameworks that are concerned with a specific topic; this, however, comes with the price that the chapters are only loosely integrated.

References

Alesina, Alberto, and Edward L. Glaeser. 2006. *Fighting poverty in the US and Europe a world of difference*, The Rodolfo De Benedetti Lecture Series. Oxford/New York: Oxford University Press.

Alkire, Sabina. 2008. Choosing domains: The capability approach and multidimensional poverty. In *The many dimensions of poverty*, ed. Nanak Kakwani and Jacques Silber, 89–119. Basingstoke/New York: Palgrave Macmillan.

Anderson, Elizabeth. 1999. What is the point of equality? *Ethics* 102(2): 287–337.

Arda, Mehmet. 2014. *Least developed countries – Development priorities and development cooperation*. Istanbul: United Nations Development Programme. http://www.idc-istanbul2014.org/notes/istanbul-19-20-june-2014-background-paper-ldcs-development-priorities-and--development-cooperation.pdf. Accessed 25 Oct 2015.

Babb, Sarah L. 2009. *Behind the development banks: Washington politics, world poverty, and the wealth of nations*. Chicago: University of Chicago Press.

Boersema, David. 2011. *Philosophy of human rights. Theory and practice*. Boulder: Westview Press.

Brock, Gillian, and Darrel Moellendorf (eds.). 2005. *Current debates in global justice*, Studies in Global Justice, vol. 2. Dordrecht: Springer.

Casal, Paula. 2007. Why sufficiency is not enough. *Ethics* 117(2): 296–326.

Crocker, David. 2008. *Ethics of global development. Agency, capability, and deliberative democracy*. Cambridge/New York: Cambridge University Press.

Deveaux, Monique. 2015. The global poor as agents of justice. *Journal of Moral Philosophy* 12(2): 125–150.

Drydyk, Jay. 2013. Empowerment, agency, and power. *Journal of Global Ethics* 9(3): 249–262. doi:10.1080/17449626.2013.818374.

Fricker, Miranda. 2007. *Epistemic injustice: Power and the ethics of knowing*. Oxford/New York: Oxford University Press.

Guio, Anne-Catherine, David Gordon, and Eric Marlier. 2012. *Measuring material deprivation in the EU: Indicators for the whole population and child-specific indicators*. Eurostat Methodologies and Working Papers. Luxembourg: Office for Official Publications of the European Communities. Accessed 25 Oct 2015.

Güven, Ali Burak. 2012. Exploring paradigm continuity: The IMF, the World Bank, and the Global Economic Crisis. *Development and Change* 43(4): 869–898. doi:10.1111/j.1467-7660.2012.01781.x.

Kelleher, J. Paul. 2015. Capabilities versus resources. *Journal of Moral Philosophy* 12: 151–171.

Langlois, Anthony J. 2008. Charity and justice in global poverty relief. *Australian Journal of Political Science* 43(4): 685–698. doi:10.1080/10361140802429288.

Miller, David. 2007. *National responsibility and global justice*. Oxford/New York: Oxford University Press.

Neuhäuser, Christian, and Julia Müller. 2011. Relative poverty. In *Humiliation, degradation, dehumanization: Human dignity violated*, ed. Paulus Kaufmann, Hannes Kuch, Christian Neuhäuser, and Elaine Webster, 159–172. Dordrecht/New York: Springer.

Nussbaum, Martha. 2011. *Creating capabilities: The human development approach*. Cambridge, MA/London: Belknap Press of Harvard University Press.

O'Neill, Onora. 2001. Agents of justice. *Metaphilosophy* 32(1–2): 180–195. doi:10.1111/1467-9973.00181.

Pogge, Thomas. 2008. *World poverty and human rights: Cosmopolitan responsibilities and reforms*. Cambridge/Malden: Polity Press.

Pogge, Thomas. 2009. How world poverty is measured and tracked. In *Absolute poverty and global justice: Empirical data, moral theories, initiatives*, ed. Mack Elke, Schramm Michael, Klasen Stephan, and Pogge Thomas, 51–65. Farnham/Burlington: Ashgate.

Pogge, Thomas, and Darrel Moellendorf (eds.). 2008. *Global justice: Seminal essays*. St. Paul: Paragon House.

Reuter, Peter (ed.). 2012. *Draining development? Controlling flows of illicit funds from developing countries*. Washington, DC: World Bank.

Schweiger, Gottfried. 2013. Recognition and social exclusion. A recognition-theoretical exploration of poverty in Europe. *Ethical Perspectives* 20(4): 529–554. doi:10.2143/EP.20.4.3.3005349.

Sen, Amartya. 1983. Poor, relatively speaking. *Oxford Economic Papers* 35(2): 153–169.

Townsend, Peter. 1985. A sociological approach to the measurement of poverty: A rejoinder to Professor Amartya Sen. *Oxford Economic Papers* 37(4): 659–668.

Walker, Robert. 2014. *The shame of poverty*. Oxford: Oxford University Press.

World Bank. 2011. *World development indicators 2011*. Washington, DC: World Bank. http://siteresources.worldbank.org/DATASTATISTICS/Resources/wdi_ebook.pdf. Accessed 25 Oct 2015.

Young, Iris Marion. 2011. *Responsibility for justice*, Oxford political philosophy. Oxford: Oxford University Press.

Part I
Human Rights and Poverty Alleviation

Chapter 2
Are We Violating the Human Rights of the World's Poor?

Thomas Pogge

Abstract In this chapter I argue that we are violating the human rights of the world's poor. To show this I proceed in two main steps. Section 2.1 sets forth a conception of what it means to violate a human right, arguing that 'human rights violation' is a relational predicate, involving right holders as well as duty bearers, with the latter playing an active role in causing the human rights of the former to be unfulfilled. Widely neglected is one very common kind of such violations involving the design and imposition of institutional arrangements that foreseeably and avoidably cause some human beings to lack secure access to the objects of their human rights. Just as one is actively harming people when one takes on the office of lifeguard and then fails to do one's job, so we are actively harming people when we seize the authority to design and impose social institutions and then fail to shape them so that human rights are realized under them insofar as this is reasonably possible. By examining the empirical evidence then I argue in Sect. 2.2 that we violate the human rights of billions of poor people by collaborating in the imposition of a supranational institutional scheme that foreseeably produces massive and reasonably avoidable human rights deficits. In the concluding part of Sect. 2.2 and the subsequent conclusion I reflect on the moral consequences for citizens in the affluent countries and present some ideas how compensation might work.

Keywords Human rights violation • Institutional arrangements • Right holders • Duty bearers

I am grateful to Tienmu Ma, John Tasioulas and Lynn Tong for many valuable comments and suggestions. An expanded version has appeared in the (2011) 14(2) *Yale Human Rights & Development Law Journal* 1.

T. Pogge (✉)
Yale University, 313 Saint Ronan Street (B2), New Haven, CT 06511-2327, USA
e-mail: thomas.pogge@yale.edu

H.P. Gaisbauer et al. (eds.), *Ethical Issues in Poverty Alleviation*, Studies in Global Justice 14, DOI 10.1007/978-3-319-41430-0_2

2.1 Introduction

Answering the title question requires explicating its meaning and examining the empirical evidence. The first task is begun in this introduction, which gives a rough account of the two groups whose relation is to be queried: the world's poor and 'we'. Part 2 then proposes a specific understanding of what it means to *violate* human rights, arguing that a human rights violation involves a specific causal relation of agents to a human rights deficit. This understanding includes not only interactional violations (perpetrated directly by agents) but also institutional violations (caused through the imposition of institutional arrangements). Based on the explication of the question in Parts 1, 2, and 3 provides evidence for the existence of a supranational institutional regime that foreseeably and avoidably produces massive human rights deficits. By collaboratively imposing this institutional scheme, we are indeed violating the human rights of the world's poor.

Following the *Universal Declaration*, we might define a poor person as one who does not have access 'to a standard of living adequate for the health and well-being of himself and of his family, including food, clothing, housing and medical care'(Universal Declaration of Human Rights 1948). This is a vague definition, but clearly includes a large percentage of the world's population. In 2011, when the average monthly income per person was $394, half the world's people were living on less than $80 per person per month (converted at market exchange rates). Most of them lacked the income necessary for basic survival and sustenance according to the *Universal Declaration*'s definition. This includes almost all those who, in 2011, belonged to the poorest quarter of humanity and thus lived on less than $30 per person per month. Even with substantially lower prices of basic necessities, their standard of living cannot plausibly be deemed adequate.[1]

By 'we' I mean citizens of developed countries who have sufficient mental maturity, education, and political opportunities to share responsibility for their government's foreign policy and for its role in designing and imposing supranational institutional arrangements. This definition takes for granted that citizens of developed countries share a collective responsibility for what their government does in their

[1] The data used in this paragraph were kindly supplied by Branko Milanovic, principal conomist in the World Bank's Development Research Group, in an email on 24 December 2014. He calculated the 2011 median as $965 per person per year and the 25th percentile as $361. Milanovic is the leading authority on the measurement of inequality, and his published work contains similar albeit somewhat less updated information (see Milanovic 2011). Inequality and poverty data are usually adjusted according to purchasing power parities (PPPs). I reject this practice as unjustified in the case of inequality because it conflicts with revealed-preference data: affluent people who could easily move to cheaper locations do not do so, and this shows that they get something of value in return for the higher prices they pay for the goods and services they consume. In the case of poverty measurement, a price adjustment is indeed appropriate. But the PPPs for individual household consumption expenditure commonly used for this purpose are inappropriate here because they reflect the prices of all the goods and services that households worldwide consume and thereby give far too little weight to the prices of basic foodstuffs, which are cheaper in poor countries but not as much cheaper as PPPs suggest. For detailed analysis, see Thomas Pogge (2010b, 79–85, endnote 127 at 213).

name. While children and people with serious mental disabilities are excluded from this responsibility, I would not want to exclude others on account of their low income or poor education. If poor or poorly educated citizens recognize such a responsibility and act on it, then who has the standing to tell them that they have no such responsibility and need not bother? On the other hand, I am also not prepared to point the finger at a laid-off steel worker or struggling single mother in today's United States, for example, and accuse her of failing to live up to her citizen responsibilities.[2] What matters here is the judgment each of us reaches about ourselves. I believe that I share responsibility for my country's policies, and I explain what human rights deficits I hold myself co-responsible for, and why. Reflecting on this analysis, you must judge for yourself whether you share responsibility for your country's policies and, if so, what human rights violations you are implicated in as a result.

2.2 What Does It Mean to Violate a Human Right?

Human rights violations involve *causal responsibility by agents* for the *non-fulfillment of a human right*. These two aspects of human rights violations are treated respectively in Sects. 2.2.1 and 2.2.3. Section 2.2.2 is a brief interlude on the normativity of human rights: their relation to morality and the law. Section 2.2.4 concludes Part 2 by discussing the concept of a human rights violation emerging from the preceding sections.

2.2.1 Non-fulfillment

A particular human right of some particular person is unfulfilled when this person lacks secure access to the object of that human right. This object is whatever the human right is a right to: for example, freedom of movement, equal political participation, basic education or freedom from assault. With regard to the human rights of the global poor, the most immediately relevant human right is the right to secure access to an adequate standard of living. But those lacking such access typically lack secure access to the objects of other human rights as well. For example, many people are compelled by poverty to enter employment relations that expose them to serious abuse by factory supervisors or domestic employers. Many women are exposed to assault and rape because they cannot afford to divorce their husband, cannot afford a secure dwelling or must fetch water from distant locations. Others are sold into prostitution by their relatives or fall prey to traffickers who abduct them or lure them abroad with the false promise of a living wage. Most poor people are

[2] This topic has been the subject of an exchange between Debra Satz and me (see Satz 2005, 50–51; Pogge 2005, 80–83).

vulnerable to humiliation, dispossession, or personal domination because they lack the means to defend their legal rights.

What then is the normative significance of the empirical distinction between fulfilment and non-fulfilment of a particular human right of a particular person? By asserting a human right to some object, one is making at least the following two claims. First, one is claiming that such secure access serves important interests of the right holder or other human beings.[3] Second, one is claiming that these important interests justify some significant duties on the part of other agents to ensure that human beings actually have secure access to the objects of their human rights. The second claim fails where security of access cannot be affected by human conduct: human beings cannot, at present, ensure immortality or perfect memory, for instance. And it also fails where the counterpart obligations would be too onerous: the importance of the interest in secure access to sexual intimacy is offset by the burdens that assuring such access would place upon others.

That a human right exists presupposes that the second claim can be defended. But it does not follow that such counterpart obligations exist whenever this human right is unfulfilled. When a person is without food or shelter, her human right to an adequate standard of living may be unfulfilled even while there are no obligations on the part of others because no one can reach her to supply what she lacks. A similar conclusion seems compelling when someone is without food or shelter in a social context where all others who could assist her are likewise desperately short. Here rendering assistance is too onerous to be required. But such scenarios do not undermine the case for the existence of the human right in question because it is not true across the board that there are never any counterpart obligations. When human beings today lack access to a minimally adequate standard of living, there typically are others who can plausibly be deemed required to help ensure access to basic necessities. So the human right asserted in Article 25 of the *Universal Declaration* is well grounded because its non-fulfillment triggers stringent obligations in some cases. This same point can be made in terms of a distinction between duties and obligations. Duties are general; obligations specific. For example, someone may have a general duty to keep her promises and a derivative obligation to return a book. A duty may generate obligations only in certain circumstances: one's duty to keep one's promises generates no obligations if one has made no promises, for instance; and one's duty to give, when one reasonably can, food to hungry persons generates no obligations when there are no hungry people or when one is desperately short of food oneself. Though there is no obligation in these situations, this does not defeat the assertion of the duty so long as this duty does generate obligations in other situations that do or can arise in the world as we know it.

What, then, are the duties correlative to a human right and, more specifically, to the human right to a minimally adequate standard of living? A good step toward answering this question involves examining the respect-protect-fulfill triad that has become a staple of international agency thinking in this area. This triad goes back to

[3] Freedom of speech and expression, for example, are important not merely to those who would communicate, but also to all those who have such communications available to them or gain when injustice and ill treatment are deterred by the fear of publicity.

Henry Shue's seminal book *Basic Rights*, which argues that each basic right gives rise to three distinct correlative duties: to avoid depriving, to protect from deprivation, and to aid the deprived (Shue 1996).

Inspired by this typology, Philip Alston and Asbjorn Eide popularized the triad in the 1980s (Alston 1984, 162, 169–174, see generally Alston and Tomaševski 1984). It was then carefully elaborated in the famous General Comment 12, adopted in 1999 by the UN Committee on Economic, Social and Cultural Rights. This General Comment says in its Article 15:

> The right to adequate food, like any other human right, imposes three types or levels of obligations on States parties: the obligations to *respect*, to *protect* and to *fulfill*. In turn, the obligation to *fulfill* incorporates both an obligation to *facilitate* and an obligation to *provide*. The obligation to *respect* existing access to adequate food requires States parties not to take any measures that result in preventing such access. The obligation to *protect* requires measures by the State to ensure that enterprises or individuals do not deprive individuals of their access to adequate food. The obligation to *fulfill* (*facilitate*) means the State must proactively engage in activities intended to strengthen people's access to and utilization of resources and means to ensure their livelihood, including food security. Finally, whenever an individual or group is unable, for reasons beyond their control, to enjoy the right to adequate food by the means at their disposal, States have the obligation to *fulfill* (*provide*) that right directly. This obligation also applies for persons who are victims of natural or other disasters (UN 1999).

These reflections largely accept two limitations widely taken for granted in the world of international relations: namely that human rights impose counterpart duties only on states and that any person's human rights normally impose counterpart duties only upon the state or states under whose jurisdiction she falls through physical presence or a legal bond of citizenship or residency. I highlight these limitations because I will later question them along with the comfortable belief they sustain: namely, that the unfulfilled human rights of impoverished foreigners abroad impose human-rights-correlative obligations only on their respective governments and compatriots and none upon ourselves.

2.2.2 *Human Rights in Relation to Law and Morality*

The two limitations are deeply entrenched in the impressive body of human rights law that has emerged since World War II both internationally and in many national jurisdictions. Nevertheless human rights are not merely part of the law but also a moral standard that all law ought to meet. Law has incorporated human rights in a way that points beyond itself: to a normativity that does not depend on the law for its existence and cannot be revised or repealed by legislative or judicial fiat or by treaties or international custom. This point is articulated in the legal separation from customary international law of *ius cogens*, a set of norms whose validity is understood to transcend the discretion of states.[4] The point is also prominent in many

[4] *Ius cogens* is generally taken to include at least norms prohibiting aggressive war, genocide, slavery, torture, military aggression and piracy.

legal documents, for instance in the very first words of the *Universal Declaration*, which call for the '*recognition* of the inherent dignity and of the equal and *inalienable* rights of all members of the human family' (my emphases) (UDHR 1948, preamble). With this formulation, echoed in frequent appeals to 'internationally *recognized* human rights', governments present themselves as recognizing certain rights in law rather than as creating these rights de novo. Their use of the word 'inalienable' reinforces this conclusion: an inalienable right is a right that its holders cannot lose, not through anything they do themselves (waiver or forfeiture), nor through anything others do, such as an alteration of the law. National and international human rights law is then not declaring itself the source of human rights but, on the contrary, asserting that all human beings have certain human rights regardless of whether these are recognized in their jurisdiction or indeed anywhere at all. Human rights are set forth in the law in a way that implies that these rights existed before they were codified and would continue to exist even if governments were to withdraw their legal recognition.

Born of the horrendous abuse of law in Nazi Germany, this self-restraint of the law is a great advance in human civilization. Endorsing it just because governments did would miss the essence of their endorsement. Governments have taken this step in a way that clearly recognizes that it is right, independent of their endorsement. They have recognized that the Nazis, had they won the war, could not have abolished human rights (though they could, of course, have systematically violated them in their law and practice). The advance should be endorsed in this spirit. The legal texts in which governments formulate human rights and explicate their correlative duties do, of course, deserve close attention. But when studying them one should understand that they are not, by their own self-conception, definitive. Whether there are human rights, what human rights there are, and what duties these human rights entail – these questions are not settled by the texts alone. Both Shue and the authors of General Comment 12 approach the questions in this spirit and I will follow their example.

2.2.3 From Non-fulfillment to Violation

What is the relationship between the non-fulfillment of a human right and its violation? Here we must differentiate the various kinds of causal pathways by which one agent's conduct may affect human rights fulfillment. General Comment 12 draws a fourfold distinction. Reconstructing it without the artificial limitation to states, one can say that human rights may give agents duties of four distinct kinds: duties to *respect* human rights, duties to *protect* (secure access to the objects of) human rights, duties to *provide* (secure access to) the objects of human rights, and duties to *facilitate* human rights fulfilment. My discussion of these four kinds of duties focuses on cases where a breach of the duty counts as a human rights violation. This excludes breaches of human-rights-correlative duties by uninvolved bystanders who can protect or provide at reasonable cost. Their failure to do this does not make them human right violators. An non-fulfillment human right manifests a human rights violation only if there are agents actively causing the non-fulfillment of the human right in question even while they could and should have known that their conduct would have this effect.

The most straightforward human rights violations involve breaches of *duties to respect*, that is, duties 'not to take any measures that result in preventing' a human being from having secure access to the object of a human right. As this negative formulation indicates, these are conceived as negative duties: duties that can be honored by remaining passive and can be breached only by taking action. They forbid any action that is reasonably avoidable and foreseeably causes some human being to be prevented from enjoying secure access to the object of a human right.

Duties to protect and duties to provide are both positive: requiring active intervention. Breaching duties of either kind does not then count as a human rights violation. The two positive duties are distinguished by reference to the type of threat that triggers them and by the mode of intervention they require. Duties to protect require agents to take *preventive* action when the fulfillment of human rights is endangered by *social* threats: by other agents who are, perhaps inadvertently, disposed to act in ways that render such access insecure. The duty requires that one render the objects of human rights secure by preventing either the potentially harmful actions or their potentially harmful effects. Duties to provide require not a blocking of the threat but a neutralizing of its harmful effects. Duties of the two kinds are substitutional in that one becomes moot insofar as the other is discharged: if UN troops break the siege of a city and thereby restore its usual food supply, the obligation to provide food to its population dissolves; conversely, if the UN provides food to the city's people, it staves off the human-rights-based obligation to break the siege.

Duties to respond to natural disasters that threaten the fulfillment of human rights are generally classified as duties to provide. Exemplified in human rights documents (including General Comment 12), this is an unfortunate practice because it obscures the fact that, as in the case of social threats, the task can be discharged in two fundamentally different ways: by preventing the harm from reaching people or by assisting them in coping with it. The common label draws attention to the latter approach; and nearly all international efforts in regard to natural disasters are indeed focused on assistance ex post rather than on (often more cost-effective) prevention ex ante. A good step towards correcting this irrational bias would break out duties to protect human beings from natural disasters as a separate category of human-rights-correlative duties.

Being positive, duties to protect and to provide are largely irrelevant to the topic of human rights violations as defined. Yet two further points should be made about them here. First, those who prevent effective conduct pursuant to a duty to protect or to provide typically breach a duty to respect and can then be labelled human rights violators. For example, those who ordered General Roméo Dallaire not to confiscate the weapons that the Interahamwe militias were assembling in Kigali in 1993–1994 were breaching their duty to respect human rights, assuming they could and should have known that Dallaire's assessment of what these weapons were intended for was essentially correct (Pogge 2010b, 168–169). Their prevention of his initiative was an *active* intervention that foreseeably led to avoidable genocide.

Second, even a failure to protect or provide can constitute a human rights violation in cases where the agent has assumed a special role that involves protecting or providing (secure access to) objects of human rights. For example, when a police officer remains passive when he sees a violent assault, he is not merely breaching his duty to protect (as a civilian bystander might), but also his negative duty to respect human rights: the duty not to assume an office and then to fail to perform its associated tasks. This is analogous to the case of promising discussed above, where the duty not to break one's promises, though negative, may generate positive obligations to do as one had promised. Likewise with the roles of police officer, lifeguard, physician and the like: one is violating human rights when one takes on such a role and then fails to meet its requirements in a way that foreseeably and avoidably renders insecure others' access to the objects of their relevant human rights.

Explicating duties to facilitate, General Comment 12 prescribes that 'the State must pro-actively engage in activities intended to strengthen people's access to and utilization of resources and means to ensure their livelihood, including food security' (UN Committee on Economic, Social, and Cultural Rights 1999). Transcending the respect-protect-fulfil triad, General Comment 12 clearly conceives duties to facilitate as distinct from duties to provide and also as important enough to be distinguished as a separate category. This reflects the recognition that the extent to which human rights are fulfilled depends on the totality of background conditions prevailing in a society. Some such background conditions are subject to human modification only in minor ways or very slowly. But the effect of even these conditions is shaped by other background conditions that are very much under human control. Of greatest importance here is the way the state structures and organizes a society. For example, the structure of a society's economy profoundly affects the distribution of income and wealth; the organization of its criminal justice system greatly influences what dangers citizens face from criminal activities; and the design of its education system makes a large difference to the opportunities various groups of citizens have to effectively participate in politics and to defend their legal rights. Badly organized societies pose massive threats to the objects of their members' human rights. In response to these threats, one can impress upon the governing elites and other citizens the importance of their duties to respect, protect, and provide. But such appeals are of limited use in a society in which members of the elite can embezzle with impunity or in which citizens who work to protect the rights of fellow citizens are persecuted and subjected to arbitrary mistreatment by organizations whose status and legal basis are murky. What such a society needs is structural reform: reorganization.

Duties to facilitate are then a crucial addition that highlights the vital importance of institutional design for human rights fulfilment. This importance is overlooked on a purely interactional understanding of human rights fulfilment which can, somewhat simplistically, be put as follows: (1) human rights would be universally fulfilled if all agents complied with their duties to respect; (2) some agents fail to do this and their disposition to violate human rights triggers duties to protect; (3) the willingness or ability of agents to comply with their duties to protect is insufficient to deter and prevent all breaches of duties to respect; (4) this fact, along with the occurrence of natural disasters which may also undermine human rights fulfilment, triggers duties to provide, that is, duties to help people overcome impediments that obstruct or render insecure their access to the objects of their human rights.[5]

The purely interactional analysis of human rights deficits must then be complemented by an institutional analysis which traces such deficits back not to wrongful conduct of individual and collective agents, but to injustice in the design of social institutions: in the rules and procedures, roles and agencies that structure and organize societies and other social systems. The two kinds of analysis are often complementary. Thus, each instance of slavery involves agents who (typically with violence or intimidation) subject a human being to their domination; and the persistence of slavery on a massive scale involves unjust social institutions such as the legal protection of property rights in persons or (in modern times) the massive reproduction of life-threatening poverty and the effective non-recognition by national legal systems of the human rights of poor foreigners from less-developed countries.[6] Similarly, each marital rape is a moral crime committed by a husband; and persistent high prevalence of marital rape exhibits institutional injustice in legislation and training of police and judicial officers.

Contrasting with these cases of complementarity, there are also many cases where institutional analysis reaches beyond interactional analysis and thus enables intelligent responses to human rights deficits that, on a purely interactional analysis, remain elusive. Thus, poverty and hunger are nowadays typically systemic: arising in the context of some economic order from the effects of the conduct of many market participants who cannot foresee how their decisions, together with those of many others, will affect specific individuals or even the overall incidence of poverty and hunger. While it is straightforward what husbands must not do in order to respect their wives' human right to physical security, it may be quite unknowable what market participants must not do to respect others' human right to an adequate standard of living. This human right can best be realized through suitable socioeconomic institutions, and the countries that have realized this right have in fact done so through appropriate institutional design.

While institutional analysis with a moral purpose goes back a long way,[7] its recent exemplar is John Rawls's (1971) great work *A Theory of Justice*. While focusing on social institutions and more specifically on the basic structure of a national society existing under modern conditions, this work's normative message is addressed to the citizens of such a national society, offering to explicate for them

[5] Such an account of 'waves of duties' is suggested in Waldron (1989, 503, 510; see also the Afterword of Shue 1996, 156). Both authors understand how important attention to the design and reform of institutional arrangements is for human rights fulfilment (see also Pogge 2009b, 113).

[6] The number of slaves today is commonly estimated to be around 27 million. 'There are more slaves today than were seized from Africa in four centuries of the trans-Atlantic slave trade. The modern commerce in humans rivals illegal drug trafficking in its global reach – and in the destruction of lives' (Cockburn 2003).

[7] For an important milestone in the Anglophone discussion see Bentham (1996[1789]).

their 'natural duty of justice' which, Rawls believes, 'requires us to support and to comply with just institutions that exist and apply to us [and] to further just arrangements not yet established' (ibid., p. 115; see also ibid., p. 246, 334). His argument for such a natural duty importantly highlights how citizens can institutionally control socio-economic deprivations and inequalities even when they cannot do so through individual protection or provision efforts. But Rawls's argument also involves a serious and highly influential flaw, namely the unthinking presupposition that citizens' duties with regard to the social institutions they are involved in designing or upholding are one and all positive duties. In an elaborate mapping exercise, Rawls explicitly classifies our natural duties in regard to institutional design as positive, likening them to the positive duties of mutual aid and mutual respect while contrasting them with the negative duties not to injure and not to harm the innocent (ibid., p. 109). Reiterating the widely shared assumption that 'when the distinction is clear, negative duties have more weight than positive ones,' (ibid., p. 114) Rawls thereby marginalizes our responsibility for the justice of our shared social institutions.

Political thinkers and jurists writing after Rawls have unquestioningly accepted his classification without recognizing how important and contestable it is. Thus General Comment 12 demands that 'the State must pro-actively engage in activities intended to strengthen people's access to and utilization of resources and means to ensure their livelihood, including food security'(UN Committee on Economic, Social, and Cultural Rights 1999). And Shue's complex formulation is also a positive one: casting our relevant responsibility as one to design institutions that avoid the creation of strong incentives to violate human rights – rather than one *not* to design or uphold social institutions that create strong incentives to violate human rights.

The problem here is not one of scope: there are no citizen duties that Rawls and his successors fail to mention. The problem concerns the duty's character and weight. On the now conventional view, a society's social institutions have important effects on the lives of its members, and the government and the citizenry therefore ought to improve these institutions so as to promote their justice (Rawls) or rights fulfilment (Shue). But this positive duty cannot explain the special responsibility agents have in regard to social institutions they themselves are involved in designing or upholding. It cannot explain, for instance, why during the colonial period the government and citizens of Portugal had a far weightier responsibility to promote the fulfilment of human rights in Brazil and Mozambique than in Mexico or Sudan.

My concern to complement this account can be introduced with a dramatic analogy. Imagine a driver who encounters a badly hurt child by the side of the road. Being local, the driver knows how to get the boy quickly to the nearest emergency room. She can see that her failure to drive him there may well cost him his life. Given all this, her duty to aid people in need generates a stringent obligation to drive the boy to the hospital.

Let us now add another detail to the story, namely that it was the driver herself who caused the boy's condition: talking on her cell phone, she hit the boy after seeing him too late and reacting too slowly. This new information does not affect the initial conclusion that she should drive the boy to the hospital. But this conclusion is now backed by an additional and weightier moral reason: if the boy dies, she will have killed him. Her negative duty not to kill thus generates another, even more stringent obligation of identical content: she must drive the boy to the hospital as fast as she safely can.

The key point of the analogy is that citizens generally have two obligations to make their society's social institutions more just. One derives from their general positive duty to promote the justice of social institutions for the sake of safeguarding the rights and needs of human beings anywhere. The other derives from their negative duty not to collaborate in designing or imposing unjust social institutions upon other human beings. In regard to a citizen's home society, the content of these two obligations is essentially the same. But they differ in stringency. Other things equal, it is worse to let an injustice persist if one is complicit in it than if one is merely an uninvolved bystander. If the injustice manifests itself in human rights deficits, then one is a human rights violator in the first case but not in the second. This provides an additional, stronger, and non-instrumental rationale for why typical Turkish citizens should focus their political reform efforts on Turkey in preference to Paraguay. If Turkey is so organized that substantial and avoidable human rights deficits persist, then Turkish citizens participate in a human rights violation. They are not similarly implicated in Paraguay's institutional injustice.[8]

General Comment 12 is right to recognize that the fulfilment of human rights is greatly affected by social institutions and right to acknowledge, by breaking out positive duties to facilitate as a separate category, human responsibilities in regard to institutional design. To this must be added, however, another category of negative duties not to collaborate in the design or imposition of social institutions that foreseeably and avoidably cause human rights to be unfulfilled. These duties are close to duties to facilitate in their focus on social institutions and the related purpose of reducing human rights deficits through institutional reform. They are close to duties to respect in their essentially negative character: it is only by breaching duties to respect or duties not to collaborate that one can become a violator of human rights.

2.2.4 *Human Rights and Supranational Institutional Arrangements*

As the foregoing shows, the concept of a human rights violation is a relational predicate, involving specific responsibilities by particular agents in regard to unfulfilled human rights. When many Paraguayans are unable to attain an adequate standard of living, then this may indicate a human rights violation on the part of Paraguay's political and economic elite insofar as they are collaborating in the imposition of

[8] Part 3 will explore the possibility that Turkish citizens may, through their government, be implicated in the design or imposition of unjust supranational institutional arrangements that contribute to Paraguay's human rights deficit.

unjust social institutions in Paraguay and also insofar as they are abusing their indigenous servants or employees. The same human rights deficit indicates merely a breach of positive duty on the part of an affluent citizen of Turkey who – even if she leaves undone things she could easily do toward protecting, providing, or facilitating secure access by Paraguayans to the objects of their human rights – is not involved in abusing them or in designing or imposing upon them unjust social institutions. And the same human rights deficit may not indicate any breach of duty on the part of impoverished citizens of Sierra Leone or indeed of most of Paraguay's poor themselves – the former are simply unable to improve the living conditions of poor Paraguayans and the latter cannot reasonably be said to be morally required to undertake political action toward realizing their own and each other's human rights when such action would be excessively risky or costly for them.

Let us recap two central points about the notion of a human rights violation. One is a call to resist the tendency to deflate the term 'human rights violation' by using it broadly to cover all avoidable cases of unfulfilled human rights. If possible, the expression should be saved from the political preachers and media windbags ever in search of stronger expressions to show that they care more than the rest. Human rights violations are not tragic events, like the destruction of a town by a meteorite, nor even culpable failures to give aid or protection. Human rights violations are crimes actively committed by particular agents who should be identified and then be persuaded to change their ways or else stopped.

The other point is that human rights violations come in two varieties, one of which has – unsurprisingly – been overlooked. There is the interactional variety, where individual or collective agents do things that, as they intend, foresee, or should foresee, will avoidably deprive human beings of secure access to the objects of their human rights. And there is the institutional variety, where agents design and impose institutional arrangements that, as they intend, foresee, or should foresee, will avoidably deprive human beings of secure access to their human rights. That the latter variety is overlooked among those who enjoy the privilege of theorizing about justice and human rights is related to the fact that its recognition would bring into full view a large crime against humanity that is now going on and in which these theorists and their readers are involved. This crime is the design and imposition of unjust supranational institutional arrangements that foreseeably and avoidably cause at least half of all severe poverty which in turn is by far the greatest contributor to the current global human rights deficit.

Consciously or unconsciously, normative theorists obscure this crime in two main ways. The traditional obfuscation presents national borders as moral watersheds. Each state is responsible for the fulfilment of human rights in its territory, and the responsibility of foreign actors is limited to (at most) a positive duty of assistance.[9]

There is an emerging contemporary obfuscation. Its emergence and success owes much to the phenomenon of globalization. Transforming the traditional realm

---

[9] John Rawls exemplified this traditional view, limited to the recognition of such a positive duty of assistance (see Rawls 1999, 106–119).

of international relations, one central component of globalization has been the creation of an increasingly dense and influential global system of rules along with a proliferating set of new international, supranational, and multinational actors. These transnational rules and actors reach deep into the domestic life of especially the poorer national societies by shaping and regulating not only the ever-growing share of interactions that traverse national borders, but increasingly also purely domestic interactions. In view of the evidently profound effects that these transnational rules and actors have on the lives of human beings worldwide, it has become ever more palpably untenable to claim for them a morality-free zone in which the concept of justice has no application.[10] So the contemporary approach does the next best thing by acknowledging a duty to *facilitate* the realization of human rights. In addition to positive duties to contribute to the remedial protection and provision of missing objects of human rights, agents are now assigned the additional positive duty to promote the realization of human rights through the improvement of institutional arrangements. As with the other two positive duties, this new duty is understood as 'imperfect', leaving its bearers much discretion over what and how much they will do. From there it is only a small step to the position the United States set forth in an 'interpretative statement' it issued in regard to the Rome Declaration on World Food Security: 'the attainment of any 'right to food' or 'fundamental right to be free from hunger' is a goal or aspiration to be realized progressively that does not give rise to any international obligations' (World Food Summit 2012).

The contemporary obfuscation represents a step forward in its acknowledgement that the proliferating supranational institutional architecture is neither causally nor morally neutral. But by assigning us, in regard to these supranational institutional arrangements, an open-ended task of improvement, the contemporary obfuscation presents this responsibility as exclusively positive and thereby reinforces a central doctrine of the traditional obfuscation: the only way foreigners can violate human rights is through violent cross-border intervention. Though recognizing that our design of supranational institutions has important effects on human rights fulfilment worldwide, the contemporary obfuscation still hides an important possibility: that the existing supranational institutional order is fundamentally unjust and 'progressive improvement' therefore an inadequate response. There was a time when people talked about the improvement of slavery – about legislative changes that might facilitate more tolerable living conditions by curbing rapes, beatings, and splitting of families, by reducing back-breaking labor, and by guaranteeing minimally adequate food, shelter and leisure. But as slavery came to be recognized as fundamentally unjust, the only adequate response to it was abolition. An institutional injustice is not something to be gradually ameliorated at one's leisure. It must be eliminated through institutional reforms as fast as reasonably possible pursuant to a negative duty not to impose unjust social institutions and, in particular, ones that foreseeably give rise to a reasonably avoidable human rights deficit. In this regard, severe poverty and slavery are on a par: when social institutions avoiding these deprivations are reasonably possible, then the imposition of social institutions that perpetuate

[10] As had been done, in the wake of Rawls, by Thomas Nagel (2005).

these deprivations constitutes a violation of the human rights of those whom these institutions enslave or impoverish.

2.3 We Are Violating the Human Rights of the World's Poor: The Empirical Evidence

We are now ready to examine my central claims: there exists a supranational institutional regime that foreseeably produces massive and reasonably avoidable human rights deficits; and by collaboratively imposing this severely unjust institutional order, we are violating the human rights of the world's poor.

Section 2.2.4 has shown how normative theorists sustain this injustice by allowing no space in their catalogues of duties for a negative duty not to collaborate in the imposition of unjust institutional arrangements. This part will show how empirical theorists sustain the injustice by arguing that globalization is good for the poor (2.3.1) and that the remaining causes of poverty are domestic to the societies in which it persists (2.3.2). Part 3 concludes with some reflections on what we ought to do in light of the actual causes of global poverty (2.3.3).

It may be useful to precede the discussion with a brief reminder of the state of human rights fulfilment today. About half of all human beings live in severe poverty and about a quarter live in extreme or life-threatening poverty. They appear in statistics such as the following: 795 million people are chronically undernourished (FAO 2015), 884 million lack access to improved drinking water (UNICEF 2015), 2.4 billion lack access to improved sanitation (UNICEF 2015), and almost 2 billion lack regular access to essential medicines (WHO 2004). Some 1.6 billion lack adequate shelter (UN – Habitat 2015), 1.2 billion lack electricity (UN – Habitat 2012), 757 million adults are illiterate (UNESCO 2015), and 168 million children are child laborers (ILO 2015). About one-third of all human deaths, 18 million each year, are due to poverty-related causes (WHO 2008).

2.3.1 Is Globalization Good for the Poor?

One way of disputing the claim that we are violating the human rights of the poor is by arguing that, because the percentage of very poor people has been declining (the first Millennium Development Goal, MDG-1, is phrased in these terms), globalization and the supranational institutional arrangements it has brought must be good for the poor. This argument employs an invalid inference. The relevant standard is not whether the lot of the poor has improved in the past quarter century of globalization, but rather whether we could have found a feasible alternative path of globalization, evolving some alternative scheme of supranational institutions, which would have led to a much smaller human rights deficit during and at the end of that period. If there is some such feasible alternative scheme, then we are violating the human

Table 2.1 Distribution of global household income 2011

Segment of world population	Share of global household income 2011 in percent
Richest 5 %	42.77
Next 5 %	19.49
Next 15 %	22.71
Second quarter	10.64
Third quarter	3.17
Poorest quarter	1.22

rights of the poor by imposing upon them the current institutional arrangements. By analogy, suppose someone denied that the institutional order authorizing and enforcing black slavery in the United States in 1845 violated the human rights of slaves by pointing out that the number of slaves had been shrinking, that the nutritional situation of slaves had steadily improved and that brutal treatment (such as rape, whipping and splitting of families) had also been in decline. Do such facts weaken, *in any way*, the claim that the institution of slavery violated the human rights of slaves? If the answer is no, then the mere fact that the world's poor were even worse off at some earlier time cannot refute the claim that the imposition of the current global institutional order violates their human rights. The relevant question is not whether and how much the global human rights deficit has been declining but rather whether and how much the design of the supranational institutional arrangements we impose contributes to the human rights deficit that remains.[11] The question is, in particular, whether the world economy could have been, or could now, be restructured so as to mitigate the existing socio-economic inequalities. The following table shows the distribution of global household income in 2011, basically unchanged from 1988.[12]

The Table 2.1 shows that, surprisingly, the world poverty problem – so unimaginably large in human terms – is tiny in economic terms. In 2011, the shortfall of the world's poor from an adequate standard of living was about 2 per cent of global household income or 1.2 per cent of world income (the sum of all gross national incomes).[13]

The distribution of global private wealth is even more unequal, with the richest 1 percent now holding 50.4 percent of all such wealth, (Credit Suisse 2015, 19) while the poorer half of humanity has been reduced to roughly 0.6 percent, about as much as the richest 67 individuals (0.0000009 percent of humanity). (Moreno 2014).

The data cannot prove conclusively that there was no feasible alternative path of supranational institutional design that would have led to considerably larger income

[11] This paragraph draws on my reply to Matthias Risse in Pogge (2005) 'Severe Poverty as a Violation of Negative Duties'. For a more extensive discussion of baselines for assessing institutional harm, see Pogge 2007b.

[12] These data were kindly supplied by Milanovic, Branko of the World Bank in a personal email communication. See Email from Branko Milanovic (n 1).

[13] This accords roughly with the World Bank's PPP-based tally which counted 3.085 million people as living in severe poverty in 2005 and estimated their collective shortfall – the global poverty gap – at 1.13 % of world income (see Pogge 2010b, 69).

and wealth shares for the global poor while still achieving a reasonable rate of global economic growth and would thereby have led to a much smaller human rights deficit. But the data do make this possibility wildly implausible.[14] Its implausibility becomes even clearer as we reflect on the strongly antidemocratic and pro-wealthy path that globalization has taken. Globalization involves the emergence of complex and ever more comprehensive and influential bodies of supranational laws and regulations that increasingly pre-empt, constrain, and shape national legislation. Such supranational rules are not formulated through the kind of transparent, democratic procedures that characterize national law-making in the countries that have reached a basic level of domestic justice. Rather, supranational rules largely emerge through intergovernmental negotiations from which the general public and even the majority of weaker governments are effectively excluded. Only an unusually small number of 'players' can exert real influence over supranational rule-making: powerful organizations, prominently including large multinational corporations and banks, as well as very rich individuals and their associations and the ruling 'elites' of the most powerful developing countries. These richest and most powerful agents are best positioned to engage in cost-effective lobbying. They can reap huge gains from favorable supranational rules and therefore can afford to spend large sums acquiring the necessary expertise, forming alliances with one another, and lobbying the stronger governments (G7, G20) that dominate supranational rule-making. Ordinary citizens, by contrast, typically find it prohibitively costly to acquire the necessary expertise and to form alliances that are large enough to rival corporate influence. In the absence of global democratic institutions, globalization sidelines the vast majority of human beings, who have no way of influencing the formulation and application of supranational rules, and greatly enhances the rule-shaping powers of a tiny minority of those who are already the richest and most powerful. (Many of them foresaw this, of course, and therefore strongly supported the ongoing globalization push.) Their interests are diverse, and so they are competing and bargaining with one another – each seeking to shape and reshape supranational rules to be as favorable as possible to itself. There are winners and losers in these contests, some elite players fail in their efforts to shape in their favor the rules that stand to impact them the most. Yet, the rules do get captured by some elite players and, as a group, they consequently grow their share of global wealth and expand their advantage over the rest of humankind. This, in turn, further increases their capacity to influence the design and application of the rules in their own favor and, unintentionally but no less inexorably, keeps the poorer half of humankind in dire poverty.

Therefore it is not surprising that the institutional design shift upward, from the national to the supranational level, is marginalizing humanity's poorer majority, who have no way of influencing supranational negotiations, and is further increasing the absolute and relative wealth and power of a tiny minority, who can monopolize such influence. The rapid global polarization of the last 20 years is a foreseeable

---

[14] For a more extensive discussion, see Pogge 2010a.

effect of a highly undemocratic globalization path and the regulatory-capture opportunities it offers.

2.3.2 *Are the Causes of the Persistence of Poverty Purely Domestic?*

Empirical theorists provide a second line of defense of the status quo by arguing that the causes of the persistence of poverty are domestic to the societies in which it persists. The observed polarization is not one phenomenon, driven by supranational institutional arrangements, but rather two phenomena: good progress in well-organized Western countries, which maintain high levels of social justice and decent rates of economic growth, and mixed progress in many other countries, which pay little attention to social justice and whose economic growth is often held back by a range of local natural, cultural, or political impediments. Two sets of empirical findings are adduced as evidence for this picture. One is that the overall gap between affluent and developing countries is no longer growing as China and India, in particular, have been maintaining long-term rates of economic growth that are considerably above those of Europe, North America, and Japan. This is taken to show that supranational rules are not biased against poor countries and that the main driver of polarization today is rising *intra*-national inequality which is under domestic control and each country's own responsibility.

In response, one might point out that, over the recent globalization period, GDP growth in the poorest countries has just barely managed to keep up with population growth. As a consequence, growth in GDP per capita has been lower in the low income countries than in the high income countries.[15] But the more important point is that the increase of intra-national economic inequality in nearly all countries is no longer under easy domestic control but rather driven by the increasingly important role that supranational rules play in constraining and shaping national legislation and in governing domestic markets for goods, services, labor, and investments.

The influence of supranational rules is in some cases direct and immediate and in other cases mediated through competition. As an example of a direct and immediate influence, consider an important part of the World Trade Organization (WTO) regime, namely the 1994 Trade-Related Aspects of Intellectual Property Rights (TRIPS) Agreement which requires WTO members to institute national intellectual property regimes that award and enforce product patents of at least 20-year duration on new medicines and thus suppress the manufacture and sale of competing generic products. This requirement massively aggravates poverty by increasing the cost of medicines that poor people, far more vulnerable to disease, have much greater need for. Often, poor people cannot afford the medicines they would have been able to

---

[15] World Bank, GDP per capita growth (annual per cent), http://data.worldbank.org/indicator/NY.GDP.PCAP.KD.ZG/countries/1W-XQ-EG-SYMA-IR-SA?display=graph Accessed 25 October 2015.

buy in the absence of TRIPS and then spend money on inferior (often counterfeit) products, or else go without medicine altogether, and suffer chronic disease or even premature death as a result, with devastating effects on their family's livelihood (Pogge 2009a, 542).

As an example of the influence of supranational rules mediated by competition, consider that the WTO Treaty, while mandating open and competitive global markets with enforcement of uniformly strong intellectual property rights, contains no uniform labor standards that would protect workers from abusive and stressful working conditions, from absurdly low wages, or from excessive working hours. It thereby draws poor countries into a vicious 'race to the bottom' where they, competing for foreign investment, must outbid one another by offering ever more exploitable workforces. Under the conditions of WTO globalization, workers cannot resist a deterioration of their terms of employment because, if they secure more humane working conditions, many of them will end up unemployed as jobs are moved abroad.

Massive increases in domestic inequality are to be expected, then, in developing countries. And we do indeed find this phenomenon in nearly all developing countries for which good data are available, countries as diverse as Argentina, Bangladesh, Costa Rica, the Dominican Republic, Ecuador, Hungary and Jamaica (UNU-WIDER 2008).

China is an especially interesting case, because it contains nearly a fifth of humanity and is the leading poster child of globalization. During the period 1990–2004, China reportedly achieved spectacular 236 % growth in per capita gross national income.[16] But the same period also saw a stunning increase in inequality. While the income share of the top tenth rose from 25 to 35 %, that of the poorest fifth fell from 7.3 to 4.3 %.[17] This means that the ratio of the average incomes of these two groups increased from 6.8 to 16.3 as average income in the top tenth rose by 370 % while average income in the poorest fifth rose by only 98 %. To be sure, an income gain of 98 % over 14 years is not bad at all. But China's poor paid a high price for it in terms of marginalization, humiliation and oppression by the emerging economic elite whose greatly expanded share of Chinese household income gives them much greater opportunities to influence political decisions, to give unfair advantages to their children, and to dominate the poor in direct personal interactions. The poor would have been much better off with more equal economic growth, even if this would have been somewhat less rapid.

We find a similar phenomenon in the other leading country of the twenty-first century, the United States. In line with the Kuznets Curve hypothesis, the US experienced gradual income equalization from the beginning of the Great Depression until the beginning of the current globalization period. Contrary to the Kuznets hypothesis, this period was followed by a dramatic income polarization that pro-

[16] Calculated from World Bank data by dividing each year's GNI (in current RMB) by China's population that year, then using China's GDP deflator to convert into constant 2005 Yuan.

[17] Distribution data for 1990 from the World Bank as cited in Minoiu, Camelia and Reddy, Sanjay (2008, 572, 577, Table 1) Distribution data for 2004 is from World Bank (2008, 68, Table 2.8.).

gressed most rapidly in the 1990s. Table 2.2 tells the story, and the data from the Internal Revenue Service (more fine-grained than those available for China) show, in particular, that the relative gains were heavily concentrated at the very top, where a mere 400,000 now earn as much as the poorest 150 million. The top 0.01 % of US households (c. 14,400 tax returns) quadrupled their share of US household income and increased their advantage in average income over the poorer half of Americans sixfold, from 375:1 to 2214:1. The richest ventile is the only one that gained ground; all other ventiles saw their share of US household income decline, with relative losses greatest at the bottom.[18]

This income polarization in the US, and the consequent economic and political marginalization of the US poor, underscore the point that increasing intra-national inequality is a widespread phenomenon that, while certainly influenced by domestic factors and resistible by domestic political processes, is favored and facilitated by the WTO globalization of the last decades. US polarization can moreover highlight a useful political point: if the poorest 90 % of the US population had a better understanding of their own interests, they would be potential partners in a coalition aimed at democratizing globalization: aimed at reducing the near-monopolistic power of the small global elite now steering the evolution of the supranational institutional architecture. To win them as allies we can appeal to their interests, but also, of course, to their commitment to human rights which are the core theme of this arti-

Table 2.2 Evolution of US household income 1928–2008

Segment of US population	Share of US household income 1928/1929	Share of US household income 1980/1981	Share of US household income 2007/2008	Absolute change in income share 1980/1981–2007/2008	Relative change in income share
Richest 0.01 %	5.01	1.33	5.54	+4.21	+318 %
Next 0.09 %	6.22	2.17	5.81	+3.64	+168 %
Next 0.9 %	11.92	6.53	10.89	+4.36	+67 %
Next 4 %	14.38	13.09	15.37	+2.28	+17 %
Next 5 %	10.48	11.48	11.39	−0.09	−1 %
Next 15 %		24.63	21.14	−3.49	−14 %
Second quarter		25.61	19.45	−6.16	−24 %
Poorest half		17.72	12.51	−5.21	−29 %

[18]The top five rows of the table present data from Saez and Piketty (2003), Tables and Figures Updated to 2014 in Excel format, June 2015, available at http://eml.berkeley.edu/~saez (accessed 25 October 2015). The remaining three rows present data provided by Robyn, Mark and Prante, Gerald 2011. 'Tax foundation, summary of latest federal individual income tax data' (Table 5). http://taxfoundation.org/article/summary-latest-federal-individual-income-tax-data-0 (accessed 25 October 2015). Because the data come from different sources, columns two to four do not quite sum up correctly. But this should not disturb the table's point which is to display the rapid polarization of the US income distribution documented in the rightmost column.

cle. Let me conclude then by highlighting some of the main features of the present supranational institutional arrangements that are especially detrimental to the realization of human rights.

I give this account in opposition to the usual rosy story which, if it acknowledges the massive persistence of severe poverty at all, explains it by two factors: corrupt and oppressive regimes in many poor countries and the 'leaky bucket' of development assistance. Both these explanations have an element of truth. But the first fails to explain the high prevalence of corrupt and oppressive regimes, and the second fails to explain why the income of the poor is not catching up with that of the rest.

My own explanation can redeploy the metaphor: the assets of the poor are like a leaky bucket, continuously depleted by massive outflows that overwhelm the effects of remittances and development assistance, which, in any case, are puny. We take great pride in our assistance, boasting, for example, of the billions we spend annually on assistance to poor countries. Yet we ignore the vastly larger amounts that we extract from the poor without compensation. Consider the following examples.

First, affluent countries and their firms buy huge quantities of natural resources from the rulers of developing countries without regard for how such leaders came to power and how they exercise power. In many cases, this amounts to collaboration in the theft of these resources from their owners: the country's people. It also enriches their oppressors, thereby entrenching the oppression: tyrants sell us the natural resources of their victims and then use the proceeds to buy the weapons they need to keep themselves in power (Pogge 2008; Wenar 2008, 2015).

Second, affluent countries and their banks lend money to such rulers and compel the country's people to repay it even after the ruler is gone. Many poor populations are still servicing debts incurred, against their will, by dictators such as Suharto in Indonesia, Mobutu in the Congo, and Abacha in Nigeria. Again, we are participating in theft: the unilateral imposition of debt burdens on impoverished populations.

Third, affluent countries facilitate the embezzlement of funds by public officials in less developed countries by allowing their banks to accept such funds. This complicity could easily be avoided: banks are already under strict reporting requirements with regard to funds suspected of being related to terrorism or drug trafficking. Yet Western banks still eagerly accept and manage embezzled funds, with governments ensuring that their banks remain attractive for such illicit deposits. Global Financial Integrity (GFI) estimates that less developed countries have in this way lost at least \$660 billion annually during the period 2003–2012 (Kar and Spaniers 2014).[19]

Fourth, affluent countries facilitate tax evasion in the less developed countries through lax accounting standards for multinational corporations. Since they are not required to do country-by-country reporting, such corporations can easily manipulate transfer prices among their subsidiaries to concentrate their profits where they are

[19] For comparison, official development assistance during this period averaged \$124 billion annually,of which only \$13.5 billion was allocated to 'basic social services', United Nations, 'Millennium Development Goal Indicators', available at http://unstats.un.org/unsd/mdg/Search.aspx?q=bss%20oda (accessed 25 October 2015).

taxed the least. As a result, they may report no profit in the countries in which they extract, manufacture or sell goods or services, having their worldwide profits taxed instead in some tax haven where they only have a paper presence. Christian Aid estimates that, during the period 2000–2015, these illict outflows have deprived less developed countries of $160 billion per annum in tax revenues (Christian Aid 2009).

Fifth, affluent countries account for a disproportionate share of global pollution. Their emissions are prime contributors to serious health hazards, extreme weather events, rising sea levels, and climate change, to which poor populations are especially vulnerable. A report by the Global Humanitarian Forum estimated that climate change is already seriously affecting 325 million people and is annually causing $125 billion in economic losses, as well as 300,000 deaths, of which 99 % are in less developed countries (Global Humanitarian Forum 2009).

Finally, affluent countries have created a global trading regime that is supposed to release large collective gains through free and open markets. The regime is rigged; it permits rich states to continue to protect their markets through tariffs and anti-dumping duties and to gain larger world market shares through export credits and subsidies (including about $265 billion annually in agriculture alone) that poor countries cannot afford to match (OECD 2009). Since production is much more labor-intensive in poor than in affluent countries, such protectionist measures destroy many more jobs than they create.

2.3.3 *What Ought We to Do?*

Taken together, these supranational institutional factors generate a massive headwind against the poor.[20] This headwind overwhelms the effects of public and private foreign aid, perpetuating the exclusion of the poor from effective participation in the globalized economy and their inability to benefit proportionately from global economic growth. This problem may be solvable through huge increases in development aid, but such continuous compensation is neither cost-effective nor sustainable. It is far better to develop institutional reforms that would reduce the headwind, and eventually turn it off. This would mean seeing the world poverty problem not as a specialist concern at the margins of grand politics but as an important consideration in all institutional design decisions.

The world's leading governments could mainstream the imperative of poverty avoidance in this way. But Western governments are unlikely to do this unless there is voter demand or at least voter approval. As of now, the opposite is the case. Even while the hardships suffered by poor people are rising (partly as a result of the US-caused global financial crisis), voters in the United States are putting foreign aid

[20] That this headwind is at most weak and uncertain has been forcefully argued by Cohen (2010). See also my reply (Pogge 2010a). With luck, this dispute will stimulate more and better empirical research on what the effects of various supranational institutional design decisions actually are.

at the bottom of the list of expenditures to be preserved.[21] Voters in Continental Europe are somewhat more supportive of foreign aid, with voters in Germany, Italy, France, and Spain holding that more of the needed budget cuts should come out of the military budget (Barber 2010). These more supportive voter attitudes are reflected in higher European outlays for official development assistance (ODA), which are 0.43 % of gross national income versus 0.19 % for the United States (UN Statistics Division 2010). Both rates are far below the Western promise of the 1970s to bring ODA rates up to 0.70 % – a promise that only five small countries (Sweden, Norway, Luxembourg, Denmark and the Netherlands) have been honoring. (In 2013, the Netherlands have left, and the United Kingdom has entered, this small group.) It should also be noted that much foreign aid is spent for the benefit of domestic exporters or 'friendly' governments; out of $135 billion spent annually on ODA, only about $15.5 billion is spent on 'basic social services,' that is, on reducing poverty or its effects (ibid.).

Citizen attitudes clearly matter. If citizens of Western states cared about the avoidance of poverty, then so would their politicians. But an individual citizen may still feel powerless to change anything and may then reject any responsibility for the massive persistence of severe poverty. This rejection clearly could not excuse a majority of citizens. Given the stakes, the members of such a majority should organize themselves or otherwise ensure that politicians understand that they must seriously address the world poverty problem if they want to succeed in politics. But if – as is actually the case – a large majority of one's fellow citizens is not ready to prioritize the world poverty problem, then there may indeed be little that a few willing citizens can do to change their country's policies and posture in international negotiations. Should citizens in this situation be considered implicated in their country's human rights violation even if they cannot prevent it?

One might argue for an affirmative answer on the following ground: such citizens could emigrate to one of the poorer countries, thereby disconnecting themselves from their erstwhile country's policies and marginally weakening this country. Emigration may indeed be a plausible decision in cases of great injustice – it made sense, for instance, for Herbert Ernst Karl Frahm (the later Willy Brandt) to leave Germany as the Nazis were consolidating power. But in developed Western societies today, democratic institutions remain basically intact, and efforts to stir the conscience of one's compatriots are not futile. Moreover, there is a far better way for citizens to avoid sharing responsibility for the human rights violations their government is committing in their name. Citizens can compensate for a share of the harm for which their country is responsible by, for example, supporting effective international agencies or non-governmental organizations. Such compensation is typically less burdensome for citizens, and it also reduces the human rights deficit in which these citizens are implicated. To make room for this compensation option, our human-rights-correlative negative duty in regard to social institutions should then

[21] A recent CNN poll (21–23 January 2011) found that 81 % of Americans are in favor of reductions in foreign aid. CNN. 2011. 'Opinion Research Corporation Poll – Jan 21 to 23, 2011'. http://i2.cdn.turner.com/cnn/2011/images/01/25/rel2d.pdf. Accessed 4 March 2011.

be amended. We ought not to collaborate in the design or imposition of social institutions that foreseeably cause a human-rights deficit that is reasonably avoidable through better institutional design – unless we fully compensate for our fair share of the avoidable human rights deficit.

How might compensation work? Suppose one accepts the earlier estimate that those lacking an adequate standard of living would need another 2 % of global household income to reach this low level of sufficiency. And suppose that your household's per capita income is about $20,000, placing you in the middle of the second ventile. Since the top two ventiles have about 62.3 % of global household income, a transfer of 3.2 % of their collective income to the poor would have been theoretically sufficient to eradicate severe poverty. Were you to reduce the global poverty gap by $640 (=3.2 % of $20,000), then you would be sure to compensate for your fair share of the harm that we, through our governments, are collectively imposing on the world's poor.[22]

2.4 Conclusion

To show that we are indeed violating the human rights of the world's poor, I have proceeded in two main steps. Part 2 set forth a conception of what it means to violate a human right, arguing that 'human rights violation' is a relational predicate, involving right holders as well as duty bearers, with the latter playing an active role in causing the human rights of the former to be unfulfilled. Widely neglected is one very common kind of such violations involving the design and imposition of institutional arrangements that foreseeably and avoidably cause some human beings to lack secure access to the objects of their human rights. Just as one is actively harming people when one takes on the office of lifeguard and then fails to do one's job, so we are actively harming people when we seize the authority to design and impose social institutions and then fail to shape them so that human rights are realized under them insofar as this is reasonably possible. As argued in Part 3, we violate the human rights of billions of poor people by collaborating in the imposition of a

[22] This calculation should be refined in various ways. First, even a just supranational institutional order, carefully designed towards human rights realization, would not avoid poverty completely, so we may not be collectively responsible for the entire poverty gap. Second, some have job-related reasons to live in an area with high prices (especially for shelter) which may reduce their fair share. Third, some people poorer than ourselves, those in the third and fourth ventiles at least, might also be expected to make compensating contributions. Fourth, people richer than ourselves should be expected to contribute more than a proportional (3.2 %) share of their incomes. You can easily find reasons for reducing your fair share. But in view of the horrendous deprivations suffered by the world's poor, in view of the near universal failure of our peers to make the required compensating contribution, and in view of our undeserved good fortune to be born among the privileged (and perhaps to be more privileged than anyone would be under just institutional arrangements), we have every reason to err on the side of overcompensation.

supranational institutional scheme that foreseeably produces massive and reasonably avoidable human rights deficits.

It is easy to walk away from this conclusion with the comment that its empirical support has not been established beyond all doubt. As I indicated above, it is certainly *possible* that no feasible alternative design of supranational institutional arrangements could have led to a smaller global human rights deficit. But to live comfortably with the belief that we have only positive assistance duties toward the world's poor, we need more than a slight doubt of my conclusion. This is especially true in light of the amazing lack of serious unbiased inquiry into the effects of existing global institutional arrangements. Are we going to tell the poor majority of our contemporaries that, as we haven't carefully examined the causal effects of the institutional arrangements we are (in collaboration with their ruling elites) imposing on the world, we cannot be certain that these arrangements are doing massive avoidable harm – and may therefore reject as insufficiently corroborated the claim that we are violating their human rights? With much evidence supporting the view that supranational institutional arrangements we are involved in imposing contribute greatly to the persistence of the huge current human rights deficit, we ought to press for more careful study of these arrangements and their effect and for feasible reforms that make these arrangements more protective of the poor. Each of us should also do enough towards protecting poor people to be confident that one is fully compensating for one's fair share of the human rights deficit that we together cause.

References

Alston, Philip. 1984. International law and the right to food. In *Food as a human right*, ed. Asbjorn Eide, Wenche Barthe Eide, Susantha Goonatilake, Joan Gussow, and Omawale. Tokyo: United Nations University Press.

Alston, Philip, and Katarina Tomaševski (eds.). 1984. *The right to food*. Leiden: Martinus Nijhoff Publishers.

Alvaredo, Facundo, Tony Atkinson, Thomas Piketty and Emmanuel Saez. 2011. Top Incomes Database. Available at http://g-mond.parisschoolofeconomics.eu/topincomes/. Accessed 2 Apr 2011.

Andrew Cockburn. 2003. 21st Century Slaves. *National Geographic*, http://ngm.nationalgeographic.com/ngm/0309/feature1/. Accessed 25 October 2015.

Barber, Tony. 2010. Strong public support for spending cuts across Europe. *Financial Times*. http://www.ft.com/cms/s/0/8f9e61c0-8ce2-11df-bad7-00144feab49a.html#axzz3pgxbLVxz. Accessed 26 Oct 2015.

Christian Aid. 2009. 'False Profits: Robbing the Poor to Keep the Rich Tax-Free'. http://www.christianaid.org.uk/Images/false-profits.pdf. Accessed 25 October 2015.

CNN. 2011. Opinion research corporation poll – Jan 21 to 23, 2011. http://i2.cdn.turner.com/cnn/2011/images/01/25/rel2d.pdf. Accessed 25 October 2015.

Credit Suisse. 2015. Global Wealth Report 2015. http://publications.credit-suisse.com/tasks/render/file/index.cfm?fileid=C26E3824-E868-56E0-CCA04D4BB9B9ADD5. Accessed 25 October 2015.

Cohen, Joshua. 2010. Philosophy, social science, global poverty. In *Thomas Pogge and his critics*, ed. Jaggar Alison, 18–45. Malden: Polity Press.

FAO. 2015. *The state of food insecurity in the world 2015*. www.fao.org/3/a-i4646e/index.html. Accessed 25 October 2015.

Global Humanitarian Forum. 2009. *The anatomy of a silent crisis*. Geneva Global Humanitarian Forum. http://www.ghf-ge.org/human-impact-report.pdf. Accessed 27 Oct 2015.

ILO. 2015. Child labour. http://www.ilo.org/global/topics/child-labour/lang--en/index.htm. Accessed 25 October 2015.

Jeremy Bentham. 1996 [1789]. *An introduction to the principles of morals and legislation*, ed. H. Burns and H.L.A. Hart. Oxford: Oxford University Press.

Kar, Dev and Joseph Spaniers. 2014. *Illicit financial flows from developing countries: 2003–2012*. Global financial integrity. http://www.gfintegrity.org/wp-content/uploads/2014/12/Illicit-Financial-Flows-from-Developing-Countries-2003-2012.pdf. Accessed 25 October 2015.

Milanovic, Branko. 2011. *The haves and have-nots: A brief and idiosyncratic history of global inequality*. New York: Basic Books.

Minoiu, Camelia, and Sanjay Reddy. 2008. Chinese poverty: Assessing the impact of alternative assumptions. *Review of Income and Wealth* 54(4): 572–596.

Moreno, Kasia. 2014. 'The 67 People As Wealthy As The World's Poorest 3.5 Billion', Forbes March 25, 2014. http://www.forbes.com/sites/forbesinsights/2014/03/25/the-67-people-as-wealthy-as-the-worlds-poorest-3-5-billion. Accessed 25 October 2015.

Nagel, Thomas. 2005. The problem of global justice. *Philosophy and Public Affairs* 33(2): 113–147.

Organization for Economic Cooperation and Development (OECD). 2009. *Agricultural Policies in OECD Countries*.

Pogge, Thomas. 2005. Severe poverty as a violation of negative duties. *Ethics and International Affairs* 19(1): 55–83.

Pogge, Thomas. 2007a. Severe poverty as a human rights violation. In *Freedom from poverty as a human right: Who owes what to the very poor?* ed. Thomas Pogge, 11–54. Oxford: Oxford University Press.

Pogge, Thomas (ed.). 2007b. *Freedom from poverty as a human right: Who owes what to the very poor?* Oxford: Oxford University Press.

Pogge, Thomas. 2008. *World poverty and human rights: Cosmopolitan responsibilities and reforms*, 2nd ed. Cambridge: Polity Press.

Pogge, Thomas. 2009a. The health impact fund and its justification by appeal to human rights. *Journal of Social Philosophy* 40(4): 542–569.

Pogge, Thomas. 2009b. Shue on rights and duties. In *Global basic rights*, ed. Charles Beitz and Robert Goodin, 113–130. Oxford: Oxford University Press.

Pogge, Thomas. 2010a. Responses to the critics. In *Thomas Pogge and his critics*, ed. Alison Jaggar, 175–191. Cambridge: Polity Press.

Pogge, Thomas. 2010b. *Politics as usual: What lies behind the pro-poor rhetoric*. Cambridge: Polity Press.

Rawls, John. 1971. *A theory of justice*. Harvard: Harvard University Press.

Rawls, John. 1999. *The law of peoples*. Harvard: Harvard University Press.

Robyn, Mark and Prante, Gerald. 2011. *'Tax foundation, summary of latest federal individual income tax data' (Table 5)*. http://taxfoundation.org/article/summary-latest-federal-individual-income-tax-data-0. Accessed 25 Oct 2015.

Satz, Debra. 2005. What do we owe the global poor? *Ethics and International Affairs* 19(1): 47–54.

Shue, Henry. 1996. *Basic rights: Subsistence, affluence, and US foreign policy*, 2nd ed. Princeton: Princeton University Press.

UN Committee on Economic, Social, and Cultural Rights. 1999. General comment on the right to adequate food. UN Doc E/C.12/ 1999/5. http://www.refworld.org/docid/4538838c11.html. Accessed 26 Oct 2015.

UN Habitat. 2012. 'Women and Urban Energy- International Women's Day'. http://unhabitat.org/women-and-urban-energy-international-womens-day/. Accessed 25 October 2015.
UN Habitat. 2015. 'World Habitat Day 2015 key housing facts'. http://www.habitat.org/getinv/events/world-habitat-day/housing-facts. Accessed 25 October 2015.
UN Statistics Division. 2010. Net ODA as percentage of OECD/DAC donors GNI. http://data.un.org/Data.aspx?d=MDG&f=seriesRowID%3A568. Accessed 26 Oct 2015.
UN Statistics Division. 2010. Net ODA, million US$ http://data.un.org/Data.aspx?d=MDG&f=seriesRowID%3A568. Accessed 26 Oct 2015.
UN Statistics Division. 2010. ODA to basic social services, million US$. http://data.un.org/Data.aspx?d=MDG&f=seriesRowID%3A568. Accessed 26 Oct 2015.
UNESCO. 2015. 'International Literacy Day'. http://www.uis.unesco.org/literacy/Pages/literacy-day-2015.aspx. Accessed 25 October 2015.
UNICEF. 2010. What we do: Water, sanitation and hygiene. http://www.unicef.org/wash/. Accessed 25 October 2015.
United Nations. 1948. Universal declaration of human rights.
United Nations, Millennium Development Goal Indicators. http://unstats.un.org/unsd/mdg/Search.aspx?q=bss%20oda. Accessed 4 Mar 2011.
Universal Declaration of Human Rights (UDHR). Proclaimed by the United Nations General Assembly in Paris on 10 December 1948, General Assembly resolution 217(III) A.
UNU-WIDER. 2008. World income inequality database. http://www.wider.unu.edu/research/Database/en_GB/database. Accessed 1 May 2012.
Waldron, Jeremy. 1989. Rights in conflict. *Ethics and International Affairs* 99(3): 503–519.
Wenar, Leif. 2008. Property rights and the resource curse. *Philosophy and Public Affairs* 36: 2–32.
Wenar, Leif. 2015. *Blood Oil: Tyrants, Violence and the Rules that Run the World*. Oxford: Oxford University Press.
WHO. 2004. WHO medicines strategy: Countries at the core – 2004–2007. http://apps.who.int/medicinedocs/pdf/s5416e/s5416e.pdf. Accessed 25 October 2015.
WHO. 2008. Global burden of disease. 2004 Update. http://www.who.int/healthinfo/global_burden_disease/GBD_report_2004update_full.pdf. Accessed 25 October 2015.
World Bank. 2008. World development indicators. http://data.worldbank.org/sites/default/files/wdi08.pdf. Accessed 27 Oct 2015.
World Bank. GDP per capita growth (annual per cent), http://data.worldbank.org/indicator/NY.GDP.PCAP.KD.ZG/countries/1W-XQ-EG-SYMA-IR-SA? display=graph. Accessed 25 October 2015.
World Food Summit. 2012. *Report of the world food summit*, Annex II, UN Doc. WFS 96/REP. http://www.fao.org/wfs/. Accessed 25 October 2015.

Chapter 3
A Decent Social Minimum as a Matter of Justice

Elena Pribytkova

Abstract The chapter is devoted to exploring a decent social minimum as a set of guarantees aimed at protecting persons from extreme poverty; enabling them to lead a decent life; ensuring their involvement in society and access to shared material and intellectual values; and, in the final analysis, providing the opportunity for their moral and intellectual flourishing. Guarantees of a decent social minimum represent an important instrument of poverty and inequality alleviation. My chapter intends to clarify the most controversial issues surrounding a decent social minimum: its content, scope, elements and relation to principles of social justice and equality. I develop an idea that it is necessary to distinguish between two interpretations of equality – distributive equality and equality of status – and analyze their interdependence. I argue then that it is equality of status that is the key idea of the demand for a decent social minimum and show that the following distributive guarantees necessarily derive from equality of status and form essential components of a decent social minimum: minimum political conditions of a decent life (equal citizenship), minimum socio-economic conditions of a decent life (decent standard of living), and guarantees of protection from extreme inequality (non-dominance and non-discrimination). Finally, while applying the principle of sufficiency conformable to equality of status, I examine the scope of a decent standard of living.

Keywords Poverty • Human rights • Social minimum • Decent life • Equality

3.1 Introduction

My chapter is devoted to exploring a decent social minimum as a set of guarantees aimed at protecting persons from extreme poverty; enabling them to lead a decent life; ensuring their involvement in society and access to shared material and intellectual values; and, in the final analysis, providing the opportunity for their moral

The research is supported by the SNSF Ambizione grant (No. 142547).

E. Pribytkova (✉)
Faculty of Law, University of Basel, Peter Merian-Weg 8, 4002 Basel, Switzerland
e-mail: e.pribytkova@unibas.ch

H.P. Gaisbauer et al. (eds.), *Ethical Issues in Poverty Alleviation*, Studies in Global Justice 14, DOI 10.1007/978-3-319-41430-0_3

and intellectual flourishing. Guarantees of a decent social minimum are globally recognized as an important instrument for alleviating poverty and inequality and have gained acceptance in international and regional human rights law as well as in legal orders of particular states. Nevertheless, there is still no agreement in contemporary legal and political philosophy, as well as in human rights law, on a set of complex issues concerning the social minimum principle. What are the content, scope and elements of a decent social minimum? How can one formulate its key idea and a justifying basis? What kind of inequality and injustice does a decent social minimum aim to combat? What measures of protection from extreme poverty and extreme inequality does it embrace? How are the demands for a social minimum and a decent standard of living interrelated? Can the internationally recognized human "right of everyone to an adequate standard of living" be considered a correct expression of a decent social minimum? These questions underlie my research.

The chapter has the following structure: first, I develop an idea that it is necessary to distinguish between two interpretations of equality – distributive equality and equality of status – and analyze their interdependence; the second part of the chapter argues that it is equality of status that is the key idea of the demand for a decent social minimum and shows what distributive guarantees derive from equality of status and form essential components of a decent social minimum; and in the third part, while applying the principle of sufficiency conformable to equality of status, I examine the scope of socio-economic guarantees of a decent standard of living.

3.2 Equality of Status or Distributive Equality?

Political philosophers often distinguish between two interrelated but at the same time substantially different meanings of equality: distributive equality and "moral equality" or, as I prefer to call it, "equality of status". For instance, John Rawls speaks about two conceptions of equality: "equality as it is invoked in connection with the distribution of certain goods, some of which will almost certainly give higher status or prestige to those who are more favored, and equality as it applies to the respect which is owed to persons irrespective of their social position" (Rawls 1971, 511). Equality of the second kind belongs to human beings as moral persons. Rawls considers it to be fundamental and to have a priority over distributive equality.

David Miller defines equality of status, or social equality, as "a social ideal, the ideal of a society in which people regard and treat one another as equals, in other words a society that is not marked by status divisions such that one can place different people in hierarchically ranked categories, in different classes for instance" (Miller 1997, 224). He addresses the question of the relationship between justice and equality – "In what sense is justice intrinsically egalitarian?" – and claims that justice is egalitarian not in the sense of distributive equality, but in the sense of equality of status.

While developing this line of argument, Elizabeth Anderson and Samuel Scheffler assert that equality is essentially not a distributive value, which requires people to have equal amounts of something, but a relational one (Anderson 1999, 313; Scheffler 2015, 22). According to this understanding of egalitarianism, distributive equality matters "only because and insofar as it is necessary in order to achieve a society of equals". On this assumption, "the relevant question in thinking about equality and distribution, is not 'What is the currency of which justice requires an equal distribution?' It is rather 'What kinds of distributions are consistent with the ideal of a society of equals?'" (Scheffler 2015, 22).

The principal premise of equality of status is that all persons as moral beings equally possess human dignity and human rights. In this sense, equality of status is the basis of the conception of human rights and has found its embodiment in Art. 1 of the Universal Declaration of Human Rights: "all human beings are born free and equal in dignity and rights". In his recent Report on extreme inequality and human rights, the Special Rapporteur on extreme poverty and human rights, Philip Alston, proposes "revitalizing and giving substance to the right to equality" (Alston 2015, para. 54–55). One cannot but support this recommendation. I believe however that the right to equality should be interpreted as the right to equality in status.[1]

It is not accidental that equality of status is often called "equality in dignity". A society of equals is a society where the equal worth and equal dignity of its members is recognized as a fundamental common standard and economic, political or cultural differences do not influence judgments about their moral status. In the context of contemporary multiculturalism, the necessity to formulate a normative core of the multidimensional concept of human dignity that is, in the words of Otfried Höffe, "indifferent in relation to the difference of cultures" (Höffe 1994, 121) is being articulated more and more insistently.[2] I consider equality of status to be capable of serving as the desired intercultural core of human dignity.[3]

On this premise, equality of status is characterized by several fundamental features: universality, inalienability, and fully-fledged membership in society. First, all

[1] My thesis does not contradict another of Alston's suggestions to put "questions of resource redistribution at the centre of human rights debates" (Alston 2015, para. 56), because I think that equality of status should shape distributive practices.

[2] For example, while developing Gerald Neuman's ideas, Christopher McCrudden formulates three elements of a basic minimum content of human dignity. According to the first two of them – the "ontological claim" and the "relational claim" – "every human being possesses an intrinsic worth, merely by being human" and "this intrinsic worth should be recognized and respected by others, and some forms of treatment by others are inconsistent with, or required by, respect for this intrinsic worth". He argues then that "there appears to be no consensus politically or philosophically" on how these claims are best understood in various societies and legal cultures (McCrudden 2008, 679–680).

[3] It looks as if Miller sees the correlation of dignity and equality of status in the same way: "So if people are to have dignity and respect in this society now, it must be the kind of dignity and respect that social equality provides" (Miller 1997, 234).

members of society are unconditionally entitled to a status of moral persons irrespective of their financial or social state. Secondly, nobody can be deprived (nor deprive oneself) of this status even if her sad financial and social state is a result of her own bad choices. Finally, equality of status implies that all persons equally enjoy human rights and are fully able to participate in all core social, political and cultural institutions and practices of society including important decision-making processes. It is necessary to emphasize that equality of status does not presuppose any equalizations, aimed at ensuring equal income, wealth, power, or prestige.

Without doubt, equality of status and distributive equality are interrelated. There is no direct connection between them however. On the one hand, distributive inequality as such is not an impediment to a society of equals. As Richard Arneson states, "the idea is that citizens might be unequal in wealth, resources, welfare, and other dimensions of their condition, yet be equal in status in a way that enables all to relate as equals" (Arneson 2013). On the other hand, equal distribution of resources, social goods or capabilities by no means ensures that equality of status is achieved. Miller is absolutely right in his statement that there are no goods or resources which when appropriately distributed should necessarily cause equality of status (Miller 1995, 199–200).

Since equality of status externalizes itself in social relations, it is determined above all by social consciousness.[4] In this context, Anderson defines equality of status as a "social relationship" (Anderson 1999, 313). Recognition and respect for a person and her dignity is capable of transforming even a non-egalitarian (from the point of view of distributive equality) society into a society of equals. The emphasis here is not on "creating" but on "realizing" equality.[5] In the meantime, material conditions of equality as such are not sufficient if members of society are not ready to recognize each other as equal moral persons.

Besides the fact that equality of status depends substantively on social consciousness, there is one more fundamental difference between the two kinds of equality. Equality of status necessarily correlates with the principle of human dignity and is inconceivable without it, whereas distributive equality as such can be compatible with any other and even opposite ideas. For example, the idea of equal distribution of material goods in USSR was combined with a total disregard for the principles of equal respect for, and equal worth and dignity of persons.

At the same time, under certain conditions, distributive strategies certainly influence equality of status. First of all, equality of status is impossible when a section of a society lives in extreme poverty,[6] marked by severe material deprivation, exclusion, powerlessness, and stigmatization of a person. But the most tragic sign of

[4] My chapter deals with equality of status in the public domain. An excellent examination of equality of status in interpersonal relationships can be found in Scheffler (2015).

[5] A prominent Russian philosopher, Vladimir Solov'ev (1853–1900), developed this idea in his conception of the right to a dignified existence (Pribytkova 2013, 119–122). It is also in tune with Miller's position (1995, 200).

[6] The focus of my chapter is not on social relationships among those in extreme poverty, but rather on relationships between those on different sides of the extreme poverty line.

extreme poverty is the feelings of indignity, worthlessness or "nobodiness" suffered by people affected by extreme poverty. The founder of the International Movement ATD Fourth World, Fr. Joseph Wresinski, succeeded in conveying these feelings: "For the very poor tell us over and over again that man's greatest misfortune is not to be hungry or unable to read, nor even to be without work. The greatest misfortune of all is to know that you count for nothing, to the point where even your suffering is ignored. The worst blow of all is the contempt on the part of your fellow citizens. For it is that contempt which stands between a human being and his rights. It makes the world disdain what you are going through and prevents you from being recognized as worthy and capable of taking on responsibility. The greatest misfortune of extreme poverty is that for your entire existence you are like someone already dead" (Wresinski 2000, 20). Beyond any doubt, those practices of distribution of social goods, resources or capabilities that cause people to lead such a miserable existence, to be considered and to realize themselves as being non-persons who cannot appear in public without shame, violate equality of status and should be eradicated.

Secondly, distributive inequalities often translate themselves into inequality of status. Those who enjoy higher power or prestige in one sphere often strive to use them for advantages in other spheres and, vice versa, the less advantaged in one domain are often discriminated against in other domains as well. The Report of the Special Rapporteur on extreme poverty and human rights gives an excellent overview of how distributive inequalities widening around the world "stifle equal opportunity, lead to laws, regulations and institutions that favour the powerful, and perpetuate discrimination against certain groups" (Alston 2015, Summary). Contemporary scholars and practitioners have proved that extreme distributive inequality negatively affects the realization of basic rights[7] and is an obstacle to poverty reduction: "high levels of inequality may create institutions that maintain the political, economic and social privileges of the elite and lock the poor into poverty traps from which it is difficult to escape" (UNRISD 2010, 6). It is evident that increasing distributive inequalities prevents people from recognizing each other as equal members of society, while furthering a division of a society into first-class and second-class citizens.[8] In this sense, Alston is right when he asserts that "extreme inequality and respect for the equal rights of all persons are incompatible" and states should "commit themselves to policies explicitly designed to reduce, if not eliminate, extreme inequality" (Alston 2015, para. 48–49).

If extreme poverty excludes any opportunity of equality of status, then distributive inequality may hamper it significantly. In other words, whereas extreme poverty, indicated by an acute insufficiency of basic social goods or resources, is directly and universally translatable into inequality of status, the convertibility of

[7] For example, the Special Rapporteur on extreme poverty and human rights provides an analysis of "detrimental effects of economic inequalities on the enjoyment of human rights" (Alston 2015, para. 26–32).

[8] For instance, a survey carried out by Oxfam in six states (Spain, Brazil, India, South Africa, the UK and the US) demonstrated that "a majority of people believe that laws are skewed in favour of the rich" (Oxfam 2014, 3).

distributive inequalities into inequality of status is indirect and culturally specific (Miller 1997, 224, 237). Since we consider a decent social minimum to provide effective institutional guarantees of equality of status, the former should be equipped with the means capable of eradicating extreme poverty and reducing extreme distributive inequality. The measures of protection from extreme poverty and extreme inequality presupposed by a decent social minimum will be in the limelight in the next part of the chapter.

3.3 Essential Components of a Decent Social Minimum

A decent social minimum is traditionally considered to be a set of socio-economic guarantees of a decent life and thereby is interpreted as a matter of distributive justice (see, for example: White 2004). I believe it is necessary to draw the line between a decent social minimum and a decent standard of living. As will be shown further, a decent social minimum embraces both distributive and non-distributive aspects; and minimum socio-economic guarantees of a decent life, i.e. a decent standard of living, represent only one of several components of a decent social minimum.

The fundamental thesis of my chapter is that it is equality of status that underlies a decent social minimum and serves as its justifying basis. Securing access to a decent social minimum is aimed not at distributing something, but first and foremost, at promoting relations between people as equals, i.e. as between fully-fledged members of society. Since certain strategies of distribution may impede equality of status or even make it impossible, a decent social minimum should include mechanisms for limiting them. In this respect, a decent social minimum comprises several important distributive guarantees that derive from equality of status, or "distributive implications" of equality of status, as Miller defines them (Miller 1997, 234). These are: minimum political conditions of a decent life directed to ensure equal citizenship; minimum socio-economic conditions of a decent life or a decent standard of living; and guarantees of protection from extreme inequality of distribution that enclose the principles of non-dominance and non-discrimination.

Let me specify briefly the distributive guarantees that arise from equality of status and form integral parts of a decent social minimum.

Equal citizenship is defined by how citizens regard themselves and one another in their political and social relationships. As Rawls asserts, equal citizens enjoy mutual respect as free and equal moral persons (Rawls 1981, 17, 43). Equal citizenship is a projection of equality of status in the political domain. As it was noted in the first part of the chapter, equality of status implies equal enjoyment of basic rights and fair and full access to all core institutions and practices including political and legal. People living in poverty are largely deprived of equal citizenship and equality of status, since they are oppressed, marginalized, excluded, silenced, and disempowered. Their financial and social state is both cause and effect of their inability to exercise their basic rights effectively, participate in significant decision-making and defend their fundamental interests. Minimum political conditions of a decent life involve guarantees of the full enjoyment of basic civil and political rights (rights to freedom of thought, conscience and religion, freedom of speech and expression, freedom of assembly and association etc.) and an "active, free, informed and meaningful participation of persons living in poverty at all stages of the design, implementation and evaluation of policies that affect them" (Sepúlveda 2013, para. 17) as well as an effective and affordable access to justice and to public and legal services (Sepúlveda 2012).

Guarantees of equal citizenship should be complemented with minimum socio-economic conditions of a decent life. At the heart of the socio-economic guarantees of a social minimum is the composite human right to an adequate, or decent, standard of living, which integrates the basic rights to adequate food, water, sanitation, housing, clothing, and health. The core international and regional human rights instruments recognize that "everyone has the right to a standard of living adequate for the health and well-being of himself and of his family, including food, clothing, housing and medical care and necessary social services" (Art. 25, the Universal Declaration of Human Rights).[9] The right to an adequate standard of living is closely interrelated with other social rights (the rights to social security, assistance and social protection), economic rights (the rights to job security and equal employment, decent work conditions, rest and leisure, just and favorable remuneration, and minimum wage) and cultural rights (the rights to education, participation in cultural life, enjoyment of the benefits of scientific progress and its applications) as well as the right to development indispensable for a dignified existence of a person.

Minimum political and socio-economic guarantees of a decent life are among the principal preconditions for establishing and maintaining a society of equals, because they aim at freeing persons from poverty and enabling them to lead a decent life; subverting oppression, exclusion, marginalization, and stigmatization of the most vulnerable social groups and individuals; promoting their legal and political empowerment and making their voices heard; ensuring their access to shared material and intellectual values and breaking barriers to their full participation in public life; and, in the final analysis, providing the opportunity for their moral and intellectual flourishing.

Since distributive inequalities are capable of translating themselves into inequality of status, social minimum guarantees should embody a certain level of protection from this unfair translation. In his conception of complex equality, Michael Walzer defends an idea of "relative autonomy" of distributive spheres, according to which inequalities in one sphere of justice are not allowed to provoke inequalities in another sphere (Walzer 1983, 10, 18). While sharing Pascal's view of tyranny as "the wish to obtain by one means what can only be had by another", Walzer formulates a non-dominance principle that forbids converting sphere-specific advantages from one sphere to another, when there is no intrinsic connection between both spheres: "*No social good x should be distributed to men and women who possess some other good y merely because they possess y and without regard to the meaning*

[9] See also: ICESCR (Art. 11), CRC (Art. 27), CEDAW (Art. 14), CRPD (Art. 28), ESC (Art. 4, 13), CFREU (Art. 34), Protocol of San Salvador (Art. 6, 7, 9, 12, 15).

of x" (Walzer 1983, 18, 20).[10] Miller suggests interpreting complex equality as equality of status: "we should read Walzer's claim as a claim about status. In a society which realizes complex equality, people enjoy a basic equality of status which overrides their unequal standing in particular spheres of justice such as money and power" (Miller 1995, 206). Miller regards guarantees of non-dominance and equal citizenship as essential distributive implications of equality of status: "distributive pluralism plus equal citizenship leads to equality of status" (Miller 1995, 208). I believe equality of status requires the principles of equal citizenship and non-dominance to be supplemented with guarantees of a decent standard of living and non-discrimination.

The protection from the tyranny of extreme inequality of distribution is directed not only against using one's high position in one sphere for an unfair dominance in the other, but also against de jure and de facto discrimination and exclusion of most vulnerable social groups and individuals from core political, social and cultural institutions and practices. An unfair dominance and discrimination are two sides of the same coin: the former imposes disadvantages on certain social groups and individuals as compared with unfair advantages of the powerful actors, while the latter makes social groups and individuals vulnerable to oppression and exploitation by the powerful actors through the denial of equal opportunities.[11]

Being essential for equality of status, the principle of non-discrimination is among the foundational rules of human rights law. The Universal Declaration of Human Rights proclaims "all are equal before the law and are entitled without any discrimination to equal protection of the law" (Art. 7). The International Covenant on Civil and Political Rights reaffirms that "the law shall prohibit any discrimination and guarantee to all persons equal and effective protection against discrimination on any ground such as race, colour, sex, language, religion, political or other opinion, national or social origin, property, birth or other status" (Art. 26).[12] This includes also a prohibition of discrimination on account of poverty. As the Committee on Economic, Social and Cultural Rights General Comment No. 20 "Non-discrimination in economic, social and cultural rights" elucidates, "a person's social and economic situation when living in poverty or being homeless may result in pervasive discrimination, stigmatization and negative stereotyping which can lead to the refusal of, or unequal access to, the same quality of education and health care as others, as well as the denial of or unequal access to public places". Therefore, "individuals and groups of individuals must not be arbitrarily treated on account of belonging to a certain economic or social group or strata within society" (para 35).

[10] It is necessary to note that the matter does not concern fair conversions of advantages from one sphere to another. It is beyond question, for example, that a good education may be a key for an interesting and well-paid job and well-deserved prestige in a particular society may be the reason to be elected into its representative body.

[11] On a definition of discrimination see Andrew Altman's article (Altman 2015).

[12] See also: ICESCR (Art. 2), CRC (Art. 2), CEDAW, CRPD, ICERD.

A former Special Rapporteur on extreme poverty and human rights, Magdalena Sepúlveda Carmona, remarks that "the theory and practice of human rights is deeply concerned with preventing powerful actors from imposing their will or interests at the expense of others through coercion, force or manipulation" (Sepúlveda 2013, para. 15). International, regional and national legal instruments and policies should both prevent unfair dominance and promote resistance to it through ensuring full enjoyment of basic rights and equal access to all core institutions and practices of society including significant decision-making processes. It is also important to add that guarantees of non-dominance and non-discrimination are implicitly implied by the political and socio-economic conditions of a decent life (equal citizenship and a decent standard of living).

Thus distributive aspects of a decent social minimum represent institutional guarantees of recognition of and respect for human dignity and equality of status. They are not exhausted by minimum socio-economic conditions of a decent life (decent standard of living), but embrace also minimum political conditions of a decent life (equal citizenship) as well as guarantees of protection from extreme inequality (non-dominance and non-discrimination). In this context, when translated into the language of human rights, the principle of a decent social minimum goes far beyond the scope of the right to an adequate standard of living and interrelated socio-economic rights and requires realization of the right to freedom from discrimination as well as other basic civil and political rights guaranteeing full participation in core institutions and practices of society including important decision-making processes.

My thesis on a decent standard of living as one of distributive guarantees of equality of status and an essential component of a decent social minimum raises the following questions: Does a decent standard of living demand equal distribution of social goods or does it call for any other distributive principle? Is the principle of equality of status capable of providing us with a criterion for determining the scope of basic socio-economic guarantees of a decent life? The next part of my chapter intends to answer these questions.

3.4 The Scope of a Decent Standard of Living

In response to the question of whether a decent standard of living requires equal distribution of social goods, one often encounters the argument: "If it is the inequality per se that is bad, then the gap between poor and rich would seem to be no worse than a same-sized gap between the life prospects of the rich and super-rich" (Arneson 2013; Frankfurt 1987, 32; Miller 1999, 199). According to a so-called "levelling-down objection", egalitarian principles as such are indifferent as to how inequality should be ended: by bringing the worst-off up or by bringing the better-off down. While invoking this objection, Joseph Raz develops an idea that poverty is not a question of inequality between rich and poor, but that poor do not have enough (Raz 1986, 227, 229, 235). The lack of a secure access to minimum socio-economic conditions of a decent life is caused, therefore, not by distributive inequality but by insufficiency.[13]

Harry Frankfurt has represented one of the most thorough justifications of the doctrine of sufficiency, along with a pointed criticism of the idea of equal distribution. In his opinion, "economic equality is not, as such, of particular moral importance. With respect to the distribution of economic assets, what is important from the point of view of morality is not that everyone should have the same but that each should have enough. If everyone had enough, it would be of no moral consequence whether some have more than others" (Frankfurt 1987, 21). In addition, under conditions of scarcity, equal distribution may be morally unacceptable (Frankfurt 1987, 31). Frankfurt considers the demand for equal distribution to be inadmissible because it distracts people from determining their own necessities and motivates them to strive for social goods absolutely irrelevant for them. Instead of measuring and comparing amounts of social goods possessed by members of society, the doctrine of sufficiency focuses on the correlation between basic needs of a particular person and social goods available to her. Frankfurt emphasizes that poverty expresses "not a quantitative discrepancy but a qualitative condition": it is not the fact that people have less resources that disturbs us but their misery (Frankfurt 1987, 32). As was shown previously in this chapter, distributive inequalities may detrimentally affect equality of status and, in this respect, may, in spite of Frankfurt's claim, definitely have moral consequences. That is why extreme inequalities should be taken under the control of other distributive instruments of a decent social minimum, i.e. guarantees of non-dominance and non-discrimination.

The scope of a decent standard of living is defined by the principle of sufficiency, which does not demand any equalization of the socio-economic state of a person above a certain minimum level.[14] With that it is equality of status that serves as a measure of what is sufficient for a decent life: "decent" in this context means sufficient for enjoying equality of status. One often distinguishes between the concept of an "absolute" minimum essential for physical survival of a person and the concept of a "socio-cultural" minimum, which ensures her involvement in society. A decent standard of living cannot be confined to guarantees necessary for a mere physical existence and freedom from extreme poverty, but implies guarantees that enable full participation in social, political and cultural life and access to shared material and intellectual values, as well as providing an opportunity for the moral and intellectual flourishing of a person.

The principle of sufficiency conformable to equality of status determines several important features of a decent standard of living.

---

[13] According to Anderson, who applies the capabilities approach to her "relational theory of equality", equality of status or "democratic equality guarantees not effective access to equal levels of functioning but effective access to levels of functioning sufficient to stand as an equal in society" (Anderson 1999, 318).

[14] Stephen Nathanson opposes the criteria of sufficiency and decency (Nathanson 2005). I proceed from the assumption that sufficiency is one of criteria of the principle of decency.

On the one hand, a decent standard of living is a non-derogable demand that should be fulfilled to the full extent.[15] In part, this idea has found its implementation in the concept of the minimum core of economic, social and cultural rights, to which minimum core obligations of states correspond. The minimum core approach helps to outline an essential level of socio-economic guarantees that should be reached by all states as a matter of priority and regardless of their level of wealth. Since a state fails to fulfil its minimum core obligations with the maximum of resources available to it, this gives rise to a subsidiary international responsibility to provide assistance in order to enable a state to secure access to the core elements of a decent standard of living (ICESCR, Art. 2). A serious disadvantage of contemporary applications of the minimum core approach lies in the fact that the interpretations of the minimum core of socio-economic rights that comprise essential foodstuffs, primary health care, basic shelter and housing, and the most basic forms of education,[16] are too narrow and sufficient merely for the physical survival of a person. For the sake of equality of status, the minimum core of socio-economic rights and corresponding obligations of states should embrace guarantees sufficient for leading a decent life and full participation in all core institutions and practices of society.

On the other hand, a decent standard of living corresponds to what Raz calls a "diminishing" and "satiable" principle, because it aims to eliminate a certain level of deprivation, "beyond which a person cannot be helped", and when the demand to eliminate deprivation is completely met it cannot be satisfied to a higher degree (Raz 1986, 235–236). Minimum socio-economic guarantees aim at promoting not a happy or good life, but a decent one. They, however, should also provide an opportunity for the moral and intellectual flourishing of a person and for pursuing what she considers to be a happy life. The demand for securing access to a decent standard of living is fulfilled when a certain minimum level of well-being sufficient for enjoying equality of status is achieved. An assessment of whether different people are capable of leading a more or less decent life is appropriate only until a minimum standard of a decent life is not equally safeguarded for all members of a given society or worldwide, since we apply our assessment to a global context. We cannot any longer estimate and compare different levels of well-being in terms of "sufficiency" or "decency", since this minimum threshold is reached. For instance, although we can say that the life conditions of a well-paid lawyer or a Nobel Prize Laureate are probably better than those of a shoemaker or a street cleaner, we cannot say that they are more decent, since the latter enjoy a secure access to a decent standard of living. In this case, their life conditions are equally decent.

To conclude, minimum socio-economic guarantees of a decent standard of living do not demand equal distribution of any social goods or resources, but rely on a

[15] Theories of justice that do not integrate a decent standard of living – for instance, John Rawls' maximin principle (Rawls 1971) and Philippe Van Parijs' highest sustainable basic income (Van Parijs 1995) – do not correspond to the principle of sufficiency, because they do not guarantee that the minimum level of well-being indispensable for maintaining a decent life can be achieved in impoverished societies.

[16] See: CESCR General Comments No. 3, 12, 13, 14, 15, 17, 18, 19, 21.

conception of sufficiency corresponding to equality of status. Being a diminishing and, at the same time, a non-derogable demand, a decent standard of living should provide for conditions sufficient not only for the physical survival of a person, but also for her leading a dignified life, her full participation in all core political, social and cultural institutions and practices of society as well as for her moral and intellectual flourishing.

3.5 Conclusion

The main ideas defended in the chapter can be summarized in the following way:

1. It is necessary to distinguish between distributive equality demanding persons to have equal amounts of something, and equality of status, which is characterized by the relation of persons to each other as to equals.
2. Equality of status is the key idea and a justifying basis of a decent social minimum. In this respect, a decent social minimum does not presuppose equal distribution of any social goods or resources. Rather, it is a demand for minimum conditions indispensable for enjoying fully-fledged membership in society irrespective of the financial or social state of a person.
3. A decent social minimum comprises important distributive guarantees that derive from equality of status: minimum political conditions of a decent life (equal citizenship), minimum socio-economic conditions of a decent life (decent standard of living) as well as guarantees of protection from extreme inequality of distribution (non-dominance and non-discrimination).
4. The scope of a decent standard of living is determined by the principle of sufficiency corresponding to equality of status. Being a diminishing and at the same time a non-derogable demand, a decent standard of living should provide for conditions sufficient not only for the physical survival of a person, but also for her leading a dignified life, her full participation in all core political, social and cultural institutions and practices of society as well as for her moral and intellectual flourishing.

References

Alston, Philip. 2015. Report of the Special Rapporteur on extreme poverty and human rights on extreme inequality and human rights, A/HRC/29/31.

Altman, Andrew. 2015. Discrimination. Stanford encyclopedia of philosophy. http://plato.stanford.edu/entries/discrimination/. Accessed 5 Sept 2015.

Anderson, Elizabeth. 1999. What is the point of equality? *Ethics* 109: 287–337.

Arneson, Richard J. 2013. Egalitarianism. Stanford encyclopedia of philosophy. http://plato.stanford.edu/entries/egalitarianism/. Accessed 5 Sept 2015.

Frankfurt, Harry. 1987. Equality as a moral ideal. *Ethics* 98: 21–42.

Höffe, Otfried. 1994. Die Menschenrechte im interkulturellen Diskurs. In *Die Menschenrechte. Herkunft – Geltung – Gefährdung*, ed. Odersky Walter, 119–137. Düsseldorf: Patmos.
McCrudden, Christopher. 2008. Human dignity and judicial interpretation of human rights. *The European Journal of International Law* 19(4): 655–724.
Miller, David. 1995. Complex equality. In *Pluralism, justice, and equality*, ed. David Miller and Michael Walzer, 197–225. Oxford: Oxford University Press.
Miller, David. 1997. Equality and justice. *Ratio* X(3): 222–237.
Miller, David. 1999. Justice and global inequality. In *Inequality, globalization, and world politics*, ed. Andrew Hurrell and Ngaire Woods, 187–210. Oxford: Oxford University Press.
Nathanson, Stephen. 2005. Equality, sufficiency, decency: Three criteria of economic justice. In *Ethical issues for the twenty-first century*, ed. Frederick Adams, 367–377. Charlottesville: Philosophy Documentation Center.
Oxfam. 2014. Working for the few: Political capture and economic inequality, briefing paper. https://www.oxfam.org/sites/www.oxfam.org/files/file_attachments/bp-working-for-few-political-capture-economic-inequality-200114-en_3.pdf. Accessed 5 Sept 2015.
Pribytkova, Elena. 2013. The human right to a dignified existence: The ethical foundations of the contemporary legal order. In *Human dignity as a foundation of law*, ed. Winfried Brugger & Stephan Kirste, Archiv für Rechts- und Sozialphilosophie 137: 117–129.
Rawls, John. 1971. *A theory of justice*. Cambridge, MA: Harvard University Press.
Rawls, John. 1981. The basic liberties and their priority. The tanner lectures on human values delivered at the University of Michigan. http://tannerlectures.utah.edu/_documents/a-to-z/r/rawls82.pdf. Accessed 5 Sept 2015.
Raz, Joseph. 1986. *The morality of freedom*. Oxford: Clarendon.
Scheffler, Samuel. 2015. The practice of equality. In *Social equality: Essays on what it means to be equals*, ed. Carina Fourie, Fabian Schuppert, and Ivo Wallimann-Helmer, 21–44. Oxford: Oxford University Press.
Sepúlveda Carmona, Magdalena. 2012. Report of the Special Rapporteur on extreme poverty and human rights on access to justice for people living in poverty, A/67/278.
Sepúlveda Carmona, Magdalena. 2013. Report of the Special Rapporteur on extreme poverty and human rights on the right to participation of people living in poverty, A/HRC/23/36.
UNRISD. 2010. Combating poverty and inequality: Structural change, social policy and politics. United Nations Research Institute For Social Development. http://www.unrisd.org/80256B3C005BCCF9/(httpAuxPages)/92B1D5057F43149CC125779600434441/$file/PovRep%20(small).pdf. Accessed 5 Sept 2015.
Van Parijs, Philippe. 1995. *Real freedom for all: What (if anything) can justify capitalism?* Oxford: Oxford University Press.
Walzer, Michael. 1983. *Spheres of justice. A defence of pluralism and equality*. Oxford: Basil Blackwell.
White, Stuart. 2004. Social Minimum. In Stanford encyclopedia of philosophy. http://plato.stanford.edu/entries/social-minimum/. Accessed 5 Sept 2015.
Wresinski, Joseph. 2000. The very poor, living proof of the indivisibility of human rights. In Extreme poverty and human rights: Essays on Joseph Wresinski, ed. Quentin Wodon, 12–32. Discussion Draft.

Human Rights Instruments

The Additional Protocol to the American Convention on Human Rights in the Area of Economic, Social and Cultural Rights (Protocol of San Salvador).
The Charter of Fundamental Rights of the European Union (CFREU).
The Convention on the Elimination of All Forms of Discrimination against Women (CEDAW).

The Convention on the Rights of Persons with Disabilities (CRPD).
The Convention on the Rights of the Child (CRC).
The European Social Charter (ESC).
The International Convention on the Elimination of All Forms of Racial Discrimination (ICERD).
The International Covenant on Civil and Political Rights (ICCPR).
The International Covenant on Economic, Social and Cultural Rights (ICESCR).
The Universal Declaration of Human Rights (UDHR).

Committee on Economic, Social and Cultural Rights (CESCR) General Comments

CESCR General Comment No. 3: The nature of States parties obligations (Art. 2, para. 1 of the Covenant).
CESCR General Comment No. 12: The right to adequate food (Art. 11 of the Covenant).
CESCR General Comment No. 13: The right to education (Art. 13 of the Covenant).
CESCR General Comment No. 14: The right to the highest attainable standard of health (Art. 12 of the Covenant).
CESCR General Comment No. 15: The right to water (arts. 11 and 12 of the Covenant).
CESCR General Comment No. 17: The right of everyone to benefit from the protection of the moral and material interests resulting from any scientific, literary or artistic production of which he or she is the author (Art. 15, para. 1 (c) of the Covenant).
CESCR General Comment No. 18: The right to work (Art. 6 of the Covenant).
CESCR General Comment No. 19: The right to social security (art. 9 of the Covenant).
CESCR General Comment No. 20: Non-discrimination in economic, social and cultural rights (art. 2, para. 2 of the Covenant).
CESCR General Comment No. 21: Right of everyone to take part in cultural life (art. 15, para. 1 (a) of the Covenant).

Chapter 4
Children's Rights, Bodily Integrity and Poverty Alleviation

Gunter Graf and Maria del Mar Cabezas

Abstract In this chapter, we explore the potential of children's rights for the alleviation of poverty with a special focus on a child's right to bodily integrity. In the first section, we analyze the children's rights discourse, which is closely connected to the Convention on the Rights of the Child of the United Nations (CRC). We recognize its importance but also detect a need to connect it more thoroughly to philosophical theories. In Sect. 4.2 therefore, we present a capability approach to children's rights and suggest that these rights should be seen as means that justice for children can be secured. We suggest four criteria to identify which capabilities/functionings are crucial in terms of social justice for children and which therefore should be protected by rights, claiming that they should (1) reflect the best available empirical knowledge, (2) be societally influenceable, (3) be objectively determinable, and (4) integrate an evolving perspective. In Sect. 4.3, we then turn to the functioning/capability of and right to bodily integrity. While not explicitly part of the CRC, such a right is helpful to identify the harms that poverty may generate to children's well-being and well-becoming in a holistic way. Finally, in Sect. 4.4 we point to the relation between a right to bodily integrity and the empowerment of children in poverty, paying special attention to the fact that it connects concerns about children's bodies with children's agency and self-relations.

Keywords Capability approach • Human rights • Children's rights • Bodily integrity • Child poverty

This research was funded by the Austrian Science Fund (FWF): P26480.

G. Graf (✉) • M.d.M. Cabezas
Zentrum für Ethik und Armutsforschung, Universität Salzburg,
Edith-Stein-Haus, Mönchsberg 2a, 5020 Salzburg, Austria
e-mail: ggraf@ifz-salzburg.at; maria.cabezas@sbg.ac.at

H.P. Gaisbauer et al. (eds.), *Ethical Issues in Poverty Alleviation*, Studies in Global Justice 14, DOI 10.1007/978-3-319-41430-0_4

4.1 Child Poverty and the Language of Children's Rights

Child poverty is one of the biggest challenges in today's world. Millions of children and their families are suffering from it and the often severe consequences it implies. One way to look at the problem and its dimension is to put it into the context of debates concerning absolute poverty and the human rights violations connected to it. According to the World Bank, for example, which measures extreme poverty by a $1.25 a day poverty line, in 2010 approximately 1.2 billion people were classified as poor in this sense (Olinto et al. 2013). Of course it is important to differentiate between different contexts and situations of the persons affected, since poverty has many faces and exists in a variety of shapes. It depends on many factors what kind of life a person can lead with $1.25 a day at her disposal and how such a lack of income translates into different kinds of deprivations like hunger, inadequate shelter or ill-health. But these numbers surely show the extent of the problem of extreme poverty. Within the group of poor people, children are a particularly vulnerable group. According to the most recent figures provided by the World Bank report from 2013, "more than one-third of the extremely poor individuals are children under age of 13, and half of children in LICs are in extreme poverty" (Olinto et al. 2013, 2). Likewise, it should not be ignored the fact that children suffer the highest rates of poverty compared to adults and that "a third of all poor in the developing world are children 0–12 years, while children are 20 % of the nonpoor" (Olinto et al. 2013, 5). In low-income-countries the data provided by the World Bank show in this report that half of all children live in poverty.

In such contexts, the language of the violation of children's rights has become influential and there are different reasons for this (Pemberton et al. 2012). First, the effects of extreme poverty on the lives of children are particularly bad and jeopardize even the most basic dimensions of their lives. In fact, many children die each year, mainly from preventable causes often linked to poverty. In 2008, there were about seven million children under the age of 5 in developing countries who died such deaths (Liu et al. 2012), a major reason being malnutrition or diseases which can be cured or prevented at comparatively little cost (Jones et al. 2003). In addition, the living conditions of many poor children do not even meet minimum standards of decency. Sharing a room with four other persons, having a mud floor, not having toilet facilities whatsoever or drinking water from open and unsafe sources is a reality for millions of children and it is very plausible and intuitive to claim that rights are violated in such circumstances. Second, the language of human rights has a political dimension not existing in other categories that are often used for analyzing child poverty such as needs or quality of life (Axford 2012). Saying that a basic human right is violated emphasises that a harm is done and that someone has to act against this injustice. In particular, the language of rights and their violations reminds us that states have a responsibility to provide the conditions that realizing the rights in question is feasible. Third, developments in the human rights framework have led to a situation in which it seems natural and important to see children as subjects of human rights. Within the twentieth century children have received growing attention in this respect, leading to the UN Convention on the rights of the child (CRC), which came into force in 1990, after it was ratified by the required number of nations. The CRC provides an ample framework of children's rights which can be used in poverty analyses and strategies to alleviate it. And when this is done it becomes obvious that global poverty is a main obstacle that these rights get realized.

But child poverty is not only a challenge for the global context and developing countries. On the contrary, in affluent societies, the figures are alarmingly high as well. In the United States, e.g., the figures concerning child poverty estimate that 14.7 million children suffer this kind of deprivation (DeNavas-Walt and Proctor 2014, 14) while more than 31 million children in the country live in low income households. Finally, according to Save the Children, "almost 27 million children in Europe were at risk of poverty or social exclusion" (Save the Children 2014, 3). These numbers give only a brief insight into the topic and it is important to look at differences between countries and the poverty concepts and measures applied in different studies. This is important for two reasons. First, child poverty figures diverge considerably between affluent societies. The circumstances in Sweden, e.g., are very different from those in France, although both count as rich countries. Furthermore, within the same country, some regions or neighbourhoods are more heavily affected by child poverty than others, leading to considerable internal heterogenities. Second, studies often apply different concepts and measures of child poverty. Child poverty can be defined and measured in a variety of ways and in comparisons one must be very careful that similar notions are put into relationship with each other. The poverty measures in the US for national statistics on child poverty, e.g. differ from those in the European Union or the ones used by UNICEF in international studies. However, even if these points are considered, it appears that children are a very vulnerable group in relation to their risk to be struck by poverty. Typically, children are more likely to be poor than adults, as the general data both by the European Union and the United States shows. In the European Union, the at-risk-of-poverty rate is higher for children than for the age group between 18 and 64 (51 million persons). In 2011 20.8 % of children under 18 were poor in this sense while only 16.0 % of adults were affected. If we look at the children (6.3 million children) under 6 years, the at-risk-of-poverty rate is at 19.3 %. In relation to the US, the NCCP estimates that around the 22 % of children are living in poverty (Jiang et al. 2015, 1).

Now, child poverty in affluent societies is typically not comparable to the global setting mentioned above. The welfare systems in place usually manage to bolster some of the worst effects of child poverty. Poor children normally do not die because of hunger and malnourishment, they have access to basic health care and go to school. Therefore, it is more difficult and contested to argue that their rights are violated by being in poverty – a form of poverty that is often called relative. Frequently, children's rights in regard to poverty are interpreted as setting minimum standards that can in fact be enforced and with such an approach it is possible to say that poverty has negative consequences for children without implying that their rights have been violated as long as some basic levels of well-being and developmental opportunities are secured (Axford 2012, 35). But again, the semantics used in the current children's rights debates allows different interpretations and can also be used in a more demanding way. In fact, the CRC can be read in such a way that makes it applicable to cases of child poverty as they occur in affluent societies. There is, for instance, article 24.1, which specifies that children have the right "to the enjoyment of the highest attainable standard of health and to facilities for the treatment of illness and rehabilitation of health" and which therefore goes far beyond the right to a minimum of health or health care. Or let us look at article 29, which refers to education. Here it says among other specifications that the education of the child shall be directed to "the development of the child's personality, talents and mental and physical abilities to their fullest potential" and "the preparation of the child for responsible life in a free society, in the spirit of understanding, peace, tolerance, equality of sexes, and friendship among all peoples, ethnic, national and religious groups and persons of indigenous origin". If child poverty in affluent societies jeopardizes these goods, and there is overwhelming evidence that it does, it is possible to speak about the violation of children's rights in such contexts with all the implications this has.

The briefly described discourse on the rights of children in regard to poverty is very valuable and opens up new perspectives in the alleviation of poverty. As subjects of human rights there is an urgent demand to counter circumstances – such as poverty – in which these rights get violated. This aspect is different from a focus on children's needs or quality of life and politically more ambitious.

However, from a philosophical point of view, there is a need to connect the discourse on children's rights to normative theories more deeply. It is true that human rights are often understood as moral rights from an ethical perspective; and as soft law from a juridical point of view. However, what is at the heart of violations of children's rights must be investigated more closely, and for this reason we will deepen our understanding of children's rights in the next section, connecting it to an influential philosophical theory: the capability approach. By doing so, we will gain a deeper understanding of the importance of the concept of children's rights, since they not only guarantee that violations of the dignity of children are avoided, but also that the demands of justice are met. Then we will argue that the functioning/capability of bodily integrity, which plays a central role in the capability approach, is of particular importance for understanding child poverty. It provides further insights into the injustices connected to child poverty and opens up perspectives how it can be alleviated in a holistic way. A right to bodily integrity therefore should play a major role in normative theorizing about poverty alleviation.

4.2 Children Rights and the Capability Approach

If we ask why children have rights, we can assume two possible meanings (Archard 2004, 53 ff.). On the one hand, children can have legal rights, meaning that they have them under the law. This usage of the term was presupposed in the section above, where some aspects of the current discourse on children's rights – with special attention to the CRC – were presented. Legal rights matter and deeply influence the lives of children. However, they do not necessarily say much about the justification or the appropriateness of these rights. On the other hand, we can look for the normative grounds to grant children rights; and it is here where the term "moral rights" is typically used. Moral rights have to be substantiated by moral arguments and are in an important sense independent from legal rights; they can depart from each other even if it should be an aim of existing legislations that they are, at least to a large degree, consistent with the demands of morality. As mentioned above, legal and moral rights do not necessarily overlap. However, we would like to suggest that many of the rights specified in the CRC are substantiated by moral arguments, which makes it a crucial document not only for legal, but also for moral concerns. There are different ways and strategies to ground moral rights. Martha Nussbaum, an important proponent of the capability approach, for example, claims that humans, and that includes children, have rights because of their dignity (Dixon and Nussbaum 2012). She argues that if we want to respect the dignity of persons appropriately, we have to grant them rights. Furthermore, she is confident that the notion of dignity plays an important part in determining what rights we should grant them (Nussbaum 2011).

In this chapter, we want to take a somewhat different route and argue that children have rights because they have entitlements of justice to well-being and well-becoming, which are best protected if children have rights. We will not analyze Nussbaum's notion of dignity and her normative justificatory strategy in detail, but simply assume that children are equally worthy members of society and that they deserve the same moral consideration as adults, a claim that is universally accepted in the capability approach (Nussbaum 2006; Biggeri et al. 2011; Sen 2007). We are aware that with this we do not solve basic puzzles about the moral status of children and human beings in general compared to other species, but for the aims of this chapter, which is concerned with children's rights violations due to poverty, such an approach seems to be promising and straightforward. Children are entitled to a just treatment and rights, both in a moral and legal meaning, are important means by which these basic entitlements can be met. Especially if the rights substantiated by a moral theory get translated into legal rights, this seems to be a very effective way to protect the justice-based entitlements of children. If a state wants to protect such an important dimension of children's well-being like education, it seems well-suited to translate that into a right to education, which the child herself or a guardian can claim if it is wrongfully denied.

But what does a society owe its children in terms of justice if we take this interpretation of the capability approach as the basis? If the goal of justice is to protect and support the well-being and well-becoming of children, it must acknowledge what is special about children. Two characteristics are of particular importance here: their special vulnerability and the fact that they are still not autonomous beings, but rather on their way to autonomy, which is only gained in adulthood (Brighouse 2002; Schweiger and Graf 2015, 26ff.). These characteristics help us understand and define child-sensitive conceptions of well-being and well-becoming, and they also provide the justificatory basis for restricting certain rights for children and treating them paternalistically, but only on two conditions. First, children share the same moral worth as adults and second, paternalist interventions have to consider the maturity, competence and level of agency of the child. The capability approach claims that the justice based entitlements of children are best understood based on their functionings (their "beings and doings") or capabilities (the real freedoms to achieve functionings), which means that they should also guide the determination of specific rights (Sen 2009, Chapter III).

So according to our understanding of the capability approach, children have rights because they demand equal concern as adults and because they have a justified entitlement of justice to their well-being and well-becoming which should be expressed in the form of rights. But what rights do they have, then? Before we answer that question, we want to make a side-step. Within the capability approach there is some discussion about whether we should care about capabilities in terms of freedoms to do something and be something or about functionings, which are the realizations of capabilities (Sen 2007, 1990; Crocker 1992). For our purpose here, we want to settle this issue with a reference to the maturity of children. A right should cover a capability, meaning a freedom, if the child is mature enough to make a decision on its own at a comparable level to an adult, and it should cover a functioning if the child fails to show that maturity. In difficult cases, an appropriate expert should decide whether the child is able to make the decision or not. That said, we now want to argue for four criteria that we should use to determine the main capabilities/functionings that need to be protected by rights as a matter of justice (see also Schweiger and Graf 2015, 42ff.). We do that at a very general and basic level, like the declaration of human rights. That leaves some room for interpretation in the exact exposition of such rights, their implementation in specific contexts, and it certainly leaves a lot of room for the establishment of further and more specific rights.

(1) This first criterion is that the chosen functionings/capabilities should reflect the best available empirical knowledge about children's lives and development, in particular their physical, mental, and social needs. This also means that the functionings/capabilities can change and be redefined if new knowledge is available; today we have, for instance, information on how children develop and on how their development is shaped by their environment, or on the various ways in which childhood and adulthood are interconnected, like the influence of growing up poor on bodily, cognitive and emotional development. (2) Secondly the chosen functionings/capabilities must be, at least partly, societally influenceable. This means that it can be guaranteed that children actually can be granted these rights. (3) Closely connected to this second criterion, the chosen functionings/capabilities should be, at least to some extent, objectively determinable and not merely subjective, i.e. not primarily dependent on the assessments, experiences and evaluations of the subjects in question. This is important because children's rights should also guide the design of institutions and policies, which demands that the well-being of different children be comparable and that the ways in which it can be influenced and changed is objectively comprehensible. (4) The chosen functionings/capabilities should incorporate

a developmental perspective. Such "evolving functionings/capabilities" reflect the "process character" of the growing-up of children (Ballet et al. 2011).

Having spelled out these four criteria we can now try to specify the relevant capabilities/functionings that need to be protected by rights. There are two options that are discussed in the literature (Sen 2004): either we define and justify a more or less fixed list of central functionings/capabilities that covers at least everything that is most important or we refrain from that Nussbaumian approach and focus on particular injustices, contexts or groups in question and try to figure out what we need to know in order to criticize, evaluate, analyze or improve the problem in question. That second approach was, for example, used by Ingrid Robeyns in her attempt to criticize gender injustices, for which she generated a specific list that fits her purpose (Robeyns 2003). There are good reasons in favor of both approaches, depending on the task in question. For our purpose to discuss poverty as a children's rights violation one important reference is the CRC. Without having the scope here to discuss it in detail, most rights spelled out there fulfill these four criteria, like for example health, education or decent living conditions. They are tremendously important for the well-being and well-becoming of children, they are societally influenceable and can be protected by state policies. Furthermore in their implementation a developmental perspective is obviously important as the health, education and material needs of children vary according to their age. But we want to try a different route in this paper and focus on a particular capability/functioning which is not mentioned directly in the CRC but of utmost importance nonetheless: bodily integrity. References to children's bodies are made several times in the CRC, for example in relation to education (§29) and decent living condition (§27), freedom from exploitation (§32) and protection from all forms of violence, neglect and abuse (§19). In the next section, we will now discuss the concept of bodily integrity. Finally, we would like to emphasize again that the concept of a right as we use it does not only demand minimal levels of decency, but actually serves the function that every human being, including children, can enjoy a life of well-being and well-becoming, which is the benchmark of justice in the capability approach.

4.3 Bodily Integrity and Child Poverty

What is bodily integrity and why does it matter? To begin with, bodily integrity is part of Nussbaum's list of central capabilities, which is a major point of reference for the discussion of valuable capabilities/functionings in the capability approach. She defines it as follows: "Bodily Integrity – Being able to move freely from place to place, to be secure against violent assault, including sexual assault and domestic violence, having opportunities for sexual satisfaction and for choices in matters of reproduction" (Nussbaum 2011, 33). For some reasons this definition is not appropriate for children since we restrict both their ability to move freely and their sovereignty over their bodies according to reasons that they are not competent enough to make decision for themselves and act on their own judgements. In order to give a more substantial concept of the bodily integrity of children we want to highlight four points in that regard.

1. Bodily integrity is itself a multidimensional functioning/capability and does at least involve health, agency and positive self-relations. Only if children are sufficiently healthy, have agency over their bodies and if they have a positive relation to their own body, is their bodily integrity satisfied. For us and also Nussbaum bodily integrity is thus not only a passive and negative concept of being protected against various harms but it is an active and positive concept, something which implies that children are active agents of their own lives and that for that reason they need their bodies to function and to have control over them.
2. Bodily integrity of children is not static but dynamic and developing, in the sense that children's bodies are in need of nourishment and care, change and develop rapidly and are the medium of their actions and manifestation as well as the tool of their agency. It is a capability/functioning that like all others is brought into existence through a combination of internal and external conversion factors.
3. Bodily integrity of children always involves the two dimensions of dependency – the need to be protected and to be cared for by others – and autonomy – being the irreplaceable body of a particular individual, which needs to be in control over that body and view it as himself or herself. Bodily integrity involves both local and global autonomy, where local autonomy refers to the ability to make choices in a particular situation and global autonomy is the ability to develop and realize a life plan that is one's own. To be protected from harm against the body and against harms that involve the body but which target the psyche of children and to have sufficient control over one's body is also necessary for children to be able to appear in public without shame or humiliation. Or to put it differently: children should be able to trust their own body, to respect it and to esteem it – not as an external object but as themselves.
4. Bodily integrity is also fruitful, in the sense of Avner de-Shalit and Jonathan Wolff, that it positively influences other capabilities/functionings and that its distortion or absence is not only harmful but hurts other areas of the well-being and well-becoming of children as well (Wolff and de-Shalit 2007). Damages related to bodily integrity are hence corrosive, they affect how children can develop other capabilities/functionings and most importantly their ability to live a life they have reasons to value.

These four aspects give more insight than the definition of Martha Nussbaum, as they try to capture what is different for children but also stay close to the intended meaning of the definition in Nussbaum's work. In what follows we will explore the relation between bodily integrity and child poverty and then discuss how poverty alleviation measures should sufficiently cover this sometimes overlooked dimension of children's rights.

Let us start with the aspect of health which is an essential part of bodily integrity. It is itself a complex functioning/capability that has aroused considerable attention within the approach (Venkatapuram 2011). Its definition is still in dispute but it certainly comprises a physical and a mental dimension and both are crucial for bodily integrity. Furthermore, it is no longer appropriate to consider it a "natural good" which is distributed first and foremost as a matter of luck as stipulated by many theoreticians in the field of social justice (Rawls 1971). The research on social determinants shows that health is co-determined by social factors, making its availability a concern of social justice. There are certainly different influences on a person's health and it is very difficult to determine causal pathways linking certain socially influenceable factors to negative health outcomes. However, the available evidence is overwhelming that child poverty is a major risk factor for ill-health, jeopardizing therefore an essential ingredient to a child's bodily integrity. The case for detrimental effects of extreme child poverty on health is so clear and obvious that we will not address it explicitly here: extreme poverty kills or reduces a child's life expectancy substantially. However, also relative poverty is proven to be linked to bad health outcomes. When it comes to its mental dimension, it has been found, e.g., to precede anxiety disorders, depression, post-traumatic stress disorder and academic underachievement and to be correlated to a variety of mental health problems and psychological disorders in adults, jeopardizing the well-becoming aspect (Nikulina et al. 2010; Evans and Cassells 2014). But it has negative influences on the well-being of children as well. Children in low socioeconomic level families are for instance more likely to show self-harming behavior such as overdose and self-injury than their non-poor peers (Ayton et al. 2003). In regard to physical health, there are many studies to be found which substantiate the negative influence of child poverty both on health in childhood and adulthood. The literature on the subject is extensive and for the purpose of this chapter we can only give some examples for illustration. There is evidence that the babies of poor mothers have lower birth weight and are born preterm, factors that are significant health risks for the infant (Dunkel et al. 2010). Another interesting finding states that child poverty is predictive of cardiovascular disease and type II diabetes (Raphael 2011). But also adult chronic disease outcomes for coronary heart disease (CHD), stroke and asthma seem to be influenced by the socioeconomic status of the child (Nandi et al. 2012; Williams et al. 2009).

Health is an important ingredient to bodily integrity, but it is not all that matters. Above, we defined it as an active and positive concept that sees children as agents of their own lives and in control of their bodies. The mentioned dimension of mental health already points into this direction. However, agency implies more. Children need a suitable environment in order to exercise their agency and given their special vulnerabilities this agency has to happen in a controlled and conducive way. Children are not small adults with a right to determine autonomously their own circumstances and appropriate agency evolves between protection and the ability to act. Now, the category of powerlessness is helpful here for our analysis since it points towards constraints of agency and therefore a lack of bodily integrity. There are different types of powerlessness of children and not all of them are problematic per se, since they are closely tied to their nature as developing and vulnerable beings in need of protection. However, all of them can be exaggerated and abused. Especially in a condition of poverty – this is the main point we would like to make here – the powerlessness of children gets reinforced, which makes it a real danger to their bodily integrity. Let us consider two dimensions of this powerlessness where the relationship is clear: powerlessness because of children's immature physical and mental competencies and economic powerlessness. Children are developing beings and in a state of special vulnerability. Because of this, they are not in a position to decide where to live, if they want to move, or which adults they want to interact with. In addition, they are dependent and not able to protect themselves from a wide set of threats, such as violence, abandonment, etc. These factors have to be interpreted according to the age and maturity of the child. However, they are relevant for all children independent of their socio-economic position. Nevertheless, poverty adds to this powerlessness in a variety of ways, jeopardizing the child's agency. Poor children often grow up in conditions where they do not get suitable opportunities to engage in activities adequate to their developmental stage and level of maturity or they do not learn how to deal with many chances and risks offered in their environment. Often the neighborhoods of poor children simply do not offer the right activities or they are too expensive to be accessible. As a result, the agency of children is often misdirected, for example when they only eat junk food or engage in criminal activities and they have difficulties with developing genuine agency towards their bodies. The other form of powerlessness that is reinforced by poverty is economic in nature. Generally, children are dependent on others in an economic sense. Indeed, children depend entirely, due to their reduced autonomy and the respective social roles, on the economic power of their caregivers, the social care systems and networks, which leads to a deep helplessness in relation to their own options in their current and future life. Non-poor children usually do not suffer from this economic dependency because their parents provide for them adequately. Children living in poverty, however, do not enjoy such privileges. For their parents it is much more difficult to give them what they need in economic goods and therefore they are likely to be excluded from many contexts where economic resources are an entry condition. Hence, they also miss opportunities to develop and exercise their bodily agency.

A third dimension of bodily integrity is to have a positive relation to oneself, which can be expressed in such connected functionings as self-confidence, self-respect and self-esteem. Positive self-relations are "fertile" in two senses (Schweiger 2014). On the one hand, they are fertile for the development of the child, because these positive self-relations are – as Axel Honneth suggests – necessary for someone to develop into an autonomous adult and realize him or herself in his or her life (Honneth 1996). Without the achievement of self-confidence, self-respect and self-esteem it is very unlikely if not impossible for a person to develop an undistorted self and to make important life choices for themselves. However, a sole focus on autonomy and the ability to live a life one has reason to value is inappropriate for children; such responsibilities would overburden them. A sole focus on development would reduce children to "adults-to-be", although it is still a necessary dimension of justice for children to have in mind what they need to achieve for well-being in adulthood. On the other hand these positive self-relations are also fertile for the actual well-being of the child and the achievement of other capabilities and functions that matter for the child during their childhood. For example, self-confidence, self-respect and self-esteem are connected to and greatly influence (physical and mental) health and the ability to participate in social activities and to engage in social relationships or learning and playing. All these are valuable functions for children, which they should be able to achieve as a matter of justice; positive self-relations influence whether and to what extent this is possible.

The available empirical evidence now suggests that children, like adults, experience poverty as humiliating and that this sometimes has devastating effects on their mental health and well-being, as well as on their self-relations (Walker 2014). Poverty causes shame; it is perceived as stigma and many children feel they are of less worth than others because of their poverty. This again triggers coping mechanisms that do not always work in the child's best interests, like withdrawal from social relations, anger and aggression, or simply giving up. Tess Ridge summarizes the empirical evidence from qualitative studies on child poverty:

> Fears about being left out or marginalized pervaded children's accounts. Poverty in childhood extracts a high emotional toll on children trying to 'fit in' and 'join in' with their peers. Children's inner fears and their experiences of feeling humiliated, sad and shamed are often hidden and they are rarely asked about their thoughts and feelings. However, sensitively conducted studies have revealed the deep emotional costs that hardship can bring to children's lives. (Ridge 2011, 76)

4.4 Poverty Alleviation and Empowerment

So far we have argued that children's rights provide an important perspective to look at child poverty. We have shown that the discourse on children's rights is already a point of reference in academic and political discussions because of the influence of the United Nations convention on the rights of the child. However, we also identified a need for a philosophical theory to ground such rights claims and we suggested that the capability approach could fulfill this function. We then turned to the concept of bodily integrity as entailed by the capability approach and the harm done to it by child poverty. In this final section, we would like to substantiate why this focus on a child's right to bodily integrity is important in the alleviation of child poverty and argue that it adds an important aspect to the discourse on the violations of children's rights through poverty.

Child poverty cuts deep and it is widely acknowledged that there is an urgent need for different agents to act if the child's body is in danger. If child poverty translates into malnourishment, abuse or neglect, it is obvious that we face a violation of children's rights and that something should be done about it. While it is true that we live in a world where many children face such problems without receiving adequate support, from a moral point of view, it is clear that we face a severe injustice in such situations. The capability approach and its notion of bodily integrity fully agree with such an analysis. The child's body is in need of protection, and unjustified and avoidable harms done to the body of the child are among the most serious rights violations. But the idea of the multidimensional functioning/capability of bodily integrity goes deeper. It connects concerns about the body with the child's agency and her self-relations. A right to bodily integrity, in our understanding, implies therefore much more than the claim that no harm to the body must be done. It has a positive connotation and means that children have to learn to effectively control their bodies and minds and to develop healthy body images and positive self-relations. Controlling the body, this has to be emphasized, does not mean that it has to be trained, kept thin and impeccable, as is maintained by neoliberal ideologies and the body politics they imply (Rose 2007). Rather, it refers to the ability to shape the body in a way that fits with one's authentic self-realization, which can happen in many ways and in accordance with a variety of conceptions of a good life. In fact, developing the perception that one's body does not have to fit prevalent ideas of beauty and perfection and that one does not have to act accordingly is one aim of the concept of bodily integrity as we have developed it here.

This functioning/capability of bodily integrity is directly relevant for an in-depth analysis of child poverty. Poor children's bodies, even if not directly harmed by violence or neglect, suffer from disadvantages. Poor children have fewer opportunities than their non-poor peers to realize the functionings/capabilities needed for having a healthy body, for shaping and controlling it the way they want and for relating positively to it. Bodily integrity therefore shows how far child poverty violates a child's right to a life of well-being and well-becoming. An analysis of single rights (e.g. to health, education, decent living conditions etc.), as is often the case in the political discourse, tends to overlook this insight that child poverty harms fundamental aspects of a child's personality and life and translates into a powerlessness regarding her own body. The functioning/capability of bodily integrity, on the other hand, points to the entanglement of these different aspects and their manifold and often indirect relationship to the body.

But what do we learn from these insights for the alleviation of child poverty? There are two interrelated aspects we consider important. First, putting the focus on the child's body and explaining a considerable part of the moral harm done by child poverty via what is done to children's bodies is a promising idea. Children's bodies are essential to them and their selves, their well-being and well-becoming, and measures for poverty alleviation have to make sure that direct harm to the body is prevented or at least that negative consequences are mitigated. Harm to the body typically generates pain and suffering, and due to the special vulnerability of children, this can have long lasting effects on the physical and psychological health of the child. We are dealing here with apparent effects of child poverty that constitute, according to a widespread view, the "core" of the problem. Malnourishment, preventable poverty related diseases or poverty related abuse and neglect are examples of what we have in mind. There are good reasons to give these issues priority in the alleviation of child poverty and to guarantee that children's bodies do not get hurt or harmed. This aspect is essential to our notion of bodily integrity as well, which sees the child's health as one of the defining functionings/capabilities. Malnourished, sick or beaten bodies are not healthy and, by definition, the child's bodily integrity is endangered in these circumstances. As we have shown above, threats to children's bodies are obvious in the context of extreme poverty. Many children in the developing world die prematurely from preventable illnesses, starve or are confronted with other, often deadly harm to their bodies. However, child poverty is also a threat to children who are affected by relative poverty. Compared to their peers, their chances to be healthy as children and to enjoy a healthy development are reduced, which constitutes, from the social justice perspective we endorse, a violation of an essential children's right (Schweiger and Graf 2015). Many of these negative effects can be alleviated or even prevented, at least to a large degree, by the institutional arrangement of a society, its laws and policies. The health system certainly has an important role to fulfill here, since giving children, who are affected by poverty effective access to the relevant services is a minimal condition that they can lead a healthy life as a child and develop into an equally healthy adult. However, the growing research on the social determinants of health powerfully shows that health is not only a matter of the healthcare provisions available to a person; it is deeply influenced by factors such as inequality, social status and hierarchies, and a society that takes the bodily integrity of all its children equally seriously has to rethink its institutional structure and relationships of power (Marmot and Wilkinson 2003; Venkatapuram 2011).

Second, however, bodily integrity as we defend it here does not content itself with measures of poverty alleviation, which protect the child's body from external dangers. It is not primarily a passive concept but addresses a child's ability to act regarding her own body and therefore includes an active component. As we have argued above, poverty affects the agency of children in a variety of ways, many of which have to be considered negative. Poor children have fewer options than their non-poor peers and usually have fewer opportunities to develop life plans and to actively shape their lives into a direction they consider valuable. These plans, naturally, involve their bodies and the way children relate to them. Enhancing the agency of children, therefore, becomes an essential matter for poverty alleviation. Different dimensions of this empowerment have to be kept in mind here, not all of which we can discuss. However, two aspects are basic and fundamental for alleviating child poverty. (a) Enhancing the agency of children in poverty is related to factors which are internal to the child in the sense that they depend on her abilities, knowledge, attitudes and skills. From a capability perspective, this means that children have to develop functionings/capabilities that enable them to live a life of well-being and well-becoming. The most powerful tool to foster these internal factors is education. All children, as developing beings, must acquire relevant functionings/capabilities over time and are in need of the right environments, attachment figures and teachers in this process. Poor children, as evidence shows, are often disadvantaged in this regard (Engle and Black 2008; Ferguson et al. 2007). Nevertheless, with the right educational opportunities they can achieve the same outcomes as their peers. One important aspect is that education provides the conditions children need for being able to participate in the labor market, which is without doubt an important means to prevent or overcome poverty. However, from the perspective of the capability approach, education is also a process in which children learn that their worth is equal to that of all other members of society and that they have a right to full inclusion and participation in society. In other words, they develop the necessary self-respect and self-esteem which allows them to stand up against injustices connected to poverty (Nussbaum 2011). At this point, the relationship they develop to their own bodies is crucial, as well. They have to be aware of the many cultural codes and prejudices connected to different body shapes and to develop a healthy relationship to their own bodies and selves that deeply affects how they perform their agency. (b) It is important to strengthen the internal factors relevant for a child's agency; equally important, however, are structural features of society, which impede the way in which poor children can exercise and enhance their agency adequately. Poor children in affluent societies, for example, are more likely to grow up in an environment that is conducive to the excessive consumption of junk food and sugary drinks and are confronted with social barriers that make social mobility extremely difficult for them (Wickins-Drazilova and Williams 2011). Here, it is not enough for poverty alleviation measures to concentrate only on the child and her abilities. Rather, the sustainable alleviation of child poverty needs to address these systemic failures as well. When approaching this topic with our notion of bodily integrity in mind, a special focus has to be put on prevailing body images and beauty ideals. Admittedly, these facets of society are a challenge to all children, their development of agency and healthy self-relations. For children in poverty, however, they pose even greater challenges. It is more difficult for them to comply with these images and ideals, which have a strong class component as well, and they are more likely to be negatively affected by them. Their "poverty vulnerability" gets thus reinforced and their chances to overcome poverty, weakened. In terms of responsibilities, this means that agents such as the media, the food and the culture industry have a much stronger link to the alleviation of poverty than is often acknowledged. They create and transport ideals of the body, which are corrosive to the agency and positive self-relations of children in poverty and therefore endanger their bodily integrity. For situations of extreme poverty, the point that structural injustices have to be fought in order to empower children and to foster their bodily integrity is equally valid. Projects focusing on the individual child, her health, agency and positive self-relations are certainly important, and the work so many NGO's are doing is indeed valuable. However, empowerment for children suffering from extreme poverty also means transforming unjust structures and asymmetrical power relationships as people in poverty often experience them. Only then will children be able to learn to lead a life they have reason to value, in which their bodily integrity is an essential ingredient.

4.5 Conclusions

In this chapter, we have tried to substantiate children's rights from a philosophical perspective by connecting them to the capability approach. We have argued that, in the approach, justice for children is best defined via children's achievement of well-being and well-becoming (which consists in the realization of functionings/capabilities) and children's rights should be seen as important tools for securing children's justice. We have presented some criteria that should guide the selection of functionings/capabilities that should be protected by rights, and we are confident that many rights specified in the CRC fulfill them. We then turned, however, to the right to bodily integrity, which is not discretely recognized in the CRC, albeit some of the rights specified in the convention relate to it. We argued that such a right to bodily integrity can be of great use to poverty alleviation in regard to children, since it incorporates an integral view of the child, relating health, agency and self-relations, and thus puts the harm done to children and their bodies by poverty in a wider perspective. Alleviating poverty while focusing on the right to bodily integrity further means transforming unjust structures and asymmetrical power relationships, which are typically part of the problem of poverty. Only then will children be able to learn to lead a life they have reason to value and to relate positively to themselves and their bodies.

References

Archard, David. 2004. *Children: Rights and childhood*, 2nd ed. London: Routledge.

Axford, Nick. 2012. *Exploring concepts of child well-being: Implications for children's services*. Bristol: Policy.

Ayton, Agnes, Hufrize Rasool, and David Cottrell. 2003. Deliberate self-harm in children and adolescents: Association with social deprivation. *European Child & Adolescent Psychiatry* 12(6): 303–307. doi:10.1007/s00787-003-0344-0.

Ballet, Jérôme, Mario Biggeri, and Flavio Comim. 2011. Children's agency and the capability approach: A conceptual framework. In *Children and the capability approach*, 1st ed, ed. Mario Biggeri, Jérôme Ballet, and Flavio Comim, 22–45. Basingstoke/New York: Palgrave Macmillan.

Biggeri, Mario, Jérôme Ballet, and Flavio Comim (eds.). 2011. *Children and the capability approach*, 1st ed. Basingstoke/New York: Palgrave Macmillan.

Brighouse, Harry. 2002. What rights (if any) do children have? In *The moral and political status of children*, 1st ed, ed. David Archard and Colin M. Macleod. Oxford/New York: Oxford University Press.

Crocker, David. 1992. Functioning and capability. The foundation of Sen's and Nussbaum's development ethic. *Political Theory* 20: 584–612.

DeNavas-Walt, Carmen, and Bernadette D. Proctor. 2014. *Income and poverty in the United States: 2013*, 60–249. Washington, DC: United States Census Bureau. Current Population Reports. http://www.census.gov/content/dam/Census/library/publications/2014/demo/p60-249.pdf.

Dixon, Rosalind, and Martha Nussbaum. 2012. Children's rights and a capabilities approach: The question of special priority. *Cornell Law Review* 97: 549–593.

Dunkel Schetter, Christine, and Laura M. Glynn. 2010. Stress in pregnancy: Empirical evidence and theoretical issues to guide interdisciplinary researchers. In *The handbook of stress science: Biology, psychology, and health*, 1st ed, ed. Richard J. Contrada and Andrew Baum, 321–343. New York: Springer.

Engle, Patrice L., and Maureen M. Black. 2008. The effect of poverty on child development and educational outcomes. *Annals of the New York Academy of Sciences* 1136(1): 243–256. doi:10.1196/annals.1425.023.

Evans, Gary W., and Rochelle C. Cassells. 2014. Childhood poverty, cumulative risk exposure, and mental health in emerging adults. *Clinical Psychological Science* 2(3): 287–296. doi:10.1177/2167702613501496.

Ferguson, Hb, S. Bovaird, and Mp Mueller. 2007. The impact of poverty on educational outcomes for children. *Paediatrics & Child Health* 12(8): 701–706.

Honneth, Axel. 1996. *The struggle for recognition: The moral grammar of social conflicts*, 1st ed. Cambridge, MA: MIT Press.

Jiang, Yang, Mercedes Ekono, and Curtis Skinner. 2015. *Basic facts about low-income children: Children under 18 years, 2013*. New York: National Center for Children in Poverty, Mailman School of Public Health, Columbia University.

Jones, Gareth, Richard W. Steketee, Robert E. Black, Zulfiqar A. Bhutta, and Saul S. Morris. 2003. How many child deaths can we prevent this year? *The Lancet* 362(9377): 65–71. doi:10.1016/S0140-6736(03)13811-1.

Liu, Li, Hope L. Johnson, Simon Cousens, Jamie Perin, Susana Scott, Joy E. Lawn, Igor Rudan, et al. 2012. Global, regional, and national causes of child mortality: An updated systematic analysis for 2010 with time trends since 2000. *Lancet* 379(9832): 2151–2161. doi:10.1016/S0140-6736(12)60560-1.

Marmot, Michael, and Richard Wilkinson (eds.). 2003. *Social determinants of health: The solid facts*, 2nd ed. Copenhagen: Centre for Urban Health World Health Organization.

Nandi, Arijit, M. Maria Glymour, Ichiro Kawachi, and Tyler J. VanderWeele. 2012. Using marginal structural models to estimate the direct effect of adverse childhood social conditions on onset of heart disease, diabetes, and stroke. *Epidemiology* 23(2): 223–232. doi:10.1097/EDE.0b013e31824570bd.

Nikulina, Valentina, Cathy Spatz Widom, and Sally Czaja. 2010. The role of childhood neglect and childhood poverty in predicting mental health, academic achievement and crime in adulthood. *American Journal of Community Psychology* 48(3–4): 309–321. doi:10.1007/s10464-010-9385-y.

Nussbaum, Martha. 2006. *Frontiers of justice: Disability, nationality, species membership*. Cambridge, MA/London: The Belknap Press of Harvard University Press.

Nussbaum, Martha. 2011. *Creating capabilities : The human development approach*, 1st ed. Cambridge, MA/London: Belknap Press of Harvard University Press.

Olinto, Pedro, Kathleen Beegle, Carlos Sobrado, and Hiroki Uematsu. 2013. *The state of the poor: Where are the poor, where is extreme poverty harder to end, and what is the current profile of the world's poor?* Washington, DC: World Bank. http://siteresources.worldbank.org/EXTPREMNET/Resources/EP125.pdf.

Pemberton, Simon, David Gordon, and Shailen Nandy. 2012. Child rights, child survival and child poverty: The debate. In *Global child poverty and well-being*, ed. Alberto Minujin and Shailen Nandy. Bristol: Policy Press.

Raphael, Dennis. 2011. Poverty in childhood and adverse health outcomes in adulthood. *Maturitas* 69(1): 22–26. doi:10.1016/j.maturitas.2011.02.011.

Rawls, John. 1971. *A theory of justice*, 1st ed. Cambridge, MA/London: Harvard University Press.

Ridge, Tess. 2011. The everyday costs of poverty in childhood: A review of qualitative research exploring the lives and experiences of low-income children in the UK. *Children & Society* 25(1): 73–84. doi:10.1111/j.1099-0860.2010.00345.x.

Robeyns, Ingrid. 2003. Sen's capability approach and gender inequality: Selecting relevant capabilities. *Feminist Economics* 9(2–3): 61–92. doi:10.1080/1354570022000078024.

Rose, Nikolas S. 2007. *Politics of life itself: Biomedicine, power, and subjectivity in the twenty-first century*, 1st ed. Princeton: Princeton University Press.

Save the Children. 2014. Child poverty and social exclusion in Europe. A matter of children's rights.

Schweiger, Gottfried. 2014. Humiliation and justice for children living in poverty. *Azafea: Revista de Filosofía* 16: 57–72.

Schweiger, Gottfried, and Gunter Graf. 2015. *A philosophical examination of social justice and child poverty*, 1st ed. Basingstoke: Palgrave Macmillan. http://www.palgraveconnect.com/doifinder/10.1057/9781137426024.

Sen, Amartya. 1990. Justice: Means versus freedoms. *Philosophy and Public Affairs* 19(2): 111–121.
Sen, Amartya. 2004. Capabilities, lists, and public reason: Continuing the conversation. *Feminist Economics* 10(3): 77–80. doi:10.1080/1354570042000315163.
Sen, Amartya. 2007. Children and human rights. *Indian Journal of Human Development* 1(2): 1–11.
Sen, Amartya. 2009. *The idea of justice*, 1st ed. London/New York: Allen Lane.
Venkatapuram, Sridhar. 2011. *Health justice*, 1st ed. Cambridge, MA/Malden: Polity Press.
Walker, Robert. 2014. *The shame of poverty*, 1st ed. Oxford: Oxford University Press.
Wickins-Drazilova, Dita, and Garrath Williams. 2011. Ethics and public policy. In *Epidemiology of obesity in children and adolescents: Prevalence and etiology*, 1st ed, ed. Luis A. Moreno, Iris Pigeot, and Wolfgang Ahrens, 7–20. New York: Springer New York. http://www.springerlink.com/index/10.1007/978-1-4419-6039-9_2.
Williams, David R., Michelle Sternthal, and Rosalind J. Wright. 2009. Social determinants: Taking the social context of asthma seriously. *Pediatrics* 123(Supplement): S174–S184. doi:10.1542/peds.2008-2233H.
Wolff, Jonathan, and Avner de-Shalit. 2007. *Disadvantage. 1st ed. Oxford political theory*. Oxford/New York: Oxford University Press.

Part II
Poverty Alleviation and Development

Chapter 5
A Human Right to Financial Inclusion

Jahel Queralt

Abstract This chapter argues that universal access to basic financial services can be defended as a human right. Its contribution is twofold. On the one hand it defines the content of this right, which I will call a human right to financial inclusion. On the other hand, it builds on two standard human rights justifications to defend this right. First it offers an interest-based argument emphasizing the value of this right to realize individual autonomy. Second, it elaborates a double linkage argument based on the supporting relationship between the proposed right and two other well-established human rights, namely, the right to an adequate standard of living and the right to development.

Keywords Poverty • Human rights • Financial inclusion • Autonomy • Right to development

5.1 Introduction

According to the most recent estimates, approximately 2.2 billion people survive on less than $2 a day. For the poorest one billion, this threshold falls to less than $1 a day (World Bank 2015a). Although we are all familiar with the dollar-a-day measurement of poverty, it is hard to imagine what it is like to live with such a meager budget. At a cursory level, it implies a hand-to-mouth existence, spending every cent on feeding our families and ourselves. But the economic lives of the poor are far more complex than that. Besides putting food on the table every day, they have to raise lump sums in order to meet other important needs – e.g. paying for

---

Previous versions of this chapter were presented at the University of Zurich and the University of Barcelona. I am grateful to these audiences, and especially to Julian Culp, Iñigo González Ricoy and Jonathan Fu, for very insightful comments and suggestions. Funding was provided by the Swiss National Science Foundation.

J. Queralt (✉)
Ethics Centre of the University of Zurich, Zollikerstr. 117, 8008 Zurich, Switzerland
e-mail: jahel.queralt@philos.uzh.ch

H.P. Gaisbauer et al. (eds.), *Ethical Issues in Poverty Alleviation*, Studies in Global Justice 14, DOI 10.1007/978-3-319-41430-0_5

children's education – and coping with emergencies – e.g. paying for a doctor or fixing accommodation. Survival at the bottom of the pyramid often involves a hectic financial life.

Hamid and Khadeja, for example, are a married couple from Dhaka that live on $70 a month – a fifth of their income is spent on rent and the rest on running their house and raising a child (Collins et al. 2009, 7). Despite having few resources, they manage a complex portfolio of financial assets and liabilities. They have reserves in different instruments ranging from home savings, remittances sent to Hamid's parents for safekeeping, a loan to a relative, life insurance, and a small amount of cash in hand. They owe money to a microfinance institution and to some relatives. In addition, they also act as informal bankers by keeping savings for others. Hamid and Khadeja have more dynamic financial activity than many of us and yet they do not have access to the (formal) financial services that have become an integral part of our economic systems, namely: credit, savings, insurance and payment services.

The economic lives of the vast majority of the world's poor are similar to that of Hamid and Khadeja. They are engaged in many financial relationships that take place in the shadows because formal financial institutions are unable or unwilling to offer them adequate services. They are financially excluded. The informal or semi-formal financial tools available to the poor – e.g. informal moneylending, savings-and-loan clubs, insurance clubs, etc. – are insufficient, insecure and usually very expensive (Banerjee and Duflo 2011). This lack of access to reliable and quality financial services compounds an already difficult situation since it increases their vulnerability to the consequences of seasonal income variation, food price shocks, crop failures and other unexpected contingencies. Staying alive below the poverty line requires good administration of small sums of money and effective strategies to cope with irregular income flows and high levels of risk. The poor are constantly facing difficult economic choices that can dramatically affect their lives. For this reason, they need – arguably more than better-situated individuals – financial services tailored to their particular circumstances.

Over the last few years, the debate about financial inclusion – the delivery of quality financial services to the poor at affordable costs – has gained momentum globally due to the increased awareness of the importance of access to formal financial services for economic growth and poverty alleviation and the development of the microfinance industry. Microfinance institutions have significantly broadened access to financial services but their success in meeting the financial needs of the entrepreneurial poor is still limited for three main reasons. First, the rapid expansion of microfinance has been accompanied by malpractices in the sector that have led in some saturated markets to over-indebtedness of clients and other disastrous results including spirals of suicides. Second, these institutions do not serve all potential customers – they fail to reach the poorest among the poor. Third, their offer is often limited to credit products (Armendáriz and Morduch 2010).

In 2013 financial policymakers and regulators from 40 low and middle-income countries signed the Maya Declaration, committing themselves to improve access to finance for the world's two billion unbanked adults. Aligning itself with this declaration, the World Bank has recently called for universal financial inclusion by 2020

(World Bank 2015b). Financial inclusion is becoming increasingly entrenched in the global development agenda but only as a policy goal – a specific target combined with concrete strategies and programs to execute them.[1] So far, only a few voices have suggested the importance of recognizing a *human right to financial inclusion*.[2] This right would complement the current goal-oriented approach to the problem of financial exclusion by creating a nondiscretionary duty for states and international institutions to secure universal access to financial services.

The right to financial inclusion could, if effectively enforced, significantly enhance the financial well-being of the poor. However, arguing for financial inclusion as a human right requires going a step further. We must be able to show that the interests at stake in the area protected by this right are of sufficient importance to deserve human rights protection. This is the main aim of this chapter. It seeks to offer a normative justification of the human right to financial inclusion based on the significance of this right in advancing individual autonomy and satisfying other well-established human rights.

My analysis is divided into five further sections. Section 5.2 clarifies the idea of financial inclusion. Section 5.3 offers a formulation of the right to financial inclusion and unfolds its content. The next two sections develop a twofold justification of this right. Section 5.4 presents an *interest-based argument* that shows the usefulness of the human right to financial inclusion to protect and enhance the fundamental interest in individual autonomy. Section 5.5 offers two *linkage arguments* that illustrate how this right contributes to the realization of other well-established human rights, namely, the right to an adequate standard of living and the right to development. Finally, a conclusion closes the chapter in Sect. 5.6.

5.2 Access to or Usage of Financial Services?

In the current debate among practitioners about financial inclusion, *non-usage* of financial services is used as a proxy for *lack of access* to these services. From a normative perspective, however, the two concepts should be clearly distinguished. While financial *usage* is the act of employing or utilizing financial services, financial *access* refers to the availability of such services. Financial inclusion is concerned with *effective access* to finance. It seeks to ensure universal availability – not usage – of affordable and adequate *basic* financial services, namely, credit, savings, insurance and payment services. Those situations where individuals are *prevented* from gaining or *unable* to gain access to these services can thus be described as cases of financial *exclusion*.

---

[1] At the time of writing this article (August 2015) there is an ongoing discussion about whether financial inclusion should be included as a specific goal in the Post-2015 agenda.

[2] See, for example the recent defense of this right offered by Kimberly Brownlee and Zofia Stemplowska (2015).

Four kinds of obstacles are responsible for much of the financial exclusion experienced by poor people in developing countries. (i) The first is the *high cost barrier* that includes both economic and non-economic costs. Economic costs are the fixed fees and interest rates charged by mainstream financial institutions, which are quite often unaffordable for the poor – e.g. the annual fees of maintaining a checking account in Sierra Leone are the equivalent of 27 of the annual GDP per capita (Demirgüç-Kunt and Klapper 2013). The charges for these services are high because for financial institutions the costs of dealing with small transactions are also high – operating savings accounts with very little money or lending small sums at common interest rates is simply not profitable. Non-economic costs, on the other hand, include intangibles like the insecurity and inconvenience of having to carry money over long distances given that most of the financially excluded live in areas that are too far away from the nearest bank branch – in Tanzania, for instance, there is less than 0.5 bank branch per 1000 km^2 (ibid.).

(ii) The second obstacle is the *bureaucratic barrier*. Documentation requirements for opening a savings account or contracting other financial services typically exclude individuals who do not have proof of address or a legal identity, informal workers lacking formal wage slips, and micro entrepreneurs operating without accounts books and traceable means of payment – most of the global poor fall into one or two of these categories.

(iii) A third hurdle is the *discrimination barrier*. Financial discrimination takes place when financial services are denied or adjusted on the basis of non-relevant factors such as race, age, gender or ethnicity. The most common form of financial discrimination is gender-based and in many developing countries it is a practice sanctioned by law (Ellis et al. 2007). Women in some Middle Eastern and South Asian countries, for example, are far less likely to get credit than men because they need a husband – or another male family member – to co-sign a loan.

(iv) Finally, the fourth obstacle is *financial illiteracy*. Poor people often turn to informal finance because they are unfamiliar with the existence and the functioning of formal financial services and they lack the necessary means to obtain the relevant information – e.g. more than two-thirds of people in Zambia are ignorant of basic financial products and 60 % of people in South Africa do not understand the concept of interest (Miller et al. 2009).

In the presence of these barriers, non-use of financial services is tantamount to lack of effective access to them – and, thus, to financial exclusion. Still, keeping the concepts of *access* and *usage* separate is important because it might be the case that individuals have the possibility of using adequate and affordable financial services but decide not to do so. From the standpoint of financial inclusion, their decision is unproblematic. They do not have financial needs – and therefore they do not use financial services – but they have the *possibility* of using financial services in an appropriate form if they wish. The case of an individual who voluntarily opts out of using affordable financial services should, however, be carefully distinguished from situations where someone decides not to use these services because she lacks adequate access to them. Individuals who do not face any of the barriers just mentioned can still experience some form of financial exclusion. Two cases of voluntary non-use of financial services will help to illustrate this point.

The first case concerns individuals that refuse to use financial services for religious reasons. This happens mainly in Muslim countries due to the Quran's prohibition of interest-based financial transactions. Many religiously minded Muslims do not use financial services because *in their present form* most of these services violate Islamic laws – in Morocco and Tunisia more than 25 % of unbanked adults mention religious reasons as the main explanation for not having a bank account (Demirgüç-Kunt et al. 2015). They experience financial exclusion because they lack access to financial services that are *adequate* in the sense of respectful of their religious beliefs. They would be financially included if Sharia-compliant financial services were available to them.[3]

The second case involves individuals who shy away from financial markets because they do not trust them. Lack of trust in formal financial institutions can have several causes but it constitutes an access problem when it is triggered by high financial uncertainty due to recent experiences of hyperinflation, bank insolvency and bank expropriation. In Peru, for example, the loss of savings experienced by many households during the economic instability of the 1980s, has left many Peruvians – lower and middle-class – with a distrust of the financial system. This has pushed them towards informal finance. In this context financial exclusion occurs because individuals lack access to financial services that are safe and reliable.

The presence of voluntary choice does not render these two cases unproblematic from the point of view of financial inclusion. In contrast with the case of someone who voluntarily opts out of using adequate and affordable financial services, these individuals have a demand for financial services. However, their situation is different from that of those experiencing one of the four barriers previously described because they are accepted in a financial system. The problem is that the products and services available in this system are inadequate to satisfy their basic financial needs. The six scenarios introduced in this section show that financial exclusion can have a variety of causes. Identifying them is important because each one demands different responses from policy makers.

In the light of what has been said in this section, three aspects of the idea of financial inclusion should be clear. First, financial inclusion is concerned with real possibilities of using financial services – i.e. with access rather than usage necessarily of these services. Second, it can be defined as a *state* or a *process* that ensures effective access to adequate and affordable financial services – or negatively, as the absence or the removal of barriers and obstacles that prevent or make access to these services difficult. Third, financial inclusion is a *distributive* dimension of financial development concerned with the availability of financial services to all.

[3] Islamic finance has been growing since the 1970s and is now considered one of the main channels to achieve financial inclusion in Muslims countries.

5.3 The Human Right to Financial Inclusion

Philosophical justifications of concrete human rights should define and clarify, from the outset, the sense in which they understand these rights. In the present context, human rights should be understood as *legal* rights – i.e. as rights that are included in the international system of human rights law or that we are morally obliged to include. This obligation can be grounded on different moral reasons that might include, but not necessarily so, a previous moral right of which the legal right is a counterpart or a specification (Buchannan 2013). In this chapter I explore several moral considerations in favor of acknowledging a legal human right to financial inclusion that ought to be protected and fulfilled by any state and the international community. I will remain agnostic about whether the right to financial inclusion also qualifies as a moral human right. Before examining the moral underpinnings of a legal right to financial inclusion, I shall first introduce the content of the right to financial inclusion.

Tentatively, the right to financial inclusion can be defined as a right to have effective access to a full suite of high-quality basic financial services – including credit, savings, insurance and payment services – at an affordable cost, without being discriminated on grounds of financial situation, race, religion, ethnicity or gender.[4] Three elements of this definition are worthy of elaboration. First, *high-quality* should be understood as an all-encompassing term that includes (i) product-fit – i.e. adequacy of the products to the needs of the clients-, (ii) client protection – e.g. prevention of over-indebtedness, transparency, mechanisms for complaint resolution, etc.- and (iii) respectful treatment – including reasonable accommodation of religious beliefs.

Second, the right to financial inclusion ensures access to a range of financial services that can be considered *basic* in the sense that they are essential to enable individuals' full participation in the mainstream economy. It is thus not concerned with the availability of more sophisticated financial products such as stocks and derivatives. The regulation of access to these products can have important distributive implications but, like other socioeconomic human rights, the right to financial inclusion only seeks to address one of the worst problems in the economic arena.

Third, the full realization of the right to financial inclusion requires universal availability of *affordable* financial services. Thus, it is fulfilled when all individuals, including the very poor, can access basic financial services at a price that is in line with their ability to pay. It obviously goes beyond of the scope of this introductory chapter to give a full account of the affordability requirement. Nevertheless, it is important to emphasize that the right to financial inclusion assigns a duty to the right holders to pay for the services they receive. It does not ensure *free* basic financial services for all – its aim is to make financial markets maximally inclusive, not to transform them into something else.

---

[4] Brownlee and Stemplowska (2015) provide a similar, albeit slightly different, definition.

As a human right, the right to financial inclusion is held by all individuals[5] and imposes nondiscretionary obligations on states and other actors. The issue of identifying the duty-bearers of a human right is usually not a simple one, but it is particularly complicated in the case of the proposed right. Financial services are provided by the financial industry and so identifying the range of businesses belonging to this industry as the primary addressees of a right to those services seems at a cursory level pretty straightforward. This, however, is doubly problematic. First, considering that human rights are typically conceived as norms addressed to states, it seriously weakens the case for a right to financial inclusion (Brownlee and Stemplowska 2015). Second, given that financial institutions operate under important economic constraints – e.g. solvency and deposit protection -, considering them as the primary duty-bearers makes the fulfillment of the right highly conditional (Sorell 2015).

For these two reasons, I suggest that the primary obligation inherent in the (putative) right to financial inclusion should be that governments take the necessary steps to create an enabling environment for a well-functioning inclusive financial system. This, in turn, entails different duties. Firstly, it creates a negative duty to refrain from directly owning and managing financial institutions with the purpose of taking bribes or engaging in other forms of rent-seeking behavior that hinders financial inclusion. Secondly, it generates a positive duty to regulate financial markets and provide incentives to financial institutions with the purpose of ensuring the progressive realization of full financial inclusion. Governments can do several things to expand financial access, for example: (i) enacting antidiscrimination laws banning private sector practices that foster financial exclusion; (ii) improving information sharing between financial institutions in order to reduce transaction costs and information asymmetries; (iii) simplifying burdensome branch regulations that prevent the expansion of financial access in rural areas, especially in developing countries; (iv) improving financial literacy and developing consumer-oriented disclosure requirements – for fees, penalties and other aspects of financial contracts -; (v) subsidizing the delivery of financial products to underserved areas or groups; (vi) imposing interest rate ceilings to protect customers from exploitation by commercial actors; (vii) mandating financial access; and (viii) providing financial services.

The proposed right would create a direct obligation for the providers of financial services to avoid practices that foster financial service discrimination – for example, requiring women to pay higher interest rates or to collateralize a higher share of the loan they request. But it should be stressed that they would not be violating this right if, in the absence of the adequate regulatory framework, they fail to provide financial services to the poor – if they did, they would not be discharging a human rights duty.

[5] This is compatible with making the *exercise* of the right conditional upon fulfilling non-discriminatory requirements that reflect standard qualifications for the use of these services – e.g. having certain age and normal capacities. In this sense, financial rights are like voting rights or labor rights.

Naturally, as a human right, the right to financial inclusion would also create secondary duties for the international community (including other states, NGOs, and supranational institutions), consisting of helping and encouraging governments to respect and protect their content. For example, donors can use specific aid modalities aimed at improving the financial systems of developing countries such as providing guidance and technical assistance to government regulators or offering funding for retail finance providers and loans for the purpose of strengthening the financial market.

5.4 Financial Inclusion and Individual Autonomy

A common justificatory approach to human rights holds that a right *R* is justified as a human right if it secures fundamental human interests (Nickel 2007; Beitz 2009). The core idea behind this view is that individuals will have a better life if they live in a society that respects and secures their human rights. Human beings have a broad range of interests but we can only consider fundamental, and thus worthy of human rights protection, those that are "recognizable as important in a wide range of typical lives that occur in contemporary societies" (Beitz 2009, 110). Even though human rights theorists do not agree on which specific interests pass this test, our interest in living as autonomous agents, or simply, our interest in autonomy is endorsed by many of them as a good candidate (Griffin 2008; Nickel 2007). The ideal of autonomy holds that individuals – adults of normal capacities – should be the authors of their own lives. They should be able to reason on the basis of their values, goals and preferences and choose freely – i.e. without coercion or manipulation – from an adequate range of available options (Raz 1986, p. 373). The interest in autonomy can thus be broadly defined as an interest in having the mental capacities to form intentions and beliefs of certain complexity and being able to use such capacities to pursue a worthwhile life (Raz 1986; Griffin 2008). The human interest in autonomy yields three more specific claims, namely: (i) the claim to assistance in the development of the ability to choose autonomously, (ii) the claim to non-interference with one's exercise of autonomy, and (iii) the claim to the creation and maintenance of meaningful opportunities for choice. These claims often have a prominent role in the justification of other human rights. It has been argued, for example, that the human right to education is necessary to satisfy (i), and that the right to freedom of expression is essential to secure (ii). Let us consider whether these three claims can generate support for the human right to financial inclusion.

First, granting people basic financial services is an important way of assisting them in acquiring the capacities to choose autonomously and, thus, satisfy claim (i). Savings and credit facilities allow individuals to have access to the resources they need in order to obtain basic goods – e.g. food, clothes, housing and education – that are necessary for the development of such capacities. Assessments of the impact of microfinance programs show that poor people use credit and savings mainly to buy food, pay school fees and cover sickness expenses – and less so to invest in small businesses, as it was initially expected (Banerjee et al. 2013). Eliminating credit constraints can substantially increase school enrollment rates (Becchetti and Conzo 2010; Dehejia and Gatti 2005) and investments in clean water connections (Devoto et al. 2011) or mosquito nets (Tarozzi et al. 2014).

In pointing to the connection between access to finance and the first autonomy claim, I do not mean to suggest that the proposed right can replace other socioeconomic rights like the right to education or the right to an adequate standard of living. Governments cannot relinquish their responsibility for ensuring these other rights arguing that food, education and other basic goods can be fostered through credit. In fact, as we will see in the next section, secure access to finance can improve the implementation of these other rights.

Second, being able to make financial choices is a dimension of individual autonomy that concerns the freedom to manage one's economic resources. Currently, many women cannot exercise this freedom because they need to be authorized by their husbands – or male relatives- to use financial services. By granting effective access to financial services, the right to financial inclusion seeks to avoid this form of interference.[6] Furthermore, the proposed right has crucial instrumental value to advance claim (ii) in a more general sense – i.e. not only concerning financial decisions. Savings and insurance help protect people against the economic consequences of health shocks, long-term unemployment and other contingencies. In doing so, they render individuals less vulnerable to exploitation and coercive offers, for whom it would otherwise be easier to take advantage of their situation.

Third, financial services make resources available to individuals to pursue their aims – e.g. developing a hobby, buying a house, travelling the world, etc. In a market economy with extensive commercialization and well-enforced property rights, the pursuit of many worthwhile goals depends upon possessing enough resources to pay for them. As G.A. Cohen has argued, lack of economic resources entails lack of freedom because money removes constraints that otherwise restrict our options – someone is unfree to take a train if she does not possess the necessary resources to pay the fare (Cohen 2011 [2001]). Financial services help individuals to enjoy options that, in the absence of economic resources, are only available in a formal sense. Moreover, they enable them to make intertemporal choices regarding these options, which is essential for life planning. Saving facilities protect people from immediate pressures to spend monetary resources thus helping them to postpone its use. Credit gives them the possibility to use resources they currently need but do not have. In short, access to financial services advances claim (iii) because it increases individuals' effective possibilities to pursue their goals and their capacity to plan their realization.

[6] A non-discriminatory legal framework is not sufficient to avoid all forms of financial discrimination against women. In the worst patriarchal societies, women might have the legal possibility to contract financial services by themselves and still be compelled by their husbands – using threat or force – to make certain financial choices. Eradicating these forms of interference requires a series of measures oriented at changing the structure of gender relationships within society and creating a gender-egalitarian ethos – of which broadening access to finance is only one.

5.5 Financial Inclusion and Other Human Rights

An alternative non-foundational strategy to justify a right to *X* as a human right is to show that it can be derived from one of several well-established human rights. This type of argument is known as *linkage-argument* and can be summarized by saying that a right *R1* should be acknowledged as human right if it provides strong support for the implementation or enjoyment of *R2*, which is already accepted as a justified human right (Nickel 2008; Sen 1999; Shue 1996). Linkage arguments rely on the idea that the realization of different human rights is highly correlated due to existing supporting relationships between them. They require strong one-way supporting relationships between two rights – not necessarily interdependence or bidirectional support (Nickel 2008). In his celebrated defense of the right to subsistence, Henry Shue claims that this right is necessary for the implementation of any other right: "No one can fully…enjoy any right that is supposedly protected by society if he or she lacks the essentials for a reasonably healthy and active life" (Shue 1996, 24–25). Amartya Sen has also used a linkage argument to defend the view that civil and political rights are decisive to prevent famines in developing countries (Sen 1999). This section offers two linkage arguments that connect the right to financial inclusion with (i) the right to an adequate standard of living and (ii) the right to development.

5.5.1 Financial Inclusion and the Right to an Adequate Standard of Living

The right to an adequate standard of living is recognized as a human right in the UDHR (art.37) and in the ICESCR (art.14). It requires, at a minimum, that people have sufficient access to the necessary means of subsistence – e.g. food, clothing, shelter, basic health care, etc. The right to financial inclusion supports this right in two important ways. First, access to finance enhances the capacities of the poor to engage in income-generating activities and to fend for themselves (Sen 1999, p. 39). Basic financial services are necessary tools for taking full advantage of the productive opportunities available and, more generally, of the benefits of a productive system. This form of economic empowerment is particularly important for the enjoyment of the right to an adequate standard of living if we understand the latter as requiring the *actual possibility to acquire* and enjoy basic goods without having to degrade oneself – e.g. by engaging in forced labor or begging (Nickel 2004).

Second, broad access to financial services can significantly improve the efficiency and effectiveness of social protection policies. Existing empirical evidence shows that social transfers made through bank accounts – instead of in cash – can help governments to reduce transaction costs and corruption. In India the use of banking services to transfer money to the poor has reduced bribe payments almost by half 47 %. In Brazil similar policies reduced administrative costs by 82 % (World Bank 2015c).

The linkage between the putative right to financial inclusion and the right to an adequate standard of living can be questioned on the grounds that some empirical evidence available shows that microcredit – the most popular finance service targeted to the poor – can, in some cases, exacerbate poverty. Extremely poor borrowers – those earning less than $1 a day – are sometimes unable to pay back their loans because they often have difficulties to save and fewer skills to turn their investment into profitable businesses. Over-indebtedness can make the lives of these individuals worse than they would have been if they had not had access to credit at all. In response to this concern, I should first say that access to finance may not an effective way to address cases of extreme poverty. Malnourished individuals who cannot engage in self-help activities need, first of all, targeted in-kind and in-cash transfers. This conclusion, however, does not invalidate the first linkage argument. Financial inclusion is not the silver-bullet solution to poverty but it still has great potential to help a large segment of the global poor who, despite not being the poorest, still face severe economic hardship.

Two additional considerations diminish the force of the objection. First, linkage arguments require a strong *net positive* support. That is, they hold as long as the negative impact of the supporting right is outweighed by the positive impact it has on the realization of the supported right – obviously, the greater the difference between the positive and negative effects the stronger the argument (Nickel 2008, p. 989). Pointing out that financial services can in some cases aggravate poverty does not debunk this first linkage argument if, in spite of these cases, it is possible to establish a relationship of *net positive* support between broad access to finance and the enjoyment of an adequate standard of living.

Second, the existing empirical evidence on microfinance is, of course, relevant to assess the strength of this argument. But we should focus on cases of well-functioning microfinance institutions that give poor people effective access to financial services of high quality and tailored to their specific needs. The right to financial inclusion secures access to *these* services and not to the abusive deals offered by some microfinance institutions that have caused horrific tragedies. When we restrict our attention to the best practices in microfinance the evidence that reduces poverty become more conclusive. For example, in Bangladesh since 1997 Grameen Bank – the microfinance organization founded by the Nobel Peace Prize-winning Muhammad Yunus – has lifted out of poverty 55 % of its long-term customers (customers for more than 5 years) (Sorell 2015).

5.5.2 Financial Inclusion and the Right to Development

The right to development has been recognized as a human right through the Declaration on the Right to Development of the UN (1986), which was followed up by the Vienna Declaration of 1993. It is a right to a process of incremental realization of all human rights, which is grounded in claims to the material resources and conditions that are necessary for the fulfillment of those rights. The specific content of the right to development is a matter of debate but there seems to be a broad consensus among scholars and legal commentators that it entails, at least, a corresponding obligation for governments to adopt and implement a "policy of economic growth that lessens resource constraints and adjusts the institutions that facilitate the realization of all or most [human] rights" (Sengupta 2007, 338). The right to development should not be seen as the aggregate of the social and economic rights of each individual, but rather as a distinctive collective right to the conditions that are necessary to protect and fulfill all human rights. Thus, one could say that it is the economic parallel of the right to self-determination in that it belongs to the same category of collective rights.

Development economists have long debated about the sources of development and economic growth. One position is that economic prosperity is mainly determined by geography – e.g. climate, natural resources, location, etc. Another holds that what matters is market integration. Yet the view that appears to have gained most acceptance is an institutional approach that holds that development is mainly determined by the quality of institutions – e.g. rule of law, stable property rights, bureaucratic capacity, independent courts, etc. According to this view, developing countries are hampered by *extractive* institutions in which a group of individuals do their best to extract resources from the rest of the population (Acemoglu and Robinson 2012). Economic development requires replacing these institutions with *inclusive* ones that "allow and encourage participation by the great mass of people in economic activities that make best use of their talents and skills and that enable individuals to make the choices they wish" (ibid., 74). A financial system that ensures broad and effective access to basic financial services is a clear example of the kind of inclusive economic institutions that are necessary for economic development – other important ones are stable property rights and rule of law (ibid.) The importance of financial institutions for economic development was highlighted by the High Level Panel on Financing for Development assigned with the task of identifying possible ways of financing these goals. In its final report it stressed that: "No country can expect to achieve equitable growth, or to meet the International Development Goals, unless it focuses on building effective domestic institutions and adopting sound policies including…a financial system that intermediates savings to those capable of investing efficiently, including microfinance borrowers, women, and the rural sector" (as cited in Risse 2005, 82). But how exactly does financial inclusion promote development? Although the macroeconomic consequences of financial inclusiveness have been less analyzed than the effects of financial depth or stability, the existing literature allows us to identify three important mechanisms.

First, the absence of adequate payment services has a negative impact on remittances – voluntary transfers of money by migrant workers to their family members and relatives in their home countries. Together with foreign aid, remittances are the largest economic inflows to developing countries. In 2013, remittances to developing countries amounted to more than $16bn. In countries like Nepal, Armenia and Haiti they represent more than 20 % of the yearly GDP. Remittances have a significant redistributive effect and in some cases they contribute decisively to reduce external debt. Underdeveloped payment systems make sending and receiving money in poor countries more expensive and thus reduce remittance flows to developing countries. For instance, while the average global cost of sending $200 is 7.99 %, the costs of sending the same amount to a developing country is 9.24 % – individual corridors can be significantly more expensive, sending 500$ from Singapore to Pakistan costs 12.33 %. The implementation of the right to financial inclusion would increase the competition among money operators and reduce the fees charged for the transmission of cash. As a consequence, the money that is now used to pay these fees could be injected into the economy.

Second, a right to financial inclusion can have a positive impact on the creation and growth of firms – mainly small and medium-sized ones – and, hence, on the aggregate economic output. In developing countries, access to finance is one the most important factors that constrains entrepreneurial activities. Under certain circumstances, the removal of this barrier has two important economic consequences. On the one hand it prompts individuals to start an entrepreneurial activity and thus increases the number of new business start-ups. On the other hand, it helps existing businesses to exploit market opportunities and to raise and pool funds for riskier investments.

Third, a growing body of literature shows that financial inclusion can be conducive to greater financial stability (Han and Melecky 2013). In the context of economic turmoil, the lack of trust in financial markets increases the risk of bank runs – i.e. correlated withdrawals of deposits by a large numbers of customers – and subsequent systemic banking crises. Financial institutions can mitigate this risk if they diversify their deposit base by involving a greater share of the population in the use of banking deposits. Greater access to bank deposits means more customers and, as a matter of fact,[7] that makes correlated withdrawals more difficult therefore improving the resilience of financial institutions and the overall economy.[8] This effect is expected to be stronger in countries that are highly integrated in global financial markets and whose citizens have low levels of trust in the financial sector – these two features are typically shared by middle-income countries, like Argentina or Peru, that have suffered repeated episodes of financial crisis.

Against the two linkage arguments developed in this section it might be objected that they are too weak a defense of the human right to financial inclusion. Both arguments show at most that broad access to finance is conducive to the realization of the two other rights, not that it is indispensable. For example, it is possible to secure access for the poor to basic goods by means of in-kind and in-cash transfers – instead of access to credit to buy them. The linkage arguments in favor of a human right to financial inclusion are seriously undermined if, as it seems to happen, this right is just one instrument among others to realize other human rights.

[7] This is not just a consequence of the law of large numbers. Retail customers are often less likely to follow financial markets and to be exposed to rumors or media coverage about particular financial institutions.

[8] Broad access to credit has a similar effect on financial stability as losses associated with small loans pose less systemic risk than losses on large loans (Adasme et al. 2006).

This objection correctly points out the strength of the connection between the supported and the supporting right affects the justificatory force of a linkage argument. These type of arguments are obviously more robust when they show that a right is indispensable for the realization of another. However, let me briefly introduce two considerations in defense of what has been said in this section. First, in the context of human rights – and in social sciences in general – relations of strict necessity are unusual. However, linkage arguments still provide a strong case when they are able to show that the supporting right is *highly useful* for the realization of the supported right (Gilabert 2010). The empirical evidence available shows that under high and medium quality implementation, the right to financial inclusion strongly supports the two other rights examined in this section. Thus, *ceteris paribus*, it seems unreasonable not to implement this right even if it had not been proved to be necessary for the realization of those rights.

Second, when assessing the force of linkage arguments, we should not only take into account the *existence* of alternatives to the supporting right but also their *feasibility* and *effectiveness* in realizing the supported right. The supporting relationship between two rights is not so weakened by the existence of other ways to pursue the supported right, if these alternatives imply higher risks or are significantly more costly (Nickel 2010). For example, even though it is conceivable to implement socioeconomic rights without a right to political participation, the absence of public deliberation makes more difficult to identify the best ways of implementing those rights in a specific context (Gilabert 2010, 429). Giving basic goods for free might be necessary in some cases but it fails to enable poor people to pull themselves out of poverty. In this chapter I argued that, under high quality implementation, the human right to financial inclusion gives people instruments that are necessary for self-sufficiency. If my case is sound, we have good reasons to believe that this right is an essential component of sustainable and dignified strategy to alleviate poverty.

5.6 Conclusion

This chapter claimed that universal access to basic financial services can be defended as a human right – and not just as a development goal – using two different strategies. The first is an interest-based argument that stresses the value of access to finance to protect and enhance individual autonomy. The second is a double linkage argument based in the existence of a supporting relation between the right to financial inclusion and the rights to an adequate standard of living and development. The combination of both arguments seeks to strengthen the case for the human right to financial inclusion but they should be seen as providing compatible but independent reasons in favor of the proposed right. As it happens with most socioeconomic rights, implementing the right to financial inclusion will be costly and many developing countries will have difficulties securing the conditions for its full realization. However, judgments concerning the feasibility of these rights should not only take into account the capacity of local states to implement them, but also the resources of the international community to fulfill its back-up duties. If the arguments offered in the chapter are sound, both sides should be required to take action to broaden financial markets.

References

Acemoglu, Daron, and James A. Robinson. 2012. *Why nations fail: The origins of power, prosperity and poverty*. New York: Crown.

Adasme, Osvaldo, et al. 2006. *Access and risk: Friends or foes. Lessons from Chile*, World Bank policy research working paper n. 4003. Washington, DC: World Bank.

Armendáriz, Beatriz, and Jonathan Morduch. 2010. *The economics of microfinance*, 2nd ed. Cambridge, MA/London: MIT Press.

Banerjee, Abhijit V., and Esther Duflo. 2011. *Poor economics: A radical rethink of the way to fight global poverty*. New York: Public Affairs.

Banerjee, Abhijit V., et al. 2013. *The miracle of microfinance? Evidence from a randomized evaluation*. Massachusetts Institute of Technology Department of Economics working paper series, Working paper. 13–09.

Becchetti, Leonardo, and Pierluigi Conzo. 2010. The controversial effects of microfinance on child schooling: A retrospective approach. ECINEQ working paper no. 2010-173.

Beitz, Charles. 2009. *The idea of human rights*. Oxford: Oxford University Press.

Brownlee, Kimberley, and Zofia Stemplowska. 2015. Financial inclusion, education and human rights. In *Microfinance, rights and global justice*, ed. Tom Sorell and Luis Cabrera, 47–62. Cambridge: Cambridge University Press.

Buchannan, Allen. 2013. *The heart of human rights*. New York: Oxford University Press.

Cohen, G.A. 2011[2001]. Freedom and money. In *On the currency of egalitarian justice and other essays in political philosophy*, ed. Michael Otsuka, 166–192. Princeton: Princeton University Press.

Collins, Daryl, et al. 2009. *Portfolios of the poor: How the world's poor live on $2 a day*. Princeton/Oxford: Princeton University Press.

Dehejia, Rajeev, and Roberta Gatti. 2005. Child labor the role of financial development and income variability across countries. *Economic Development and Cultural Change* 53: 913–932.

Demirgüç-Kunt, Asli, and Leora Klapper. 2013. Measuring financial inclusion: Explaining variation in use of financial services across and within countries. In *Brookings papers on economic activity*. Washington, DC: The Brookings Institution.

Demirgüç-Kunt, et al. 2015. Financial inclusion in Africa: Obstacles and opportunities. In *Oxford handbook of Africa and economics: Policies and practices*, ed. Célestin Monga and Justin Yifu Lin, 388–400. Oxford: Oxford University Press.

Devoto, Florencia, et al. 2011. *Happiness on tap: Piped water adoption in Urban Morocco*, NBER working paper 16933. Cambridge, MA: National Bureau of Economic Research.

Ellis, Amanda, et al. 2007. *Gender and economic growth in Kenya: Unleashing the power of women*. Washington, DC: World Bank.

Gilabert, Pablo. 2010. The importance of linkage arguments for the theory and practice of human rights: A response to James Nickel. *Human Rights Quarterly* 32: 425–438.

Griffin, James. 2008. *On human rights*. Oxford: Oxford University Press.

Han, Rui, and Martin Melecky. 2013. *Financial inclusion for financial stability: Access to bank deposits and the growth of deposits in the global financial crisis*. Washington, DC: World Bank.

Miller, Margaret, et al. 2009. *The case for financial literacy in developing countries: Promoting access to finance by empowering consumers*. Washington, DC: OECD/World Bank/DFID/CGAP.

Nickel, James. 2007. *Making sense of human rights*, 2nd ed. Malden: Wiley-Blackwell.

Nickel, James. 2008. Rethinking indivisibility: Towards a theory of supporting relations between human rights. *Human Rights Quarterly* 30: 984–1001.
Nickel, James. 2010. Indivisibility and linkage arguments: A reply to Gilabert. *Human Rights Quarterly* 32: 439–446.
Raz, Joseph. 1986. *The morality of freedom*. Oxford: Clarendon Press.
Risse, Mathias. 2005. What do we owe to the global poor. *The Journal of Ethics* 9: 81–117.
Sen, Amartya. 1999. *Development as freedom*. Oxford: Oxford University Press.
Sengupta, Arjun. 2007. Poverty eradication and human rights. In *Freedom from poverty and human rights*, ed. Thomas Pogge. Oxford: Oxford University Press.
Shue, Henry. 1996. *Basic rights: Subsistence, affluence, and U.S. foreign policy*, 2nd ed. Princeton: Princeton University Press.
Sorell, Tom. 2015. Is there a human right to microfinance? In *Microfinance rights and global justice*, ed. Tom Sorell and Luis Cabrera, 27–46. Cambridge: Cambridge University Press.
Tarozzi, Alessandro, et al. 2014. Microloans, insecticide-treated bednets, and Malaria: Evidence from a randomized controlled trial in Orissa, India. *American Economic Review* 104: 1909–1941.
World Bank. 2015a. Poverty overview. http://www.worldbank.org/en/topic/poverty/overview. Accessed 14 Sept 2015.
World Bank. 2015b. Overview: Universal financial Access by 2020. http://www.worldbank.org/en/topic/financialinclusion/brief/achieving-universal-financial-access-by-2020. Accessed 10 Sept 2015.
World Bank. 2015c. Financial inclusion and access to finance. Remarks made by Wield Bank Managing Director and Chief Operating Officer Sri Mulyani Indrawati at 11th ASEAN Central Bank Governors Meeting. http://www.worldbank.org/en/news/speech/2015/03/21/remarks-world-bank-managing-directro-coo-asean-central-bank-governors-meeting. Accessed 18 Sept 2015.

Chapter 6
Is Globalizing 'development' Ethical? A View from the Pacific

Joy Paton and Elisabeth Valiente-Riedl

Abstract As the Millennium Development Goals (MDGs) drew to a close in 2015, it was apparent that Small Island Development States (SIDS) did not fare well in achieving their goals for eradicating poverty. This chapter investigates development progress in the Pacific, providing a case study from Papua New Guinea (PNG) focused on the experience of poverty alleviation under the MDG framework. It points to an ethical conundrum for the international community whereby the 'development' process displaces and sometimes destroys existing social economies; yet, traditional systems for social and economic provisioning often constitute a necessary safety net for the poor in developing economy contexts. The Pacific SIDS development experience with foreign aid and volatile markets in international trade is one that threatens culturally specific means for socio-economic reproduction. The chapter therefore directs attention to the complex forms of livelihood that might form part of a creative and just approach to development and poverty alleviation. Further, it suggests hybrid institutional forms can maintain the integrity of culture in development rather than sacrificing it to the one-size-fits-all globalizing construct that characterized the MDGs and which continues in the newly sanctioned Sustainable Development Goal framework.

Keywords MDG/SDG • SIDS • Poverty alleviation • Development • Capability approach

---

J. Paton (✉)
Department of Political Economy, The University of Sydney, Merewether Building H04, Sydney 2006, NSW, Australia
e-mail: joy.paton@sydney.edu.au

E. Valiente-Riedl
Department of Sociology, The University of Sydney, Old Teachers College A22, Sydney 2006, NSW, Australia
e-mail: elisabeth.valiente-riedl@sydney.edu.au

H.P. Gaisbauer et al. (eds.), *Ethical Issues in Poverty Alleviation*, Studies in Global Justice 14, DOI 10.1007/978-3-319-41430-0_6

6.1 Introduction

In re-articulating its global development paradigm, the international community paid particular attention to the emerging economies of small island development states (SIDS). The Millennium Development Goals (MDGs), which were the key framework informing development practice for the previous 15 years, concluded at the end of 2015 (which happened to be named the 'Year of Small Island Development States'). Its successor framework, the Sustainable Development Goals (SDGs), was positioned to reenergize the international development pact and its machinery to combat global poverty. However, the SDG framework does not depart significantly from the MDGs in terms of its philosophical underpinnings and ethical implications, thereby maintaining problematic aspects of the MDG poverty alleviation agenda.

As the MDGs drew to a close, it was apparent that SIDS had not fared well in terms of poverty alleviation. Unlike many emerging economies in Asia, Africa and Latin America, countries in the Pacific region are not making significant progress towards their development goals. In the case of many small island state emerging economies, poverty persists and development has faulted. Yet, the development path expressed in the MDGs (and now SDGs) which has led to this 'failure', sits uncomfortably alongside the realities of existing social economies in some areas of the Pacific. Arguably, these already provide the institutional basis for both formal and informal livelihoods thereby posing a potential challenge to the very conception of poverty at the core of international frameworks for development and poverty alleviation.

Institutional structures organizing the production and distribution of the material (economic) means for life are central to the sustainability of any society or community (Paton 2011:15; Polanyi 1977:31). Yet, in the 'development' process, these existing social economies, with their traditional systems for the provisioning of food, clothing, shelter and so on, are displaced and often destroyed. Regrettably, in an era of 'global community' that otherwise purports to honor and preserve cultural specificity, 'development' represents a tandem process that threatens it. This ethical tension is highlighted through a consideration of the 'capability' concept developed by Amartya Sen (2004). Bringing a culturally sensitive lens to the idea of capability permits a critical examination of the strategies for poverty alleviation stemming from development orthodoxies institutionalized through international policy frameworks.

Sen's (1989) work is acutely concerned with individual freedoms and people's capacity to translate them into functioning in everyday life. However, his ideas point to some radical implications when we think about capability and livelihoods in meta-cultural terms. This is because it opens up the opportunity for consideration of enabling institutional forms beyond the current development orthodoxies. The capability lens enriches an examination of the challenges facing SIDS, supporting a deep meta-cultural critique which reveals both the limits of prevailing development strategies as well as the potential scope for hybrid or even autonomous forms of development. The ethical tensions arising from the experience of poverty alleviation in the Pacific are evident in the small island state of Papua New Guinea (PNG) which provides a relevant case study for consideration of the tensions and challenges of 'development' in SIDS of the Pacific region.

In PNG, the culturally specific forms of economic activity and organization that prioritize traditional or local knowledges over the imperatives of the global economy represent indigenous means for both formal and informal livelihoods. What might constitute 'poverty' and 'development' in the PNG context is therefore contested, as is the very meaning of 'economy' itself. PNG is an agriculturally based economy where subsistence production and collective institutions, such as traditional forms of land tenure, already provide effective mechanisms of social provisioning. The facilitation of livelihoods in this way challenges the development model implicit in the MDG/SDG agendas which assume a 'profit', rather than 'provisioning', view of economic activity (Paton 2010; 2011:24; Nelson 1993).

This chapter takes up the concern with poverty alleviation in the context of a changing global development regime that remains wedded to key tenets of the MDGs. It begins by surveying development trends in historical context before examining the MDG-based strategies which guided international development practice for 15 years and now continue in the SDG framework. This is followed with an investigation of development progress in the Pacific and a detailed case study of PNG. Ethical tensions arising from social and economic reproduction in pursuit of the MDGs are shown to challenge the integrity of the MDG/SDG frameworks. These 'pro-poor growth' strategies marginalize and threaten the very viability of indigenous organizational structures which constitute a necessary social safety net for the poor in developing, or emerging, economy contexts such as PNG. Furthermore, the chapter suggests hybrid institutional forms can maintain the integrity of culture in development rather than sacrificing it to a one-size-fits-all globalizing construct.

6.2 Evolving Development Paradigms

Historically, determining a country's level of economic development was typically dependent upon the monetary measure of Gross National/Domestic Product (GNP/GDP), which is commonly captured by the notion of 'economic growth'. The idea of 'Development' as a specific policy goal aimed at transforming so-called 'underdeveloped' or 'Third World' economies, stems from the period after World War Two when unprecedented levels of economic growth characterized the global economy until the 1970s (Arndt 1989:3). Rapid growth was experienced by the rich industrialized economies of the West and also by many 'developing' countries, too. Yet the latter continued to be characterized by widespread poverty and a generalized low standard of living, notwithstanding increased per capita incomes. Despite this (relatively recent) history, there continues to be widespread international acceptance of the argument that development, understood as economic growth or rising GNP, is a prerequisite for eliminating poverty.

With economic growth designated as the central aim of policy, a consensus on the introduction and maintenance of market mechanisms inevitability follows. Where non-market production[1] predominates, or only embryonic market-based production is present, a structural transformation of such societies into market-based economies is required to enable integration into global networks of production and trade. Since the 1970s, the language of the market has provided a common foundation for articulating development across the globe through the free-market oriented 'Washington Consensus'[2] and later the more radical form of 'neo-liberalism'. In this view, the engine of economic growth constitutes an international regime of free trade where development is fueled by trade liberalization, foreign direct investment, export led growth, privatization of public sector entities and reliance on so-called trickle-down distribution (von Frantzius 2004:471).

However, the model of development embodied in this perspective failed to eradicate global poverty as promised, and instead perpetuated widening gaps in the global economy between developed and emerging economies. It has consequently been widely challenged as a 'development' agenda. This is because something more than mere growth in GNP is needed to secure development which embodies a qualitative character not captured in monetary measures. For example, minimal or even negative growth, such as during times of economic recession, can be present in 'developed' economies; while elsewhere rising levels of GNP can co-exist with widespread poverty and 'underdevelopment'. As Sen (1989:42) argues, high GNP per capita does not necessarily enhance the quality of life, nor remove other problems of poverty such as "premature mortality, escapable morbidity [or] overwhelming illiteracy".

The 'something more' needed for development is a set of pro-active policies aimed directly at poverty, without which widening inequalities within (and between) countries will accompany the growth-based development process. Development cannot be left to 'the market' alone. It is in this context of concern about the limitations of quantitative measures as indicators of social and individual well-being that more complex understandings of development and the goals of development policies began to emerge in the 1990s. This 'broadening' of the development agenda toward what has become known as the 'human development' paradigm, was spearheaded, not surprisingly, outside the traditional domain of 'development economics', underpinned by the philosophical critique of Amartya Sen.

6.2.1 The Contribution of Amartya Sen

Sen (1989) has been influential in broadening the understanding of development as necessarily involving a greater range of concerns than economic growth. The commonly used default measure of GNP is judged as an inadequate 'indicator of

[1] That is, production for needs (use value) rather than production for the market (exchange value).

[2] A set of prescriptions for addressing crises in developing economies which was jointly promoted by the Washington based US treasury, the World Bank and the IMF.

development' by Sen (1999:2) because it reflects the potential 'means' (and only one at that) rather than the valuable 'ends' of development. GNP itself is not a useful measure for gauging the kinds of lives people actually live nor does it reveal information about the distribution of national income or the quality of life in terms of people's health, education or general freedoms (Sen 1989:42). As well as rejecting GNP (i.e. a measure of the capacity to produce commodities), Sen (1999:3) also rejects other commonly held ways of understanding development such as rising personal incomes, industrialization, or social modernization.

Instead, Sen (1999:37) posits that development should be understood as the "enhancement of human freedom" and its concomitant abeyance of deprivation. It is a process of expanding the substantive freedoms and opportunities people have to improve the quality of their lives. Focusing on people's capacity to choose and achieve what they want to do and be "provides a firm basis for evaluating living standards and the quality of life" (Sen 1989:54). Rather than pursuing increased GNP as an end in itself, such a perspective subsumes income goals within the overarching goal of 'freedom', which becomes both the ends and means of development. Ultimately, a person's freedom to make choices 'between different ways of living' reflects their capability, thus for Sen (1989) development should be a process of capability expansion.

The capability approach also provides a context within which the problems of market inefficiencies and distributional inequalities that accompany 'economic development' can be discussed. It provides a way of assessing the "effectiveness of the means" in achieving identified ends (Sen 1989:43). In other words, 'capability' offers a way of evaluating policies for social change such as those marshalled in the "planning of economic development" because only with appropriate planning, might rising national income (GNP) underpin development (Sen 1989:41). For example, poverty is viewed as a form of capability deprivation (Sen 1999:39, 87), but even guaranteed access to a social minimum (for basic needs) does not necessarily equate to capability expansion; it is, in and of itself, an inadequate indicator of 'development' and individual well-being (Sen 1989:54).

For the 'basic needs' element of the 'human development' paradigm to meet the capability criterion, the availability of certain means (commodities and resources) needs to be converted into ends that fulfill quality of life goals. In addition to the various opportunities for achievement a person may command (i.e. their 'capability'), any evaluation of human well-being must therefore also consider what people actually achieve (Sen 1989:44). In this, the capability approach looks beyond 'what money can buy' in any objective sense. However, it is not the case that Sen rejects the role that economic growth and industrialization might play in the enhancement of human freedom. Rather, the capability approach posits that they have to be judged as instruments for that purpose, rather than ends in themselves (Sen 1989:42).

In other words, rising GNP and technological advancement should be "appraised…in terms of their actual effectiveness in enriching the lives and liberties of people" (Dreze and Sen 2002:3). As it turns out though, these 'instruments' are indeed central to the kind of multi-faceted development Sen (1999:40) articulates in his capability framework. Ultimately, his message about development is simple.

Industrialization and growth in a nation's aggregate income (GNP) do not make for development; they are a necessary but insufficient condition. Such 'means' must be harnessed to institutions that guarantee and enhance people's capability (freedoms and opportunities) to achieve their chosen outcomes. Capability brings in the social and political dimensions of human experience thereby removing poverty from simple measurements based on income deprivation.

In this sense, the influence of Sen on the new orthodoxy of human development is palpable, as evidenced in the introduction of the annual UN Human Development Report (HDR) and the Human Development Index (HDI) established in 1990. Spanning qualitative (HDR) and quantitative (HDI) assessments of 'human development', these initiatives aim to institutionalize a capabilities framework. They seek to drive and measure a much more complex understanding of development than was evident in the market-centered focus of the 'Washington Consensus'. The current human-centered "New York consensus" (Fukuda-Parr 2003:310) is manifest in the 'multi-criteria' approach to development evident in the Millennium Development Goals and continued in the Sustainable Development Goals.

6.3 The New Millennium Development Strategies

Launched in 2000, the Millennium Development Goals (MDGs) belonged to a growing list of global coordination initiatives targeting key issues such as poverty. Unlike previous global efforts, the MDG program received broad-based support for its wide ranging and sustained approach (Nelson 2007:2046). Indeed, the MDGs represented an unlikely consensus between the diverse institutions of the United Nations (UN) system. These include the International Monetary Fund (IMF) and the World Bank, as well as developed and developing country governments, the private sector and civil society. In building on the human development framework, the MDGs similarly reflected Sen's capability approach in their concern with a more complex understanding of development. However, compared to the HDIs, they included more detailed targets and drew on more indicators, including the World Bank's income poverty metric[3] (Saith 2006:1172).

The broadening of development cooperation brought with it the promise that the concept of development, and its associated strategies and mechanisms for implementation, might also be broadened. Such aspirations were reflected in the *United Nations Millennium Declaration* (United Nations General Assembly 2000) where 'development', once primarily articulated as an economic concern, was reconceived within a 'human rights' framework. Despite the constraint of limited goals[4] and

[3] The international poverty line for 'extreme poverty' of living on less than US$1/day.

[4] The eight goals in the MDGs addressed income poverty and hunger (MDG1), education (MDG2), gender equality (MDG3), child mortality (MDG4), maternal health (MDG5), diseases (MDG6), environmental sustainability (MDG7) and global development cooperation (MDG8). Under the SDG framework, these have been expanded to 17 goals whereby the original MDG agenda is now

their articulation through quantitative targets, the MDGs spanned a wide range of concerns. At their core was a broad-based attack on multiple dimensions of global poverty that included, but moved beyond, economic goals and mechanisms. From a capability perspective, the MDGs made significant advances by expanding understanding of the condition of poverty beyond economic concerns alone.

Yet, the articulation of MDG1 and the broader market-based development strategy espoused by the MDG framework, indicates the conception of poverty remained wedded to the very economic development orthodoxies that the framework promised to move beyond.[5] There was limited consideration of different mechanisms and strategies, including alternative institutional structures, for meeting needs and achieving development goals. This ensured the MDGs remained closely aligned to the market-based economic measures and imperatives of the global economy. The narrow approach was clearly revealed in the poverty alleviation strategies that guided realization of the MDG goals that emanated from the UN 'Millennium Project', an independent advisory body directed by development economist Jeffrey Sachs.

6.3.1 MDG Strategies for Poverty Alleviation and Development

The Millennium Project's 2005 report, *Investing in Development*, provided a roadmap for achieving the MDGs. It reflects a strong market-based (capitalist) growth strategy and served as a blueprint for MDG poverty alleviation. The report supported "the scaling up of…official development assistance" and strengthened market liberalization, particularly regarding market barriers for developing country exports (UN Millennium Project 2005:xx–xxii). Furthermore, it recommended developing country governments use "MDG-based poverty reduction strategies" and that these be "aligned" with the IMF Poverty Reduction Strategy Papers (PRSPs)[6] (UN Millennium Project 2005:xx). This reflects an obvious effort to streamline MDG implementation with existing strategies and mechanisms for poverty reduction.

extended to include aspirations for: 'no poverty' (SDG1); 'zero hunger' (SDG2); 'good health and wellbeing' (SDG3); 'quality education' (SDG4); 'gender equality' (SDG5); 'clean water and sanitation' (SDG6); 'affordable and clean energy' (SDG7); 'decent work and economic growth' (SDG8); 'industry, innovation and infrastructure' (SDG9); 'reduced inequalities' (SDG10); sustainable cities and communities' (SDG11); 'responsible consumption and production' (SDG12); 'climate change' (SDG13); 'life below water' (SDG14); 'life on land' (SDG15); 'peace, justice and strong institutions' (SDG16), and; 'partnerships for goals' (SDG17) (see https://sustainabledevelopment.un.org).

[5]The emphasis on 'economic growth' is now made explicit under the SDG framework in Goals 7 (growth) and 8 (industrialisation).

[6]The PRSPs outline a policy framework for poverty alleviation which developing countries submit to the IMF when seeking loans.

In Sachs'schema, the condition of "extreme poverty" was diagnosed as a "lack of access to basic needs" (Sachs 2005:293). This advanced a distinct approach to poverty alleviation whereby basic needs, seen as critical to development, were identified and targeted. This approach is clearly reflected in the MDG framework which identified and set time-bound goals and targets across a series of basic needs including health, education and gender equality. It was also an approach commensurate with that introduced by the International Labour Organization (ILO) in the late 1970s, where a 'basic needs' model complemented rather than rejected the prevailing economic orthodoxy of the time by orienting growth policies toward "the supply and distribution of essential goods and services" (Lisk 1977:187).

Thus, the primary mechanism for development has not fundamentally changed. Indeed, the MDG development strategy became more, not less, focused on integration into the global capitalist economy. Sachs (2005:244–45) explicitly attributed the condition of extreme poverty – synonymous with basic needs deprivation – to problems in the process of capital accumulation[7]. In this view, household incomes are insufficient for savings or payment of taxes because they are predominantly used for consumption. As a result, two key sources of capital investments – household savings and government investments (through tax revenue) – are strained. This, according to Sachs (2005:245), leads to a vicious cycle where lack of capital undermines economic growth, which in turn, stunts the incomes needed to spur capital accumulation.

Such a diagnosis reflects a fundamental misunderstanding of the historical processes of capitalist development (see Wood 1999) and is reminiscent of earlier prescriptions for growth-led development which emerged in the 1950s (see Lewis 1955). These were further championed under the 'Washington Consensus' promotion of market led growth and development. The point of difference in the MDGs 'New York Consensus' was the effort to pursue economic growth as a vehicle for achieving certain ends – those defined as basic needs – rather than pursuing growth as an end in itself. In this way, a substantial shift in the development paradigm was effected. However, while 'basic needs deprivation' of the MDG framework echoes 'capability deprivation', it is differentiated from Sen's framework in its explicit focus on (market) commodities over (human) capacities.

To kick-start the growth process, the MDG strategy of development cooperation emphasized aid as a necessary mechanism. Sachs (2005) followed the tradition of the Washington Consensus in endorsing the role of international aid as central to development. He thereby supported an export-led growth model while insisting that escape from the poverty trap would necessitate a strategy of "trade plus aid" (Sachs2005:281). Furthermore, Sachs (2005:244) suggested that the "poorest of the poor…lack the minimum amount of capital necessary" to get onto the "development ladder". Yet, donor funding as a vehicle for achieving the MDGs represents much more than the transfer of finance to spur development efforts: aid in itself

[7] Sachs (2005:244–45) refers to six types of capital that are lacking in conditions of extreme poverty: human capital, business capital, infrastructure, natural capital, public institutional capital and knowledge capital.

represents a blueprint for development, and one predicated on distinct ideological and policy frameworks.

MDG-based development must therefore be understood through its key driving mechanisms, such as aid. MDG8, the "global partnership for development", packaged the emphasis on aid in a continued commitment to an open market trading system (UN Millennium Project 2005:xix). The call for donor funds to support the MDGs was strengthened with a clear pledge to support development through a "new partnership between developed and developing countries" (United Nations 2002:2). Yet this dichotomous positioning effectively polarizes and stereotypes 'rich and powerful' developed countries against 'poor and corrupt' developing countries. It tends to "ghettoize the problem of development and locate it firmly in the third world" implying the fundamental issue of development is one of "absolute levels of living" (Saith 2006:1184).

Given the wealth of literature that implicates developed countries in causing or contributing to poverty, the idea that developed countries can and will champion development is in itself contestable.[8] In this context, it should be noted that the Official Development Assistance (ODA) recommended under MDG8 was typically 'tied-aid' (Saith 2006:1186). Through this mechanism, developing countries become increasingly dependent upon and indebted to their 'global development partners'. This not only brings a high debt servicing burden, but also a suite of policy directives as conditions of the loan. Thus the policy agenda behind the aid industry became embodied in the MDG development model and is nowhere more apparent than the small island nation states of the Pacific.

6.4 Globalizing Development Fails the Pacific

Broadly, the Asia-Pacific region emerged as a strong performer across the MDG development metric (see ADB et al. 2015:2). However, the diversity of the region does not lend itself to regional analysis. Asia and the Pacific are arguably "largely incompatible as regions", with the former housing the globe's largest countries (China and India) and the Pacific comprising a plethora of small island developing states (SIDS) (Feeny and Clarke 2008:198). Indeed, falling levels of poverty in China and India alone largely account for global progress on poverty reduction, and were isolated in regional data on poverty presented for *The Millennium Development Goals Report 2015* (United Nations 2015:14).

Accordingly, the Pacific as a sub-region offers a counter-narrative to the broader 'Asia-Pacific' MDG story. It also serves as an important example of the challenges that globalizing development projects like the MDGs/SDGs present for developing

[8] See the work of dependency theorists including the pioneering work of Andre Gunder Frank (1966) on poverty and, more recently, the ongoing tensions between North and South evident in successive UN summits for international cooperation on 'sustainable development' where developed economies have failed to follow through on their enabling commitments (Paton 2011:84).

countries. In the Pacific, especially, this includes the inability to track data and where data is collected, performance ranges between poor and mixed results (see ADB et al. 2015). Indeed, stalling MDG progress necessitated a revision of goals and an acceleration of interventions across many Pacific states. This was the case despite the maintenance of relatively high-levels of foreign aid, a central pillar of the MDG development frame.[9] The Pacific countries have been identified as some of the largest aid recipients in the world, relative to the size of their populations and economies (Feeny and Clarke 2009:37).[10]

Arguably, while official data suggests the Pacific 'failed' the MDGs, it is also possible to suggest that the MDG model failed the Pacific. The Pacific Island states accentuate the difficulties some countries and regions face in attempting to implement global goals and metrics. In the first instance, the Pacific suffers a stark deficit in its data collection capacity, being lower than that of the Asia-Pacific at large, with even greater gaps registered in comparison to some other regions (ADB et al. 2015:54). This makes it difficult to track progress in the Pacific across most benchmarks, and in turn, longitudinal measurement cannot inform the design of many development interventions as it does in other regions. As a result, the lack of statistical capacity produced an incomplete MDG assessment for the Pacific.[11]

Yet, tracking the MDG performance of Pacific SIDs is significant as much for the results that are present as for those missing. The Pacific at large seems not to have met global development aspirations for the new millennium either in terms of progress or its meaningful measurement (see ADB et al. 2015:2). However, consideration of the local contexts marginalized in global sentiments usefully fleshes out an alternative to the 'off track' picture painted by official MDG reports. To this end, reflection on the MDG experience of Papua New Guinea highlights the myriad tensions increasingly defining the globalizing development project including the problems of global goal setting and measurement. These were central features of the MDGs and are intensified in the 'metrics' paradigm of the SDGs (ADB et al. 2015:58).

6.4.1 PNG 'off track'?

Papua New Guinea is a small island developing state in the Pacific which comprises more than 600 islands and lays claim to over 850 language groups; each is denoted by identifiable 'wantoks' or clans, with commensurate diversity in cultural identity

[9] ODA did, however, fall short of the MDG8 target for developed countries to commit 0.7 % GNI and flows into the region were generally considered inadequate for MDG benchmarks (ADB, UNESCAP and UNDP 2014:6,8).

[10] In 2005 Pacific countries received $142US of aid per capita compared to $13US for Asian countries (Feeny and Clarke 2009:37).

[11] In the *Asia-Pacific Regional MDGs Report 2014/15*, 19 Pacific countries were tracked across the three targets for MDG-1 (the Goal for income poverty and hunger). This should have produced 57 entries. However, only six entries are made: three for Fiji, two for PNG and one for Vanuatu (ADB, UNESCAP and UNDP 2014:2).

and traditions (Cammack 2007:6). This culturally, linguistically and socio-economically diverse country highlights some of the ethical dilemmas that 'one-size-fits-all' development models continue to present in their ambition to catapult all states onto a homogenous development path. The globalizing development project strains the fabric of an existing hybrid social economy, tied to culturally relevant articulations of livelihood that run counter to the market-based growth model favored by conventional development wisdom.

Since independence from Australia in 1975, PNG has experienced sustained external development support.[12] Significantly, aid funding, including under the MDG umbrella, imposes its own brand of development. Australia, the primary aid funding source for PNG, not only channels funds into the small island developing state, but these funds act as a conduit for development orthodoxy. In relation to achieving MDG1, AusAID[13] (2005:19) asserted that aid is effective for growth "when it is used to build the policies, institutions and social infrastructure needed to improve economic decision making and productive processes". This statement highlights the level of structural intervention accompanying the flow of aid funds, which target the creation and maintenance of particular growth enabling institutions. Its noteworthy too, that from 1999 Australia transitioned to a fully 'tied aid' model for ODA dispersed to PNG (DNPM PNG 2010:225–226).

Despite the flow of aid monies into PNG, the small island state maintained a poor track record for the duration of the MDG lifecycle. In PNGs first 'Progress Report' tracking its MDG performance, achievement of MDG's 1–7 was considered '[v]ery unlikely' (Government of PNG 2004a:41). By 2007, the *MDG Monitor* (UNDP 2007) labelled PNG progress 'off track' for the target date of 2015. By 2014, for the 17 targets for which there was data available (of a total of 22), PNG was considered an 'early achiever' across four targets (all MDG6 targets and one MDG7 target[14]), but for the remaining 13 either 'slow' (seven targets) or 'regressing/no progress' (six targets) (ADB et al. 2015:2). This 'failed' performance is hard to reconcile with the legacy of debt from aid funding.

Aid dependence and the burden of debt servicing have been flagged as major concerns for PNGs development aspirations, including for achieving the MDGs. In 2004 PNGs debt burden was equivalent to 71 % of GDP and syphoned off much of the public budget (DNPM PNG 2010:226). This imbalance, occurring at a critical time for MDG investment, proved controversial. The second and final PNG Progress Report in 2010 explained that heavy debt servicing obligations were judged by many "as the most important impediment for development and the most important

[12] At independence, Australia contributed 40 % of PNG's budget in aid (DFAT 2014:1). In the 1980s and early 1990s Official Development Assistance (ODA) represented over 10 % of PNGs Gross National Income (GNI), a figure which has decreased over time (4.5 % of GNI in 2013) (see World Bank 2015). Broadly, between 1990 and 2004 the growth of debt outstripped economic growth; this has since stabilised as a result of stronger economic growth (DNPM PNG 2010:226).

[13] Note: today Australian aid is administered as part of the broader mandate of its Department of Foreign Affairs and Trade (DFAT).

[14] MDG6 targets HIV/AIDS, Malaria and other diseases and MDG7 targets environmental sustainability.

challenge with regards to the achievement of the MDGs" by virtue of limiting the resources available to invest in key areas like health and education (DNPM PNG 2010:226). In contrast, there was also concern over 'excessive donor dependency' noting that in 2004 MDG6 activities were 96 % donor funded and MDG7 activities also had minimal government contribution (DNPM PNG 2010:225).

It appears that neither aid nor the MDGs brought 'development' to PNG, raising the question whether this combined formula (now embodied in the SDGs) serves as a suitable fit for PNGs social economy; likewise, whether the phenomenon of 'development' in PNG is well understood. The MDGs emphasized a 'big push' market-based development strategy, articulating a specific model for development that emphasizes the growth of formal markets. Yet opportunities in formal markets remain limited. In PNG, the biggest export earnings are derived from extractive industries meanwhile the biggest employment opportunities are found in agriculture, fisheries and forestry (DNPM PNG:16–17). Here, smallholder growers dominate the production of 'cash-crops' (Warner and Omuru 2008:6) but incomes derived from these commodities are notoriously unreliable for sustaining livelihoods (on coffee, see Riedl 2009 and Valiente-Riedl 2013).

Moreover, the growth of monoculture farming for some commodities like palm oil works to limit the opportunities for growers to diversify their crops (see Anderson 2008:63), including undermining important informal markets that rely on access to land. In contrast to formal market opportunities, vibrant markets for food, craft and clothing exist, which all feature strong participation from women (Anderson 2008:61). Indeed, the National Research Institute (NRI), which conducted a survey of informal-sector activity across four provinces in PNG, identified that incomes in informal markets outweigh minimum wages awarded in some foreign-owned processing plants (Sowei et al. in Anderson 2008:62). However, in terms of addressing MDG1 (now articulated across the first two goals of the SDG framework), both informal and formal markets pale next to the vital infrastructure that subsistence agriculture provides.

A deeper understanding of PNGs social economy makes visible a hybrid of formal and informal markets as well as subsistence living. Hybrid livelihoods are the meeting point between cultural institutions and global markets where, arguably, dueling development pathways exist. In PNG some 87 % of the population lives in rural areas with only a small proportion of people participating in the cash economy (Government of PNG 2004a:7, 11; Government of PNG United Nations Development System 2007:11). Strong labor force participation (both males and females) in subsistence agriculture ensures that "most rural households have a significant level of income in kind" (DNPM PNG 2010:54–55). Of course, 'in kind' income does not translate easily into dollar figures. Not surprisingly, in PNG the number of people living under the country line poverty metric remains high, recorded as 37.5 % in 1996 and 39.9 % in 2009 (see ADB et al. 2015:65)[15].

[15] Note, the latest figure for the international poverty line for 'extreme poverty' (US$1/day) has not been updated since 1996 (ADB et al. 2014:65). The international poverty line itself has been

Equally, it is not surprising that the PNG government spoke out against the imposition of the MDG conception of poverty given generally low participation in the cash economy and prevalence of subsistence livelihoods. In 2004 the PNG government worked to revise MDG targets in line with its "national context and realities" (Government of PNG 2004a:2), which included the goal of *increasing* subsistence production of agriculture by 34 % (Government of PNG 2004a:12). In 2010, this revised target was reinforced[16] amid a strong rejection of the MDG conception of poverty in the context of a country with "an abundance of food" (DNPM PNG 2010:23).[17] Importantly, PNGs rejection of the income-poverty concept is significant because the MDG/SDG formula points to enabling formal markets (including in the new SDG framework a very specific focus on 'economic growth' in SDG8), whereas PNG realities point to maintaining hybrid sources of livelihoods and enhancing opportunities from within.

The maintenance of hybrid sources of livelihoods in PNG is directly enabled by culturally articulated institutions, perhaps most importantly, that of land. These are enshrined in the PNG Constitution which emphasizes "Papua New Guinean forms of social, political and economic organization" (Government of PNG 1975:s5). Included here is the aspiration that "traditional villages and communities remain as viable units of Papua New Guinean society, and for active steps to be taken to improve their cultural, social, economic and ethical quality" (Government of PNG 1975: s5[4]). PNG law protects customary land tenure (Government of PNG 2004a; Government of PNG 2004b:10), whereby land is passed through a clan by either a patrilineal or matrilineal system of allocation (Anderson 2008:61). Indeed, 97 % of land falls under customary ownership facilitating broad-based access to land (DNPM PNG 2010: 17).

Maintenance of customary land title directly underpins subsistence livelihoods and informal markets in PNG, as well as alternative production units such as cooperative enterprises.[18] The PNG Ministry of Trade and Industries supports cooperatives, arguing they contribute to national economic development and incomes, improve import and export capacity and land-use productivity, and reduce land conflicts (CSU n.d.). Cooperatives support hybrid livelihoods by facilitating participation in formal markets while maintaining cultural integrity and traditional

---

revised numerous times and accordingly, concerns have been raised about its accuracy (see Robeyns 2005:33).

[16] It was also acknowledged that PNG lacks capacity to monitor even the revised target incorporating subsistence production (DNPM PNG 2010: 42).

[17] Instead, the concept of "poverty of opportunities" was put forward, which refers rather "to vulnerability, lack of opportunities, choices and access to services" (DNPM PNG 2010:36). According to this conception of poverty, alternative measures in and beyond the MDGs become relevant, including employment, food security and malnutrition, education and literacy and household facilities (DNPM PNG 2010:39–48). The separation of 'hunger' (SDG2) from 'poverty' (SDG1) in the SDG framework goes some way in acknowledging these sorts of concerns from SIDS like PNG.

[18] Cooperatives are defined as "…an autonomous association of persons united voluntarily to meet their common economic, social, and cultural needs and aspirations through a jointly-owned and democratically-controlled enterprise" (ICA 2007).

forms of 'welfare'. However, customary title runs counter to the institutional structures that support growth in formal markets where the importance of attracting foreign investors underscores individual property rights. Unsurprisingly, the introduction of Westernized property tenure in PNG has broad-based support from key donors like AusAID and the World Bank (see Anderson 2006:139).

Although the orthodox development model is underpinned by an individual property rights regime, a shift away from customary land title in PNG is problematic. It threatens hybrid livelihoods and possible development alternatives, but also the (limited) welfare provisioning capacity of the state. The Government of PNG already relies on Church and community groups to deliver 50 % of health and education services in rural PNG (DNPM PNG 2010:19). Shifting away from customary land title would also threaten the maintenance of the 'wantok'[19] system in PNG, which maintains familial ties and collective culture as an alternative and informal system of welfare provisioning. Although this cannot take the place of government welfare provisioning, it does provide an important and accessible grassroots capacity if 'development' is to be embraced.

6.5 Ethical Dilemmas and Challenges in Re-articulating Global Development

The privatized model of property rights is core to the Western model of development and therefore the foundation upon which the MDG/SDG frameworks were built. Yet it remains implicit and rarely discussed in a critical way, despite being implicated in questions about cultural justice and self-determination in development. In threatening customary land rights in PNG and other SIDS of the Pacific region, global development runs counter to alternative models of social and economic reproduction that provide 'parallel' systems for provisioning. These may well constitute a more suitable and just 'boost onto the development ladder' than the cultural dislocation and poverty that is invoked when access to traditional forms of subsistence are removed. Herein lies a core ethical dilemma of the global development regime: the development process brings about the poverty it is supposed to address.

Development must necessarily be based on the structural transformation of societies into market-based economies but at the same time, such transformations bring about the creation of poverty as a structural phenomenon. In other words, development creates poverty just as it creates affluence; they are two sides of the capitalist coin. People may be 'poor' by western standards but be free from hunger because they have access to subsistence within traditional forms of social and economic provisioning. It is when they are denied this access, such as with the privatization of land and other productive assets necessary to market economies, that they have the potential for poverty thrust upon them. As eloquently articulated by

[19] The DNPM PNG (2010:19) defines this as "PNGs safety net, whereby family and clan members are required to support each other".

Vandana Shiva (1989: 10), being poor (a characteristic of individuals) does not necessarily equate to poverty which is a structural phenomenon associated with the institutions of capitalism.

In the process of dispossessing people from their community lands, private property rights distort or remove traditional access to subsistence thereby bringing about the structural deprivation associated with poverty. This is a trend becoming noticeably present in the Pacific. In the case of PNG, the increasing push for a commercial land market threatens broad-based access to land under current customary land tenure arrangements, which in turn, threatens livelihoods based on subsistence agriculture (Anderson 2006). For Shiva (1989: 179), the embrace of international capitalism in this way brings about 'mal-development' for emerging economies rather than 'progress' as it generates much hardship and forces people into market participation (dependency) if they are to survive. Sen (1999: 31) too, acknowledges the tensions between tradition and development, but draws quite different conclusions.

Sen is much more strident in his critique of the economic underpinnings of development definitions than he is of economic growth per se; and by extension, the (capitalist) institutions necessary to it. He rejects the idea that increased growth is synonymous with development, but does not reject the need for growth. Indeed, he suggests a trade-off between tradition and wealth (growth in GNP) has to be made. For Sen (1999: 31), this trade-off is a constitutive element of development planning and one that must be confronted by "the people directly involved" if traditional ways of life have "to be sacrificed to escape grinding poverty". In this, he poses an ethical dilemma: give up culture or stay poor. Yet this dichotomous proposition, reflecting Sen's liberal worldview, is one that belies the implications of his own capability framework.

In creating the capability perspective as one intimately linked to individual 'freedom', Sen's (1999) ideas are directly embedded in a liberal value system, albeit one more broadly defined than the current laissez-faire *neo*-liberalism. Indeed, Sen's work echoes the social (welfare) liberalism which emerged in the nineteenth century as liberal theorists in the West sought to confront the poverty and inequality that grew out of the economic transformations associated with industrialization and urbanization in early capitalism. Their policies of 'social reform' (Freeden 1978) institutionalized the redistribution of wealth from increasing GNP to provide protective mechanisms that ensured a social safety net for the poor and disadvantaged (those without a market income). In this way, policies of redistribution served to enhance people's capability, even if modestly, in using GNP to generate freedom from hunger.

Sen's (1989:12) capability framework emphasizes the freedoms and capacities of individuals to function and to live the life they choose. Yet in practice, the choice 'between different ways of living' remains within the parameters of a market-based liberal democracy. However, when Sen points to the social structures and institutional fabric that shape agency in any given cultural context, he gives to 'capability' a more general (universal) applicability. Indeed, Sen (1999: 53) acknowledged the importance of diverse institutions for people's freedoms when he argued in *Development as Freedom* that "there is a need to develop and support a plurality of institutions …[which can] incorporate private initiatives as well as public arrangements and also more mixed structures, such as nongovernmental organisations and cooperative entities".

Individual capabilities are effectively dependent on enabling social structures and should be open to renegotiation within different social contexts and across different time periods (Sen 2004:77). While it seems that the institutions Sen has in mind are those of liberal democracy, his ideas nevertheless point to some radical implications when we think about social context in meta-cultural terms. Thought about in this way, capability opens up the opportunity for consideration of institutional forms beyond market-based (developed) economies. The Pacific SIDS, such as PNG, have viable alternatives in their unique systems of social and economic organization. The existing social economy supports both formal and informal sources of livelihood, raising questions about both the measurement of poverty and the appropriateness of MDG/SDG-based development to address it.

To some extent, a capability approach is already reflected in the globalizing development agenda through its widening of the conceptions of poverty. This seeks to trace multiple dimensions of 'capability deprivation' beyond the orthodox focus on 'income deprivation' as synonymous with poverty. However, a failure to provide space for alternative strategies for development is evident given the focus on market-based economic growth spurred by foreign aid funds. Thus a 'trade plus aid' strategy commensurate with a 'New York meets Washington consensus' prevails in development circles. However, a capability lens helps to challenge the conclusions drawn from the MDG measurement regime and indicates it is important to look carefully at what it means for a country to be 'off track' in its progress toward goals set under international frameworks like the MDG/SDGs.

6.5.1 An MDG 'Report Card'

The Millennium Development Goals pioneered an unprecedented shift in the visibility of 'development' on the world stage and now warrant reflection for their globalizing development mission. They promised to broaden understanding of poverty and in turn, conception of the 'development project'. They also promised to re-articulate and re-energize the momentum for delivering development globally. In this sense, two clear understandings of the MDG framework as a 'globalizing' mission emerge: first, in the development agenda it espoused; and second, in the consensus model it pioneered. The MDG framework mobilized broad-based support for pushing through a global development agenda. However, the extent to which the development model promulgated departs from the pre-existing 'one-size-fits-all' orthodoxy is contestable.

Indeed, 'development' disappointment in culturally and socio-economically diverse countries underscores the failure of the MDG Project to provide representative and diverse development solutions. This is highlighted by the fated MDG record of the Pacific vis-à-vis other regions and the ways in which freedom from hunger are measured and achieved (MDG1/SDG2). These belie the existence of functioning social economies and the efforts of SIDS like PNG in maintaining their cultural traditions to escape the specter of poverty, rather than trading them off for wealth (*contra* Sen). Importing the Western model of development denies people their traditional freedom from hunger in exchange for market dependence: once instituted, there is no freedom from the (capitalist) market. In this, contemporary global development differs little from historical forms of colonization – it merely shifts the apparent locus of colonization onto the governments of developing countries themselves.

Instead of diversity in development, the MDGs entrenched development more deeply into a market-based set of metrics and this is being extended in the SDGs through its proposed 'Data Revolution' (ADB et al. 2015:58). A key part of the institutional narrowing effect is the emphasis on quantitative targets and 'measuring performance'. Such indicators reflect 'technologies of governance' because they not only set particular standards for monitoring, rewarding and penalizing performance, but they also generate "a 'knowledge effect' where the indicators intended to reflect a concept effectively redefine it" (Fukuda-Parr et al. 2013:59). As such, the conception of poverty and in turn the dynamic of development proposed, are best traced to the conceptions underpinning the logic of the indicators themselves. Furthermore, it should not be the sophistication of measurement design or the volume of data collected that is central.

Rather, the critical question of metrics must be *what* is actually being measured and whether this is meaningful for understanding how the lives of real people are, for better or worse, being impacted. Ultimately, any re-articulation of the global development agenda must confront the limitations of a data driven, top-down, one-size-fits-all paradigm and open up the space for genuine localized bottom-up models of development. The ethical concern here is the way in which the MDG/SDG development model ruptures pre-existing mechanisms for social provisioning without which a social collective (society) could not exist. The 'developed' (capitalist) economies resolved this rupture historically in the institutional compromises of the 'welfare state' (Paton 2011:174). However, these took many decades, even centuries, to mature, during which time poverty and hardship were experienced by the majority of people.

Today, emerging economies like PNG and other Pacific SIDS are asked to not only sacrifice their traditional institutions for provisioning, but also the cultural specificity that gives them value. It is here that the ethical tensions in the global development agenda are laid unavoidably bare. They stem from the conceptualization, design and implementation of poverty alleviation strategies that depend on a development process that is itself an initiator of (structural) poverty. SIDs are the central focus here precisely because they highlight the contradiction in development-based approaches to poverty alleviation. This is not a question of 'stopping development', but rather to lay the basis for understanding why poverty and affluence go together and why traditional or customary mechanisms for social provisioning need to be protected and maintained while new mechanisms are established.

Maintenance of appropriate welfare institutions is not only a moral issue for the individual, as important as that is. It is also a structural issue because no country can escape the poverty trap without mechanisms that secure the capability of its people through (sustainable) systems of social provisioning (production of food, clothing, shelter and so on). For SIDS in the Pacific, the development experience with foreign aid and volatile markets in international trade is one that threatens existing capability derived from culturally specific institutional arrangements. It is therefore necessary to direct attention to the complex forms of livelihood that might form part of a creative and just approach to development and poverty alleviation. Sanctioning the cultural dislocations that otherwise accompany development is an ethical conundrum that must be a consideration in any re-articulations of international development cooperation for poverty alleviation.

References

Anderson, Tim. 2006. On the economic value of customary land in Papua New Guinea. *Pacific Economic Bulletin* 21(1): 138–152.

Anderson, Tim. 2008. Women roadside sellers in Madang. *Pacific Economic Bulletin* 23(1): 59–73.

Arndt, Heinz W. 1989. *Economic development: The history of an idea*. Chicago: The University of Chicago Press.

Asian Development Bank (ADB), United Nations Economic and Social Commission for Asia and the Pacific (UN ESCAP) and the United Nations Development Programme (UNDP). 2015. Making it happen: Technology, finance and statistics for Sustainable Development in Asia and the Pacific, Asia-Pacific Regional MDGs Report 2014/2015. http://www.adb.org/sites/default/files/publication/159951/asia-pacific-regional-mdg-report-2014-15.pdf. Accessed 1 Sept 2015.

AusAID. 2005. *A global partnership for development: Australia's contribution to achieving the millennium development goals, 2005 progress report*. Canberra: AusAID. www.ausaid.gov.au/publications/pdf/mdg_report.pdf. Accessed 19 May 2010.

Cammack, Diana. 2007. Chronic poverty in Papua New Guinea. www.chronicpoverty.org/publications.details/chronic-poverty-in-papua-new-guinea. Accessed 8 June 2011.

Cooperative Societies Unit (CSU). n.d. Cooperative societies unit of Papua New Guinea: Information pamphlet. Boroko. (obtained in-country in December 2004).

Department of Foreign Affairs and Trade (DFAT), Australian Government. 2014. A new direction for Australian aid in PNG: Refocusing Australian aid to help unlock PNGs economic potential. 14 October. http://dfat.gov.au/geo/papua-new-guinea/development-assistance/Documents/png-aid-assessment-summary-paper.pdf. Accessed 28 Aug 2015.

Department of National Planning and Monitoring (DNPM) of Papua New Guinea. 2010. Millennium development goals Second National Progress Comprehensive Report for Papua New Guinea 2010. http://www.pg.undp.org/content/dam/papua_new_guinea/docs/MDG/UNDP_PG_MDG%20Comprehensive%20Report%202010.pdf. Accessed 1 Sept 2015.

Dreze, Jean, and Amartya Sen. 2002. *India: Development and participation*. Oxford: Oxford University Press.

Feeny, Simon, and Matthew Clarke. 2008. Achieving the millennium development goals in the Asia pacific: The role of international assistance. *Asia Pacific Viewpoint* 49(2): 198–212.

Feeny, Simon, and Matthew Clarke. 2009. *The millennium development goals and beyond: International assistance to the Asia Pacific*. Basingstoke: Palgrave Macmillan.

Frank, Andre. 1966. The development of underdevelopment. In *Paradigms in economic development: Classic perspectives, critiques, and reflections*, ed. Rajani Kanth, 149–160. London: M.E. Sharpe.

Freeden, Michael. 1978. *The new liberalism: An ideology of social reform*. Oxford: Oxford University Press.

Fukuda-Parr, Sakiko. 2003. The human development paradigm: Operationalizing Sen's ideas on capabilities. *Feminist Economics* 9(2–3): 301–317.

Fukuda-Parr, Sakiko, Alicia Yamin, and Joshua Greenstein. 2013. The power of numbers: A critical review of MDG targets for human development and human rights. *Development* 56(1): 58–65.

Government of PNG. 1975. Constitution of the independent state of Papua New Guinea. www.ilo.org/aids/legislation/lang--en/docName--WCMS_117452/index.htm. Accessed 8 June 2011.

Government of PNG. 2004a. Millennium development goals: Progress report for Papua New Guinea 2004. Government of PNG. www.undppc.org.fj/_resources/article/files/PNG_MDG_report_2004.pdf. Accessed 8 June 2011.

Government of PNG. 2004b. *The medium term development strategy: 2005–2010, November 2004*. www.aciar.gov.au/publication/EXT02. Accessed 13 Nov 2009.

Government of PNG United Nations Development System. 2007. *A partnership for nation-building: United Nations Country Programme Papua New Guinea 2008–2012*. Online. Available HTTP: www.undp.org.pg/documents/UNCP/UNCP12.pdf. Accessed 13 Nov 2010.

ICA. 2007. *Statement on the co-operative Identity*. www.ica.coop/coop/principles.html, last updated 26/5/2007: Retrieved 8/8/07.

Lewis, William A. 1955. *The theory of economic growth*. London: Allen and Unwin.

Lisk, Franklyn. 1977. Conventional development strategies and basic-needs fulfilment: A reassessment of objectives and policies. *International Labour Review* 115(2): 175–191.

Nelson, Julie A. 1993. The study of choice or the study of provisioning: Gender and the definition of economics. In *Beyond economic man: Feminist theory and economics*, ed. Marianne A. Ferber and Julie A. Nelson. Chicago: Chicago University Press.

Nelson, Paul J. 2007. Human rights, the millennium development goals, and the future of development cooperation. *World Development* 35(12): 2041–2055.

Paton, Joy. 2010. Labour as a (fictitious) commodity: Polanyi and the capitalist 'Market Economy'. *Economic and Labour Relations Review* 21(1): 77–88.

Paton, Joy. 2011. *Seeking sustainability: On the prospect of an ecological liberalism*. London: Routledge.

Polanyi, Karl. 1977. In *The livelihood of man*, ed. Harry W. Pearson. New York: Academic.

Riedl, Elisabeth. 2009. Fair trade: Evaluating opportunities for smallholder coffee growers in Papua New Guinea. *Pacific Economic Bulletin* 24(2): 122–140.

Robeyns, Ingrid. 2005. Assessing global poverty and inequality: Income, resources, and capabilities. *Metaphilosophy* 36(1–2): 30–49.

Sachs, Jeffrey. 2005. *The end of poverty: How we can make it happen in our lifetime*. London: Penguin.

Saith, Ashwani. 2006. From universal values to millennium development goals: Lost in translation. *Development and Change* 37(6): 1167–1199.

Sen, Amartya. 1989. Development as capability expansion. *Journal of Development Planning* 19: 41–58.

Sen, Amartya. 1999. *Development as freedom*. Oxford: Oxford University Press.

Sen, Amartya. 2004. Capabilities, lists, and public reason: Continuing the conversation. *Feminist Economics* 10(3): 77–80.

Shiva, Vandana. 1989. *Staying alive: Women, ecology and development*. London: Zed Books.

UN Millennium Project. 2005. Investing in development: A practical plan to achieve the millennium development Goals. New York. www.unmillenniumproject.org/reports/fullreport.htm. Accessed 9 May 2011.

UNDP. 2007. MDG monitor: Papua New Guinea. United Nations development program. www.mdgmonitor.org/country_progress.cfm?c=PNG&cd=598. Accessed 11 May 2011.

United Nations. 2002. Report of the International Conference on Financing and Development. Monterrey, Mexico, 18–22 March 2002. New York. www.unmillenniumproject.org/documents/aconf198-11.pdf. Accessed 10 May 2011.

United Nations. 2015. The millennium goals report 2015. New York. http://www.un.org/millenniumgoals/2015_MDG_Report/pdf/MDG%202015%20rev%20(July%201).pdf. Accessed 1 Sept 2015.

United Nations General Assembly. 2000. United Nations millennium declaration. Resolution 2, Session 55, United Nations 2000, New York. www.un.org/millennium/declaration/ares552e.htm. Accessed 13 Nov 2009.

Valiente-Riedl, Elisabeth. 2013. *Is fairtrade fair*. Eastbourne: Palgrave Macmillan.

von Frantzius, Ina. 2004. World summit on sustainable development Johannesburg 2002: A critical analysis and assessment of the outcomes. *Environmental Politics* 13(2): 467–473.

Warner, Bob, and Eric Omuru. 2008. PNG commodity prices – an opportunity not to be missed. *Pacific Economic Bulletin* 23(1): 1–15.

Wood, Ellen M. 1999. *The origin of capitalism*. New York: Monthly Review Press.

World Bank. 2015. Data: Net ODA Received (% of GNI). http://data.worldbank.org/indicator/DT.ODA.ODAT.GN.ZS?page=4. Accessed 31 Aug 2015.

Chapter 7
Animals in International Development, Ethics, Dilemmas and Possibilities

Max Kelly

Abstract This chapter explores the role and perceptions of animals in international development efforts and the possible contradictions between differing priorities of agencies involved in international charitable efforts. Although there is a wide range of purposes for a charitable organization, as shown in the (England and Wales) Charities Act 2011 (c.25) and having one purpose does not preclude a second, organizations concerned with animal welfare are quite distinct from those working for poverty alleviation in the developing world (and indeed the developed world). A fun and novel gift of a donkey may equally be perceived as a cruel, environmentally unsustainable and misguided development effort, a valuable asset, or a burden to a household struggling to feed existing mouths. Exacerbating this situation is the fact that much of the debate around animals in a developing context is heavily polarized between livestock welfare, and animal rights, with a very limited middle ground.

This chapter analyzes the underlying tensions between human development, animal welfare, and poverty alleviation, exploring cultural tensions, philosophical tensions and where areas of common ground may be found, with specific reference to development programming. The chapter is framed by contemporary debate on ethics and international development. International development interventions are driven by human welfare concerns, within the broader context of an increasingly globalized world economy. There is a danger in not engaging with ethical considerations with regard to animals and development, as there are potentially complex, interrelated and unintended outcomes. Such outcomes include rising inequality for those who depend on livestock for livelihoods in a business-as-usual scenario of increasing production and intensification; a focus on animal welfare in isolation, with potential accusations of forcing limitations on animal production on low income communities and countries;, and, finally, a moral debate surrounding the issue of whether it is reasonable to require animal welfare standards of people who live in poverty, as a pathway out of poverty. Discourse and practice needs to engage with how to link debate on international development with ethics of livestock production, beyond animal welfare, with global sustainability as core.

M. Kelly (✉)
International and Community Development, Faculty of Arts and Education, Princes Highway, Warrnambool 3280, Vic, Australia
e-mail: max@deakin.edu.au

H.P. Gaisbauer et al. (eds.), *Ethical Issues in Poverty Alleviation*, Studies in Global Justice 14, DOI 10.1007/978-3-319-41430-0_7

Keywords International development • Development ethics • Animal welfare • Livestock • Food production

7.1 Introduction

Theories and practice of international development are complex and contradictory (Thomas 2004), but at a broad level development is promoted as something akin to 'good change' (Chambers 1995, 174). Thomas (2004) argues that development is often reduced to the practices of various development agencies and actors seeking to reduce poverty and driven by the recently concluded (but far from achieved) Millennium Development Goals. The very ambiguity of what development may be is discussed, and heavily critiqued, by development theorists (cf Sachs 1992; Sen 1999; Rist 2014; Peet and Hartwick 2015) from a range of theoretical positions, linked to how desirable change in society may be achieved, and what the impact of significant investment in development interventions over decades actually is. Of course, international development is about human development. The very basis of the notion of development is either personal, societal or world development (Gasper 2014). Deneulin (2013) polarizes views of development between those who predominantly contextualize development from a human rights perspective (NGOs and the UN) and those who perceive development predominantly as increase in wealth or income poverty reduction (World Bank and IMF). Although debatable, this does focus on the complexity of some common core understanding of what a desirable state or society may actually be. The post MDG development agenda, enshrined in the Sustainable Development Goals (SDGs) formally adopted in September 2015, links the poverty reduction agenda of the MDGs with broader global agendas, namely environmental concerns of sustainability, inequality, and justice. However, the fundamental principle underpinning large-scale development interventions, as well as being enshrined in the SDGs is inarguably that of economic growth.

So whatever the particular status of most of the debates surrounding development, and despite the existence of alternative development paradigms, the predominant model of development currently is of course underpinned by a neoliberal economic paradigm, driven by ever increasing globalization of the world economy. The linear thinking embedded in the modernization paradigm is the progression 'towards' a state of development', a paradigm that Hoffstaedter (2011, 17) argues is concurrent with the 'domesticating logic' of the neoliberal agenda (capturing all aspects of our lives within the sphere of free market economics). The links between the global economic market based system and 'developing' or 'least developed' countries, and the significant broadening of the development agenda from the MDGs to the SDGs, open a space for discussions of forms and impacts of development on global and local sustainability. Agriculture, food and land use are central concerns both for human welfare, environmental sustainability, and economic growth.

The influence of neoliberal growth models underpinned by free markets has specific relevance for animal production systems across the globe. Support for agriculture had languished somewhat over the past couple of decades, particularly through the 1990s (Trotter and Gordon 2000). However, from the mid 2000s, the importance of agriculture to economic growth and therefore development is now firmly back on the agenda (de Janvry and Sadoulet 2002; World Bank 2007; Anríquez and Stamoulis 2007). In many developing countries the base of the economy is subsistence agriculture, and economic growth can include a move to increase productivity, to diversify agricultural production, and moves to commercial production. Sustainable intensification is the most recent catch cry (FAO 2014). This is the principle area in which international development interventions collide with animals. The various forms that agricultural development may take however relate to the overall treatment of animals in the farm sector at least. At one level there is considerable focus on increasing productivity in the subsistence or small farm sector with increasing technology, and locally relevant improvements (see for example Vanlauwe et al. 2014). Within a differing perspective there is the possibility of the increasing intensification and commercialization of agriculture, which of course has entirely different connotations, particularly in reference to animal welfare under these intensive systems (see for example White 2014). This contrast between smaller scale, more localized agriculture and industrial farming resonates with contemporary debate in the developed world, and there is a strong and logical link. This chapter explores the tensions between human development, animal welfare, and poverty alleviation exploring cultural tensions, philosophical tensions and where areas of common ground may be found. The chapter first briefly addresses the contemporary challenges in discussing ethics in the context of the development 'industry'. This contextualizes the subsequent discussions on the evolution and complexities of livestock production globally. The final section explores some of the contractions, possibilities, and dilemmas of a focus on livestock production as a pro poor development strategy, for agricultural development and economic growth, and for food security. This chapter focuses on animals for productive human purposes (livestock) rather than companion animals, or non-domesticated animals. Small scale production systems also form a core focus. However the nature and shape of animal production systems in a smallholder or subsistence farming system is perhaps not so clear. What may also not be so clear in a developing world context is the clear distinction between farm animals and other uses.

7.2 Ethics in International Development

Development in the context of this chapter is that which occurs beyond an immanent process, an intentional investment in attempting to promote human development. Corbridge (1998, 36) makes reference to a very generalized concept of a developmental mainstream that assumes a 'broadly positive relationship between economic growth and human development'. He notes the considerable focus on the form that development interventions take, at the expense of the moral basis of international solidarity. However, interventions in the name of development have unquestionably an ethical dimension in addition to the empirical and theoretical (Crocker 1998). Discussions of ethics in international development discourse are relatively limited, and occupy an interesting space between development theory, and philosophy. Discussions on the 'moral agenda' (Corbridge 1998, 37) can be understood in terms of an implicit and inbuilt view of the world as either more (north) or less (south) developed, rich and poor, majority and minority world or other binaries that underpin the transfer of resources from the 'uppers' to the 'lowers' (Chambers 2007, 7). This transfer of resources can be either benevolence or beneficence, and Smith (2001, 131) notes that a major ethical and practical issue is how to turn benevolence into beneficence, which requires sacrifices on behalf of those in a position of advantage. Although an in-depth analysis of development ethics is beyond the scope of this chapter it is useful to explore some key themes. Crocker (1991, 457) asks a range of questions of an ethical enquiry, related to the 'normative or ethical assessment of the ends and means of Third World and global development'. A core concern with development ethics is the human cost, or the 'calculus of pain' and the 'calculus of meaning' embedded in Berger's Pyramids of Sacrifice (Berger 1974). Gasper (2014) notes the requirements to explore the implications of the costs and benefits of economic development, inclusion and exclusion, distribution and harm, risks and rewards, both to humans and the environment. Equally, as Corbridge (1998, 48) asks:

> how ethical or moral is it to condemn modernisation and Western science without first explaining the possible benefits of these monoliths, and without signaling a personal willingness to live without their apparent benefit

Development ethics and discussions of ethical and moral courses of action fall somewhere between normative ethics and applied ethics. Regan (2014) notes that development ethics could easily be perceived primarily an academic pursuit, however the contribution of ethical debate to aspects of development such as the Human Development Index (from the work of Sen (1999) among others), and discussions on power relations, contexts, cultures, institutions and so on, are there, if often implicitly. The application of ethics discourse to development appears therefore to be both limited to quite academic debate in academic literature, but conversely deeply embedded in everyday theory and practice of development through complex considerations of how to embed 'good change' into people's everyday lives, through investment of a variety of resources, both benevolent and beneficent. This chapter starts from a position whereby development interventions are understood as being far more complex than economic investment for economic growth for human development impact. This is exacerbated by an increasing focus on climate change as a result of human 'development'. The shift to a more global focus through the SDGs should require a concurrent shift in thinking within development, engaging much more with the 'wicked' problems, climate change, conflict, environmental/land degradation, malnutrition in all its forms (including obesity) and so on. While this may be occurring in some ways, for example climate change discourse is now a global endeavor, as is related but separate discourse and practice around disaster risk management. However, aid budgets in isolation cannot address the global and interrelated nature of many of the most complex problems that are resistant to change, and the livestock sector is one where there are significant global and interconnected issues. This is unpacked further in the following sections.

7.3 Changing Perspectives of Animals in the Developed World

Animals can have a range of uses to humans, including productive assets, food source, cultural values, social standing, pets, sporting engagement etc. Animals play a wide variety of roles, however few in the 'developed' or minority' world rely directly on animals for our survival, and most in this context would have the capacity (as well as the legal obligation) to care for animals with which we interact for any reason.

Although the next section discusses some of the basic discussions concerning animals in society, it is useful to review quickly the historical notion of what the relationship between humans and animals may be. Some (particularly Peter Singer 2001) argue that historically in the Judeo-Christian tradition animals were simply possessions, with humans ruling "*over the fish of the sea and the birds of the air and over every living creature that moves on the ground*" (Genesis 1, 28). However others argue that Christianity does in fact promote an ethic of stewardship which should involve a concern for animals (Attfield 1983). Videras (2006) argues that these are entirely literal readings of the bible and there are much deeper issues at stake, such as the impact of religion on various social and political reasonings that must be taken into account when assessing people's perceptions of their relationship with animals. This debate links in well with Fraser's (2001) discussions around the evolution of attitudes towards animals, and associated mythology. However most of this debate takes place in a developed world context, and in English Law through the eighteenth and nineteenth century animals were treated as possessions. Interestingly, the UK was the first country to implement animal welfare legislation with the 1822 Cruel Treatment of Cattle Act (Public General Act 3, George IV, 71). This was repealed by the Cruelty to Animals Act of 1849 in England reframing animals from insensate objects or strictly possessions to having some degree of protection through anti cruelty laws, strictly targeting cruelty (but what is cruelty?) and only if there was no conflict of interest with human needs or wants (Singer 1985).

Beyond this general trend towards increasing concern for humane treatment of animals, there really was little change until the 1960s where in the UK community concern about livestock intensification prompted the setting up of a technical committee to inquire into animal welfare. The resulting Report (Brambell 1965) is the basis of modern animal welfare, leading to the development by the Farm Animal Welfare Council of the five freedoms of animals (FAWC 1993), namely freedom from hunger and thirst; discomfort; pain, injury or disease; freedom to express normal behavior; and freedom from fear and distress. However, globally animal welfare legislation is highly variable. In Australia there is no federal level legislation for animal welfare (it's a state/territory responsibility), except for international trade. There are however a wide range of animal welfare standards at a national and global level. These demonstrate a changed focus, shifting from being a tool for homogeneity to being a strategic tool for accessing markets (value adding) (Miele and Bock 2007).

Primarily, it is the demand side that drives the increase globally in animal welfare standards. However increased concern with animal welfare often hits a stumbling block when confronted with farm animals and farming practices, as agricultural use of animals rarely sits comfortably with the kind of treatment we may be comfortable with in our companion animals. This is particularly true of intensive animal production systems. Perspectives of intensive practices are somewhat contradictory. Intensive systems concentrate greenhouse gas emissions, and toxic waste products, often in places where mitigation measures are hard to enact. Significant numbers of intensive livestock production units in developing countries are located in peri-urban areas in proximity to factors of production, and markets (FAO 2006). However, there are economies of scale in industrial production that allow meat production to increase in line with demand.

In terms of the agricultural sector there are interesting debates about the drivers of intensification in agricultural production. The increasing demand for livestock for consumption across the developed world was driven by industrialization and urbanization. However a primary driver seems to be the requirement for ever lower retail meat prices. To achieve ever tightening margins, there needs to be "production efficiencies" which rarely have any relationship to animal livelihoods and wellbeing (Lusk and Norwood 2008), Moreover, while agricultural practices have historically sought and succeeded in obtaining lower retail meat prices, corresponding production efficiencies have generally not been principally concerned with the well-being effects on farm animals (Tonsor et al. 2009; Lusk and Norwood 2008).

However over the last century and particularly over the last 30 odd years there has been a massive upsurge in public interest in the role animals play in society. Much of this is branded as the animal rights movement although there is, as in any widespread debate, a huge diversity of opinion from the extreme end of animal liberationists, through animal welfare, so on, through meat eating society, the hunters and further out to the extremes at this other end. However, the animal liberation movement or animal rights really are no longer outside the mainstream of society, and animal welfare, animal rights, ethics and many related but perhaps equally broadly understood topics have become a theme of both academic and public debate. There has been considerable interest through mass media, and of course the antics of the celebrities, particularly celebrity chefs (think Jamie Oliver's various crusades) bringing the issue of animal well-being into our living rooms. This of course comes after perhaps 40 years of exposure to anthropomorphized animals in both reality and fiction (Jane Goodall, Dianne Fossey, Skippy, Lassie, Flipper, or even the world of David Attenborough bringing in the lives of animals to our living rooms). Miele and Bock (2007) identify two core issues in reflecting on changes towards thinking on animals, "*the growing ambivalence of humans to use animals for food production and the great malleability of the concept of animal welfare*" (Miele and Bock 2007, 5).

This malleability of concept seems particularly important and there are large inconsistencies in the use of language employed around ethics, animal rights, animal welfare, and so on, which appears both to disguise perhaps deeper debates that may be less palatable to the general public who are becoming increasingly involved in the debate. Francione (1996a) argues that what the nineteenth century theory of animal welfare represents is however still very much the basis of the animal rights movement today (or at least the practical end of the movement). He argues that animal rights as they should be understood are entirely removed from human needs, or demands or desires but that animals rights are the position where animal interests are protected *absolutely* and this occurs regardless of any loss to the human species. Nussbaum (2007, 6) argues that we have "an ethical sensibility that is only weakly and inconsistently developed in this area". The traditional animal rights position is of course completely at odds with any discussion regarding the use or exploitation of animals for any reason, including food, or work but as Francione (1996a) also points out, the modern animal rights movement understands animal rights to be the ideal state of affairs, a state which can only be achieved through ongoing fights to increase animal welfare. This kind of disjuncture between power, justice, rights discourse, and welfarist discourse, whether this is the traditional welfarist utilitarian view, or the "new welfarist" incremental change approach (Francione 1996b), causes perhaps the first major point of concern for development practitioners. Miele and Bock (2007) succinctly summarize the complexity of the issue:

> animal welfare is associated with genetic robustness in a lab, in the market it is linked to high quality; for consumers it is associated with ethical choice, better taste and healthier products; for farmers it is the care for their animals and it is part of their vocation; for animal rights movements it is the respect for natural animality, traditional small-scale production and so forth. (Miele and Bock 2007, 6)

This of course relates to Nussbaum's (2007) criticism of our weak and inconsistent ethical sensibilities around animals. Society may be aghast at the cruelty meted out to an animal in obvious distress, but will not relate this in any way to buying their steak that evening. Current conceptualizations of acceptable animal use in UK legislation has not changed in the last century – that while humans may subjugate animals, they may not cause them unnecessary harm (Brambell 1965; FAWC 2009). This is probably also of course a direct relation to the speciesist debate with differing levels or spheres of animals in the consciousness of many humans. From a speciesist view of the world, humans are at the top of the heap and companion animals (dogs, cats) are closer to the top than for example, cattle, sheep, or pigs. As a whole, we live in a society where animal welfare may mean more room in cages for chickens, or less constriction of pregnant sows, or the humane destruction of animals, but apart from a minority, fails to recognize that vast numbers of animals are destroyed hourly for our consumption pleasure, a 'willed blindness' about the impact of our production and consumption of meat (Gjerris 2015). This contradiction is explored further later in the chapter.

7.4 Livestock in the Developing World, Globalization and the Economic Imperative

Livestock contributed only 1.5 % of Gross Domestic Product (GDP) globally in 2005 (FAO 2006). However, livestock provides a livelihood, and source of food for almost a billion people. In the developing world, livestock is often part of a multi-functional agricultural system (FAO 2009). The trend in the developed world has been increasing consumption of animal products to a current plateau in Pork, Sheep, and Beef products, although not in Poultry, which continues to rise. The link between affluence and meat consumption is shown conclusively in most studies (Delgado et al. 1999; Delgado 2003). The demand for meat and dairy products across the developing world is forecast to continue strong growth, requiring what Delgado et al. (1999) referred to as a 'livestock revolution' to meet this demand. However the final level of meat consumption (and the types of meat consumed) also shows regional diversity (York and Hill Gossard 2004; Pingali 2007). Pingali's work explored the westernization of diets, due, he argues due to the "*globalization and the consequent global interconnectedness of the urban middle class*" (2007, 285). Indicative figures show that meat consumption is disproportionally concentrated in developed countries with a global average of 41.2 kg/capita carcass weight equivalent food consumption of meat (2005 figures, cited by FAO 2009), but with the industrialized countries eating more than 95 kg/capita and sub-Saharan Africa around 13 kg/capita (2005 figures, cited by FAO 2009).

The greatest growth in meat consumption, primarily due to increasing affluence, urbanization, population growth and rising income, is in Asia with China a major contributor to livestock demand (FAO 2009; Ali and Pappa 2015). The reason for the importance of this debate around changing consumption habits lies in the production requirements to meet demand. If, as will happen if development results in increased affluence in a country, dietary habits or preferences change to include a greater consumption of meat and dairy products in general, then production must grow significantly. However the composition of the diet is hardly fixed, and as Pingali (2007) argues, if the global connectedness of the middle class results in a "westernized" diet globally, then agriculture must be intensified and production made more efficient. In short the developing world must adopt similar agricultural practices including livestock production systems, which have evolved in response to demand and economic conditions to be dominated by large scale, predominantly intensive production methods (FAWC 2009). However, the level of meat consumption in the developed world is problematic for a number of reasons, not least the health implications of obesity epidemic (cf. Wang and Beydoun 2009).

Globally, livestock production systems are moving towards specialization and intensification (Fraser 2001). The move to more intensive or industrialized farming systems is more than just scaling up, but a fundamental restructure of the livestock production system. Industrialized production is predominantly single produce based 'landless' farming, and moves agriculture away from multifunctionality (with associated benefits) to a commodity specific enterprise. This loses any sense of integration in production, with an associated decline in alternative livestock functions (draught power, cultural values, source of manure), as consumer of other crop residues and natural pasture. In traditional mixed enterprises, there can be a much higher reliance on local resources, and more effective use of resources, whereby non food outputs can acts as inputs into other parts of the system (FAO 2009).

Intensification and structural changes in the livestock system is likely to negatively impact smallholders, and small production units, the most. Some authors (De Haen et al. 2003; Pingali 2007) note the technological advances that provide transferable economies of scale. However, in particular in the poultry industry, and likely in other areas 'in the absence of deliberate action, small-scale producers will eventually be put out of business by competition from large-scale producers, especially since the better-off producers will scale up' (Pingali 2007, 290).

Herein lies the crux of the problem. By various means there is a circular logic which shows that development, as currently pursued, will or should produce economic growth, leading to increased demand for livestock products, which in the long run can no longer be efficiently produced by small holder farmers in the developing world, which leads therefore to a vast increase in the numbers of livestock produced in intensive systems.

7.5 Opportunities, Benefits, and Dilemmas of Livestock Production Systems

The first point of tension, both in terms of what we accept in the "Western" world, and in what we promote through development interventions in the name of human development, is whether we accept intensive production methods as the principal model. As noted, increasing demand is leading to intensification in the livestock sector. Livestock production systems are conceptualized as either (1) grazing systems (extensive or intensive); (2) Mixed Farming Systems (rain fed or irrigated); and (3) industrial systems. Each have positive and negative aspects. Grazing lands occupy around 26 % of the earth's (ice free) land (FAO 2009). In Latin America forest area has been reduced by 40 % in the last four decades in conversion to grazing land (FAO 2015). Mixed grazing farming systems link cropping and livestock with related synergies of production. Industrial farming systems are those where at least 90 % of the feed comes from other enterprises (FAO 2009). Despite the physical remove between industrial or intensive systems and the land that supports it, around 33 % of global cropland is devoted to producing feed for industrial systems (Steinfeld et al. 2006).

A starting question is therefore whether factory farming is an acceptable environment for animals to be reared for slaughter (or milking). This in itself is a primary question on which all further issues, questions and discussions hinge. In this way it is also the hardest issue to discuss in any reasonable way as it appears to be the most problematic. Given the lack of one particular tradition of ethical reasoning in what in most of the developed world is a multicultural society, it is unlikely that there could be a consensus on either reasoning or actions globally. Across the spectrum of moral positions on the human animal relationship there seems to be at least a little disquiet about factory farming. The human animal relationship is evolving, and changing and this is happening in concert with a plateauing of meat consumption in the developed world. However we are still a long way from being clear on what an acceptable moral or a practical position is. In terms of future decisions however, key players in the livestock sector call for intensification as the only reliable means to meet demand across the developing world, with amendments to practices to avert some of the more catastrophic environmental issues (FAO 2006). Varying degrees of focus on family farms (FAO 2014), 'sustainable intensification' (Tilman et al. 2011) notwithstanding, intensification is progressing at significant rate, with little coherent policy direction.

Bringing economics into this area is even more problematic, particularly when the issue becomes one of economies of scale and efficiencies in production. Smallholder livestock production cannot compete with industrial or commercial farms, and there is quite a major contradiction in promoting livestock development in subsistence economies as part of development interventions when this may in fact put small-scale farmers out of business. Accepting that investment in small scale livestock innovations in small and medium mixed enterprises can contribute to livelihoods, many subsistence and small scale producers are unlikely to be able to meet market requirements to enter the value chain and will therefore become uncompetitive. The act of promoting development for poverty alleviation can actually increase poverty. This issue, and particularly more specifically the issue of requiring or promoting animal welfare in developing countries, has come onto the international trade agenda with the Doha round of negotiations of the WTO allowing "non trade" issues to be discussed which includes animal welfare. This is raised under the topic of allowing green box subsidies for increased costs of production to meet animal welfare standards (WTO 2015). Concerns are raised however about who bears the cost of these higher standards, to meet EU and other requirements (Marimpa 2013). It seems likely that the state will have to pay most of it and this is of course extremely problematic for developing countries. The final costs will be passed on to developing countries' governments who will simultaneously be obliged to reduce export subsidies by the same external forces. This is really pushing the cost of social decisions onto other countries.

How do market forces determine animal treatment? Ransom (2007) argues that agri-food organizations adopt animal welfare standards to access markets (often with relevance to corporate social responsibility). This identifies what the FAWC

(2009) call a 'major transfer of economic power within the food supply chain, from the supply to the demand side' (p.i). Despite the power of supermarkets in the food chain, consumer demand for higher standards in animal welfare is likely to influence production decisions. Consumer demand is not always driven by welfare concerns per se.

In many instances animal welfare is driven primarily again by human need, whereby animal welfare is used as a way of maintaining a level of animal health. The two options here are a reduced likelihood of pathogens entering the food chain (McIntyre et al. 2009) and better animal welfare producing healthier and safer food (no antibiotics or hormone use, less fat content in free range chickens etc.). Animal husbandry and related welfare from this perspective is simply a means to an end. However intensification of farming systems is shown to be a cause of the emergence or re-emergence of infectious diseases (Horrigan et al. 2002). So there is a health imperative for promoting animal welfare standards, although it bears little or no relationship to any understanding of the human – animal relationship outside of human needs. It does appear to be the most consistently cited reason for engaging with animal welfare issues in developing countries. However it has a major limitation which is that the treatment of animals is only a cause of concern under threat of disease, so the primary driver is not how we treat our animals but rather what the impact of various animal husbandry regimes are.

From a sustainability perspective it becomes even more complex. A core question is whether the breeding and consumption of animals is sustainable from an environmental perspective and from the perspective of a food secure planet. The impact on planetary resources of intensive animal production is well documented. The FAO (2006) summarize some of the core environmental issues resulting from livestock production globally, including greenhouse gas emissions of 37 % of methane and 65 % of nitrous oxide emissions globally. Deforestation is estimated to account for an additional 17 % of greenhouse emissions (IPPC 2007). Further environmental issues include water use, pollution, biodiversity loss, land degradation, and so on. Environmentally differing production systems have differing environmental impacts with intensive systems leading to unsustainable land livestock ratios that lead to soil nutrient overload and pollution issues. Given the increasing importance of climate change in all aspects of discussion, it is also worth noting here that climate change may impact heavily on the way we produce animals. Changing climatic conditions can reduce the availability of suitable grazing land, water, and energy required for livestock production. Also the contribution of livestock to climate change through emissions cannot be overlooked. Also given the majority of people affected by climate change will be in the developing world, and the current largest consumption for meat is from the developed world there is a strong imperative to reflect on our policies and practices in livestock production consumption and promotion in the developing world.

From a food security perspective, livestock production is not the most efficient use of resources in terms of energy output per resource or energy input. This is an incredibly complex area of argument but it can be argued both ways. An economist may argue that vegetarianism will not solve world hunger (Leathers and Foster

2008), whereas the anti factory farming lobby can provide equally compelling data to demonstrate that every kilogram of meat produced requires several kilograms of grains, and multiple liters of water. Both arguments are equally compelling but both are equally simplistic, given the complex interrelationships between resources, food production, nutritional needs, environmental issues, and our global market economy means that food security is a multi-dimensional issue and cannot be simplified down to whether one eats meat or not. However the multi-dimensional nature of poverty, which drives food security in many cases, can be traced back to economic factors.

Food sovereignty is a further point of relevance in food production and sustainability. Animals in industrialized countries have been deliberately selected for their productive potential, and their potential to withstand intensive livestock systems. Friesians, or Holstein Friesians are extremely high milk producers, although less useful as beef animals so the vast majority of dairy animals are Holstein Friesians. Across the Indian sub-continent, buffalo milk is strongly preferred, but of course there are serious limitations on intensification of buffalo milk farming – their fecundity, their irregular udders which can defy milking machines (and therefore the core notion of mechanization for efficiency), issues with production levels, issues of letdown leading to oxytocin injections prior to each milking, and probably only a personal issue, but their general overall grumpiness! So should Buffaloes be abandoned in favor of more productive cattle? Should Buffalo be selectively bred to reduce variation, particularly in udder and teats…?

The selective breeding of animals to maximize efficiency in intensive systems has led to major overall reduction in animal genetic diversity in intensive systems. In dairy production Holstein dominates production in the US, and Holstein Friesian in the UK. Leghorn chickens are the industrial chicken; the Large White and Landrace are core breeds for pig production (Notter 1999). Loss of genetic diversity has consequences for any species. The loss of specific characteristics that have evolved in different areas over different times can be difficult as decreased diversity leads to increased disease susceptibility, and decreased adaptation. Although rare breeds societies may be concerned with the extinction of breeds the overall issue is far greater than breed extinction, being both loss of breeds, and loss of genetic diversity within breeds (Notter 1999). Reduced genetic diversity in intensive farming can be also driven by the decisions of a few multinational companies (for example in the poultry sector) that govern an industry.

In terms of understanding or debating the ethics of animals in "western" societies, Europe, America, Australia (the meat eating, capitalist societies of choice perhaps?), Nussbaum (2007) argues that the utilitarian voice (Peter Singer) is somewhat limited in its capacity to fully understand the complexities of animals. The very basis of our perceptions of and discussions surrounding animal ethics and animal welfare can be even more problematic when applied in a "Non Western" context. Bailey (2009) argues strongly that the very notion of ethics is driven by a range of assumptions common to western ethical theory – and which are quite the antithesis of "Eastern" values. Ethics seems to have lain in the domain of the philosopher for an extended period but recent concerns with ethics and welfare in the scientific journals shows a move towards combining ethics with science (cf. Arnold 2011; Jagers and Duus-Otterström 2008; Jamieson 1996).

If we examine the anthropomorphic perspective, in most literature this identifies humans as the most important species on the planet – the speciesist debate, as mentioned earlier seems to underpin most of the "Western" thought. Fraser (2001) argues that cultures possess an animal mythology which he refers to as the "*fundamental popular beliefs and values about animals which often embedded in a cultures art and stories, which influence how people view animals, and what they judge to be proper conduct towards them*" (Fraser 2001, 176). Our mythologizing of animals gives them a relative position within our value system which allows us to have a dog as part of the family, whilst eating steak for dinner, and setting a mouse trap under the sink to get rid of a pesky visitor.

Part of this mythology is the notion of the "virtuous pastoralist" (Fraser 2001, 180) whether this is the somewhat romanticized version of the Australian stockman, or the agrarian ideal of the family farm living in harmony with nature. Fraser argues that modern animal production systems will be trusted by the public, if it at least tries to conform to this ideal. This mythology has been somewhat dented by the likes of Mad Cow Disease, where consumer responses to the fact that BSE (and CJD) arose from feeding animal offal to feedlot cattle were hardly positive.

Miele and Bock (2007) argued earlier that there was an increasing reluctance to use animals for food production, or at least it would seem an increasing engagement with the means of food production. Fraser (2001) would argue that this corresponds to fluidity in our mythologizing of animals – influenced by science in his opinion, but driven primarily by a decreased gap between humans and other species. Herein lies perhaps the core of the issue in terms of development activities – how do we discuss, perceive or even debate logically the issue of animal ethics, animal welfare, animal rights, and the human animal relationship in our dealing with the developing world, if we are so far from any sense of rationality in (Western) discourses and practices?

At one end of the spectrum, animal welfare appears to be of limited concern to development because the very nature of developing economies requires a focus on a basic standard of living for humans, and therefore to generally preclude non cost efficient animal welfare standards in intensive animal production. However this is very general and somewhat misleading. Poultry farming across the developing world is primarily industrial (FAO 2006) and the increased demand for meat will lead to strong decisions on future production systems. At the other end of the scale, there are vast numbers of subsistence or small scale farmers who rear animals for a variety of purposes, many in situations which can be seen either to be better than intensive systems (not caged, etc.) but also worse in that care of animals is often contingent on differing understandings and knowledge of what animal care is required.

In broader terms it is interesting to review what animal welfare may be in developing countries. There seems to be a general consensus that animal welfare is poor in developing countries. The British Veterinary Association (Wensley undated, NP) provides some interesting guidelines for vets going to do voluntary work overseas, including the call that people in developing world may either perceive animal welfare as something that is a developed world luxury, or aspire to the same heights of animal welfare as the developed world country (Britain) from which the vet hails. This is backed by a suggestion to demonstrate Britain's animal friendly culture by bringing plenty of photos of "*pets in homes, of nest-boxes provided for birds and other wild animals*, etc.". This is a selective quote, although it does portray a general sense of the developed world as being a very cruel place for animals, and the UK at least as being a very animal friendly culture, which may be true of companion animals, but less so in relation to meat production. However there is increasing evidence of interest in and commitment to animal welfare in parts of the developing world. The increasingly urban consumers in many developing countries are demonstrating purchasing increased awareness of animal welfare, and nationally there have also been moves to implement good agricultural practices and livestock management in diverse countries such as Namibia, Argentina, Thailand, and India, Columbia, Costa Rica and Brazil (Bowles et al. 2005; WSPA undated).

Given the situation in the developed world, where despite considerable debate about animals' rights, and so on, the main issue is not about the ethics of the human animal relationship and the role and rights of animals. Rather it is about the ethics of how we treat our farm animals before we eat them. As a society we appear to accept our position in the animal spectrum, with varying levels and values ascribed to different species according to our perceptions of their utility. Animal welfare therefore has received substantial attention from animal welfare scientists, vets and others to determine what animal welfare means from the perspective of animal physiology, behavior, physical and mental health, and husbandry.

7.6 Developments in Practice: Actors, Programs, and Animals…

There are a vast number of development actors, from the developed world individuals (contributing either their tax dollars through government funded programs, or their direct money through charitable donations to NGOs), through international Donors (Government, Non-Government, Multilateral), onto the development agencies themselves (international NGOs, Multilaterals, Bilaterals, national and local NGOs) and of course the government and judiciary of the developing country. Each of these sources comes with their own philosophical and ethical mores fairly firmly entrenched, whether explicit or not.

The role of NGOs has increased exponentially over the last 20 years with an enormous diversity of both large international, smaller, and national and local NGOs. If we think about who we know that works in international development, the likes of OXFAM, World Vision, CARE, Concern, etc., spring to mind – all of whom are of course primarily concerned with the relief of poverty, the promotion of human wellbeing, and justice. The picture that springs to my mind is the cute picture of donkeys goats and other animals that you can sponsor through a variety of gift options. The portrayal of the differing descriptions of purposes in the (England and Wales) Charities Act of 2006 identifies types of charitable organizations, of which poverty alleviation and animal welfare are two. Having one purpose does not necessarily preclude a second. However, organizations concerned with animal welfare appear to be quite distinct from those working for poverty alleviation in the developing world. Although Australia does not formally legislate charitable purposes, the Australian Tax Office has some pretty detailed guidelines for what constitutes a charitable organization (for tax purposes), which observe relatively closely the categories above – with animal protection quite distinct. The reason for bringing this up is of course the fact that many NGOs actually deal with animals as part of their overseas development efforts, but it seems that how they operate there has no influence on their charitable status. There is little at the international level that I can find to guide any interactions with animals in development programming. A review of large NGOs in the development space where livestock programming is either a primary or secondary programming focus, shows very little evidence of animal welfare policies and their implementation.

7.7 Conclusion

Different countries have varying cultural and ethical attitudes towards animals, and husbandry practices. The impact of high animal welfare standards on the relative competitiveness of their agriculture may be very different. European Communities Proposal on Animal Welfare and Trade in Agriculture to the WTO 2000

The relevance of this in overall understandings of how we engage with animals in international development becomes clearer as we think about what we are promoting in livestock development. Intensification, commercialization, productivity, and economic growth are at the heart of the current development model. However it is not necessarily or even primarily poverty reduction and human wellbeing that is the target. The current situation in regard to human animal interactions in the developed world, although complex, seems to hinge primarily on debates as to the role and use of animals in our society, with a growing awareness, probably more so in the European Union, of animal welfare issues at the very least. However, as Nussbaum has suggested, our weak and inconsistent ethical sensibilities in regard to animal interests means that on the whole the consumption of meat across the developed world is still extremely high, and the use and killing of animals for human needs is still the norm. Therefore, the mainstream or majority position is not so much a debate about the ethical treatment of animals in regard to the human-animal relationship, and the rights or otherwise of animals, but is firmly about the ethical treatment of animals before we kill them, ensconced mainly in an animal welfare discourse. The speciesist debate rages between the philosophers but in the rest of the world we are still top of the food chain, with varying values of different species. Our mythologies are firmly entrenched. The implications of this for animal production systems are of course immense. Given the globalization of world trade, and given economic rationalism as the basis of our modern living, intensive systems are not only economically efficient but increasingly the only way to compete as a primary producer.

So our worldview is complex, and definitely diverse, but driven by economic factors that on the whole (excluding the vegetarians or those who are willing to pay a premium for meat produced in regulated and "animal friendly" environments) do not promote a production environment that may be considered "ethical". Given the plateauing of meat consumption across the developed world and forecasts that the real inflation adjusted price of meat will continue to fall, it seems possible that consumers will exercise their buying power in ways that may contribute to increased animal welfare (albeit still for consumption) but this seems as likely to be driven by health concerns as much as concern for non-human animals.

The developing world is moving in the same direction – with pretty much the same drivers of economic rationalism, and increasing urbanization, population growth, and income. There is an increased demand for meat products, and an associated rise in meat production requiring further significant livestock production. Given existing production systems the required increase in livestock production in developing countries appears likely to be environmentally unsustainable, socially problematic, potentially reversing efforts to improve human welfare in small scale and subsistence farming communities, possibly exposing us to more risk averse futures due to declining genetic diversity, problematic from a policy perspective in relation to food security, and food sovereignty.

These factors are all underpinned by concerns about the human animal interface, which although primarily driven by consumer concern, and academic debate in the developed world, also is strongly driven by a range of context specific social, cultural, economic, and environmental factors in each community, region, and state in the developing world. Reorienting livestock production systems requires innovative thinking, both on the supply side, and the demand side.

Development interventions at the current time are driven by human welfare concerns. As discussed earlier there is a danger in not engaging with what livestock production, animal welfare, and 'good change' means in a global context. A focus on intensification may have a negative overall impact on poverty reduction and equality in developing countries. A focus on animal welfare can lead to one of two options – the first is a misreading of the situation and accusations of forcing limitations on animal production on low-income communities and countries. The second is a moral debate surrounding the issue of whether it is reasonable to require animal welfare standards from people who live in poverty. Environmentally, socially, and morally the debate about animals as livestock needs to engage with the complexity of the issue. Interactions between sustainable development, human-animal interactions and development programming and practice by the wide variety of organisations and individuals in international development should at the very least be driven by thoughtful reflection on bigger picture issues, such as the ethics of human animal interactions, and the link between development ethics, animal ethics and actions on the ground, both in the developed and developing world. This should form the basis of our modern agricultural ethos. Otherwise we are just "business as usual" which is possibly one of the core things that most agree on. It is unlikely to produce desired benefits for either humans or animals.

References

Ali, Jabir, and Evangelia Pappa. 2015. Global meat market: Structural changes across geographical regions. *South Asia Research* 35(2): 143–157.

Anríquez, Gustavo, and Kostas Stamoulis. 2007. Rural development and poverty reduction: Is agriculture still the key? *Agricultural Development Economics Division (ESA). 1/4. Journal of Agricultural and Development Economics* 5–46.

Arnold, Denise G. (ed.). 2011. *The ethics of global climate change*. Cambridge, UK: Cambridge University Press.

Attfield, Robin. 1983. *The ethics of environmental concern*. New York: Columbia University Press.

Bailey, C. 2009. A man and a dog in a lifeboat: Self-sacrifice, animals, and the limits of ethical theory. *Ethics & the Environment* 14(1): 129–148. doi:10.2979/ete.2009.14.1.129.

Berger, Peter L. 1974. *Pyramids of sacrifice: Political ethics and social change*. New York: Basic Books.

Boston, Massachusetts U.S.A. 1998. https://www.bu.edu/wcp/Papers/OApp/OAppCroc.htm. Accessed 20 Aug 2015.

Bowles, D., R. Paskin, M. Gutiérrez, and A. Kasterine. 2005. Animal welfare and developing countries: Opportunities for trade in high-welfare products from developing countries. *Revue scientifique et technique-Office international des épizooties* 24(2): 783.

Brambell, Roger. 1965. *Report of the technical committee to enquire into the welfare of animals kept under intensive livestock husbandry systems*, 2836. London: HMSO Cmnd.

Chambers, Robert. 1995. Poverty and livelihoods: Whose reality counts? *Environment and Urbanization* 7(1): 173–204.

Chambers, Robert. 2007. Words, power and the personal in development. In *Language and development: Africa and beyond*, ed. Coleman Hywel. Addis Ababa: British Council.

Corbridge, Stuart. 1998. Development ethics: Distance, difference, plausibility. *Philosophy & Geography* 1: 35–53. doi:10.1080/13668799808573631.

Crocker, David A. 1991. Towards development ethics. *World Development* 19(5): 457–483.

Crocker, David A. 1998. *International development ethics*. Boston: Twentieth World Congress of Philosophy. https://www.bu.edu/wcp/Papers/OApp/OAppCroc.htm. Accessed 20 Aug 2015.

De Haen, Hartwig, Stamoulis Kostas, Shetty Prakash, and Pingali Prabhu. 2003. The world food economy in the twenty-first century: Challenges for international co-operation. *Development Policy Review* 21(5/6): 683–696.

de Janvry, Alain, and Elisabeth Sadoulet. 2002. World poverty and the role of agricultural technology: Direct and indirect effects. *Journal of Development Studies* 38(4): 1–26.

Delgado, Christopher L. 2003. Rising consumption of meat and milk in developing countries has created a new food revolution. *Journal of Nutrition* 133(11): 3907–3910.

Delgado, Christopher L., Mark W. Rosegrant, Henning Steinfeld, Simeon Ehui, and Claude Courbois. 1999. The growing place of livestock products. In *World food in the twenty-first century*. MSSD Discussion Paper. 28, Washington, DC: International Food policy Research Institute.

Deneulin, Severine. 2013. Ethics and development: An introduction from the perspective of the capability approach. *Geography Compass* 7(3): 217–227.

FAO. 2006. *Livestock's long shadow: Environmental issues and option*. Rome: FAO.

FAO. 2009. FAOSTAT, statistical database of the food and agriculture organization of the United Nations. http://faostat.fao.org. Accessed 4 Aug 2015.

FAO. 2014. *State of Food and Agriculture. Innovation in family farming*. Rome: Food and Agriculture Organization of the United Nations. http://www.fao.org/3/a-i4040e.pdf. Accessed 4 Aug 2015.

FAO. 2015. *Livestock's role on deforestation*. Rome: Food and Agriculture Organization of the United Nations. http://www.fao.org/agriculture/lead/themes0/deforestation/en/. Accessed 20 Aug 2015.

Farm Animal Welfare Council (FAWC). 1993. *Second report on priorities for research and development in farm animal welfare*. Tolworth: Farm Animal Welfare Council. MAFF [Now DEFRA, 1a Page Street, London].

FAWC. 2009. *FAWC report on farm animal welfare in great Britain: Past, present and future*. Department for Environment, Food & Rural Affairs. Available at: https://www.gov.uk/government/publications/fawc-report-on-farm-animal-welfare-in-great-britain-past-present-and-future. Accessed 7 Sept 2016.

Francione, Gary L. 1996a. *Rain without thunder – the ideology of the animal rights movement*. Philadelphia: Temple University Press.

Francione, Gary L. 1996b. Animal rights and animal welfare. *Rutgers Law Review* 48: 397.

Fraser, David. 2001. Farm animal production: Changing agriculture in a changing culture. *Journal of Applied Animal Welfare Science* 4(3): 175–190.

Gasper, Des. 2014. Ethics and development. In The companion to development studies, 3rd ed, ed. Robert B. Potter and Vandana Desai, 47–50. Abingdon: Routledge.

Gjerris, Mickey. 2015. Willed blindness: A discussion of our moral shortcomings in relation to animals. *Journal of Agricultural and Environmental Ethics* 28(3): 517–532.

Hoffstaedter, Gerhard. 2011. Religion and development: Australian faith-based development organisations (ACFID). Research in Development Series, Report 3. http://www.acfid.asn.au/resources-publications/publications/acfid-research-in-development-series/religion-and-development-australian-faith-based-development-organisations. Accessed 4 Aug 2015.

Horrigan, Leo, Robert S. Lawrence, and Polly Walker. 2002. How sustainable agriculture can address the environmental and human health harms of industrial agriculture. *Environmental Health Perspectives* 110(5): 445–456.

IPCC (International Plant Protection Convention). 2007. Summary for policymakers. In *The physical science basis. Climate change 2007*, ed. Susan Solomon, Dahe Qin, Martin Manning, Z. Chen, Melinda Marquis, Kristen Averyt, Melinda Tignor, and Henry L. Miller. Cambridge, UK: Cambridge University Press.

Jagers, Sverker C., and Göran Duus-Otterström. 2008. Dual climate change responsibility: On moral divergences between mitigation and adaptation. *Environmental Politics* 17(4): 576–591.

Jamieson, Dale. 1996. Ethics and intentional climate change. 33/3: 323–336. In *Climatic change*, ed. Michael J. Langford. 1989. Animal welfare and human welfare. *Applied Animal Behavior Science* 22: 95–103.

Leathers, H.D., and P. Foster. 2008. *The world food problem: Toward ending under nutrition in the third world*, 4th ed. Boulder: Lynne Rienner Publishers.

Lusk, Jayson L., and Bailey F. Norwood. 2008. Public opinion about the ethics and governance of farm animal welfare. *Journal of the American Veterinary Medical Association* 233: 1121–1126.

Marimpi, Maria. 2013. EU *policy on animal welfare: Benefits and costs*. https://onamacrolevel.wordpress.com/2013/11/13/policy-on-animal-welfare-benefits-and-costs/. Accessed 5 Aug 2015.

McIntyre, Beverly, Hans R. Herren, Judi Wakhungu, and Robert T. Watson ed. 2009. Agriculture at a crossroads: A synthesis of the global and sub-global IAASTD reports International Assessment of Agricultural Knowledge, Science and Technology for Development (IIASTD).

Miele, Mara, and Bettina Bock. 2007. Competing discourses of farm animal welfare and agri-food restructuring, (editorial). *International Journal of Sociology of Food and Agriculture* 15(3): 1–7.

Notter, David R. 1999. The importance of genetic diversity in livestock populations of the future. *Journal of Animal Science* 77: 61–69.

Nussbaum, Martha. 2007. Facing animal complexity. *Harvard Review of Philosophy Lecture, "Facing Animals"*. Harvard University.

Peet, Richard, and Elaine R. Hartwick. 2015. *Theories of development: Contentions, arguments, alternatives*. New York: Guilford Press.

Pingali, Prabhu. 2007. Westernization of Asian diets and the transformation of food systems: Implications for research and policy. *Food Policy* 32(3): 281–298.

Ransom, E. 2007. The rise of agricultural animal welfare standards as understood through a neo-institutional lens. *International Journal of Sociology of Agriculture and Food* 15(3): 26–44.

Regan, Matthew. 2014. Development ethics: Hiding in plain sight, blog post, the compass. http://blog.chemonics.com/development-ethics-hiding-in-plain-sight. Accessed 14 Aug 2015.

Rist, Gilbert. 2014. *The history of development: From western origins to global faith*, 4th ed. London: Zed Books.

Sachs, Wolfgang (ed.). 1992. *The development dictionary*. London: Zed.

Sen, Amartya. 1999. *Development as freedom*. Oxford: Oxford University Press.

Singer, P. (ed.). 1985. *Defence of animals*. Oxford: Blackwells.

Singer, Peter. 2001. *Writings on an ethical life*. New York: The Ecco Press.

Smith, J.M. 2001. Responsibility to distant others. In *The Arnold companion to development studies*, ed. V. Desai and R. Potter, 131–134. New York: Oxford University Press.

Steinfeld, Henning, Gerber Pierre, Tom Wassenaar, Vincent Castel, Mauricio Rosales, and Haan Cees de. 2006. *Livestock's long shadow: Environmental issues and options*ed. Food and Agriculture Organization of United Nations.

Thomas, Alan. 2004. The study of development. Paper prepared for DSA Annual Conference, Church House, London.

Tilman, David, Christian Balzer, Jason Hill, and Belinda L. Befort. 2011. Global food demand and sustainable intensification of agriculture. *PNAS* 108(50): 20260–20264.

Tonsor, Glynn T., Christopher Wolf, and Nicole Olynk. 2009. Consumer voting and demand behavior regarding swine gestation crates. *Food Policy* 34(6): 492–498.

Trotter, Bruce, and Ann Gordon. 2000. Charting change in official assistance to agriculture. *Food Policy* 25(2): 115–124.

Vanlauwe, Bernard, Danny Coyne, James Gockowski, Stefan Hauser, Jeroen Huising, Cargele Masso, Generose Nziguheba, Marc Schut, and Piet Van Asten. 2014. Sustainable intensification and the African smallholder farmer. *Current Opinion in Environmental Sustainability* 8: 15–22.

Videras, J. 2006. Religion and animal welfare: Evidence from voting data. *The Journal of Socio-Economics* 35(4): 652–659.

Wang, Youfa, and May A. Beydoun. 2009. Meat consumption is associated with obesity and central obesity among US adults. *International Journal of Obesity* 33(6): 621–628.

Wensley, Sean. Undated. Contributing to animal welfare in developing countries. British Veterinary Association, Guidance notes from the BVA Overseas Group.

White, Anna. 2014. African farming is the new frontier for brave investors: Sub Saharan Africa is the promised land for long term speculators. *The Telegraph*. http://www.telegraph.co.uk/finance/economics/10901154/African-farming-is-the-new-frontier-for-brave-investors.html. Accessed 12 Oct 2015.

World Bank. 2007. *World development report 2008 – Agriculture for development*. Washington, DC: World Bank.

World Trade Organization. 2000. Committee on agriculture special session: European communities proposal on animal welfare and trade in agriculture. Available online.

WTO. 2015. *Agriculture – Negotiations backgrounder – Domestic supports*. Available at: https://www.wto.org/english/tratop_e/agric_e/negs_bkgrnd15_ph2domest_e.htm. Accessed 7 Sept 2016.

York, Richard, and Marcia H. Gossard. 2004. Cross-national meat and fish consumption: Exploring the effects of modernization and ecological context. *Ecological Economics* 48(3): 293–302.

Chapter 8
The Sustainable Development Goals: Pitfalls and Challenges Where We Now Need to Start Making Progress

Gottfried Schweiger

Abstract In this chapter, I will provide a philosophical commentary on the Sustainable Development Goals (SDGs), which will play a key role in global poverty reduction in the next 15 years. In particular, I will focus on five issues: possible trade-offs, the task of prioritization, the vagueness of the SDGs, the required coordination to implement the SDGs and the establishment of a system of sanctions against actors who fail to achieve the SDGs. Firstly, moving forward with measures to realize the SDGs will most likely demand trade-offs between certain goals; therefore, it is urgent to identify which trade-offs are likely to occur and understand how to choose those goals that should be pursued under such circumstances. Secondly, in addition to possible trade-offs, it is likely that some goals are more easy to achieve than others and that states, as well as international institutions, will have to decide where to invest the money. This probably means that some goals will be prioritized over others, with investments focused more on their achievement, at least in the short-term. Thirdly, although the SDGs cover 17 goals with a total of 169 targets, many of them are still very vague. It will be necessary to set measureable and feasible benchmarks, which can be used to track progress. Fourthly, the SDGs are ambitious and, therefore, the possibility that they will not be achieved is, unfortunately, rather high, especially if the vagueness of some of the targets is not exploited in order to achieve at least low levels of progress. Until now, not much is known about the strategies behind achieving the SDGs and how this global effort will be coordinated, as well as whether the current global framework of institutions is fit for that task. Fifthly, it is certain that, if the SDGs fail the poor and other vulnerable populations, there will be no fearful consequence for other populations, particularly those in rich countries.

Keywords Sustainable development goals • Global poverty • Global justice • Accountability • Empowerment

---

G. Schweiger (✉)
Centre for Ethics and Poverty Research, University of Salzburg,
Mönchsberg 2a, 5020 Salzburg, Austria
e-mail: gottfried.schweiger@sbg.ac.at

H.P. Gaisbauer et al. (eds.), *Ethical Issues in Poverty Alleviation*, Studies in Global Justice 14, DOI 10.1007/978-3-319-41430-0_8

8.1 Introduction

The SDGs will certainly play a key role in the efforts to move towards a world that is more just, provided that they are successful. The SDGs were recently approved by the United Nations (UN) and its member states in the UN resolution "Transforming Our World: The 2030 Agenda for Sustainable Development" on September 25th 2016. The SDGs are the successors of the Millennium Development Goals (MDGs), which have been lauded as much as criticized (see, for example, Langford et al. 2013). The SDGs, however, are also much more than just the "new" MDGs, because they go far beyond the scope of the MDGs, in that they are more progressive and ambitious, while, importantly, they focus on a much wider range of issues. They cover 17 goals with a provisional total of 169 targets[1] (as of March 2016), as well as many more indicators[2] to measure these goals. The areas covered range from poverty and inequality to education and health, and from industry and infrastructure to climate change and peace. Within these broad goals, the SDGs set out certain targets to be achieved by 2030, which is the general timeframe for the SDGs. For example, Goal 1, "End poverty in all its forms everywhere", is further defined by seven targets, such as "By 2030, eradicate extreme poverty for all people everywhere, currently measured as people living on less than USD 1.25 a day" or "By 2030, reduce at least by half the proportion of men, women and children of all ages living in poverty in all its dimensions according to national definitions". The SDGs seemingly cover all problems that the world faces today, with a focus on those who are the most vulnerable and who have the most to lose if no progress is made. That is certainly a good thing, which deserves recognition and support. Still, several questions need to be addressed if the SDGs are to become a success, not only from a public relations perspective.

The aim of this paper is neither to question the SDGs in general, nor examine each and every goal and target set out. Some goals and targets may be missing that ought to be included, while others may be set too low. But the SDGs are what we have now and the opportunity to change the goals or targets has passed (see, for example, Pogge and Sengupta 2015b). Instead, I want to focus on issues that are still open and that need to be debated. This is because the issue has become more prominent now that the UN's member states, which signed off the SDGs, and other international institutions, which play a key role in development, have to begin by designing, coordinating and implementing policies to achieve the SDGs, as well as track their progress. My chapter takes an exploratory approach without offering much in the way of answers to the complex and pressing questions surrounding the SDGs, not least because I assume that we need detailed discussions in order to do

[1] Along with much more background information, the goals and targets are explained on the website for the SDGs: https://sustainabledevelopment.un.org/.

[2] The Inter-agency and Expert Group on Sustainable Development Goal Indicators (IAEG-SDGs) of the UN has been working on this matter and has already presented a first list of indicators. They can be found on the website for the IAEG-SDGs: http://unstats.un.org/sdgs/.

so. Instead, getting a clearer picture of which pitfalls and challenges lie ahead of us is the modest aim of this chapter.

8.2 Dealing with Trade-Offs

The broad range of goals and targets covered by the SDGs is one reason for their appeal, as well as represents one major step forward compared to the MDGs, which covered only eight goals that focused on developing countries. The SDGs acknowledge the interrelation of issues, such as poverty and climate and conflict, and that making progress, particularly for the most vulnerable, demands that they are tackled. But this broad range is also problematic because it is reasonable to assume that the different goals and targets are not in complete harmony with each other, such that achieving one target may hurt the chances of achieving other ones. This may be the case because one target is much more expensive, thereby leaving insufficient funds for other targets, or that the resources in which states are able or willing to invest are generally scarce and not enough to achieve all the targets. Moreover, there may be situations in which a certain target can be more easily achieved if it is done in a way that hurts other targets or in which achieving one target results in a conflict with other targets. Furthermore, trade-offs can occur in the long run, meaning that investing in one goal will only have an impact on others after some time. I want to discuss three examples to explore trade-offs that might occur because of this scenario.

Goal 1, which aims to end poverty in all its forms everywhere, is of particular interest given that it moves beyond an explicit focus on developing countries by also targeting poverty in the developed world, such as in the European Union (EU) or the USA. It demands the eradication of severe poverty (measured by a poverty line of USD 1.25 per day) and the reduction of poverty at least by half including within developed states with reference to their respective national poverty lines. Assuming that all targets are of equal importance, which is something that I will question in the next section, it appears evident that, on the one hand, reducing poverty in developed countries will need much more funds than eradicating severe poverty, while, on the other hand, developed countries are also more inclined to invest in domestic poverty reduction because it helps them in elections, pushing their own economies etc. Developed countries are even more under pressure in times of economic downturns, rising unemployment and poverty rates or other crises, such as the task of integrating significant numbers of refugees. Under such circumstances, which we are now experiencing in Europe, it is even harder to reallocate funds for development aid and global poverty eradication. Given that the SDGs themselves stipulate that states are also committed to significantly reducing domestic poverty, this gives them another reason to focus primarily on domestic policies. The situation is even more complicated when one takes into account the fact that developed countries also have incentives to reallocate funds in order to help each other, rather than fund poverty reduction in developing countries with they have few economic, social or political ties. Given that they are all part of the EU and the eurozone, it makes sense for Germany and France to help Greece to get back on its feet and invest in social protection there, even though, from a global perspective, the vast amounts of money that are needed to rebuild Greece would impact negatively on poverty reduction in developing countries a great extent. This said, I do not want to criticize the SDGs for having targets that focus both on poverty in developed countries and on severe poverty in developing countries as part of an overarching goal to end global poverty. But we have to be aware that both these targets might come into conflict with each other when it comes to allocating funds and efforts.

Another possible conflict, which can lead to a trade-off between goals and targets, concerns the situation where achieving one target may harm the prospects for another. Poverty reduction, whether measured globally in terms of a USD 1.25 per day poverty line or measured in terms of a domestic poverty line of 60 % of the median income, which is the approach taken by the EU, can be achieved in many different ways, as well hurt other goals and targets. The creation of bad, unhealthy and unsafe jobs is a case in point. Although it can reduce poverty measured by income or consumption, because having a bad job puts money into the pockets of the poor, it also increases the risks of ill health or early death, which is seemingly in violation with Goal 3, "Ensure healthy lives and promote well-being for all at all ages", and particularly Goal 8, "Promote sustained, inclusive and sustainable economic growth, full and productive employment and decent work for all". While the creation of such bad jobs might be easier and faster to achieve, it comes with possible negative consequences in the long run. Similarly, economic growth as we know it is still largely based on ways of production that severely hurt the environment and, in turn, those people who have to live in polluted areas or whose land has disappeared because of climate change. Achieving poverty reduction and combatting climate change, which is set out in Goal 13, "Take urgent action to combat climate change and its impacts", might not easily go hand in hand, such that developing countries may have some good reasons on their side to prioritize poverty eradication even if it hurts the environment and exploits natural resources (an extensive discussion can be found in Moellendorf 2014).

The third example of a possible trade-off exists within certain targets. Again, if you look at the target to reduce poverty by half according to national measures, it can be achieved in a way that severely hurts the other half who will remain in poverty while accomplishing the SDGs. It is much cheaper to lift the better off 50 % of the poor above the poverty line than to invest in the bottom 50 %, which consists of people who have a long way to go before they will be out of poverty. A concrete definition of whom counts as poor is crucial here (Ruggeri Laderchi et al. 2006). A similar trade-off might happen within one of the targets that is concerned with migration under Goal 10 "Reduce inequality within and among countries". One of the targets for this goal aims to "facilitate orderly, safe, regular and responsible migration and mobility of people, including through the implementation of planned and well-managed migration policies". This can be interpreted in several ways, some of which, possible those favoring developed countries the most, will take such a form that certain vulnerable groups will be legally denied the option to come to developed countries, which will be justified by these countries in reference to domestic problems (poverty, the pressure on social protection systems etc.) and that letting in too many, particularly the "wrong" migrants, will hurt their chances in achieving other goals and targets to which they are committed under the SDGs. Moreover, the establishment of policies that allow regular and safe migration can also have negative effects, as evidenced by the "brain drain" or "care drain" (for example, Gheaus 2013).

8.3 Setting Priorities

Recently, Francesca Pongiglione (2015) has argued that it is necessary to set out priorities within the SDGs; otherwise, it would be hard to mobilize resources and to move from a "wish list" towards concrete policies. The issue of trade-offs, which I have discussed before, already signals one reason for such priorities, namely, to give guidance about where to invest money first and foremost, as well as how to allocate money if it is scarce and limits the chances of all targets being achieved. I want to bring forward two more reasons for prioritizing, followed by a discussion of three criteria for prioritizing certain goals or targets.

The most important consideration when prioritizing certain goals and targets is whether they are, for good reasons, more important to achieve, based on different available measures. Essentially, the consensus, supported by most normative theories, is that ending the preventable deaths of children under 5 years old is more important than access to tertiary education, which is certainly also important and valuable. If we are forced to decide – I am not concerned on which level we have to make that decision here and for what reasons – whether we should invest in saving the lives of children or the university system, then we should go for the first option. But, even if I am right in assuming that most will agree with such a priority, we still need to discuss the relevant criteria, mainly because other priorities are not so clear-cut but also because different moral reasons will come into play here. Some will go for a cosmopolitan interpretation of the SDGs, while others will be more cautious and argue that states have legitimate reasons to be focused on achieving those goals that matter the most to their citizens. This reflects is a normative decision, which is not settled but can severely influence the implementation and success of the SDGs. The second reason why we need to set priorities is because resources are scarce. That is maybe untrue for the world as a whole, because there is abundant money in private hands, but it seems that states will not be seeking money from the rich anytime soon. The realization of the SDGs will, therefore, largely depend on what the states, together the global institutions they fund, have available. That money will not increase; as it looks right now, it will more likely decrease since many states face economic difficulties and are drowning in sovereign debts. If resources are scarce, politicians will have to make decisions about where to invest. But money is not the only scarce resource that is important to the success of the SDGs. It is also knowledge and research. The SDGs will only become a success if we know enough about the reasons and causes behind the problems that they aim to eliminate, as well as ensure that progress is tracked following the investment of resources and evaluate the pros and cons of certain measures taken. Another scarce resource is attention. The SDGs are a political issue right now; but, if they are to become a true success story, the public will also need to be brought on board, given that they are the ones who will finance the delivery of the SDGs with their taxes and, therefore, have a legitimate interest to know what is being done with their money. Some will ask, "Why is my state helping to build schools in Africa while the unemployment rate here is so high?" The state should not make the mistake of keeping the SDGs hidden from the public, nor keep them in the dark about what the state is planning to do in order to achieve those goals and targets, as well as upon which goals and targets the state intends to focus resources. On what grounds should goals and targets be ranked, then? I want to briefly discuss four of them.

A first criterion that could be used concerns the prioritization of those goals that are both intrinsically and instrumentally valuable. Pongiglione (2015) discusses one example of such a goal relating to education. As she writes, being educated is such a value in itself for the person who receives education, which is a known protection against poverty. Pongiglione is right that not all goals and targets contained in the SDGs are intrinsically valuable, nor do they have the same effect on others. I have mentioned that the means to achieve on goal or target can severely hurt the achievement of others. One pressing matter prompted by Pongiglione's proposal is certainly that intrinsic values differ, while it is reasonable to think that the achievement of a purely instrumental valuable goal and target has such a great influence on others that are intrinsically valuable enough that we should prioritize them, even if they are not intrinsically valuable themselves. A similar idea has been formulated by Wolff and de-Shalit (2007), who say – from the perspective of the capability approach – that we should prioritize the fostering and development of fruitful functionings, which are helpful in developing and sustaining other functionings and capabilities, as well as prioritize the eradication of "corrosive disadvantages", which have negative effects on other capabilities and functionings. One prominent example in this regard is health (see the commentary on health equity and the SDGs in Tangcharoensathien et al. 2015). Health is the prerequisite for many other valuable aspects of life or makes it at least easier to achieve them, such as education, work, movement and political participation. Likewise, ill health is corrosive and can lead to an accumulation of disadvantages. Thus, we should prioritize our efforts to protect health, especially in children, and help people to become healthier.

A second possible criterion could focus on efficiency. Efficiency itself is too vague to serve as a criterion, so it needs to be specified. In one interpretation, prioritizing those goals and targets that are instrumentally valuable is efficient because, in this way, the progress towards more than one goal can be positively influenced. But this is not the only possible understanding of efficiency. It could also refer to investing money where the greatest gain can be expected, whether or not in relation to other goals and targets. As said, achieving the target to end severe poverty is possibly cheaper than halving poverty by national definitions in developed countries. This can translate into reasoning that would claim that it is more efficient to invest, say, USD 1 billion in the eradication of severe poverty because, by doing so, 100 million severely poor people can be helped, whereas it only will help one million poor people in a country like Germany. Such arguments have a long tradition and are found in the basics of the recent rise in "effective altruism" (Singer 2010). Another type of efficiency would be to invest in children, rather than adults, because compensating for the long-term effects of poverty, malnutrition or unsafe water during childhood is more costly in later life. A similar argument has been put forward by Martha Nussbaum and Nathalie Dixon in relation to prioritizing the protection of children's rights (Dixon and Nussbaum 2012). Another important example for thinking about efficiency is that of a triage as used in medical emergencies. The triage principle suggests that we divide patients into three groups: those who are severely wounded but have little chance to be saved, even if many resources are invested; those who are severely wounded but can be saved if resources are invested; and, finally, those who are less severely wounded and need only minor treatment and resources. Triage suggests prioritizing the second group in order to maximize outcomes and because more people can be saved this way, even if that implies that patients in the first group will die (see the discussion in Miller 1999).

The third criterion that I want to discuss focuses on needs. Needs-based approaches are not new in discussions about global poverty. A basic needs approach would claim that we should prioritize those goals and targets that are essential for basic needs. This would, in effect, put the target of ending severe poverty above that of halving poverty in developed countries, as doing so would most likely prioritize the target to end hunger and establish universal access to clean water and sanitation above goals such as reducing inequality, which do not necessarily have a negative effect on the sufficient fulfillment of basic needs. Prioritization based on needs is possible in more than one variation: it can be argued that we should prioritize certain needs over others or that we prioritize the clustering of needs over others. This can yield different results because, in the first case, we will prioritize those who lack access to safe water over those who are mildly malnourished; whereas, in the latter case, we will prioritize those who are mildly malnourished and also lack education and adequate shelter over those who lack access to clean water, but who are not necessarily deprived of other basic needs. Such clustering of deprivations is not easy and highly disputed as is the ordering of needs to this extent.

Finally, a fourth criterion that could be applied refers to vulnerability. Not all people living on this planet have the same needs or are vulnerable to the same extent to threats such as violence, poverty, climate change etc. The SDGs sometimes refer to vulnerable groups such as children, the poorest or pregnant women. The vulnerability of these groups has different roots and causes. Children are more vulnerable because they lack certain competencies, because their developing bodies and minds have particular needs, and because they are dependent on others to a greater extent. The vulnerability of women and girls can only partly be traced back to physiological needs, such as regarding their reproductive health, as it is largely based on societal norms that undermine their status, reinforce discrimination, endorse violence against women and girls, and view them as less valuable. Other groups are vulnerable because of the space they inhabit, which is in danger of becoming a desert due to climate change or being under water within the next few decades. Thus, prioritizing that is related to vulnerability will also produce different results based on the normative assumptions in the background, as well as what kinds of vulnerability are given more weight.

8.4 Reducing Vagueness (and Become More Ambitious in the Process)

It has been noted by many that the SDGs are vague, even though they are comprehensive and cover a lot of ground, with 17 goals and 169 targets and many more indicators. In my estimation, the vagueness does not apply to all goals and targets equally. Some are more or less precise, such as the target to end all severe poverty measured by USD 1.25 a day.[3] Others are so vague that it seems like an invitation to interpret it as one sees fit; for example, Target 10.4: "Adopt policies, especially fiscal, wage and social protection policies, and progressively achieve greater equality". Greater equality of what or between whom? Which policies should be adopted? Is a country like the USA equal enough, in which wealth is distributed in such a way that basically 80 % have nothing and 20 % have everything, with the top 1 % owning more than one third of the total wealth? Or do the SDGs demand, which the USA signed off on, that everyone has an equal share or that the top 1 % should have no more than, say, 10 % of the total wealth? Such vagueness is dangerous for three reasons. Firstly, it leaves the door wide open to interpretations that everything is more or less acceptable as it is. That danger might be higher in relation to the application of the SDGs in developed states, which already have achieved a higher level of welfare and social protection and equality, even though those achievements are under great pressure now. If the SDGs are to make progress here, it will be necessary to formulate the goals and targets more precisely, as well as set out feasible and reasonable benchmarks that allow to track progress. It is not enough to simply aim for more equality, less gender discrimination and better social protection if it is not made clear what that means. Secondly, being vague makes it possible to sell little progress as sufficient. It is too early to be overly pessimistic or optimistic about the SDGs and what states and global institutions will do to achieve them, but they will certainly try to avoid failure or at least to make it look like they failed because they did not do enough. Having vague goals and targets makes it easier for those responsible for the SDGs to say that they made progress, even it that progress was very little. This opens the door for some forms of "cheating", such as changing the benchmark about what constitutes progress. Consider, for example, healthcare and the formulation of Target 3.8, "Achieve universal health coverage, including financial risk protection, access to quality essential healthcare services and access to safe, effective, quality and affordable essential medicines and vaccines for all". Is

[3] Vagueness also comes into play for this target when it comes to measuring who falls below the poverty line and who has been pushed above it through policy measures.

that compatible with a system that allows private persons to opt out of medical insurance or access the privatized medical sector, in which patients with more money and better insurance receive better treatment? Maybe a state could develop a robust plan to make progress in that area; but, after encountering budget problems and the opposition of important lobby groups, they back off, only achieving a small amount of progress and being unable to reach people in low socioeconomic positions, for example. Is that enough for the SDGs? Shall we allow this state and its government to celebrate this as an achievement? Thirdly, vagueness makes it almost impossible to track progress independently and to hold states responsible. That calls for the formulation of indicators (for example, Hák et al. 2016), which is underway, as well as benchmarks. It is one thing to say that we track progress in access to healthcare by the proportion of people having insurance and another thing to say that we have achieved that target when at least 90 % of the population are covered by medical insurance. Furthermore, those benchmarks need to be made public and they need to find their way into the public debate and civil society. It should not be in the hands of the states and global institutions, such as the UN or the World Bank, alone to track progress. Independent institutions, universities, non-governmental organizations (NGOs) and researchers should also be involved and actively invited to participate in keeping track of the implementation of the SDGs. Moreover, we can only have a reasonable discussion about the best ways to achieve the SDGs if our aims are clear.

The process to reduce vagueness is certainly a difficult one. On the one hand, it demands that agreement is reached on questions where disagreement is common. This is more often the case for all those goals and targets that are important for developed states, which are, in general, I would say, formulated vaguely; meanwhile, most goals and targets that are primarily concerned with issues in developing countries are more precise. It also seems that it is easier to formulate more concrete goals and targets in some areas that appear to be more "technical" and less prone to ideological disputes, such as reducing general mortality rates or deaths by traffic accidents, or improving access to primary education for all children. In sensitive areas, such as inequality, social protection, decent jobs for all or housing, the formulation is often so vague that it is basically not possible to track whether targets and goals have been achieved or even missed at all. The formulation of more concrete and precise targets and goals will demand an interdisciplinary effort, which should also involve public debate and active engagement with different stakeholders. On the other hand, some states will certainly block or be at least reluctant to reduce vagueness because they will fear that important policy decisions will be taken out of their hands. Whilst nearly everyone will agree, and all states in fact have agreed to that by signing off on the SDGs, that access to affordable housing is important, a more precise formulation of that target and the implementation of a benchmark, which can be used to measure it, can have a wide ranging impact on domestic policies.

The reduction of vagueness is not only a technical question (see, for example, ICSU and ISSC 2015). It involves questions about ethics, morality and justice too. Without a discussion about normative goals, which should be achieved, we cannot move from indicators to benchmarks and, in turn, to a real definition of progress. Here philosophers have already made major contributions, but these need to find their way into the mechanisms that are now set in motion. By reducing vagueness and formulating more precise benchmarks, the SDGs can also become more ambitious than is the case right now. Some of the clear goals and targets are certainly already ambitious, especially given that the sad fact that we have not made much progress in the past, while more could be done. Most commentators who have criticized the low ambitions of the SDGs have focused on the most vulnerable, namely, the global poor living in severe deprivation (Pogge and Sengupta 2015b). I want to add to that by stating that becoming more precise and more ambitious is also necessary in respect of developed countries and the people living in poverty there, who are socially excluded, have few chances of moving up the socioeconomic ladder and are more often in ill health.

But the criticism of being too vague is not only important for the conceptualization of the goals, targets, indicators and the benchmarks that we need to track progress, which was one weakness of the MDGs (Saith 2006). Maybe even more problematic is the vagueness in regard to the responsibilities that come with the SDGs. Thus, in the last two sections, I will examine questions regarding the implementation of the SDGs at the local, domestic and global level.

8.5 Make It a Joint Effort

The SDGs do not say much about how they are going to be achieved, although one goal and a set of targets are concerned with partnership, namely, Goal 17: "Strengthen the means of implementation and revitalize the global partnership for sustainable development". However, most details concerning the implementation of the SDGs are unresolved as of now. For example, "Getting Started with the Sustainable Development Goals: A Guide for Stakeholders", published by the Sustainable Development Solutions Network (2015) proposes that the SDGs demand a joint effort and the integration of different stakeholders, namely, national governments, regional governments, local authorities, civil society organizations, businesses, academic institutions and development partners, but without going into any details about how such a coordination should and can look like, as well as which stakeholder should be responsible for what. Some scholars, for example, Thomas Pogge and Mitu Sengupta (2015b) or Sakiko Fukuda-Parr (2016) have thus raised doubts about the success of the SDGs because of the aforementioned vagueness, which allows states to pick and choose, and because there is no implementation model that has been agreed upon nor are there any built-in enforcement mechanisms.

Making the SDGs a joint effort involving all concerned stakeholders will require several interrelated tasks: firstly, we need to come up with a way to attribute responsibilities in a feasible, reasonable and fair manner, and in a way that makes progress most likely and reduces the possibilities of failure, whether it be because actors are overburdened, because there are loopholes that are too numerous or too big loopholes, or because it is made too easy to shift responsibilities around and stall actions in the process. This also means that we face technical, political and ethical questions here. To answer the ethical ones, philosophy has produced more than one way to attribute responsibilities. Iris Young, for example, has argued that, besides basing responsibility on causation, we should also look for those actors who are powerful, have an interest in tackling the problem or are benefiting from the existence of the problem that needs to be solved (Young 2011). Her "social connection model", which she developed mainly for individuals can be one way to approach responsibilities within the global community of states that signed off on the SDGs.

Secondly, coordination is necessary on many levels and between many actors. The aforementioned report by the Sustainable Development Solutions Network is correct in stating that the SDGs will involve many different institutions and people working at different levels. This is also a difference, and shows progress, compared to the MDGs, which were focused on North-South relations within the paradigm of development aid. Now that the SDGs apply to all countries, and in turn have a much broader scope, this paradigm is surely not enough. On the one hand, developed countries face their own challenges at home, which they cannot ignore under the SDGs. They cannot shunt the SDGs to a small development department that each country runs, while continuing with business as usual. On the other hand, the SDGs are not only about "classical" poverty reduction in developing countries, as they also envision a more equal world and better lives in many dimensions. They are concerned with the climate, poverty, democracy, education, gender equality and decent work and social protection for all, and they aim for peace. If all this is also to be achieved, the development aid structures, as we know them and as they have been criticized at length (Güven 2012), are not fit for purpose; they simply will not do the job. The coordination will not be simple, as states and institutions will have competing interests, some of which I mentioned in the first section of this chapter. The coordination should also not be dominated by development technocrats, but truly aim to involve different actors, with different views and competences.

Thirdly, be aware of inequalities between actors. The SDGs are facing a world of huge inequalities, between states and within them. The development paradigm, as we know it, is shaped by these inequalities, which allow the richer and developed states to apply force one-sidedly and secure themselves favorable agreements and policies with developing countries. During the 'golden years' of neoliberalism in the 1980s and 1990s, Structural Adjustment Programmes (SAPs) enforced radical free market policies by deregulation and privatization and the abolition of trade barriers, as long as they benefitted richer countries and their industries. The threat of financial disciplinary measures and exclusion from the global community was, and always is, in the background. Today, the Bretton Woods institutions 'negotiate' Poverty Reduction Strategy Programmes (PRSPs) with states to reach their goals in poverty reduction; although, as Paul Cammack (2004) and other critics (Rückert 2007) point out, these are ultimately not concerned with the well-being of those in poverty, but with the creation of a worldwide capitalistic market of labor and goods, as well as the inclusion of as many of the world's population in the process of capitalistic accumulation. The SDGs need to change that and move towards greater equality between states. For example, the UN Conference on Trade and Development (UNCTAD 2015) argues that, in order to make the SDGs a success, it is necessary to change the one-sided trade and investment policies in place right now. It claims that the systemic problems of international investment agreements need to be addressed, that there is a huge imbalance between the rights and obligations of states and investors, that the often-criticized investor–state dispute settlement system needs to be reformed, and that investment agreements need to contribute to the goals and targets of sustainable development.

Fourthly, transforming and changing the global structures and institutions should be aimed for. Many have criticized the global institutional design, especially the trade order, as unfair and as one major obstacle to achieve a more just world (most prominently, maybe, in Pogge 2010). The SDGs do not say much about institutional reforms, although one can interpret some goals and targets in such a way that they more or less necessarily involve such reforms. Thomas Pogge and Mitu Sengupta (2015a) have raised similar concerns, mentioning, for example, the failure of the SDGs to address illicit financial flows, which are hurting developing countries the most and also have a severe negative impact on developed countries (Reuters 2012). Another crucial issue is the push for free market reforms, which are often attached to development aid, and it is feared that the SDGs will continue that scenario. For example, Mark Langan (2015) has recently examined budget aid from the EU to African countries, which was given on condition that poverty reduction under the MDGs was achieved by means of donor leverage for free market reforms that were, in fact, detrimental to the needs of poorer citizens. He called such policies 'neocolonial'.

Fifthly, make the people relevant. The SDGs aim for better living for all and, in particular, they aim to leave no one behind, which refers to the most vulnerable and most deprived on this planet. But the SDGs should not only seek a better outcome for those groups; they should also involve them in the way they are achieved and give them ample opportunity to participate in designing, implementing and evaluating related measures and programs. Monique Deveaux has recently argued that most theories of global justice focus on institutional actors, such as the UN or the World Bank, and that they forget to involve programs and initiatives led and organized by poor and deprived people themselves (Deveaux 2015). The SDGs use positive and encouraging words that imply that all different stakeholders should be involved, including so-called major groups: namely, women, children and young indigenous peoples, NGOs, local authorities, workers and trades unions, business and industry, the scientific and technological community, and farmers.[4] Discussions

[4] More information can be found on the Stakeholder Engagement page of the SDGs: https://sustainabledevelopment.un.org/majorgroups. The UN resolution for the SDGs highlights the importance of partnership and the involvement of all different groups right from the beginning: "We are determined to mobilize the means required to implement this Agenda through a revitalized Global Partnership for Sustainable Development, based on a spirit of strengthened global solidarity, focused in particular on the needs of the poorest and most vulnerable and with the participation of all countries, all stakeholders and all people. The interlinkages and integrated nature of the Sustainable Development Goals are of crucial importance in ensuring that the purpose of the new

about topics, such as participatory research and poverty alleviation, empowerment and locally-driven development, are not new (see, for example, Alejandro Leal 2007; Cornwall and Brock 2005; Drydyk 2013; Koggel 2013), and the modes of participation mentioned were also aimed for with the MDGs; therefore, it remains to be seen if the SDGs can make a substantial move forward in that direction, or if partnerships and stakeholder involvement are just buzzwords once more.

8.6 Implement a System to Reward Progress and Sanction Failure

The final issue that I want to discuss is that of holding actors responsible for the progress or failure of the SDGs. The states signed off on them, but they do not have to fear much if they fail to deliver. Even if the situation is worse in 2030 in many areas, such as a more unequal world or poverty rates rising in many states, no one has to face much more than a little blame by the public (but, in order to avoid bad public relations, states will likely try to make even a failure look like a progress by exploiting the vagueness of the SDGs, or shift the blame elsewhere). It is general and often noted problem that the enforcement of international treaties is difficult and that states are very reluctant to accept possible sanction mechanisms. There are several issues involved, which go beyond the SDGs:

Firstly, state sovereignty is important in many aspects. States do not want to bind themselves and limit their opportunities to act in several areas (although they do that quite often in other treaties). Indeed, there are some normative arguments to support this statement, although I would tend to favor a substantial limitation of state sovereignty under the premise of a more just global order (for arguments in that direction, see Ronzoni 2012). Secondly, which institution would hold states responsible for failing to achieve the SDGs? Would that be the UN, which is often criticized for being a 'toothless tiger', in particular when it comes to the more powerful and richer states. These states, which have to shoulder the most efforts if the SDGs are to become a success, and rightly so, because, as I have argued before, they not only have the power to do that but they are also, at least partly, responsible for the situation being so bad to begin with. Therefore, a system of rewards and sanctions will be most important for those powerful states, even though they are also those states that have the most incentive, as well as power, to block the implementation of such a system or even resist it. They have much to lose and little to gain. Thirdly, a system of rewards and sanctions needs to be based on meeting the challenge of making it a joint and coordinated effort, so that it is clear whom is responsible for what, as well as reduce vagueness; otherwise, it is unclear what counts as success or failure in the

---

Agenda is realized. If we realize our ambitions across the full extent of the Agenda, the lives of all will be profoundly improved and our world will be transformed for the better" (https://sustainabledevelopment.un.org/post2015/transformingourworld).

first place. Both questions, as seen in the previous sections, are critical, but equally difficult to solve.

A system of rewards and sanctions should be one in which change is effectively supported, while also rewarding those the most that have made the most progress. Going beyond traditional forms of incentives (and coercive actions) for developing countries to fulfill poverty reduction targets is in the spirit of the SDGs to be a truly global initiative. Moreover, the SDGs should aim to reward change that is sustainable and measurable and reaches the most deprived and vulnerable, thereby truly leaving no one behind. It will also demand the institutionalization of new ways of holding the rich and developed countries responsible, as well as take some power away from them. They should not be able to escape responsibility too easily. The implementation of such a reward and sanction systems needs to be as transparent and independent as possible, not in the hands of powerful states or institutions dominated by them alone. It will be crucial that "neutral" actors, the public, civil society organizations, academic institutions and those living in poverty are also mobilized to evaluate the progress that states and other institutions are making in order to achieve the SDGs. These states and institutions should be held accountable, at least in terms of public opinion, and that it is made clear to politicians and other decision-makers that their actions are critically examined; otherwise, they will be called out if they fail to realize what they promised. Another important step forward would be to enhance the SDGs with a connection to human rights (Pogge and Sengupta 2015a), as well as rights that can generally be claimed in court. Thus far, those for whom the SDGs are actually made, the people whose lives are in need of improvement, have basically no tool with which to hold states responsible. Eric Friedman (2016) has proposed, with particular regard to health, that it is necessary to bring judicial accountability to the SDGs. He argues for the establishment of a Framework Convention on Global Health (FCGH) in the form of a global treaty, with the goal of establishing a regime of compliance and accountability to the human right to health under the SDGs. This would allow individuals to go before the court if their state fails to be on track with the SDGs and, in common with other human rights, a special rapporteur would assist individuals and groups to have their rights protected.

It should not be forgotten that a system of rewards and sanctions is also in danger of becoming a tool to push certain policies, which might be hurtful or only serve particular interests of powerful states. We have seen similar scenarios play out in recent decades, when development policies and trade agreements were forced upon weaker, developing states, and which mainly favored richer states. That also happened in the name of valuable goals such as poverty reduction, economic growth and inclusion, all of which are present in the SDGs (Vestergaard and Wade 2013). A reward and sanction system should instead try to reduce inequalities between states, as well as empower developing countries to hold those richer and more powerful states to account.

8.7 Conclusions

In this commentary I have tried to highlight a few of the important issues that surround the implementation of the SDGs. I am leaning towards a positive attitude towards the SDGs and hope that they will become a success story, not from a public relations perspective, but from the perspective of those people who need them to become a success so that they can escape poverty and live better lives, free of deprivation and severe hardship. But that will certainly demand efforts that go way beyond what we have done so far in order to move towards a more just world, especially from those who currently profit the most from injustices, such as poverty, exploitation of humans and resources, warfare, failing institutions or forced agreements.

References

Alejandro Leal, Pablo. 2007. Participation: The ascendancy of a buzzword in the neo-liberal era. *Development in Practice* 17(4–5): 539–548. doi:10.1080/09614520701469518.

Cammack, Paul. 2004. What the World Bank means by poverty reduction, and why it matters. *New Political Economy* 9(2): 189–211. doi:10.1080/1356346042000218069.

Cornwall, Andrea, and Karen Brock. 2005. What do buzzwords do for development policy? A critical look at 'participation', 'empowerment' and 'poverty Reduction'. *Third World Quarterly* 26(7): 1043–1060. doi:10.1080/01436590500235603.

Deveaux, Monique. 2015. The global poor as agents of justice. *Journal of Moral Philosophy* 12(2): 125–150.

Dixon, Rosalind, and Martha Nussbaum. 2012. Children's rights and a capabilities approach: The question of special priority. *Cornell Law Review* 97: 549–593.

Drydyk, Jay. 2013. Empowerment, agency, and power. *Journal of Global Ethics* 9(3): 249–262. doi:10.1080/17449626.2013.818374.

Friedman, Eric A. 2016. An independent review and accountability mechanism for the sustainable development goals: The possibilities of a framework convention on global health. *Health and Human Rights Journal* 18(1). http://www.hhrjournal.org/2016/01/an-independent-review-and-accountability-mechanism-for-the-sustainable-development-goals-the-possibilities-of-a-framework-convention-on-global-health/.

Fukuda-Parr, Sakiko. 2016. From the millennium development goals to the sustainable development goals: Shifts in purpose, concept, and politics of global goal setting for development. *Gender & Development* 24(1): 43–52. doi:10.1080/13552074.2016.1145895.

Gheaus, Anca. 2013. Care drain as an issue of global gender justice. *Ethical Perspectives* 20(1): 61–80. doi:10.2143/EP.20.1.2965125.

Güven, Ali Burak. 2012. Exploring paradigm continuity: The IMF, the World Bank, and the global economic crisis. *Development and Change* 43(4): 869–898. doi:10.1111/j.1467-7660.2012.01781.x.

Hák, Tomáš, Svatava Janoušková, and Bedřich Moldan. 2016. Sustainable development goals: A need for relevant indicators. *Ecological Indicators* 60: 565–573. doi:10.1016/j.ecolind.2015.08.003.

ICSU, and ISSC. 2015. Review of the sustainable development goals: The science perspective. International Council for Science (ICSU). http://resourcecentre.savethechildren.se/sites/default/files/documents/sdg-report.pdf#page=9.

Koggel, Christine M. 2013. A critical analysis of recent work on empowerment: Implications for gender. *Journal of Global Ethics* 9(3): 263–275. doi:10.1080/17449626.2013.818383.

Langan, Mark. 2015. Budget support and Africa-European union relations: Free market reform and neo-colonialism? *European Journal of International Relations* 21(1): 101–121. doi:10.1177/1354066113516813.

Langford, Malcolm, Andy Sumner, and Alicia Ely Yamin (eds.). 2013. *Millennium development goals and human rights: Past, present, and future*, 1st ed. Cambridge: Cambridge University Press. http://ebooks.cambridge.org/ref/id/CBO9781139410892.

Miller, David. 1999. *Principles of social justice*, 1st ed. Cambridge, MA: Harvard University Press.

Moellendorf, Darrel. 2014. *The moral challenge of dangerous climate change: Values, poverty, and policy*, 1st ed. New York: Cambridge University Press.

Pogge, Thomas. 2010. *Politics as usual: What lies behind the pro-poor rhetoric*. Cambridge/Malden: Polity.

Pogge, Thomas, and Mitu Sengupta. 2015a. The Sustainable Development Goals (SDGS) as drafted: Nice idea, poor execution. *Washington International Law Journal* 24(3): 571–588.

Pogge, Thomas, and Mitu Sengupta. 2015b. The sustainable development goals: A plan for building a better world? *Journal of Global Ethics* 11(1): 56–64. doi:10.1080/17449626.2015.1010656.

Pongiglione, Francesca. 2015. The need for a priority structure for the sustainable development goals. *Journal of Global Ethics* 11(1): 37–42. doi:10.1080/17449626.2014.1001912.

Reuter, Peter (ed.). 2012. *Draining development? Controlling flows of illicit funds from developing countries*, 1st ed. Washington, DC: World Bank.

Ronzoni, Miriam. 2012. Two conceptions of state sovereignty and their implications for global institutional design. *Critical Review of International Social and Political Philosophy* 15(5): 573–591. doi:10.1080/13698230.2012.727306.

Rückert, Arne. 2007. Producing neoliberal hegemony? A neo-gramscian analysis of the Poverty Reduction Strategy Paper (PRSP) in Nicaragua. *Studies in Political Economy* 79: 91–118.

Ruggeri Laderchi, Caterina, Ruhi Saith, and Frances Stewart. 2006. Does it matter that we do not agree on the definition of poverty? A comparison of four approaches. In *Understanding human well-being*, 1st ed, ed. Mark McGillivray and Matthew Clarke, 19–53. Tokyo: United Nations University Press.

Saith, Ashwani. 2006. From universal values to millennium development goals: Lost in translation: From universal values to MDGs. *Development and Change* 37(6): 1167–1199. doi:10.1111/j.1467-7660.2006.00518.x.

Singer, Peter. 2010. *The life you can save: How to play your part in ending world poverty*, 1st ed. London: Picador.

Sustainable Development Solutions Network. 2015. Getting started with the sustainable development goals: A guide for stakeholders. Sustainable Development Solutions Network. http://unsdsn.org/wp-content/uploads/2015/12/151211-getting-started-guide-FINAL-PDF-.pdf.

Tangcharoensathien, Viroj, Anne Mills, and Toomas Palu. 2015. Accelerating health equity: The key role of Universal Health Coverage in the sustainable development goals. *BMC Medicine* 13(1). doi:10.1186/s12916-015-0342-3.

UNCTAD. 2015. *World investment report 2015: Reforming international investment governance*. Geneva/New York: UNCTAD. http://unctad.org/en/PublicationsLibrary/wir2015_en.pdf.

Vestergaard, Jakob, and Robert H. Wade. 2013. Protecting power: How Western States retain the dominant voice in The World Bank's Governance. *World Development* 46: 153–164. doi:10.1016/j.worlddev.2013.01.031.

Wolff, Jonathan, and Avner de-Shalit. 2007. *Disadvantage*, Oxford political theory, 1st ed. Oxford/New York: Oxford University Press.

Young, Iris Marion. 2011. *Responsibility for justice*, Oxford political philosophy, 1st ed. Oxford: Oxford University Press.

Part III
Poverty and Poverty Alleviation in the Welfare State

Chapter 9
Relative Poverty as a Threat to Human Dignity: On the Structural Injustice of Welfare States

Christian Neuhäuser

Abstract In this chapter I argue that the pressing issue that wealthy societies face today is not merely economic inequality, but rather prevalent and increasing relative poverty. I will first analyze the concept of poverty with a special focus on relative poverty and not, as is common in contemporary political philosophy, with an exclusive view on absolute poverty. It will be argued that poverty should be seen as problematic from a moral point of view because it undermines self-respect and thereby violates the dignity of persons. Self-respect depends on the ability to look after oneself in important matters and the ability to respect oneself as an equal member of society. For people living in relative poverty both are impossible or at least extremely hard. In a second section, I will argue that the normatively problematic character of relative poverty as a threat to human dignity gives us a strong reason to assign the responsibility for eradicating relative poverty to the appropriate agents. As we will see in this chapter, it is the state that bears primary responsibility for enabling people to escape relative poverty. In a third part, I will argue that it is not irrelevant which measures are used to help people to get out of their poverty. Different measures are humiliating to a different degree and respect for the dignity of relatively poor people demands the choice of the least humiliating measure. In the light of this normative background, I will argue that welfare is better than charity and a reorganization of the economic structure, as far as possible, even better than welfare.

Keywords Relative poverty • Self-respect • Human dignity • Welfare • Economy

---

C. Neuhäuser (✉)
Institut für Philosophie und Politikwissenschaft,
Emil-Figge-Straße 50, 44227 Dortmund, Germany
e-mail: christian.neuhaeuser@tu-dortmund.de

H.P. Gaisbauer et al. (eds.), *Ethical Issues in Poverty Alleviation*, Studies in Global Justice 14, DOI 10.1007/978-3-319-41430-0_9

9.1 Introduction

The increasing economic inequality in democratic and wealthy societies is a controversially discussed issue.[1] For some, it seems to be the price we have to pay for liberty. For others, inequality is an evil to be abolished. I will argue that the pressing issue that wealthy societies face today is not merely economic inequality, but rather prevalent and increasing relative poverty. One might think that this does not make a difference as relative poverty is just one side of economic inequality. After all, it is its dynamic linkage with the distribution of national income that defines the concept of relative poverty. However, it does make a difference whether one talks about relative poverty or about inequality. First of all, not every type of income inequality is connected with relative poverty. There can be a certain degree of inequality which does not yet lead to poverty. Second, poverty is a normative concept while inequality is not. Hence, an analysis of the concept of poverty can help to understand in which way, and why, relative poverty and along with it certain forms of inequality, but not necessarily others, are morally problematic.

I will first analyze the concept of poverty with a special focus on relative poverty and not, as is quite common in contemporary political philosophy, with an exclusive view on absolute poverty. It will be argued that poverty should be seen as problematic from a moral point of view because it undermines self-respect and thereby violates the dignity of persons. Self-respect depends on the ability to look after oneself in important matters and the ability to respect oneself as an equal member of society. For people living in relative poverty both are impossible or at least extremely hard. In a second section, I will argue that the normatively problematic character of relative poverty as a threat to human dignity gives us a strong reason to assign the responsibility for eradicating relative poverty to the appropriate agents. As we will see in this chapter, it is the state that bears primary responsibility for enabling people to escape relative poverty. In a third part, I will argue that it is not irrelevant which measures are used to help people to get out of their poverty. Different measures are humiliating to a different degree and respect for the dignity of relatively poor people demands the choice of the least humiliating measure. In light of this normative background, I will argue that welfare is better than charity and a reorganization of the economic structure, as far as possible, is even better than welfare.

[1] In particular the recent book of Thomas Piketty (2014) stirred up the public debate. In philosophy, the question of the social injustice of inequality has a long tradition. For an overview see Stuart White (2006).

9.2 Relative Poverty, Self-Respect and Human Dignity

Inequality per se is not necessarily a moral problem.[2] There are many inequalities which are morally irrelevant. Some people have more hair, others less; some are redheaded or blonde. Some people are tall, others short. Some have many siblings, others none at all. Further, there are many inequalities, which ought to be morally irrelevant, but become problematic only because they are misused as a reason for discrimination. Well known examples are differences in skin color, ethnicity, religion or sex. However, there are also inequalities which are inherently problematic – such as inequality of opportunity or in legal status, unequal health coverage, unequal access to political participation and an unequal recognition of one's dignity.

In which of those three categories does economic inequality fall? Is it morally irrelevant, is it misused as a reason for discrimination or is it an inherent moral problem? I find it difficult to answer this question in general. If one defends an egalitarian theory of justice, one believes that income and wealth are directly relevant in terms of justice. Hence, economic inequality always constitutes a moral problem. According to this approach, every form of economic inequality at least demands some sort of justification, otherwise it is unjust.[3] According to this position, it might be that at first it does not seem to be a problem, that a 'simple' millionaire has a lot less money than a multimillionaire. But this only appears to be irrelevant in light of other and more urgent problems of justice. According to strict egalitarians, it indeed would be a problem of justice in need of justification if all people were millionaires and only some of them multimillionaires.

Against this strict egalitarian position it can be argued that a society of millionaires is a society of affluence, and according to Hume in such a society problems of justice would have vanished.[4] It might be that people still would not have access to all the goods they could possibly ask for and in this respect there would still be inequality. But it might be plausible to say that they would have access to all economically acquirable goods in which they can have a minimally reasonable interest. The egalitarian might insist that every form of economic inequality is a problem of justice, even in a society of millionaires. To such an egalitarian it simply does not matter on what level of abundance inequality emerges and it does not matter how luxurious the unfulfilled wishes or interests might be. Otherwise, the egalitarian would have to admit that it is not inequality itself which is problematic, but rather other things, which are connected to inequality, such as social discrimination or unequally distributed political power.

I do not want to engage this difficult issue raised by the position of the strict egalitarian. Instead, I will be exclusively concerned with the argument that economic inequality can have morally problematic effects. Identifying such effects is

---

[2] Even those egalitarians, for whom equality is of intrinsic value, normally limit this claim to certain goods (or capabilities). E.g. Larry Temkin 1993, p. 7.

[3] Stefan Gosepath (2004) among others calls this the presumption of equality.

[4] Cf. Hope (2012) for a concise formulation of this idea originally dating to David Hume.

sufficient to label the respective inequality itself as morally problematic. That is exactly what the concept of relative poverty is intended to communicate and what constitutes its advantage over mere inequality from a moral point of view. Relative poverty describes a specific form of inequality that has certain morally problematic effects. Thus, relative poverty should be understood as a thick concept which has not only descriptive but also normative content.[5]

Understanding relative poverty as a thick concept also seems to be appropriate because this corresponds with the common understanding of poverty. According to ordinary language, poverty is something bad and usually ought to be avoided. To be sure, there are people who voluntarily choose to live in poverty. But those people normally are seen as extraordinary; they might even be admired, because they freely carry this burden. Thus, poverty still is bad and voluntary poverty appears to be completely different from involuntary poverty only because of the bravery of those people who choose to face it voluntarily.[6]

In any case, understanding poverty as a thick concept helps to explain why poverty normally is seen as the more serious moral problem when compared to mere economic inequalities that do not constitute poverty. In what follows, I want to build on this common understanding of poverty and describe absolute as well as relative poverty as a threat to human dignity. Other forms of economic inequality, in contrast, do not imply a threat to dignity. Therefore, forms of economic inequality are less problematic in terms of justice.

But is that true? Can poverty be understood as a threat to human dignity? It seems to make a lot of sense for absolute poverty but not necessarily for relative poverty, which I am concerned with here. If one accepts, however, that relative poverty indeed is a form of poverty and not only inequality, it might become clearer in what respect it is connected to human dignity. In order to establish this connection, I want to describe shortly why absolute poverty is a threat to dignity before explaining why relative poverty really is poverty, just like absolute poverty. Thereby it becomes clear, or so I hope, in what way relative poverty is a threat to dignity as well. However, although both forms of poverty can be conceptualized as threats to dignity, we will also see that absolute poverty is the more serious moral problem.

According to a common understanding, human dignity is nonvolatile but it is still possible to degrade, dehumanize and humiliate human beings, in short to violate their dignity.[7] Dignity is violated if the basic self-respect of a person as a human being is undermined.[8] Self-respect as a human being, as I understand it here, has two dimensions (Stoecker 2011). First, it can be understood as self-regard which rests on autonomy and the ability to look after oneself in important matters. It is a

[5] According to the standard terminology 'thick concepts' combine evaluative and descriptive content in their meaning. Cf. Roberts (2013).

[6] Amartya Sen (1987) makes this point using the example of hunger and fasting.

[7] This position is especially popular in the German-speaking world. That is because the German constitution starts with claiming that the dignity of man is inviolable. Cf. Rosen (2012, 77–80).

[8] This conceptualization of dignity as constituted by self-respect is established especially by Peter Schaber (2004, 2008, 2010) and Ralf Stoecker (2003, 2011).

controversially discussed issue whether it always has to count as a violation of dignity if a person is unable to look after herself in important matters. Maybe, the absence of self-regard in this sense constitutes a violation of dignity only if other people are able to help the affected person to develop the necessary capabilities. But, it might also be that it is irrelevant for what reason a person is unable to look after herself regarding important matters. Then such an inability always violates her dignity. According to this second line of thought, an ongoing dementia would be a violation of dignity, but according to the first position it would not. I will abstract from this difficult question because it is not relevant to the issue of relative poverty. It seems reasonable to assume that it is possible to help poor people out of their poverty. At least, the current efforts in this direction are so weak that there is no reason whatsoever to believe otherwise.

Self-regard as the ability to look after oneself is just one side of the double meaning of self-respect. Self-respect is also about being able to respect oneself as a person of equal or even equally noble status in one's society. The idea that lies behind this dimension of self-respect is that all human beings have the right to be respected as equals solely by virtue of being human. Thus, they also have a right to respect themselves as persons of equal status.[9] Whether they actually are able to do so, often depends on social factors such as other people expressing their respect towards them. If one is not respected as an equal person by others, one's self-respect is likely to suffer. The stronger the disrespect, the stronger one's insecurity normally gets. Additionally, one is justified in seeing oneself as disrespected in such cases because one is entitled to the respect of others as an equal human being.[10]

Self-respect is based on the ability to look after oneself and on being recognized as an equal person which depends on being respected by others. This double meaning of self-respect explains the way in which absolute poverty is a threat to human dignity, or so I think. Absolute poverty is usually measured on the basis of purchasing power. If a person has less than 1.25 or 2 dollars purchasing power per day to live on, she is absolutely poor. Worldwide, about one or two billion people fall into this category.[11] Absolute poverty is a threat to human dignity because affected people cannot look after themselves in an important respect: they have too little money to be free from existential material threats. Because other people, at least collectively, are able to help them to escape their poverty, their passivity constitutes a collective violation of their status as equal human beings.[12] Additionally, absolute

[9] Kolnai (1995) elaborated on the meaning of nobility which is to be found in the term of dignity. However, his concept has extremely elitist elements. A distinctly more egalitarian interpretation is provided by Waldron (2012). For an overview see Neuhäuser and Stoecker (2014).

[10] This argument is developed by Avishai Margalit (1996).

[11] In that way it was presented in the groundbreaking book of Thomas Pogge (2008). Today, in international politics, US$ 1.25 is the common demarcation. Accordingly, there was a reduction in absolute poverty. In the last 20 years, absolute poverty roughly diminished about 700 million (in absolute terms). According to the UN (2013), this reduction goes back nearly exclusively to the reduction in poverty in these five countries: China, Indonesia, India, Pakistan and Vietnam.

[12] Conceptualizing absolute poverty as a threat to human dignity directly leads to a general positive duty to eradicate poverty.

poverty often is connected to other forms of violating the right to equal respect. For example, one can take advantage of other people's misery by exploiting them and forcing them into humiliating work. This second connection between self-respect and disrespect of others is not a necessary but a contingent one. It is possible that nobody takes advantage of poor people's misery by exploiting them.[13] But, of course in reality it happens very often and the only reliable prevention against this danger consists in overcoming absolute poverty.

If this position just sketched is defensible, absolute poverty is a threat to human dignity because absolutely poor people have too little money to live a dignified life. This is where relative poverty might be similar to absolute poverty. The conceptualization of absolute poverty as a threat to human dignity makes use of the idea mentioned earlier, that poverty should not be understood as a descriptive concept only, but as a thick concept with normative content. This also suggests [to understand] relative poverty as a thick concept which includes normative content in a similar way to the normative content in the thick concept of absolute poverty. Relative poverty then has to be conceptualized as also constituting a threat to human dignity. This, by the way, could have the additional advantage of providing a justification for the definition of poverty lines. If poverty were a purely descriptive concept, poverty lines would be completely arbitrary. Instead, it is suggested here that the two dimensions of self-respect define where to draw the lines of relative and absolute poverty. Accordingly, one would have to discuss whether 1.25 or 2 dollars are an adequate demarcation for absolute poverty. People having 3–4 dollars per day to live on may also be absolutely poor because they are still exposed to existential material threats.[14]

If it is true that the normative character of poverty can be grasped through its property of being a threat to human dignity, as outlined in the case of absolute poverty, then this would also have to apply to relative poverty. Being relatively poor would also have to mean having too little money for a dignified life. As we have seen, in the case of absolute poverty the linkage with dignity seems plausible because absolute poverty constitutes an existential threat to personhood. But, does relative poverty also constitute an existential threat? If this is not the case, then it might turn out that there is no relative but only absolute poverty and, in addition, social inequality. For someone who is sympathetic to that outcome it seems to be easy to argue that relative poverty is not connected to existential threats of any kind. Relative poverty is often measured in relation to the relative income level of a country. According to a standard developed by Peter Townsend and adopted by the EU and the OECD, people with less than 60 or 50 % of the average income are relatively

[13] I think here one can see clearly why exploitation is related to taking advantage of a vulnerability, as Jonathan Wolff (1999) and Allen Wood (2004, 249) argue. Loss of dignity constitutes an especially strong vulnerability.

[14] Measuring poverty in terms of purchasing power of course is burdened with many problems. It is still used in public and normative discourse for its simplicity and symbolic value. For policy questions other measurements have been developed like the Human Poverty Index or more recently the Multidimensional Poverty Index. Unlike the Human Poverty Index the Multidimensional Poverty Index is only applied to developing countries and not able to grasp the concept of relative poverty, which is a weakness, I think. Cf. Alkire et al. (2015).

poor.[15] With respect to some countries, relatively poor people are far above the threshold of absolute poverty and, thus, do not face existential threats or so it seems. In Germany, for instance, in 2013 people with less than 973 Euros per month were relatively poor according to the 60 % standard.[16] Those people have much more than absolutely poor people with only 30–60 Euros per month. And they apparently do not have to face existential threats which are due to their poverty. In other countries it might be that relatively poor people find themselves below the threshold of absolute poverty and are facing existential threats. However, that simply means that they are absolutely poor no matter how much other members in their society own. In this case, the concept of relative poverty does not seem to have any additional informational value because it is absolute poverty that threatens the dignity of the affected people.

Against reducing relative poverty to mere inequality I want to argue for the position that relative poverty constitutes a threat to dignity. This threat might not be existential, as is the case with absolute poverty, but rather of a more social nature. Because of their poverty, relatively poor people are in danger of being socially excluded and of being treated as second class citizens (Margalit 1996, 225–231). The concept of relative poverty is designed to grasp this danger of social exclusion and social degradation, or so I think. Because of this, relative poverty is incompatible with the idea of human dignity according to which all people have a right to be treated and respected as equal human beings. This is so because, within a given society, respect as an equal person must take the form of respect as an equal member of this society, or to be more precise, as a member of equal social rank. There is no other option, because if someone is in fact a member of a certain society, then it is impossible to disentangle this person's identity as a human being from her identity as a member of her society.[17] For in which sense could it be possible for other members of her society to consider her not as an equal member of their society, although she in fact is a member, but still see her as an equal human being?

However, even if one accepts that dignity and self-respect depend on being recognized as an equal member of society, it is still unclear how exactly this recognition of basic equality depends on relative income. According to my conceptualization of it, relative poverty only constitutes a systematic violation of basic equality and a threat to dignity if equal recognition somehow depends on relatively equal incomes. How then are social exclusion and degradation related to income? I think the answer to this question is rather simple. In most societies, social belonging and social status are expressed and communicated symbolically through material goods.[18] The

[15] Cf. Townsend (1979, 1993); for an overview see also Lister (2004).

[16] See for the data: https://www.destatis.de/DE/ZahlenFakten/GesellschaftStaat/EinkommenKonsumLebensbedingungen/LebensbedingungenArmutsgefaehrdung/Tabellen/Einkommensverteilung_SILC.html (last access: 07.07.2015).

[17] Without being able to explain this in more detail, this seems to me like a minimal condition of narrative unity of the person as John Christman (2004) describes it.

[18] For comparison, see the hypothesis that consumption can be important for the constitution of identity: Eva Illouz (2007, 43–61), Benjamin R. Barber (2007, 167 ff.).

symbolic communication of gradual differences of material status can turn into categorical differences of social status, if the ability to purchase material goods widely differs due to an increasing gap between the rich and the poor. I think on an everyday basis this phenomenon is well-known. One just has to think of the categorical differences that are communicated in different areas of our daily life, e.g. by referring to first and second class in public transport, basic and prestige hotels, or public or premium patients in hospitals.

Given that these examples are not only very rare and extreme phenomena, the symbolic discrimination they communicate consolidates into clearly recognizable categorizations of citizens of different social rank.[19] They thereby enable social exclusion and the degradation of people to second class people. This is reason enough, or so I believe, to assume that relative poverty systematically contributes to the violation of dignity. However, it is important to realize that this relationship between the public communication of material status and the degradation of people is a contingent one, at least to a certain degree. It still is possible to imagine a society in which people communicate their equal respect for one another, despite large differences in income. But I assume that in reality, we will observe various forms of disrespect in fairly all societies with significant inequality.[20] Even though, a society with relative poverty but without violation of dignity is not unthinkable and conceptually not impossible, it does not seem very likely that it could exist in reality. The more so as disrespect does not need to be communicated on purpose. Even if people only aim at showing their own high social status, communicating another person's minor status will be the unintended consequence of such everyday vanity.

To be sure, because the relation is a contingent one, my thesis that relative poverty constitutes a violation of dignity is empirically falsifiable. A more detailed sociological analysis could unfold that in many societies such a relation does not exist. Further, a future society of almost perfectly virtuous people is possible in which everyone fully respects everybody else despite considerable differences in wealth by voluntarily forgoing symbolic communication of different social ranks through material goods. As said, although such a society is possible, I do not think that it is very likely. Wealth is exceptionally suitable for communicating a high social status. Moreover, it is unlikely that all or only most human beings, as they really are, will voluntarily desist from making use of this form of communication of social status. If it really turns out that this form of communication is abolished in a certain society, this probably would also mean that relative poverty is nonexistent in this society. Probably people would simply not strive for wealth anymore. In any case, such a society would be very different from our present market societies.[21]

In summary, what I tried to show here is that in given affluent societies relative poverty is a threat to dignity because it leads to social exclusion and the treatment

[19] The common differentiation of upper, middle and lower class is a fine illustration of this fact.

[20] The work of Avner de-Shalit and Jonathan Wolff (2007) shows clearly that the affected people themselves are quite aware of this fact.

[21] Macpherson (2010, 271–278) argued in 1962 that capitalist societies are market societies. This claim was recently taken up and popularized by Michael Sandel (2012).

of relatively poor people as subhuman or second class beings. If this thesis is accepted, two things are achieved. Firstly, it is shown that relative as well as absolute poverty are, in fact, both forms of poverty and therefore in a strong sense morally problematic because both violate human dignity or at least threaten it. In both cases, people have too little money or resources or goods or capabilities to live a dignified life.[22] At the same time, it becomes evident why absolute poverty is the more serious moral problem. It deprives people of their existential and not only of their social basis of self-respect. Moreover, the relation between absolute poverty and degradation is a necessary and not only a contingent one as in the case of relative poverty and degradation.

Secondly, it is revealed that relative poverty – maybe in contrast to social inequality in a wider sense – is an urgent problem of justice. Relative poverty implies a violation of dignity, whereas other forms of wrongful inequalities do not imply such a violation. For instance, if I contingently earn less money than a colleague because she was better in negotiating her salary, this might be unjust. One could argue that salaries ought not to be dependent on negotiation skills but rather on other factors such as desert or need. But such a difference in income does not threaten my dignity, since the rather small difference deprives me neither of my ability to look after myself nor of the basis of my self-respect. From this it follows that in comparatively well-ordered states, which do not carry the burden of absolute poverty, the eradication of relative poverty takes priority over dealing with other forms of income inequality.[23]

9.3 Structural Causes of Relative Poverty

If it is true that relative poverty is a threat to human dignity and often constitutes a violation of it, then eradicating it seems to be a duty of justice. This leads to the question of who is the bearer of this duty and accordingly primarily responsible for eliminating relative poverty. There are three intuitively possible answers, that all find some support. It could be the state in which relative poverty takes place; it could be the relatively poor people themselves; and it could be relatively rich people as private persons. I will argue that it is the state which bears the primary responsibility for eradicating relative poverty. It is normally assumed that those agents, who have caused it in a culpable way, also bear the primary responsibility for dealing with a moral problem (Moore 1998). I will argue that relative poverty

[22] I leave it open, whether goods or needs or resources or capabilities are the best metric for justice and dignity because I think this question is not central for the issues discussed here, although later I will rely on the capability approach. See for an overview over the discussion of what the right metric of justice is: Brighouse and Robeyns (2010). Money on the other hand, surely is only a means to an end, but an exceptionally good one because of its nearly universal transferability, as Friedrich August Hayek (1944/2007, 125) has emphasized.

[23] In this respect, I am following an idea of Amartya Sen (2007, 2009): In different contexts, fundamental forms of injustice are to be identified and their elimination should be given priority.

predominantly has structural causes. Because states create and uphold those structures the primary responsibility for eradicating relative poverty is theirs. However, there is also a secondary responsibility of citizens, relatively poor people included, to enable states to assume their primary responsibility and to step in where this is not possible.

Iris Young objects to this standard approach and the strong relation between causation and responsibility. She calls for separating the responsibility for justice from the question of causation (Young 2011, 109–111). According to her, it is not the agents causing an injustice who are primarily responsible for eliminating it, especially in complex cases involving political structures, because it is difficult and sometimes impossible to identify those agents. Instead, the responsibility should go to those agents who are connected to the injustice in some other way, who are able to deal with the injustice and who possess a certain willingness to take on this responsibility (ibid., 112). Young's reasons for her position seem to be completely pragmatic and consequentialist in nature. According to her, trying to figure out who can be held accountable on the grounds of culpable causation often leads to nothing more than a fruitless moral debate without end. The agents involved start to play a political game of shifting blame away from themselves and towards others. Young argues, with reference to Hannah Arendt, that in such a situation people start to care only about their own morally clean slate and not about effectively eliminating serious cases of injustice such as relative poverty (ibid., 76–77).

However, I think that already from a pragmatic point of view, Young's argument is not convincing. A collective effort against relative poverty can only be successful, if most agents involved accept their fair share of the burden. If that cannot be achieved and if too many agents engage in free-riding, other agents will hardly be willing to contribute (Neuhäuser 2014). For this reason, the question of causal involvement remains relevant for questions of a forward-looking moral responsibility. It is important for a just distribution of responsibility and a distribution of responsibility is important for an effective policy. Only, if most of those agents who bear a responsibility due to their causal involvement are forced to accept their responsibility or if at least it is clear that they cannot be forced to do so, will other agents be willing to contribute. Who then are the agents responsible for relative poverty due to their causal involvement? According to one answer that is prominent in neoliberal thought, it is the relatively poor people themselves. It is their individual responsibility to rectify their situation, neoliberals and conservatives say, because they themselves have caused it.[24] Another answer, which is also widespread in public discourse, states that it is the responsibility of the rich to eliminate relative poverty through charity, because they exploit the poor or profit from their exploitation.[25] I believe that both answers are mistaken, a few exceptions notwithstanding. Rather, it is the primary responsibility of states to eliminate relative poverty. This is

[24] See for instance: Mead (1997), see for an overview over the idea of personal responsibility and its use in politics: Brown (2009).

[25] The reference to exploitation is important, because it establishes that the rich contribute to the poverty of the poor. It might still be that the rich have a secondary responsibility to help, but this

so because it is the social institutions, established and sustained by the state, that produce relative poverty.

Because relative poverty is a structural problem the primary responsibility to remedy poverty lies with the state and not with the poor people themselves or with rich agents, who could be either individuals or corporate agents like churches and companies. To be sure, rich agents have an indirect responsibility because they have a responsibility to pay taxes, not least because they benefit from the existing structures and thereby from relative poverty. As will be shown in the third section, poor people are entitled to receive help through the welfare state and not in the form of charity. However, to justify this argument, it has to be shown that relative poverty generally traces back to structural causes and not to either individual failures of the relatively poor or to a morally objectionable exploitation by the rich, which lies within their own discretion.

A number of related reasons support the claim that in most cases social structures cause relative poverty and not some kind of individual irresponsibility of the poor or the rich. In a capitalist system, labor is regarded as an economic good traded in labor markets. Hence, most people's primary source of income is distributed according to the mechanisms of supply and demand. Their willingness and ability to work are not the only reason for getting a job; in fact, they are not even the central reason. Moreover, getting a job does not automatically lead to escaping relative poverty. Instead, it is necessary to get a job with good pay which ensures a freedom from relative poverty. It is important to see that in the labor market the desire or preference for well-paid jobs only constitutes the supply side. To achieve equilibrium, it is required to also have a market creating demand. Under normal conditions in capitalist societies there is an excess supply of desire for good jobs.[26] Hence, the demand side can choose among those who offer to work in a good job according to properties it deems to be of importance.

By looking at this market mechanism we begin to see that the capability to convert one's willingness to work into a good job, which pays above the relative poverty line (in full time employment), often depends on structural factors. This, obviously, is crucial for arguing that relative poverty is caused by social structures. Amartya Sen's capability approach gives us the vocabulary to further elaborate this idea. According to Sen, it always depends on certain conversion factors whether someone is actually able to convert certain goods into an effective capability to achieve a certain functioning. Sen distinguishes personal, social and environmental conversion factors (ibid. 1992, 19–38, 1999).[27] It depends on these three factors whether one is able to convert ones desire to work in a well-paid job into actually getting such a job. Since environmental factors probably are only important in

---

would not be based on accountability and those other agents who cause the poverty would still have a primary responsibility to eradicate it.

[26] According to ILO (2014), worldwide there are more than 200 million unemployed people looking for work with a tendency for this figure to rise. Hence, excess supply of labor or sufficient work ability seems to be a normal condition in our current economic system.

[27] For an illuminating discussion of the capability approach as developed by Sen: Crocker (2008).

special cases when it comes to getting a good job, it should suffice to focus on personal and social conversion factors in order to show that the individual capability to secure a well-paid job is strongly influenced by structural factors.[28]

It can only be the direct responsibility of an individual person to secure a good job if there are no adverse conversion factors which are beyond her influence and prevent her from getting such a job. If relative poverty normally is due to such adverse conversion factors beyond the influence of the poor, it follows that those poor people are not responsible for their relative poverty. The responsibility instead falls on those agents who are also responsible for the creation and perpetuation of adverse social and personal conversion factors. Hence, for my argument it is important to show in what way social and personal conversion factors are beyond the influence of the poor.

An individual agent, who is relatively poor, obviously cannot be responsible for the unfavorable social factors which prevent her from converting the willingness to work in a well-paid job into the functioning to do so. However, it has to be shown that it is those unfavorable social factors that make it impossible or at least very difficult to escape relative poverty. I think, there are a number of arguments which strongly suggest the relevance of unfavorable social conversion factors. Firstly, Gerald Cohen has shown in his work that the capitalist market structure has the tendency to produce a distribution of income due to which a lot of people remain relatively poor (Cohen 1989). To be sure, this structure enables at least some people to escape their poverty. According to a famous argument of Cohen, it might even be possible that every person is potentially able to escape relative poverty. The problem is that although every poor person might be able to escape, not all of the relatively poor can escape. Cohen infers from this that one cannot reasonably expect poor people to escape or even want to escape their misery, because this would mean that they are expected to betray their own class (Cohen 1979). I would like to add that doing so would also be a form of opportunism. One's own effort to escape relative poverty will be more successful the fewer people who are trying to escape as well. A good example here is attempting to climb the social ladder via higher education. This often is accompanied by a devaluation of higher education, if too many people decide on this strategy of escaping poverty (cf. the classical study of Pierre Bourdieu 1998).

Secondly, Iris Young goes a step further than Cohen by doubting that for many people it is actually possible to escape relative poverty. She gives the example of a single mother who cannot accept a better paid job in another suburb because the distance between her place of employment and her place of residence would be too far for her to be able to also drop her child off at school. Even with that new job she could not afford to move to the more expensive suburb where the new employment is located. She is trapped in relative poverty because a new and more well-paid job

[28] At first sight, one could argue that environmental factors can also be decisive, e.g. in case of famines. However, Amartya Sen (1981) has shown convincingly that even in these cases social conversion factors are crucial, because famines arise from a barred access to food markets due to lack of income.

as a possible escape is blocked owing to structural reasons. It is important to see that this is a structural problem because it arises due to unfavorable social conversion factors and not due to problematic personal circumstances. For it is the social relation between rental prices, commuting time and school locations that prevents the mother from escaping relative poverty. Young insists that there are many cases like this example (Young 2011, 22–27).

On the assumption that these structural problems will prove to be robust in the light of empirical investigations, they support a strong argument against the prejudice that most relatively poor people are individually responsible for their poverty. However, one could insist that at least in some cases it is personal and not social conversion factors that hinder an agent from converting her willingness to work into the capability of securing a well-paid job. A person might not be able to do exhausting work or not be willing to move to another place, for instance. It is also possible that a person has been unemployed for a long time and has somehow come to terms with it. But it does not follow that such an agent is also responsible for these personal attitudes. Again, the capability approach offers an explanation: for it is quite possible that a person simply lacks those personal and especially mental capabilities that are necessary to handle her situation differently and maybe more productively.[29] In this case, it is by no means clear that she can be held responsible for lacking those capabilities. This depends on the relevance of external influences that might be accepted as an excuse or justification for lacking those personal capabilities which are necessary to be able to secure a good job. Consider a person being affected by unemployment on grounds of a grave illness and especially the mental burden this illness creates. Is this person responsible for lacking those mental capabilities that might be needed to secure a well-paid job, even if most agents normally do possess those capabilities? The answer seems to be a decisive "no".[30]

From those examples it follows, I think, that anybody who wants to argue for the responsibility of relatively poor people to get out of their poverty is confronted with two heavy burdens of proof. First, she must show that there are no unfavorable social conversion factors impeding a conversion of the willingness to work into actually being able to secure a good job. Second, it must be shown that personal conversion factors really fall into the area of the responsibility of the individual person. Those two burdens of proof seem to suffice for considerably weakening the argument that most or many relatively poor people are individually responsible for their misery.

There is still another aspect to be considered. If it is true that relative poverty threatens self-respect and is humiliating, then the responsibility of the state arises even in those cases where relatively poor people are individually responsible for their misery. This is so, because the right to the social foundations of self-respect cannot be forfeited, since self-respect is constitutive of dignity and it is the general

[29] Referring to Marx, Sen (1993, 2009, 163) argues that such an attitude might go back to an objective illusion and is not within the responsibility of the agent.

[30] In a legendary study Marie Jahoda et al. (1975) analyze the effects of structural unemployment on those affected. They come to the conclusion that it leads to massive changes in personality.

duty of the state to protect dignity. To be sure, it might be that someone does not make use of this right. If someone chooses to remain in relative poverty, which might have been caused by herself or not, then this choice can be understood as voluntarily not making use of the right to the social foundations of self-respect.[31] But, if someone cannot escape relative poverty anymore on her own even though she wants to, the right to the social foundations of self-respect still applies. In this case, it is irrelevant whether this person was personally responsible for getting into relative poverty. Her right to receive help in developing those capabilities that are necessary for escaping relative poverty remains.

In conclusion, there is much to say in favor of holding other agents and not the relatively poor people themselves responsible for the elimination of relative poverty. In the beginning of this chapter I said that rich agents and states are other possible candidates. Who then is primarily responsible for eradicating relative poverty? Moreover, what exactly can poor people expect from those agents?

9.4 Charity, Welfare and a Just Economic Structure

The last section has shown that, in general, it is not the relatively poor people themselves who are responsible for eradicating their poverty. Two other potential candidates for this responsibility are the state and rich people. There is much to be said for seeing the state and not rich people as bearing the primary responsibility. As we have seen, to a large extent unfavorable social conversion factors and social roots of unfavorable personal conversion factors keep individual agents from converting their willingness to work into actually securing such a job. It is the state that creates and upholds the basic institutional structure of a society and thereby the social roots of conversion factors. Since the state plays this crucial role, it also is the state that bears the primary responsibility for eradicating relative poverty.

However, it is important to see that there is a second strong reason against attributing the primary responsibility for eradicating relative poverty to the rich. Such an attribution of responsibility leads to a culture of charity as it is known from past societies in Europe and as it is still prevalent in the United States. The problem of charity is that it eliminates one form of humiliation by replacing it with another. This is so, because charity does not eliminate the threat to dignity and self-respect of relatively poor people. They continue to be unable to look after themselves due to structural reasons. They remain passively dependent on the beneficence of others. Moreover, charity establishes a hierarchical relation between solicitant and benefactor which makes it extremely difficult to mutually respect each other as equal

[31] Here, I use the phrase given by John Rawls (1971/1999, 438), who argues that the social foundation to self-respect is a basic good and maybe the most important one. Rawls does not argue, however, that freedom from relative poverty is a social foundation to self-respect.

members of society in the sense of respecting each other as people of equal rank and nobility, especially when this structure becomes permanent.[32]

Since charity has a humiliating quality and since states cause the unfavorable structure which forces poor people to endure their poverty, the state bears the primary responsibility for eliminating poverty. However, the question remains in which way the state ought to eliminate relative poverty. There seem to be two possibilities. The first alternative points at the central role of welfare states and the establishment of a strong right to transfer payments. The second alternative calls for a modification of the basic social structure in such a way that no relative poverty arises. At first sight, the second alternative seems to be preferable because it appears to be less humiliating. Not only charity, but also transfer payments threaten poor people's self-respect because those people continue to be unable to take care of themselves when it comes to the provision of basic goods. To be sure, transfer payments are less humiliating than charity, since the poor have a legal claim to these transfer payments. They are not forced into the position of a solicitant. Hence, their equality in status is not damaged, at least in theory. Admittedly, in practice it depends on how the social institutions of the state operate. They have to treat relatively poor people not as solicitants but as citizens who claim benefits to which they are entitled. Unfortunately, in reality many states continue to make active use of a mechanism of degradation or at least let it happen within their departments, which in both cases is degrading.[33]

Although it appears to be less humiliating, it is still unclear whether the second alternative of a structural reform really is preferable to welfare, at least in non-ideal theorizing. This also depends on what reform of the economic structure could look like and the moral consequences of such a reform.[34] A widespread objection against reforming the economic structure in favor of the poor points at the importance of economic growth. Far reaching interferences with relatively free markets cause a considerable loss of efficiency and therefore a decrease in the accumulation of goods, or so the argument goes. But, even if we suppose this to be true, the normative status of this objection remains unclear. If the problem only consists of not maximizing overall social welfare, this is not a sufficient reason. For an increase in welfare of one group does not justify threatening the dignity and self-respect of the poor, if the increase in welfare of the first group has nothing to do with the requirements of their self-respect and dignity. If, therefore, an increase in welfare of this other group is not needed to enable them to look after themselves with respect to basic goods, and if it does not secure their status as equal members of society, then from a moral point of view it is categorically less important than helping the poor. Welfare benefits for the relatively well-off in wealthy countries such as Germany, Austria or Switzerland do not seem to be related to their dignity and self respect. It

[32] This argument is also brought forward by Margalit (1996, 235–240) and Walzer (1983, 278).

[33] In the German language, there is a miscellany of reports by unemployed people complaining about the humiliating attendance in employment centers: Montag (2012). A more scientific study about the same problem regarding the suburbs of Paris was conducted by Bourdieu et al. (1999).

[34] This argument is consistently utilized by Friedrich v. Hayek (1960/2006, 224 ff.).

might be true that decreasing economic growth due to the reform of the economic structure might decrease their affluence. But, this is no argument against such a reform if the reform really does help the poor to escape their poverty and humiliating situation.

Still, respective structural reforms could turn out to have problematic implications so that the alternative solution of strengthening the welfare state is to be preferred. There are two types of reasons that speak in favor of this assumption. First, structural reforms could have external effects on people in other societies. An example could be restrictions on international trade as part of the reforms designed to eliminate relative poverty. Such a measure might worsen the prospects of the absolutely poor and thus much more disadvantaged people. I am not claiming this to be true. There are also economists arguing that free trade is not necessarily beneficiary for absolutely poor people (Stiglitz 2003; Rodrik 2012 and other authors). This example is only supposed to indicate that the normative weight of such external effects ought to be considered with respect to reforms of the economic structure in a wealthy state.

The second reason concerns the potentially humiliating nature of structural reforms. Those reforms ought not to be humiliating because this would only mean replacing one humiliation with another that might be even worse. For instance, Friedrich August von Hayek argues that certain regulations of income might lead to a massive restriction of occupational choice. People would not be willing anymore to do exhausting work, such as the work of a surgeon, if they could earn the same money as a philosopher, for instance. In order to make sure that people take those jobs that are most useful for society, according to Hayek, the government would have to assign them to those jobs.[35] If this argument is correct – and again, I do not want to claim its accuracy – a structural reform which includes a strong regulation of income and a restriction of the occupational freedom of choice would not be acceptable (Cohen 2008, 222). The abandonment of the freedom of occupational choice surely is a more serious assault on self-respect than relative poverty.

Those examples show that thoughtful consideration is required to figure out which structural reforms are not humiliating and thus desirable, and how much of a welfare state needs to remain in order to abolish poverty. It is important to emphasize once more that even a considerable reduction of privileges of some well-off people is no relevant argument against structural reforms. This is true as long as no basic rights, including basic freedoms, are violated. To give a simple example: that some owners of sports cars cannot continue to indulge into speeding anymore is no reason against speed limits on highways, because no basic freedoms are affected. Insofar as this is not the case, further measures of redistribution of wealth, such as

[35] Hayek (1960/2006, ch. 18). While John Rawls (1971/1999, 151) apparently accepted this argument of Hayek, Gerald Cohen (2008, ch. 5) vehemently opposes it, stating that such drastic measures are not necessary. Instead citizens just need to act in accordance with the moral principles of egalitarianism.

higher taxes on income, capital and inheritance, are appropriate measures to reduce relative poverty as long as they are effective instruments.[36]

Finally, I want to draw attention to an important thought of Iris Young. She argues that the elimination of injustices such as relative poverty is the responsibility of all capable agents (Young 2011, 113). Against this general statement I argued that it is the state that causes the injustice of relative poverty and thus has the primary responsibility to eradicate it. But, if public institutions cannot or do not want to comply with this responsibility, it transfers to other agents. This also leads to a secondary responsibility for individual citizens to oblige the state to comply with its responsibility. It is not completely clear how far such a secondary responsibility of other agents reaches and what these agents are entitled to do in this respect. These questions need further consideration. However, it is clear that relatively poor people also have this secondary responsibility, as Young emphasizes. Maybe it even applies to them particularly, because they are the ones who are negatively affected and, therefore, might have a special right to force the state to accept its responsibility to eradicate relative poverty.

References

Alkire, Sabina et al. 2015. Multidimensional poverty measurement and analysis: Chapter 5 – the Alkire-Foster counting methodology. *Oxford Poverty & Human Development Initiative Working Paper* No. 86.

Barber, Benjamin. 2007. *Consumed: How markets corrupt children, infantilize adults, and swallow citizens whole*. New York: W. W. Norton & Company.

Bourdieu, Pierre. 1998. *The state nobility: Elite schools in the field of power*. Stanford: Stanford University Press.

Bourdieu, Pierre, et al. 1999. *Weight of the world: Social suffering in contemporary society*. Stanford: Stanford University Press.

Brighouse, Harry, and Ingrid Robeyns. 2010. *Measuring justice: Primary goods and capabilities*. Cambridge: Cambridge University Press.

Brown, Alexander. 2009. *Personal responsibility: Why it matters*. London: Continuum Publishing.

Christman, John P. 2004. Narrative unity as a condition of personhood. *Metaphilosophy* 35(5): 695–713.

Cohen, Gerald A. 1979. The labor theory of value and the concept of exploitation. *Philosophy & Public Affairs* 8(4): 338–360.

Cohen, Gerald A. 1989. *History, labour, and freedom: Themes from Marx*. Oxford: Oxford University Press.

Cohen, Gerald A. 2008. *Rescuing justice and equality*. Cambridge, MA: Harvard University Press.

Crocker, David A. 2008. *Ethics of global development: Agency, capability, and deliberative democracy*. Cambridge: Cambridge University Press.

Destatis. Statistisches Bundesamt. https://www.destatis.de/DE/ZahlenFakten/GesellschaftStaat/EinkommenKonsumLebensbedingungen/LebensbedingungenArmutsgefaehrdung/Tabellen/Einkommensverteilung_SILC.html. Accessed 07 July 2015.

[36] Piketty (2014, 512–518) argues for higher taxes on income and capital. His argument has (re) opened the discussion on this much contested topic.

Gosepath, Stefan. 2004. *Gleiche Gerechtigkeit. Grundlagen eines liberalen Egalitarismus.* Frankfurt am Main: Suhrkamp.
Hayek, Friedrich August. 1944/2007. *The road to Serfdom*. Chicago: University of Chicago Press.
Hayek, Friedrich August. 1960/2006. *The constitution of liberty*. London: Routledge Publishing.
Hope, Simon. 2012. The circumstances of justice. *Hume Studies* 36(2): 125–148.
Illouz, Eva. 2007. *Cold intimacies: The making of emotional capitalism*. Oxford: Blackwell Publishing.
ILO. 2014. *World of work report 2014: Developing with jobs*. International Labor Office. http://www.ilo.org/global/research/global-reports/world-of-work/2014/WCMS_243961/lang--en/index.htm. Accessed 05 Jul 2015.
Jahoda, Marie, et al. 1975. *Die Arbeitslosen von Marienthal. Ein soziographischer Versuch über die Wirkungen langandauernder Arbeitslosigkeit*. Frankfurt am Main: Suhrkamp.
Kolnai, Aurel. 1995. Dignity. In *Dignity, character and self-respect*, ed. Robin S. Dillon, 53–75. London: Routledge Publishing. originally Philosophy & Public Affairs 1976/6.
Lister, Ruth. 2004. *Poverty*. Cambridge: Polity Press.
Macpherson, C.B.. 1962/2010. *The political theory of possessive individualism: From Hobbes to Locke*. Oxford: Oxford University Press.
Margalit, Avishai. 1996. *The decent society*. Cambridge MA: Harvard University Press.
Mead, Lawrence. 1997. From welfare to work. In *From welfare to work: Lessons from America*, ed. Alan Deacon, 1–55. London: IEA Health and Welfare Unit.
Montag, Torsten. 2012. *Gehirnwäsche Arbeitsamt: Arbeitslose klagen an – 77 Schikanen der Arbeitsagentur*. Books on Demand.
Moore, Michael S. 1998. Causation and responsibility. *Social Philosophy and Policy* 16: 1–51.
Neuhäuser, Christian. 2014. Forward-looking collective responsibility. *Midwest Studies in Philosophy* XXXVIII: 232–251.
Neuhäuser, Christian, and Ralf Stoecker. 2014. Human dignity as universal nobility. In *The Cambridge handbook on human dignity*, ed. M. Düwell et al., 298–310. Cambridge: Cambridge University Press.
Piketty, Thomas. 2014. *Capital in the 21 century*. Harvard: Harvard University Press.
Pogge, Thomas. 2002/2008. *World poverty and human rights*. Cambridge: Polity Press.
Rawls, John. 1971/1999. *A theory of justice*. Harvard: Harvard University Press.
Roberts, Debbie. 2013. Thick concepts. *Philosophy Compass* 8(8): 677–688.
Rodrik, Dani. 2012. *Globalization paradox: Democracy and the future of the world economy*. New York: W. W. Norton & Company.
Rosen, Michael. 2012. *Dignity*. Harvard: Harvard University Press.
Sandel, Michael. 2012. *What money can't buy: The moral limits of markets*. London: Penguin.
Schaber, Peter. 2004. Menschenwürde und Selbstachtung. Ein Vorschlag zum Verständnis der Menschenwürde. *Studia Philosophica* 63: 93–119.
Schaber, Peter. 2008. Der Anspruch auf Selbstachtung. In *Begründung von Menschenwürde und Menschenrechte*, ed. Wilfried Härle and Bernhard Vogel, 188–201. Freiburg: Herder.
Schaber, Peter. 2010. *Instrumentalisierung und Würde*. Münster: Mentis.
Sen, Amartya. 1981. *Poverty and famines: An essay on entitlement and deprivation*. Oxford: Oxford University Press.
Sen, Amartya. 1987. The standard of living. In *The standard of living. Tanner lectures in human values*, ed. Geoffrey Hawthorn, 1–48. Cambridge: Cambridge University Press.
Sen, Amartya. 1992. *Inequality re-examined*. Harvard: Harvard University Press.
Sen, Amartya. 1993. Positional objectivity. *Philosophy & Public Affairs* 22: 126–145.
Sen, Amartya. 1999. *Development as freedom*. Oxford: Oxford University Press.
Sen, Amartya. 2007. What do we want from a theory of justice? *Journal of Philosophy* 103: 215–238.
Sen, Amartya. 2009. *The idea of justice*. Harvard: Harvard University Press.
Stiglitz, Joseph. 2003. *Globalization and its discontents*. London: Penguin.

Stoecker, Ralf. 2003. Menschenwürde und das Paradox der Entwürdigung. In *Menschenwürde – Annäherung an einen Begriff*, ed. Stoecker Ralf, 133–151. Wien: öbv & hpt.
Stoecker, Ralf. 2011. Three crucial turns on the road to an adequate understanding of human dignity. In *Humiliation, degradation, dehumanization*, ed. Paulus Kaufmann et al., 7–17. New York: Springer Publishing.
Temkin, Larry. 1993. *Inequality*. Oxford: Oxford University Press.
Townsend, Peter. 1979. *Poverty in the United Kingdom*. London: Penguin.
Townsend, Peter. 1993. *The international analysis of poverty*. New York: Harvester Wheatsheaf.
United Nations. 2013. *The millennium development goals report 2013*. UN. http://www.un.org/en/development/desa/publications/mdgs-report-2013.html. Accessed 17 July 2015.
Waldron, Jeremy. 2012. *Dignity, rank, and rights*. Oxford: Oxford University Press.
Walzer, Michael. 1983. *Spheres of justice: A defense of pluralism and equality*. New York: Basic Books.
White, Stuart. 2006. *Equality*. Oxford: Blackwell Publishing.
Wolff, Jonathan. 1999. Marx and exploitation. *Journal of Ethics* 3(2): 105–120.
Wolff, Jonathan, and Avner de-Shalit. 2007. *Disadvantage*. Oxford: Oxford University Press.
Wood, Allen W. 2004. *Karl Marx*. London: Routledge Publishing.
Young, Iris. 2011. *Responsibility for justice*. Oxford: Oxford University Press.

Chapter 10
Suffering Within, Suffering Without: Paradoxes of *Poverties* in Welfare States

Helmut P. Gaisbauer and Elisabeth Kapferer

Abstract One major rationale of welfare states is poverty alleviation. Poverty that is in fact (more or less effectively) encountered by social policy measures can be termed included poverty. Included poverty is heuristically captured by concepts of relative poverty and reflected in social statistics. Since poverty in affluent societies is highly stigmatized and poses an enormous threat to their social identity poor people in general try to hide their neediness at all costs. Consequently included poverty reflects a state of paradoxical visibility: welfare state poverty is visible to (or in) social statistics and policy but invisible socially. One could term this the paradox of relative poverty. Quite the opposite seems to be true for forms of poverty in European welfare states that are not yet (or still not) integrated into the welfare state poverty paradigm, forms like spreading homelessness, irregular migrants without papers, begging migrants or street children: such poverty is mostly invisible for social statistics and policy but immensely visible socially – the paradox of neglected or absolutely excluded poverty. Both paradoxes bring different hardships for the affected poor and both pose distinctive challenges to poverty research and poverty alleviation that must be thoroughly reflected upon and analyzed.

Keywords Poverty alleviation • Included poverty • Excluded poverty • Welfare states • Social visibility • Shame

10.1 Introduction: From Relative and Absolute Poverty to Included and (Absolutely) Excluded Poverty

Poverty researchers in affluent societies who investigate poverty within their societies are repeatedly somewhat under pressure to explain to the general public why relative poverty is "real" poverty and – in contrast with the destitution of a billion "Third-world-poor" – not just "moaning at a high level", complaining about inequalities that are simply more or less common to affluent societies. In political

H.P. Gaisbauer • E. Kapferer (✉)
Centre for Ethics and Poverty Research, University of Salzburg,
Mönchsberg 2a, 5020 Salzburg, Austria
e-mail: helmut.gaisbauer@sbg.ac.at; elisabeth.kapferer@sbg.ac.at

H.P. Gaisbauer et al. (eds.), *Ethical Issues in Poverty Alleviation*, Studies in Global Justice 14, DOI 10.1007/978-3-319-41430-0_10

discourse this regularly mutates into arguments of politically instrumentalized envy of the lower classes instead of accepting poverty to be a question of social justice.

Furthermore, in fact, dramatic and appalling numbers of hundreds of millions of people starving to death and living in destitution are a *skandalon*, a *stumbling block*, not only from a moral and politico-ethical point of view, but also for the proper understanding and conceptualization of the notion of poverty in affluent societies. Is an old person living in a 45 m^2 flat in contemporary Austria without a telephone, without a TV set and financially unable to meet an unexpected expense of about 900 Euros really poor compared to a hungry woman in the Philippines, a mother of three children, without proper shelter who cannot afford to visit a doctor while suffering from a curable disease? Do their situations have so much in common that they can justly be subsumed under the same notion of poverty?

The academic answer to such kinds of questions has been the conceptualization of poverty as poverty-in-society, hence, as relative poverty meaning to live a life essentially beneath the standard level of societal normality. According to this, relative poverty means a lack of access to standard goods and services and an accompanying lack of access to participation in social life (often including work in the first place). Relative poverty is an extremely important concept to capture poverty in affluent societies (and, one has to add from a normative point of view, should also be the leading concept for global poverty).

For reasons that we will clarify in the remainder of this section we suggest terming this a concept of included poverty, since the heuristic premise of such a concept is still membership – membership within a given society, however marginal the position one obtains within it might be, so that the dimensions perceived as crucial for a good life or well-being in this society cannot be met. Of course such a heuristic does not preclude an understanding of social exclusion being one dimension or form of included poverty, since the common normative reference point is still a legally constituted and legitimate claim of membership and hence the consequential duty of a bureaucratic system is to mitigate the situation of such excluded poor people (members).

In parallel to this important development in the heuristics of poverty a less "societal" or "inclusive" concept of poverty prevailed outside the affluent parts of the world: this is the concept of absolute or extreme poverty, currently measured as having less than 1.9 US$ a day at one's disposal (Cruz et al. 2015). Absolute poverty is a concept that was introduced by the President of the World Bank Group, Robert McNamara, in the early 1970s as a condition of life so degraded by disease, illiteracy, malnutrition, and squalor as to deny its victims basic human necessities (Mack et al. 2009). We comprehend the very notion of absolute poverty as a somewhat "unsocial" idea as it models the poor person as an individual consumer or – according older conceptions – as an individual struggling for subsistence outside a societal framework which owes social rights to him or her. Admittedly there are more inclusive concepts now, e. g. the Multidimensional Poverty Index, MPI, that takes into account poor health, lack of education, inadequate living standard, lack of income (as one of several factors considered), disempowerment, poor quality of work and threat from violence (c.f. Alkire and Santos 2013).[1] From a normative point of view it is important not to accept an artificial divide between poverty (and social rights) in affluent societies and in non-affluent ones. Instead it is crucial to underline that full social protection by social rights is a normative goal for the whole human family, which includes, as a matter of course and in particular, the world's most vulnerable. Normatively speaking we should hence aim – in the long term – to arrive at a concept of relative poverty as the normative benchmark of well-being on the global level.

Having said that, it is in turn of utter importance to note that there are an increasing number of arguments that the concept and measure of relative poverty is not (or probably not anymore?) sufficient to depict the full reality of poverty in affluent societies. In this criticism the shortcomings of the concept and its related methodologies are tackled as insufficient and unacceptably blind to different groups with the most vulnerable being at the heart of what can be called the "overlooked poor" (Schockaert et al. 2012; Nicaise and Schockaert 2014; Gaisbauer and Sedmak 2014).[2] This chapter aims at contributing to this discussion.

One reason for such neglect of the most vulnerable is what could be termed the "methodology-trap", the fact that the most important social statistics rely on panel data which presupposes households as basic units of reference and measure. This, in turn, precludes all people from data collection who do not live in such households – often these people are highly vulnerable: for example homeless people, prisoners, elderly people in nursing homes, refugees, or undocumented migrants. Nicaise and Schockaert have proved both: that it is possible to adjust the methodologies in such a manner to include highly vulnerable groups in the statistics and that such inclusion has a considerable effect on the data (Nicaise and Schockaert 2014). From an ethical point of view such exclusion equates to a second order neglect – not only do such groups stay invisible in the data but such invisibility also precludes them from effective poverty alleviation and, hence, pushes them even deeper into despair. This also deprives them of a different, positive future (Gaisbauer and Sedmak 2014). Clearly, one could find arguments to defend the prevailing methodology. From a utilitarian perspective one could argue that it is too costly to include a relatively small number of poor people into the social statistic – money that could be better spent to help other people out of poverty. This is not the ethics we would like to defend. Rather we are concerned with a momentum that even in poverty research and poverty alleviation is further excluding the most vulnerable, for different reasons (Øyen 2009).

To be sure, this is also true for measures of poverty that are better at capturing severe forms of poverty, like material deprivation, as well as – for a number of reasons – for measures of absolute poverty. The described methodology-trap is only one explanation; it is especially important to us because of its critical politico-ethical

[1] The MPI has been developed by OPHI, Oxford Poverty & Human Development Initiative, and is based on the so called Alkire Foster Method. For more information see: http://www.ophi.org.uk/policy/multidimensional-poverty-index/

[2] See also Tendayi Bloom's contribution in this volume.

underpinning as it contributes to making the most vulnerable in affluent societies invisible in social statistics, and subsequently also in public and related policy discourses on poverty.

It is this shortcoming that fuels our general research question in this contribution: does it make sense to speak of absolute poverty in affluent societies in order to overcome this specific form of poverty neglect?

What can the tentative answers to that sort of question be? From an ethical point of view it is clear that either there has to be a one-fits-all-argument about why poverty is a moral evil, or you have to discern different 'forms' of poverty and term them differently in order to evaluate their ethical value. We want to make an effort to show that poverty is one moral evil (as humiliation of dignity) but that there are different forms and paths of how poor people are effectively humiliated by poverty. Especially in affluent societies one should distinguish between poor people who are integrated into the "poverty bureaucracy" (i.e. having been accorded membership-status) and outsiders or outcasts whose existence rather depends on the mercy of others. Can we find convincing reasons to term the integrated ones as the relative poor and the latter ones as the absolute poor?

We find some arguments that such terminology might be misleading. Firstly, the opposition of relative and absolute poverty is not a full one: it has been forcefully argued by Schweiger that there is always an absolutist core in the concept of relative and a relative core in the concept of absolute poverty (Schweiger 2013). Secondly, Bradshaw and Mayhew (2011) found the very term absolute poverty unconvincing, at least in the European context. They propose referring to extreme poverty instead.

Despite some skepticism our aim is to follow the idea of a concept of absolute poverty in affluent societies on the premise that such societies do grant social rights that are fundamentally ("absolutely") refused to certain people, who are, thus, the *absolutely excluded poor*. The difference between the included poor and the absolutely excluded poor lies in their access to fundamental social rights. This exclusion from social rights brings them different experiences of poverty: the absolutely excluded poor are not able to hide their neediness from the general public. They suffer from life-problems that are close to that of the absolute poor in the so called less and least developed countries: hunger or serious malnutrition, unsafe (illegal) or missing shelter, no papers, i.e. no bureaucratic existence, diseases not taken care of and other health problems, lacking access to sanitation facilities etc. Such experiences make poverty a brutish exercise in mere subsistence and survival, definitely qualifying for the term of extreme or absolute poverty.

Urging for such differentiation we want to shed light on the suffering of groups of the most vulnerable poor that are often ignored and hence, paradoxically, invisible in public and social-politics discourse. In order to render our arguments more precisely we start from the insights of Robert Walker et al. who portray the experience of poverty as a shaming existence, and who argue with Amartya Sen that shame lies at the absolute core of poverty. Following the important insights and arguments of this strand of literature it will be crucial for our argument to see whether included poverty and absolutely excluded poverty are experienced in different ways, i.e. whether people affected by the one or the other do experience different forms and grades of shame or if respectively they are being shamed in different contexts.

Additionally we have to discuss what such a differentiation means for the moral evaluation of poverty. Are the two proposed concepts of poverty really different, seen from an ethical point of view? Is absolutely excluded poverty morally worse than relative poverty? Answers to this question lead to questions of an ethics of poverty alleviation.

With reference to ethical approaches that view poverty as a violation of human dignity, the linking concept between literature on poverty-shame and this position of social ethics is self-respect. Against this background, in our specific interest to disentangle different experiences of included and excluded poor people it will be crucial – so we hope to show – to reflect on privacy and distance.

10.2 Poverty as Violation of Human Dignity

Poverty research has to date arrived at a considerable and persistently increasing number of influential and convincing conceptualizations of poverty. Thus we have a wide range of different accounts we can adopt and contribute to.[3] For the purpose of our chapter we follow a growing body of philosophical literature that advocates an understanding of poverty as a humiliation or a serious threat to human dignity. To our knowledge, this influential idea has been firstly discussed in political philosophy by Avishai Margalit (1998) in his seminal book *The Decent Society*. Subsequently the idea was picked up and developed further by others with central reference to the notion and concept of self-respect.[4]

Such ethical conceptions of poverty operate with the probably strongest pragmatist background possible – all relevant UN Resolutions on Poverty refer to poverty as a violation of human dignity (Cf. Sepúlveda 2012; United Nations 2012). As an ethical conception it is formulated rather generally, leaving room for different interpretations concerning the differentiation between absolute (or severe) and relative conceptions of poverty, which, in turn, is important to our intention.

The classical account on human dignity in connection with poverty was brought forward by Peter Schaber (2011) who argues that human dignity is a normative property of the human person. Consequently it can paradoxically be violated by circumstances or actions but is at the same time inviolable in general. Following this – and Neuhäuser (2010) – we consider dignity to be the claim to self-respect of

[3] Such a plurality of accounts can weaken the societal and political impact of academic poverty research. The international network *Academics Stand Against Poverty* (ASAP – www.academicsstand.org) tries to counter this weakness by forwarding a Global Poverty Consensus Report done in cooperation with Comparative Research Programme on Poverty (CROP): cf. Cimadamore and Lange 2015.

[4] Interestingly this focus on self-respect is in line with John Rawls' statement that self-respect is "perhaps the most important primary good" a theory of justice as fairness has to consider (Rawls 1971, 440).

every human being. Drawing on a Kantian account of autonomy this conception defends self-respect "to be the effect" of realizing the right to live one's own life; "in order to respect oneself, one must be able to live a life of one's own choice and to interact with others as an independent being" (Schaber 2011, 156). Poverty then is a humiliation of dignity exactly because it deprives the poor person of self-respect due to dependence on others and the inability to stand up to them.

Schaber resumes the discussion with an argument about absolute poverty by stating that such poverty deprives the poor person of the means and conditions to live one's own life and argues for a *right to subsistence* (including rights to unpolluted water, adequate food, adequate clothing, adequate shelter, and minimal preventive health care) and a *right to basic education*: "Only when these rights are fulfilled is one able to lead a life in self-respect" (Schaber 2011, 156).

With an interest in applying this account to poverty in affluent societies Neuhäuser interprets these two aspects of self-respect as (i) the ability to look after oneself in important matters and (ii) being able to respect oneself as a person of equal or even equally noble status in one's society.[5] For the purpose of differentiation of absolute and relative poverty he suggests, as we understand it, to see the former as the existential basis, and the latter as the social basis of self-respect. On those grounds he understands absolute poverty as a threat to human dignity because absolutely poor people lack the means to live a dignified life, a condition that constitutes an existential threat to personhood. Consequently, within Neuhäuser's account of poverty as humiliation of dignity, absolute poverty necessarily constitutes degradation and humiliation. While absolute poverty deprives people of their existential basis of self-respect, relative poverty is a threat to dignity because it leads to social exclusion and the treatment of relatively poor people as subhuman or second class human beings. In contrast to absolute poverty the relation between a socioeconomic position of relative poverty and degradation is not a necessary but a contingent one – degradation is an (often cumulative or "corrosive" rather than a direct) effect of social practices. Still, such practices and their effects on self-respect and self-esteem for Neuhäuser are "incompatible with the idea of human dignity according to which all people have a right to be treated and respected as equal human beings." (ibid.).

To further clarify: in social practice, and especially in poverty alleviation, measures of downright degradation as humiliation of human dignity might be the exception rather than the rule. It is of importance to note that not every violation of moral norms and each practice of shaming the poor equates automatically to a fully-fledged violation of human dignity. In this vein Schaber (2011) deliberately proposes to exclude attacks on self-esteem from the qualification "violation of dignity". Surely not every undermining of self-esteem of a poor person qualifies for such violation of dignity in the strong sense. On the other hand we have dispose of a lot of convincing descriptions available that substantiate the assumption that the attacks on self-esteem have corrosive effects on identity so that – at some stage or other – a poor person gives up the struggle for respect and dignity, breaks down and loses her self-respect. In such a case even the cumulative effects of moral misconduct by

[5] Cf. Neuhäuser's contribution in this volume.

others, societal and administrative stigmatization, or other forms of denigration constitute – in sum – humiliation of dignity (Neuhäuser and Müller 2011). Obviously it is not easy to draw a sharp and universal demarcation line between practices that bring about negative effects for self-respect and self-esteem that account for a downright humiliation of dignity and those that do not. *A fortiori* it is important to further reflect on this issue.

Two important points are appropriate to be made: Firstly, both propositions to conceptualize poverty reflect on absolute poverty, both stretching beyond the usual rather simple (or, as they are referring to a mere bio-physical survival, "somatic"[6]) definition. Schaber does so by also reflecting on the mental-intellectual issue (education) and Neuhäuser by paralleling the conception with a societal specification (relative poverty). In fact such conceptions would not work on a lower level of mere "physical existence" since they refer to the notion of self-respect, which implies a concept of man which is all-but solipsistic. Self-respect heavily relies on the "Other", and is, hence, a concept that only makes sense with regard to man-in-society. Self-respect is normatively as well as directional an inherently societal value or attitude. This, in turn, strengthens the concept of poverty as a humiliation of dignity by way of deprivation of self-respect since there is considerable consensus in poverty research that poverty itself – while at the same time, however, having an absolute core, as we stated above – is inherently relative.

Secondly, since the concepts build on the attitude and value of self-respect they decidedly understand poverty as a matter of subjective experience rather than an objective phenomenon that can be measured independently from how people perceive their situation. This opens debates that have been conducted extensively elsewhere (Shaw 1988; Madden 2000; Notten and De Neubourg 2011). In order not to neglect the important theoretical problems connected with such an approach we propose explaining a situation where people, according our normative assumptions, could be expected to feel poor, denigrated, embarrassed or excluded *and do not* – for whatever reasons (adaptive preferences, adherence to other norms) – in terms of (personal) resilience and/or (societal) pathology. In our understanding the normative value of a situation where an objective poor person does not feel poor is far from clear. In turn, what we gain from such a position is that it enables us to take theoretically seriously the experience of poor people, which subsequently brings in norms, structures and practices of the given society.

To prepare the ground for our question of whether there are severe forms of poverty in affluent societies that are systematically different to what is measured and meant by the concept of relative poverty, we propose to link our poverty concept with recent propositions by Robert Walker et al. to understand (the experience of) poverty as an experience of shame and to further elaborate the relation between self-respect and poverty.

[6] Stefan Sell dismisses such a concept of absolute poverty as "veterinary-medical", (cf. Sell 2002, 15).

10.3 The Poverty-Shame Nexus

There is considerable literature on poverty that is especially concerned with the painful experience of poverty-related shame, with the conditions, actions and policies that generate such shame in different cultures and the attempts and strategies poor people adopt to escape from it (Chase and Walker 2012; Walker et al. 2013, 2014; Chase and Bantebya-Kyomuhendo 2015b). Obviously, since shame and self-respect are closely interrelated, the same holds true for shaming, denigration and humiliation. We propose bringing together these two strands of literature on poverty as a threat to human dignity and its painful experience.

Both Sen (1983, 159) and Alkire (2002) identified the "ability to go about without shame" as a fundamentally important capability which was situated at the "irreducible absolutist core in the construction of poverty". Sen argues that whereas the material resources needed to prevent one from feeling ashamed vary across cultures and level of socio-economic development, the actual experience of poverty-induced shame and its impacts are universal and invariant (Chase and Bantebya-Kyomuhendo 2015a, 4).

It is important to understand what we would term the "double-reflective nature" of shame. Walker et al. describe it as "co-construction": shame has an external as well as an internalized dimension, both are bound (factually or putatively) to an observing or monitoring or gazing Other who, by way of visually perceiving the neediness and helplessness of the poor person, constitutes the situation of being shamed (Chase and Walker 2012). Co-construction means that additionally there is an indispensable second arena of this very act of shaming – the reflective self of the poor, who mirrors the situation back to the other. In fact, shame appears in the reflecting poor person, with the Other being the cause and the (possibly unconscious or not) witness and mirror to the very act of shaming. Only if the person being shamed feels the shame, e.g. physically speaking blushes, does the act of shaming take place and the person being shamed is trapped, so to speak, within the embarrassing situation. This is what Jean Paul Sartre cast into his well-known aphorism: "My shame is my confession" (1978, 350).

Taking this as a starting point, Walker et al. hold that "people in poverty generally feel ashamed at having failed to live up to society's expectations that, for the most part, they have internalized as their own." (2014, 65f.) Moreover, people in poverty "are also shamed by those around them, sometimes deliberately by way of reproach and, at other times, inadvertently as when people act out of pity or ignore poverty and those who experience it. They similarly suffer stigma, bureaucratized shame manifest in the framing, structures, and implementation of policy that is often reinforced by the discriminatory actions of others: neighbors, employers, and financial institutions." (Walker et al. 2014, 66). Poverty-shame is co-constructed by the individual and society.

Walker et al. propose understanding the 'poverty-shame nexus' according to the heuristic model mapped out in Fig. 10.1 (Walker et al. 2014, 65f.):

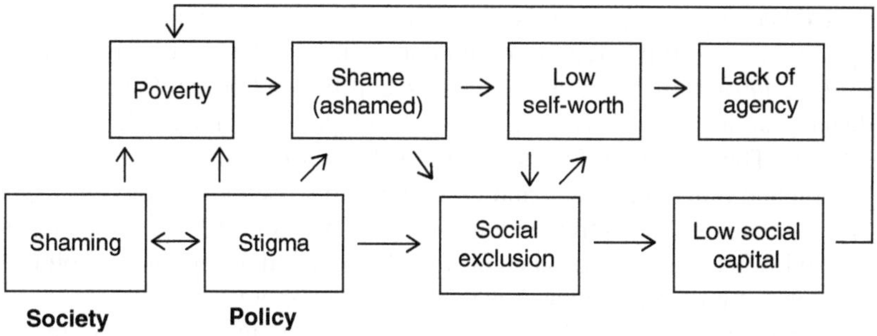

Fig. 10.1 The poverty-shame nexus

It is crucial to note that Walker et al. also refer to the undermining of self-respect by poverty-related shame. "*Shame lowers a person's sense of self-worth that, in turn, limits their agency and overall self-efficacy*." (Walker et al. 2014, 66).

10.4 Stigma Management

And, of course, people who suffer from poverty-related shame have to adapt to this situation by way of stigma-management. Generally speaking one could argue that a poverty-caused experience of shame is utterly painful and thus commands immediate reaction. This is, e.g., why a person who feels shame wishes "to sink into the ground", to flee the situation, to become invisible. Recurring or lasting experiences of shame can have corrosive effects on the human identity; such experiences heavily challenge self-respect and dignity.

In this context Walker et al. state that: "Individuals' attempts to manage shame may be counterproductive: anger; depression and despair; over-indebtedness; or even, on occasion, to sustain an income, criminal behavior. A perhaps more common response is to choose social isolation and to avoid associated social obligations, a strategy that is sometimes enforced by others as social exclusion. This not only lowers self-esteem but also reduces social capital that might have been called upon in times of crisis or exploited to generate economic opportunities. Low self-esteem and limited social capital potentially introduce [...] [a] negative feedback-loop [...] through which shame serves to perpetuate poverty by reducing human agency." (Walker et al. 2014, 66).

Walker et al. (2014, 120ff) report different forms of responses to poverty-related shame. After having successfully secured basic survival "a great motivation [for the respondents] was to avoid the glare of shame by appearing to be normal, to be part of the majority, and not to be seen as being poor or the poorest of the poor." Strategies typically began with attempts to 'stay normal' applying instrumental responses seeking to reduce the impact of poverty, maximizing resources and minimizing expenditure in the short-term, and working towards a more stable income in the future, and keeping up appearances. This is what Walker et al. termed attempts *to be and appear normal*. If this repertoire did not work or make sense respondents tried *to avoid the normal* by withdrawing from social life and psychological avoidance and disintegration. Strategies typically ended with pretence and deceit, if other strategies failed. This set of strategies was termed *resisting the normal* by anger and resignation and reflecting blame and Othering.[7] This phenomenology of responses to poverty-related shame is tremendously important to our discussion. Our point is that the divide between included and absolutely excluded poverty is the point where this typology of possible responses is not eligible anymore.

To once again refer to Walker et al.: "[R]espondents first made sure, insofar as they could, that they and their families had sufficient food to eat, somewhere to live, and adequate clothing. Beyond these acts of survival, a great motivation was to avoid the glare of shame by appearing to be normal" (2014, 121). This is, in our opinion, exactly the point where the difference between relative and absolute poverty in affluent societies becomes visible: a person is in absolute excluded poverty when she or he is not able to fulfill the acts of survival unseen by society and pretend to be part of the common majority. She or he does not succeed anymore in staying socially invisible as a needy person, but, on the contrary, is forced to make his or her need public in order to survive. We would like to term the experience when a person out of need has to quit effective stigma-management, and, instead, for the first time has to display her or his neediness to the public as the "Rubicon experience of public shame". The following testimonies illustrate that point.

10.5 The Rubicon Experience of Public Shame: Testimonies

The Bulgarian-Austrian writer Dimitré Dinev described his Rubicon experience when fleeing from Bulgaria to Austria in poetic words; remarkably his experience took place in a refugee camp:

> *So we went to visit this hostel and soon found the room and the door we were looking for. But we couldn't find a doorbell of any kind, there didn't seem to be one. There wasn't a name on the door either so we weren't quite sure what to do next. It took us a while to actually summon the courage to just knock. For someone like me who has never had to beg, has never found out what it is like to make that journey will never know what the soul goes through in that moment. Someone like me has no idea of the steep and stony slopes to be scaled, no idea of the chasms of misery one has to scramble out of and no idea of those inner storms of protest to be overcome so that the hand can be stretched forward and that first plea can be made.*[8] (Dinev 2010, 18)

[7] In contrast to Ruth Lister, to whom Walker et al. refer and who introduces 'Othering' as a way of (however delusive) socio-moral self-reassurance that usually occurs from top to bottom, they consider 'Othering' as a strategy actually coming into effect amongst and between people 'at the bottom', suffering from poverty.

[8] Translated by Deborah Fölsche-Forrow from: "*Wir besuchten also das kleine Wohnheim, fanden das Zimmer, standen vor der Tür. Eine Tür ohne Glocke und ohne Namensschild. Es hat eine Weile*

Michael, one of three formerly homeless men portrayed in an independent 2008 movie on homelessness in Vienna, tells the audience how he ended up on the street: after a period of time being unable to pay the bills and refusing to open his letters, Michael was due for eviction. After another sleepless night anticipating the forthcoming shaming of being finally forced out by the authorities of what, however empty (including the refrigerator), used to be his own four walls and his home, in a sort of a desperate rearing up of agency he left the flat – leaving behind his keys, knowing that there was no way back. Having spent a further day without food and shelter he was left with no other option than to panhandle in Vienna's biggest shopping street. Michael remembers how hard it was to sit down and to lift a coffee mug for the first time in his life to his shopping fellow citizens. Besides having strong feelings of shame he feared that someone out of this bypassing crowd might recognize him personally and thereby embarrass him even more. Both experiences, the humiliation of losing his place as well as of having to beg have burnt themselves into his psyche (Zechmeister 2008).

Similarly, Kathrin Hartmann (2012) portrays a woman, a physician by training, a mother of six children, who is forced to queue to get free food at a foodbank in a small German town after her husband had abandoned the formerly wealthy double-income family. Before queuing for the first time – the line of waiting people unfortunately sprawling deeply into a public street – she literally orbited the whole block three or more times, struggling with the decision to finally get involved with and rely on this charity service. Similar to Michael in our example above, one of her fears was that friends or neighbors could make her out in the midst of this desperate crowd. The experiences of both people portrayed here have resonated with what Stefan Selke (2013) has found in a survey in Germany of many households receiving social welfare and depending on services like foodbanks. As a result of over a hundred interviews he conducted, Selke reports that the decision whether to use this kind of service or not is deeply grueling and a powerful source of experiences of poverty-related shame and humiliation, also leading to conflicts between spouses and within families that weaken the people involved even more.

Our examples show people who were forced to cross the Rubicon from a rather non-overt, hidden – or, as we termed it, included – poverty to a socially visible form of neediness by their immediate distress. In Michael's case this meant an evident and radical transformation of his overall situation and the falling into excluded poverty.[9] In the second case the stressful step to expose her neediness publicly was risk-taking for the portrayed person in order to at least stabilize or possibly even improve the family's situation. In a sense one could argue that she traded one risk

gedauert, bis wir uns trauten anzuklopfen. Wer in seinem Leben nie betteln musste, hat auch nie erfahren, was für eine Reise die Seele durchmachen, was für steile Hänge sie erklimmen, in welch tiefe Abgründe sie stürzen, welche Stürme sie ertragen muss, bevor sie mit Gesten und Lippen die erste Bitte zu formen imstande ist".

[9] Michael's example gives hints of how such acting can also be seen as self-exclusion. Obviously, however, there are good arguments to assess his decision to leave the flat and his piles of debts not as a free choice but commanded rather by external circumstances.

against the other, but that would supposedly morally downplay how desperate and hopeless she must have been. As an asylum seeking refugee Dimitré Dinev was rather "swept away by the Rubicon" when leaving his home, and was "clambering out of the tide" when having his Rubicon experience.

Obviously the experience and circumstances of poverty give their ruthless limit to strategies of stigma-management and responses to shame. Furthermore such responses are overwhelmingly dictated by efforts to hide neediness and hence to efforts to save a minimum of nobility[10] and self-respect. The Rubicon-experience represents the collapse of such efforts. How can we translate this divide into our concept of poverty as humiliation of dignity?

10.6 Self-Respect and Privacy

If questions of visibility and poverty-related shame are to be crucial to the differentiation between different forms of poverty in affluent societies one should reflect on the relation between dignity and privacy.[11] We propose understanding included poverty as a status or circumstance (*Lebenslage*) in which individuals still can uphold crucial aspects of privacy: to have a secure and securing shelter where they can live a private life, enabling as much distance between fellow-citizens as one needs to uphold a basic self-respect and civic identity and oases of self-respect: having an address, and a home which represents independence and civic self-determination. More or less such an idea of privacy equates to what Walker et al. portrayed as the precondition of (successful) responses to poverty-related shame (food, shelter, adequate clothing). In contrast, absolutely excluded poverty means circumstances where individuals lack such a respected address and the possibilities of upholding important aspects of privacy (as well as a self-determined general distance) from their fellow-citizens and – an especially crucial point – from the public authorities and officialdom. Such a visibly deprived and exposed social position equates to a subhuman status, which precludes a dignified life by definition.

This is not to say that included poverty is by no means a violation of dignity, and that individuals inflicted by included (relative) poverty do not suffer from their situation in a way that threatens or even precludes self-respect, too. Part of their pain stems from their struggle to uphold the facade and clearly not all responses by far to poverty-related shame are productive or instrumental to overcome poverty but instead push them even deeper into poverty. (Beyond that, loneliness is a hard and common experience a lot of poor people suffer from.)

How then do *privacy* and *distance*, as the two proxies for socially invisible, hidden poverty that allows for holding up civic nobility in some way, and *self-respect*

[10] A term introduced to this discussion by Christian Neuhäuser; see his chapter in this volume.

[11] The German sociologist Sighard Neckel strongly advocates understanding infringed privacy as lying at the core of shame (Neckel 2009, 112).

relate to each other? We understand self-respect, in a similar way to Schaber and Neuhäuser, as a reflection of human autonomy and dignity.

By referring to a well-known typology of respect introduced by Stephen D. Hudson (1980)[12] we would like to add to this theorizing by distinguishing three types of self-respect: (i) institutional self-respect, (ii) obstacle self-respect and (iii) evaluative self-respect – an application prepared by Clemens Sedmak (2013, 30 ff) elsewhere.

(i) Self-regard can appear as *institutional self-respect.* Such self-respect reflects the special form of (institutional) respect a person has for all other people (and hence also for herself) and the respect she experiences from all others as an individual by virtue of their status as a human being. Thus institutional self-respect expresses a kind of "membership", a belonging to a community, in this case to the family of mankind. Each person represents mankind in her very unique way. Institutional respect entails respectful behavior based on human rights considerations, or the golden rule, or the moral imperative, or the like, and in such a way respects human dignity. Institutional self-respect is self-regard based on experiences of such respectful behavior and a respected position that allows – at least theoretically – one to understand oneself as a respected representative of humankind. To be treated in a way that does not live up to this ideal means to be treated as subhuman.

(ii) Self-regard can be connected to the idea of taking oneself seriously as an individual that can be an obstacle to actions or the will of other people. *Obstacle self-respect* means to see and respect oneself as a legitimate source of moral claims that have to be respected by others.

(iii) Self-respect (or self-esteem) can also be linked to the capability of self-assessment, the ability to realize and to value one's very own abilities, skills and achievements. One major impediment to such evaluative self-respect are conditions and experiences that hinder the proper development of an overall sense of one's abilities and achievements, such as poor and coercive working conditions (Sedmak 2012, 122ff).

We understand these types not as mutually exclusive but take – as Hudson suggested – *institutional* self-respect as a category that fully feeds into or corresponds to human dignity and hence can be seen as the crucial category for our aim, while *obstacle* self-respect alternatively expresses the norm of fundamental equality within the overall idea of dignity and *evaluative* self-respect expresses the idea of agency (which is especially important in the context of poverty alleviation).

[12] Hudson introduced four types of respect in order to prepare the ground for modern theories of respect-for-persons: (i) Evaluative-respect; (ii) Directive-respect; (iii) Institutional-respect; (iv) Obstacle-respect. According to his suggestions theories of respect-for-persons could focus on directive-respect and/or institutional respect with obstacle-respect supplementing them (Hudson 1980, 70).

How does this typology of self-respect fit into the attempts to portray poverty as a violation of dignity? And how does privacy/distance add to the understanding and theorizing of included and absolutely excluded poverty in affluent societies?

We propose understanding poverty as deprivation of institutional self-respect. Poverty humiliates human dignity because and insofar as it deprives individuals of such basic self-respect. On this basis we can understand the moral evil of poverty. Emotionally such (poverty-related) lack of institutional self-respect generally translates into poverty-related shame. Poverty-related shame goes along with and further solidifies the feeling of not being respected as an individual representative of humanity, i.e. living a normal life.

As we have seen, such shame is co-constructed, comprising of the individual (and "inner")-level of an evaluative component which takes the shape of self-accusation when not able to live up to the norm of independence and autarky. This explains a low level of self-worth and self-esteem, as Walker et al. proposed. We might call it a lack (or desperately low level) of evaluative self-respect. Moreover, poor people mostly lack even the possibility of developing an overall sense of one's abilities and achievements. Furthermore, lack of evaluative self-respect causes a lack of personal agency; it deprives the individual of the means and personal condition to stand up against her or his situation and against others. Thus, poverty deprives poor people of the possibilities and the ability to see and respect oneself as a legitimate source of moral claims that have to be respected by others. We termed this obstacle self-respect, which comes close to Neuhäuser's concept of self-respect on a social basis, the feeling of being a full and equally noble member of society.

Above we mentioned different forms of responses to poverty-related shame by poor people, the first being to try "to stay normal" by virtue of instrumental responses and the struggle for keeping up appearances, the second avoiding the normal by withdrawal from social life and psychological avoidance and disintegration, and the third resisting the normal by anger and resignation and reflecting blame and Othering (Walker et al. 2014, 120 ff). Our point is now that the difference between included and absolutely excluded poverty is the point where this whole typology of responses is not applicable anymore, because of a fundamental lack of privacy and the preconditions of normal social distance. It does not make sense to try to stay normal and to control your expenses and it does not work to keep up appearances if you are homeless and have to sleep rough. Withdrawal from social life is not up for discussion for a poor person like panhandling migrants depending on the charity of others to survive the next few days. Likewise, for a mother who has to queue at a food bank in order to manage to feed her family, blaming the homeless for her tragic situation does not provide a successful psychological strategy that contributes positively to her struggle for nobility.

In reverse, again following the described typology, to obtain a decent place to live, to have access to basic nutrition and adequate clothing, may put poor people in a condition where they can keep up appearances and maintain the struggle for normality. It also allows them to enjoy privacy and, somewhat tragically or at least paradoxically, at the same time also to withdraw from society and social obligations and hence opens a way to resist the normal by anger, resignation or blaming others for their bad living. Still, as in the case of withdrawal from society and subsequently suffering from loneliness and despair, such possibilities lead to harm and agony. However, such experiences are different from the experiences absolutely excluded poor people have.

Generally we conclude from that, that relative or included poverty is a deprivation of institutional self-respect at least in the form of a deprivation of obstacle self-respect.[13] We understand such poverty as a condition where people are not necessarily publicly stricken into "acts of survival". It is a condition in which people are struggling to be normal, to make instrumental responses, to keep up appearances – or to avoid or resist the normal if struggling to be normal is no option anymore.

Absolutely excluded poverty, in turn, is deprivation of basic goods (secured by effective social rights) in such a manner that people suffering from it are publicly stricken into acts of survival. In this way, absolutely excluded poverty is extensively embarrassing; it forces poor people to ongoing "self"-humiliation.[14]

We conclude that in affluent societies welfare state provision allows included people to uphold important dimensions of decent living even if it does not always, i. e. in the case of included relatively poor people, tackle all relevant dimensions. What distinguishes included poverty from absolutely excluded poverty is that the latter is a condition that forces people to self-humiliation. Included poverty is a (humiliating) part of normality, whilst absolutely excluded, i.e. extreme poverty, is the publicly visible abnormal. The former allows for some privacy and distance from fellow citizens, the latter makes a person a social alien who is forced into acts of survival and is absolutely dependent on the generosity of unknown Others. The former still means a humiliation of dignity, as we have seen above, especially because it deprives poor people of obstacle self-respect that, e.g. according to Peter Schaber's definition of dignity, is an inherent dimension of a good life. The latter is a deep and constant humiliation of dignity on the basis of total deprivation of institutional self-respect. Rough sleepers, migrant panhandlers or other most vulnerable groups have no reason to understand their general situation as independent, autonomous and fundamentally equal to their fellow citizens. Absolutely excluded poor people are the outcasts of our affluent societies.

It is important to add that not every included as well as not every absolutely excluded poor person does suffer from overall poverty-related shame. Walker et al. (2014, 85ff) reflect on conceiving poverty without shame. Backed by empirical data Juho Saari and Olli-Pekka Ryynänen (2015) have shown only recently that a considerable group of absolutely excluded people in Finland do not feel poverty-related shame vis-à-vis their social network. This is not to mean that they are not absolutely excluded poor or are not poor at all, but it depends on their internalized norms

[13] This comes close to what Neuhäuser theorizes in his chapter as lack of civic equality or nobility.

[14] The quotation marks express the proposition to understand such acting as not being one of free choice but rather enforced by the overall situation; hence, one should refrain from ideas of blaming the victim for the situation, as has been done constantly during the centuries by referring to such persons as "shameless".

whether a poor person is embarrassed by making his or her need public or not, and – of course – on the core values of the reference group (social network, neighbors etc.). Saari et al. found that younger people do feel less shame than older ones; people who have rather pessimistic expectations of their personal future have higher levels of shame compared to people who still hope for a transformation of their situation. Investigating into attitudes of recipients of social assistance in Germany, Klaus Dörre found that the ones who suffer most from the poverty stigma are those recipients of German social welfare (*Hartz-IV*) who fully share the aspirations assumed as positive by the labor market's "activation regime". The more they struggled to prove that they are not lazy, useless or unambitious the more they suffered from the (as they perceive them) personal setbacks, represented by years of unemployment, low-wages, short term occupations ("One-Euro-Jobs") etc. (Dörre 2013). The question of what this means for our research question leads us to consider our *desiderata of research*. Certainly further reasoning must address the questions of norms and values, questions of personal resilience and social pathologies at a societal level. Notwithstanding the outcome of such reasoning one fact seems to be clear: even if the individual "opts out" of the co-construction of poverty-related shame by free choice, resilient behavior or just another form of exclusion – what still remains disastrously in place is society's share in exclusion and humiliation: this is the poverty-stigma, deeply engraved in discourse, policies and bureaucratic procedures.

10.7 Concluding Remarks: The Paradoxes of (In-)visibility: Challenges to Poverty Alleviation

In this chapter we argue that poverty in affluent societies has two faces. The first can be portrayed as follows: there are people stricken by poverty who have access to different sorts of poverty alleviation measures, protected by social rights. We term this included poverty. Despite alleviation, such a state of affairs represents a humiliation of dignity because they are deprived of the basis of self-respect; in most cases people afflicted by included poverty are suffering from different hardships and from poverty-related shame.

Besides that there is a second face of poverty we termed absolutely excluded poverty, which means severe poverty that is frequently excluded from common poverty statistics and consequently also from welfare state measures which can be legally claimed. Consequently people stricken by such severe forms of poverty are without sufficient help and assistance to keep up an appearance of normality. In other words, they lack the means to hide their neediness and despair. In contrast, people stricken by absolutely excluded poverty have to struggle for survival in public, exactly because they are dependent on the generosity of others. People suffering from such forms of poverty are forced to actively reveal their neediness – which takes the form of public self-degradation.

The crucial difference between included and absolutely excluded poverty is that the latter lacks privacy as the last resort or island of self-respect. People suffering from absolutely excluded poverty lack the means to uphold an appearance of normality. Thus they are socially visible. Such people cannot uphold a civic identity but are members of outcast groups, or in the language of (German) sociology *Sozialtypen* – the homeless, beggars, drug addicts, and lately: refugees. As outcasts they lack the possibility to "dive into the masses" and become invisible as individuals but instead they stay visible. In other words they are deprived of the means to maintain a civic distance from their fellow citizens – which comes close to the most severe forms of humiliation like violence or torture, maybe exactly because its goes without a visible perpetrator.

This is not to say that people suffering from included poverty always suffer less, but their circumstances are different. At least, such people have some chance to keep up appearances and maintain their struggle for self-respect. Clearly, to have to struggle at all, for reasons of poverty, already opens a path for humiliation of dignity. The most obvious consequence of this humiliating effect of poverty may be a general lack of obstacle self-respect that hinders poverty-stricken people from feeling equally noble with the rest of their neighbors or other fellow citizens. Additionally, of course, there is the far-reaching lack of evaluative self-respect that rests on achievements in life and their recognition by others. Both have corrosive effects on institutional self-respect, and make poverty stricken people feel dependent on others, with low self-esteem and without many reasons and agency to stand up against others. Suffering from poverty-related shame rather they withdraw from social contacts. A lot of included poor people suffer from loneliness and despair.

We can characterize political, public and academic interest in those two groups of poverty-stricken people as somewhat paradoxical: included poor people are visible in social statistics, within the poverty-bureaucracy and – rarely – in the media discourse, mostly in the form of numbers and statistics, but are (still) invisible in public. Their poverty-related shame is (and is often taken as) a private problem. On the contrary, absolutely excluded poor people are most visible in public, but are invisible in the statistics (not least because of the initially described 'methodology-trap'), and consequently, in welfare state measures of poverty alleviation. They are invisible also in the political discourse that frames the topic of poverty or in the media, where they are mostly neglected as poor people who witness a humiliation of dignity but are, if at all, mostly portrayed as outcasts.

This paradox of the (in-)visibility of poverty in affluent societies clearly challenges the practice of poverty alleviation and its theoretical underpinning. If our reconstruction and conceptualization of included and absolutely excluded poverty is to the point then three crucial points follow from that.

Firstly, we have to reconstruct our concepts of poverty "from below", in order to overcome the heuristic invisibility of the most vulnerable. Secondly, this task needs to be accompanied by a merging of so far separated public and political discourses that overcomes the public labelling of outcast groups and their exclusion from discourses on poverty. Thirdly, and of utmost importance, we have to consider the points of entry of humiliating practices (in vocabulary, structures and acting) in poverty alleviation efforts, that constitute and underline the stigma of poverty. We would win most if we could considerably mitigate the stigma of poverty.

References

Alkire, Sabina. 2002. *Valuing freedoms. Sen's capability approach and poverty reduction*. Oxford: Oxford University Press.

Alkire, Sabina, and Maria Emma Santos. 2013. A multidimensional approach: Poverty measurement & beyond. *Social Indicators Research* 112(2): 239–257. doi:10.1007/s11205-013-0257-3.

Bradshaw, Jonathan, and Emese Mayhew. 2011. The measurement of extreme poverty in the European Union. European Commission, Directorate-General for Employment, Social Affairs and Inclusion.

Chase, Elaine, and Grace Bantebya-Kyomuhendo. 2015a. *Poverty and shame: Global experiences*, Oxford: Oxford University Press.

Chase, Elaine, and Grace Bantebya-Kyomuhendo. 2015b. Introduction. In *Poverty and shame: Global experiences*, ed. Elaine Chase and Grace Bantebya-Kyomuhendo, 1–18. Oxford: Oxford University Press.

Chase, Elaine, and Robert Walker. 2012. The co-construction of shame in the context of poverty: Beyond a threat to the social bond. *Sociology* 47(4): 739–754. doi:10.1177/0038038512453796.

Cimadamore, Alberto D., and Lynda Lange. 2015. The Global poverty consensus report. Academics Stand Against Poverty (ASAP) & Comparative Research Programme on Poverty (CROP).

Cruz, Mario, James Foster, Bryce Quillin, and Philip Schellekens. 2015. Ending extreme poverty and sharing prosperity: Progress and policies. Policy Research Note 15/03. Washington: Development Economics World Bank Group.

Dinev, Dimitré. 2010. *Barmherzigkeit. Unruhe bewahren*. St. Pölten: Residenz.

Dörre, Klaus. 2013. Soziale Wirkungen strenger Zumutbarkeit. Erwerbsorientierung im Zeitverlauf. In *Bewährungsproben für die Unterschicht? Soziale Folgen aktivierender Arbeitsmarktpolitik*, International Labour Studies = Internationale Arbeitsstudien, vol. 3, ed. Klaus Dörre, Karin Scherschel, and Melanie Booth, 257–286. Frankfurt: Campus Verlag.

Gaisbauer, Helmut P., and Clemens Sedmak. 2014. Neglected futures. Considering overlooked poverty in Europe. *European Journal of Futures Research* 2(57): 1–8. doi:10.1007/s40309-014-0057-2.

Hartmann, Kathrin. 2012. *Wir müssen leider draussen bleiben: Die neue Armut in der Konsumgesellschaft*. München: Blessing Verlag.

Hudson, Stephen D. 1980. The nature of respect. *Social Theory and Practice* 6: 69–90.

Mack, Elke, Michael Schramm, Stephan Klasen, and Thomas Pogge (eds.). 2009. *Absolute poverty and global justice: Empirical data, moral theories, initiatives*. Farnham: Ashgate.

Madden, David. 2000. Relative or absolute poverty lines. A new approach. *Review of Income and Wealth* 46(2): 181–199. doi:10.1111/j.1475-4991.2000.tb00954.x.

Margalit, Avishai. 1998. *The decent society*. Cambridge/London: Harvard University Press.

Neckel, Sighard. 2009. Soziologie der Scham. In *Scham*, ed. Alfred Schäfer and Christiane Thompson, 103–118. Paderborn: Ferdinand Schöningh.

Neuhäuser, Christian. 2010. Zwei Formen der Entwürdigung: Relative und absolute Armut. *Archiv für Rechts- und Sozialphilosophie* 96(4): 542–556.

Neuhäuser, Christian, and Julia Müller. 2011. Relative poverty. In *Humiliation, degradation, dehumanization: Human dignity violated*, ed. Paulus Kaufmann, Hannes Kuch, Christian Neuhäuser, and Elaine Webster, 159–172. Dordrecht: Springer.

Nicaise, Idesbald, and Ingrid Schockaert. 2014. The hard-to-reach among the poor in Europe: Lessons from Eurostat's EU-SILC survey in Belgium. In *Hard-to-survey populations*, ed.

Roger Tourangeau, Brad Edwards, Timothy P. Johnson, Krik M. Wolter, and Nancy Bates, 1246–1279. Cambridge: Cambridge University Press.

Notten, Geranda, and Chris De Neubourg. 2011. Monitoring absolute and relative poverty: 'Not Enough' is not the same as 'Much Less'. *Review of Income and Wealth* 57(June): 247–269. doi:10.1111/j.1475-4991.2011.00443.x.

Øyen, Else. 2009. The paradox of poverty research: Why is extreme poverty not in focus? In *Absolute poverty and global justice: Empirical data, moral theories, initiatives*, ed. Elke Mack, Michael Schramm, Stephan Klasen, and Thomas Pogge, 259–271. Farnham: Ashgate.

Rawls, John. 1971. *A theory of justice*. Cambridge, MA: Cambridge University Press.

Saari, Juho, and Olli-Pekka Ryynänen. 2015. *Always look on the dark side of the life – The worst off in the best country in the world. Paper given at the Conference Absolute Poverty in Europe, August 28/29*. Salzburg: Centre for Ethics and Poverty Research.

Sartre, Jean-Paul. 1978. *Being and nothingness: A phenomenological essay on ontology*. New York: Pocket Books.

Schaber, Peter. 2011. Absolute poverty. In *Humiliation, degradation, dehumanization: Human dignity violated*, ed. Paulus Kaufmann, Hannes Kuch, Christian Neuhäuser, and Elaine Webster, 151–158. Dordrecht: Springer.

Schockaert, Ingrid, Ann Morrissens, Sebastiano Cincinnato, and Idesbald Nicaise. 2012. *Poverty between the cracks*. Brussels: Complements and Corrections to EU-SILC for Hidden Groups of Poor People. http://www.combatpoverty.be/SILC-CUT_sam%20-%20EN.pdf. Accessed 15 Oct 2015.

Schweiger, Gottfried. 2013. Absolute und relative Kritik der Armut. *Zeitschrift für Philosophische Forschung* 67(2): 263–286. doi:10.3196/004433013806915715.

Sedmak, Clemens. 2012. Working poor: Poorly functioning societies? In *Arm trotz Erwerbstätigkeit. Working poor in Österreich*, ed. Walter J. Pfeil and Clemens Sedmak, 115–138. Vienna: ÖGB-Verlag.

Sedmak, Clemens. 2013. *Mensch bleiben im Krankenhaus: zwischen Alltag und Ausnahmesituation*. Wien: Styria Premium.

Selke, Stefan. 2013. *Schamland: Die Armut mitten unter uns*. Berlin: Econ.

Sell, Stefan. 2002. Armutsforschung und Armutsberichtberichterstattung aus Sicht einer lebenslagenorientierten Sozialpolitik. In *Armut als Herausforderung: Bestandsaufnahme und Perspektiven der Armutsforschung und Armutsberichterstattung*, 11–42. Berlin: Duncker & Humblot.

Sen, Amartya. 1983. Poor, relatively speaking. *Oxford Economic Papers* 35(2): 153–169.

Sepúlveda, Carmona Magdalena. 2012. *The guiding principles on extreme poverty and human rights*. New York: Human Rights Council of the General Assembly of the United Nations. http://daccess-dds-ny.un.org/doc/UNDOC/GEN/G12/154/60/PDF/G1215460.pdf?OpenElement. Accessed 5 Oct 2015.

Shaw, Beverley. 1988. Poverty: Absolute or relative? *Journal of Applied Philosophy* 5(1): 27–36. doi:10.1111/j.1468-5930.1988.tb00226.x.

United Nations. 2012. Guiding principles on extreme poverty and human rights. New York: United Nations. http://www.ohchr.org/Documents/Publications/OHCHR_ExtremePovertyandHumanRights_EN.pdf. Accessed 5 Oct 2015.

Walker, Robert, Grace Bantebya Kyomuhendo, Elaine Chase, Sohail Choudhry, Erika K. Gubrium, Nicola Jo Yongmie, Ivar LøDemel, et al. 2013. Poverty in global perspective: Is shame a common denominator? *Journal of Social Policy* 42(02): 215–233. doi:10.1017/S0047279412000979.

Walker, Robert, Grace Bantebya-Kyomuhendo, Elaine Chase, Sohail Choudhry, Erika K. Gubrium, Ivar Lødemel, Yongmie N. Jo, et al. 2014. *The shame of poverty*, Oxford: Oxford University Press.

Zechmeister, Alexander. 2008. *Weit Unten – Einmal Straße und Zurück*. Vienna.

Chapter 11
Exclusion from Healthcare in Spain: The Responsibility for Omission of Due Care

Rosana Triviño, David Rodríguez-Arias, and Txetxu Ausín

Abstract For almost 30 years, until 2012, Spain had benefitted from a public healthcare system with universal coverage. That year, a new law denied ordinary healthcare for undocumented adult migrants. This law is in blunt contradiction to the idea that healthcare is a fundamental human right. We argue in this chapter that not only a deep and flagrant injustice results from that law, but also an ineffective health system, because important population groups remain out of health control, treatment and prevention, and because denying healthcare to undocumented migrants has not been translated into significant savings. This situation has provoked a strong backlash, from the Spanish society at large and, in particular, among health professionals who have decided to become conscientious objectors against the governmental request to withdraw healthcare from undocumented migrants. Interestingly, in this case, claims of conscience are not associated with personal interest or convictions—as they usually are—but rather with an ethical decision by professionals to take care of their patients, regardless of their administrative status. Promoting social justice is a foundational purpose of welfare states. When they fail in this objective, conscientious objection may become an instrument of last resort to uphold people's rights.

This work has been sponsored by the Spanish Ministry of Economy and Competitiveness through its research projects *KONTUZ!* (FFI2014-53926-R, www.kontuz.weebly.com), *Bioethics and Citizenship* (FFI-2012-32827, www.bioeticayciudadania.weebly.com), and *The discourse of biorights. Philosophical and legal foundations, features and implementation* (DER2014-52811-P).

R. Triviño (✉)
Facultad de Dereito (Filosofía do Dereito), Universidade da Coruña,
Campus de Elviña, s/n, 15071 A Coruña, Spain
e-mail: rosanatrivino@yahoo.es; rosana.trivino@udc.es

D. Rodríguez-Arias
Departamento de Filosofía I, Facultad de Filosofía, Universidad de Granada,
Edificio de la Facultad de Psicología, Campus Universitario de Cartuja s/n, 18071 Granada, Spain
e-mail: dra@ugr.es

T. Ausín
CCHS, CSIC, Institute of Philosophy, Albasanz 26-28, 28037 Madrid, Spain
e-mail: txetxu.ausin@cchs.csic.es

H.P. Gaisbauer et al. (eds.), *Ethical Issues in Poverty Alleviation*, Studies in Global Justice 14, DOI 10.1007/978-3-319-41430-0_11

Keywords Spain • Public healthcare system • Law • Migrants • Social justice

11.1 Introduction

One of the greatest achievements of democracy in Spain has been the creation and consolidation of a public healthcare system that implemented the right to health protection enshrined in the 1978 Spanish Constitution (Art. 43). Its subsequent legislative development[1] progressively secured the right to healthcare for all inhabitants residing in the country, without exception.[2] Thanks to this formulation, the Spanish National Health System has significantly contributed to the achievement of high levels of social cohesion.

Such a system has been possible mainly because the full funding of the healthcare system came under the control of General State Budgets, meaning that healthcare services were decoupled from individual contributions to Social Security. The right to health protection was thus configured as a right of citizenship. The previous model, during Franco's dictatorship, of 'insured' and 'beneficiaries'—a system which left the most vulnerable populations in the hands of charities[3]—was thus superseded.

However, this situation has changed dramatically since the commencement, in 2012, of a Decree: the *Real Decreto-ley 16/2012, de medidas urgentes para garantizar la sostenibilidad del Sistema Nacional de Salud y mejorar la calidad y seguridad de sus prestaciones* [Law by Royal Decree16/2012, *on urgent measures to ensure the sustainability of the National Healthcare System and enhance the quality and safety of its services*], hereinafter RDL16, hastily approved after a brief debate in Congress and thanks to the parliamentary majority of the conservative *Partido Popular* (Popular Party). According to this law, undocumented migrants will not be covered by the public healthcare system, free of charge, unless they are minors, pregnant women, are in an emergency situation, or have contagious diseases.[4]

While we focus on the migrant population in this work, it is important to note that there are also other population groups with Spanish nationality who have been excluded from the healthcare system, such as those who have resided more than 3 months abroad or have been long-term unemployed. Interestingly, several regions in

[1] Basically, *Ley General de Sanidad* (1986), *Ley de Cohesión y Calidad del Sistema Nacional de Salud* (2003) and *Ley General de Salud Pública* (2011).

[2] Regarding migrant people, the *Ley Orgánica 4/2000, de 11 de enero, sobre derechos y libertades de los extranjeros residentes en España y su integración social*, included in its articles 3 and 12 migrants' right to health protection under the same conditions as Spaniards.

[3] In relation to the evolution and success of healthcare in Spain, see: C. Muntaner et al. 2012.

[4] Despite the exceptions that RDL16 includes, it is alarming that in practice, there are abundant cases in which adequate assistance to pregnant women, children or people in emergency situations is not being provided. Since 2012, in the region of Valencia alone, 1,252 cases have been detected in which healthcare access has been illegally denied (ODUSALUD 2015, 5).

Spain, such as Andalucía, Valencia, País Vasco, Navarra and Baleares have taken different measures to counteract the effect of RDL16, which generates in turn significant inequalities within the country with respect to the situation of the affected population, both migrants and nationals (Delgado del Rincón 2014, 221–228; ABC.es 2015).

In March of 2015, 9 months before the Presidential Elections, the Popular Party announced, through the Health Minister, Alfonso Alonso, the government's intention to provide a renewable 'special card' so that migrants could be treated for free in primary care by a general practitioner. The government based its new decision on "public health reasons", "in order to not saturate emergency services", and justified it by claiming that it is "more sensible and reasonable" (Rejón 2015). At the end of August of 2015, the requirements proposed for undocumented migrants to acquire their special card were being enrolled in a specific register and registered at the Town Hall for a minimum of 6 months. Importantly, this new measure is not a rule, but a recommendation, since healthcare services are the responsibility of each of Spanish region, which could bypass the government suggestion, provided they do not conflict with the European framework (Sevillano 2015c).

The modifications introduced by RDL16 have involved not only a serious restriction of undocumented population's access to healthcare, but also a radical paradigm shift in the essence of the Spanish health system, a model originally based on the pillars of solidarity, equity and accessibility (Rodríguez et al. 1999). In practice, the law implies that healthcare is no longer public, universal and free for all residents of the country, but only for those who are insured (and their dependents or beneficiaries). Under the heading of an alleged financial unsustainability, the law advocates for substantial changes in both the consideration of the recipients and the provision of benefits (Simón Lorda 2014, 111–112) since many people have no choice but to pay for certain private health services not covered by the public service.

Some have argued that that RDL16 is based on false premises and that hidden motivations can be identified to enact measures whose consequences are of concern not only for undocumented migrants, but for the Spanish society at large.

Important reactions against the law have emerged. Various government and non-governmental institutions have clearly spoken out against the measures it involves. Moreover, a professional movement among healthcare professionals has emerged from the enrooted belief that healthcare is a positive right and providing it when possible, without discrimination, a professional duty. Those professionals have considered conscientious objection as a way to defend such ethical convictions.

The legislation issued in Spain regarding health coverage might be in blunt contradiction to healthcare as a fundamental human right enshrined in article 25 of the 1948 Universal Declaration of Human Rights, further developed by the 1966 International Covenant on Economic, Social and Cultural Rights (art. 12), which Spain has signed and ratified without reservations. That claim is supported by the belief that healthcare is a minimum requirement for any person in order to attain sufficient control of her capacities and abilities, which will ensure full use of her autonomy. The duty to protect and care for human beings' health is a logical corollary to the basic and fundamental right to life, as there is no right to life without the availability of a reasonable standard of health and wellbeing, that depends—at least in a significant proportion—on the provision of social services and medical care.

Throughout this work we intend to reflect on several key issues. In the first part, we will expose the reasons why we think that RDL16 indeed violates the right to healthcare and represents a setback in one of the major Spanish social achievements. To do this, inconsistencies, prejudices and undesirable consequences associated with the measures proposed in the law will be identified. In the second part, we consider that exclusion from healthcare in Spain involves the nonfeasance of public authorities and causes evident harmful effects on individuals, groups, and the society in general. To the extent that it foreseeably creates negative outcomes and avoidable loss of life, we will argue that the law involves a moral and legal responsibility related to an undue inaction. Finally, we will comment on the ethical implications for healthcare professionals and their recourse to conscientious objection in response to the regulation concerning the denial of services to undocumented migrants.

11.2 Truths and Lies About Migrants and Healthcare

Despite of the right to health protection being considered a human right by the United Nations and being included in many national constitutions around the world, restricting access to healthcare services has been frequently used by European countries as a measure to avoid the presence of undocumented migrants in their territories (HUMA Network 2010, 3). In the case of Spain, several institutions have alerted the government that the healthcare reform violates international human rights agreements, as well as the European Social Charter. Both Magdalena Sepúlveda, Special Rapporteur of the United Nations, and the European Committee on Social Rights, have warned that the crisis cannot serve as a pretext for restriction or denial of access to healthcare. She and the Committee have underlined that the Spanish Constitution acknowledges access to healthcare as a positive duty, including obligations to migrants, regardless of their legal status, and the fact that we must respect this criterion which was also established by the Council of Europe (Sevillano 2014). Responding to Sepúlveda, the Spanish government has argued that RDL16 is not discriminatory, since it deals with the legality of residence in the country and not with national origin. However, as the Special Rapporteur has noticed, "this argument reflects a misperception of the principle of non-discrimination" (Sevillano 2014), which constitutes a basic principle of human rights that cannot be ignored by appealing to economic pressures.

Besides the Spanish government's lack of compliance with its ethical and constitutional commitments on human rights, the economic arguments used in support of the law can also not be taken very seriously. Budget constraints and austerity measures deployed to justify healthcare restrictions have not been supported by data demonstrating their actual effectiveness (Olías 2014) nor by a detailed analysis of the indirect costs and bad consequences that could result and, in fact, have resulted from them.[5]

The Spanish government's discriminatory policies might have been tolerated by many citizens because they perceive undocumented migrants as intolerable free riders. However, such a picture is misleading to the extent that it is weakly supported by prejudices and false assumptions about migrants' motivations and behavior, and their use of the national healthcare services. First, not all migrants are alike in their movement. As Thomas Nail has noted:

> For some [migrants], movement offers opportunity, recreation, and profit with only a temporary expulsion. For others, movement is dangerous and constrained, and their social expulsions are much more severe and permanent. Today, most people fall somewhere on this migratory spectrum between the two poles of 'inconvenience' and 'incapacitation'. But what all migrants on this spectrum share, at some point, is the experience that their movement results in a certain degree of expulsion from their territorial, political, juridical, or economic status. Even if the end result of migration is a relative increase in money, power, or enjoyment, the process of migration itself almost always involves an insecurity of some kind and duration: the removal of territorial ownership or access, the loss of the political right to vote or to receive social welfare, the loss of legal status to work or drive, or the financial loss associated with transportation or change in residence. (Nail 2015, 2)

Additionally, healthcare is not among the main motivations that drive migrants to choose a country, or to remain there. According to a study by *Médicos del Mundo*, only 6 % of undocumented migrants argued health reasons for their choice of destination. Of that 6 %, 15.7 % suffered from chronic health problem that they knew before migrating, mostly being symptomatic complaints without accurate diagnosis or common diseases (Médicos del Mundo 2009, 9). In other words, less than 1 % of all undocumented migrants may travel as a form of health tourism.

Second, it is important to keep in mind that the Spanish healthcare system is not financed through Social Security contributions, but with direct taxes—whose distribution is determined in the State Budget—and also indirect taxes (VAT, taxes on alcohol, tobacco and fuels, for example). This means that nationals *and* migrants alike, including those who are undocumented, support the national healthcare cost. In fact, it has been shown that the tax contribution of migrants is greater than the social spending that they may cause (Moreno y Bruquetas 2011). If this is correct, it might turn out that, among all the individuals who live in Spain and contribute economically to the maintenance of a highly respected healthcare system, some of them are excluded from its benefits.[6]

[5] Since RDL16 came into force, several cases have been reported of health services neglecting and discriminating against patients with curable diseases, such as tuberculosis, including a few cases resulting in the death of the patient directly linked to exclusion. Several professional institutions and NGOs are collecting evidence to denounce the situation and defend migrants. In this regard, see, for example: ODUSALUD 2012–2015; No a la Exclusión Sanitaria-Cantabria 2012–2015; Amnesty International 2013; Médicos del Mundo 2014; Yo Sí Sanidad Universal 2014.

[6] Such unfair imbalance between what migrants give to the Spanish healthcare system and what they receive from it is particularly notorious in the domain of organ transplantation: while undocumented migrants can—and often are—organ donors, they cannot legally be recipients.

Third, there is no conclusive data proving that the healthcare restriction to undocumented migrants has resulted or could eventually result in significant savings. This is for two main reasons. On the one hand, the number of undocumented migrants in Spain may be smaller than usually thought (González and Miyar 2011, 46); on the other hand, migrants rarely seek medical care, contrary to the widespread perception among some citizens and politicians (Moreno y Bruquetas 2011). The latter is due to various factors, including migrants' age and general good health—it generally covers a young population—, the lack of information and time, cultural and language barriers, and the fear of being discovered and deported if they attend a medical facility. The living conditions of this population make it such that using healthcare services is usually not among their priorities. This has been demonstrated by numerous studies (Gimeno-Feliu et al. 2009; Hernando et al. 2009; Regidor et al. 2009; Calderón-Larrañaga et al. 2011; Moreno y Bruquetas 2011), which significantly differ from the estimates made by the Ministry of Health.[7]

Fourth, there is evidence suggesting that denial of primary care to migrants may be having backlash effects on the Spanish economy. Neglected patients suffering from treatable diseases, e.g. mild infections, often evolve into emergency cases requiring hospitalization. It has been repeatedly shown that the use of hospital emergency services is more expensive than ordinary services.[8] As mentioned before, the government is currently considering providing primary healthcare to undocumented migrants so as to "not saturate the emergency services", among other reasons (Rejón 2015). This recent economic proposal, depicted by some as "electioneering",[9] leaves many unresolved issues, for instance, whether general practitioners may request complementary tests and specialized diagnosis and treatments (Médicos del Mundo 2015; Sevillano 2015a). Otherwise, migrants would be forced again to use emergency rooms to access to this kind of services. Problems like this make us suspect that the new measure is insufficient to offset the deficits caused by RDL16.

Likewise, it can be argued that the systematic questioning of the healthcare sustainability of the system is based on inaccurate arguments. The cost of the Spanish health system in relation to its GDP remains among the lowest in the OECD countries (OECD 2015). At the same time, the clinical outcomes are comparable to those of more advanced countries (Beltrán et al. 2009, 5), which would mean that the

[7] Previous Ministry of Health, Ana Mato, estimated that health costs caused by undocumented migrants amounted to 500 million euros (Prats 2012).

[8] About the cost of the healthcare exclusion of irregular migrants, see the recent information from the European Union Agency for Fundamental Rights (FRA 2015). As a sample, the cost of a general emergency in Madrid is 180 euros compared to 39 euros of a primary care consultation without complementary tests, or 57 euros in the event that this consultation includes additional tests. Data from *Orden 629/2009, de 31 de agosto, de la Consejería de Sanidad, por la que se fijan los precios públicos por la prestación de los servicios y actividades de naturaleza sanitaria de la red de centros de la Comunidad de Madrid.*

http://www.madrid.org/wleg/servlet/Servidor?opcion=VerHtml&nmnorma=5958&cdestado=P. Accessed 12 July 2016.

[9] This measure was announced on the 31st of March, 2015, only 2 months before of the elections in several regions in Spain. See Sevillano 2015b.

system scores high in efficiency. A common conclusion of the 'unsustainability argument' attributes the responsibility for the Spanish accumulated debt to the healthcare system itself, as if it was a particular problem of this kind of public services. This sort of reasoning obviates many factors, including the disproportionate investment in unnecessary equipment and infrastructures with populist purposes (e.g. inappropriately huge hospitals in relatively unpopulated regions),[10] the lack of health impact assessments, and the non-democratic political framework where the reforms leading to privatization have been undertaken (Moreno 2013).

Finally, the Spanish government has frequently mentioned the need for a European convergence in this area to justify its proposed healthcare access restrictions (Europa Press 2014). This argument is also false for several reasons: first, the regulation and financing of healthcare is a national responsibility, not a decision to be adopted by the organs of the European Union. Second, healthcare exclusion of migrants does not occur in other surrounding countries such as Portugal, France, Italy or Belgium. The Agency for Fundamental Rights of the European Union has declared that "excluding migrants in an irregular situation from healthcare endangers their lives and well-being, increases the cost of future emergency treatment and can also potentially pose a health risk to the wider community" (FRA 2011, 7). Additionally, the Fundamental Rights Agency notes that RDL16 violates international obligations as the *International Covenant on Economic, Social and Cultural Rights*, which commits signatory States to protect and respect the right to healthcare without discrimination and without regression. The Committee on Economic, Social and Cultural Rights of the United Nations also expressed its concern about the Spanish law before it came into force, recommending that healthcare reform should not limit the access to healthcare for people living in a State, regardless of their administrative status (CESCR 2012).

The reasons expounded above show that the measures taken by the Spanish government do not follow from available evidence suggesting reasonable hope for actual benefits to Spanish society, but from the hardly justifiable assumption that citizenship and residence status determine people's access to and enjoyment of human rights.

This being said, the detected inconsistencies of the adduced arguments in support of recent healthcare restrictions leaves intact some real challenges the Spanish national health system faces, including its disproportionate spending on unnecessary infrastructures, the provision of drugs with little therapeutic value, the use of advanced technologies that may not be satisfactory in terms of cost-benefits, the excessive medicalization of Spanish society, or the performing of certain preventive activities with high costs and controversial utility (Rey del Castillo 2011, 27–59; Simón Lorda 2014, 114–116). Therefore, our point here is not so much intended to deny the appropriateness of reforms to address these and other inefficiencies that actually affect the system, but to draw attention to the limited real savings recent

[10] Some authors have even identified a 'healthcare bubble' (Beltrán et al. 2009, 5; Puig Junoy 2011).

reforms have achieved at the expense of undocumented migrants' right to healthcare.[11]

11.3 Real Consequences

The arguments just developed reflect the view that RDL16 unjustifiably fosters the segregation of a particular group of the population whose access to healthcare services is denied due to their administrative situation. We would like to highlight now a number of negative consequences that follow at different levels from such policy:

1. The effectiveness of the public health policies is reduced, since part of the population is excluded from the conventional health system. For example, chronic infectious diseases, such as tuberculosis or HIV, could remain undetected and certain controlled viruses could become resistant without treatment. This problem has been prognosticated by the Special Rapporteur of the UN, who declared that the law not only violates the human rights of the affected individuals, but also involves an increased risk for public health (Sevillano 2014).
2. The proliferation of cheating practices, such as sharing the same healthcare card among different users. In those cases, the information from medical records would cease to be useful, and could even become dangerous for patients, who could receive inadequate interventions (García Pedraz 2012). In this sense, it is not difficult to imagine the explosive mix of the medical history of a person with low levels of glucose 'used' by a diabetic person, for example, or the wrong prescription of an antibiotic to a person allergic to such medication.
3. As mentioned before, the decrease in the medical efficacy in terms of health and resources if migrants are not allowed to use primary and specialized healthcare following the usual channels, with the resulting increase in costs due to the use of emergency services. It seems that this risk has been already acknowledged by the government, which pretends to avoid the overuse of emergencies with a new card for migrant people that hypothetically would facilitate their access to primary healthcare (Rejón 2015).
4. The shift of the central and regional governments' responsibilities to NGOs in order to mitigate the lack of protection generated (de Benito 2012). This deviation would require a great increase of NGOs incomes and would imply, in practice, the replacement of duties that belong to the State, and should arguably remain its duty, one of the risks being the construction of a parallel system of care based on supererogatory charity, rather than mandatory respect for patients' rights. In practice, it is the dismantling of the Social State and a dereliction (by

[11] Several regions have established legal ways to circumvent the state mandate and to continue providing healthcare to this population (Delgado del Rincón 2014, 221–228). As a result, these differences among Spanish regions introduce additional elements of inequality in the public healthcare system.

undue inaction) on the part of public authorities that has significant adverse effects on the welfare of the population.

5. The increasing vulnerability of the most disadvantaged groups within an already vulnerable population, such as undocumented migrant women in situations of abuse, or sexual slavery, since the restriction of access to primary healthcare makes the detection of that kind of unjust situation even more difficult (Lema 2013, 109–110).
6. The reinforcement of a xenophobic culture and racist attitudes amongst the population, since the objective of the law is to guarantee the sustainability of the healthcare system avoiding overburdening that undocumented migrants allegedly provoke—according to mythical but seemingly widespread beliefs.

11.4 Denying Healthcare as a Positive Right

A report emitted by the *European Committee on Social Rights* in 2014 found the Spanish Decree to be regressive (ECSR 2014), following various similar declarations made by other international and European human rights bodies. The Committee reminded the Spanish government that "states have positive obligations in terms of access to healthcare for migrants, whatever their residence status" (ECSR 2014, 13). Article 11 of the European Charter obliges states to ensure universal access to healthcare, that is to say that the health system must be accessible to all of the population without discrimination of any kind.

The Spanish government has consistently ignored the directives and recommendations made by international agencies in this area. Since the healthcare reform was passed, various international human rights protection agencies have underlined that it contravenes international standards with regard to human rights and have consequently called on Spain to modify RDL16 so as to guarantee access to healthcare for all people without discrimination. In May 2012 the *United Nations Committee on Economic, Social and Cultural Rights*, in addressing the reform, called on the state to ensure access to health services for all persons residing in its territory, regardless of their administrative situation, so as to comply with the principle of universality in the provision of health services (CESCR 2012). In June 2013, the *United Nations Special Rapporteur on Contemporary Forms of Racism, Racial Discrimination, Xenophobia and Related Intolerance* recommended that the health reform measures adopted in the context of the economic crisis be revised so as to guarantee access to healthcare among migrants, regardless of their migratory status (HRC 2013). In December 2013, the *European Commissioner on Human Rights*, in a report on the impact of austerity measures and reforms on human rights in Europe, reminded states that periods of financial difficulty, such as those currently being experienced by Spain and other European states, are not emergency situations that automatically entail the restriction of social and economic rights and the deterioration of the situation of socially vulnerable groups (COE 2013). Instead, they should be seen as opportunities to adjust national human rights protection systems and to improve the efficiency of national social security and social protection systems (COE 2013).

The economic crisis must not serve as a pretext to restrict or deny access to healthcare in a way that affects the very essence of this right. The *European Committee on Social Rights* reiterates that governments are obliged to adopt all necessary measures to ensure that the rights set out in the Charter are effectively guaranteed during the crisis, particularly given that people need this protection even more in such times (ECSR 2014). In the same vein, the Committee reaffirms what has already been established by the supervisory bodies of both United Nations and European human rights treaties: contexts of economic crisis do not reduce the human rights obligations of a state and governments must analyze the impact of measures planned in response to a crisis, in particular with respect to the most vulnerable groups, in consultation with pertinent organizations. Furthermore, the *United Nations High Commissioner for Human Rights* reminded all states party to the *International Covenant on Economic, Social and Cultural Rights* that austerity policies and other measures adopted by states in times of economic crisis must comply with obligations derived from the Covenant: any measure that could impede the progressive realization of economic, social and cultural rights must be temporary and limited to the period of the crisis; it must be strictly necessary and proportionate; the measure cannot be discriminatory and must take into account all possible alternatives, including fiscal policy measures, to guarantee the necessary services to alleviate inequities that may arise in times of crisis (HCHR 2013).

11.5 Care Duties, Omissions and Responsibility

As essentially social beings, we humans are fragile and dependent on what is outside ourselves—others, institutions and sustained and sustainable environments—. Vulnerability acquires for us a social role (not a mere contingency or a subjective disposition) and hence the positive social obligations arise to minimize instability and its differential distribution, to demand basic support (food, shelter, work, healthcare, education, mobility, expression) and to reduce avoidable damage (Butler 2006).

We are a social species, with reciprocal links (rights and duties), built on the interdependence (Mackenzie and Stoljar 2000; Aramayo and Ausín 2008); not a group of solitary individuals whose mutual obligations are limited to not invading other people's space. Care-related obligations by the (social) state come into play here, as in the case of healthcare systems. These can be characterized as 'due cares' (due actions) because the action is an expected event within a social context of values and guidelines (Jescheck 1993). In that context, the omission that causes or enables harm (Hanna 2015), as in exclusion from healthcare, qualifies as an 'undue inaction'. In the criminal legal sense, the idea of 'nonfeasance' refers to bringing about a result by not avoiding it, by violating a special duty, which equates with its causation—the prototypical example is the crime of failing to assist. Here the question not only of intentional omission but of neglect and abandonment comes into play.

In our case, faced with the lack of government accountability, some healthcare professionals have actively responded to the needs of the migrant population. Besides the already mentioned social, political and economic problems, the law has serious ethical implications for healthcare professionals. These ethical implications directly affect healthcare professionals' duties, to the extent that failing to take care of people who require it violates the code of professional ethics, shared morality—values such as equity and solidarity—, and international Human Rights treatises.[12] For this reason, the *Sociedad Española de Medicina de Familia y Comunitaria* (SEMFyC), the most representative medical organization in primary healthcare, encouraged general practitioners to become conscientious objectors in order to ensure provision of healthcare to undocumented migrants (SEMFyC 2012, 4–6). The SEMFyC argues that the law violates the code of medical ethics on several points, including the physician's duty not to abandon their patients, the duty to ensure the welfare of both the patient and the community, and to avoid discrimination. Such an initiative has been supported by the *Organización Médica Colegial* (CGCOME 2012). Several NGOs and citizen platforms are coordinating similar actions.[13] Unlike other more widespread manifestations, this novel form of conscientious objection does not imply opposition to provide services which are contrary to healthcare professionals' moral convictions—an omission or a negative moral duty—, but rather the willingness to carry it out precisely in order to respect those convictions—an action or a perceived positive moral duty—(Triviño 2014b, 121–127). We believe that recourse to conscientious objection in this context is fully justifiable.[14]

11.6 Conclusions

The exclusion from healthcare of wide sectors of the Spanish population, not only undocumented migrants but also poor and unemployed people, constitutes a breach of the Social State model as generally defined in the Spanish Constitution in its Article 1: "Spain is hereby established as a *Social* and Democratic State…

[12] The Medical Code of Ethics (CGCOME 2011) establishes the following obligations: Art. 5. 3. "The physician's main loyalty is that one that he owes to his patients and his patient's health must come before any other convenience (…)"; Art. 6. 1. "All physicians, whatever their specialty or type of exercise, should provide emergency aid to the sick or the injured"; Art. 6.2. "The physician will not abandon any patient requiring his care, even in situations of catastrophe or epidemic, unless he was compelled to do so by the competent authority (…)".

[13] Among others, Platform "Yo Sí, Sanidad Universal", Médicos del Mundo, Platform "No, Gracias, Amnesty International and *Red Acoge*.

[14] The development of the arguments to justify this unusual form of conscientious objection exceeds the objective of this chapter. About this question, see: Triviño 2014a, 176–191.

(emphasis added)". Its Article 43 stands that the right to health protection is recognized, and Article 128 remarks that the entire wealth of the country shall be subordinated to the general interest, so provision of essential services ought to be reserved to the public sector. Besides, the replacement of duties that belong to the State—and should arguably remain theirs—involves the development of a parallel system of care based on supererogatory charity and NGOs. Exclusion from healthcare is a profound shift of paradigm regarding the right to healthcare in Spain that goes against many statements and declarations on Human Rights signed by our country.

The outcome of the reform is not only to commit a deep and flagrant injustice, but also to create a healthcare system that is harmful, ineffective and inefficient.

The State is shamelessly neglecting important segments of the population, and causing harm—especially to the most vulnerable—by an ethically reprehensible omission of care. The governments in Spain are responsible for increasing the vulnerability of these sectors, and for generating their precarious living conditions. The effectiveness of public health policies is reduced, since part of the population is excluded from the conventional healthcare system, and there are increasing costs due to the use of emergency services and the proliferation of cheating practices.

Life is fundamentally dependent upon anonymous others. The human condition of interdependence and vulnerability should be the basis of reimagining—instead of destroying—the possibility of community and, therefore, the reinforcement of the Social State and responsibility to others.

The situation described in this chapter has provoked a strong backlash, largely from Spanish society and, in particular, among health professionals, who have chosen to break the rules and provide basic healthcare to the excluded population. There is still hope to recover the public and universal Spanish healthcare system that has offered such good results, both technical and social, in its recent democratic history.

References

ABC.es. 2015. Así es la asistencia sanitaria a los 'sin papeles' según la comunidad en la que residan. *ABC.* http://www.abc.es/sociedad/20150826/abci-asistencia-sanitaria-comunidades-201508251319.html. Accessed 12 July 2016.

Amnesty International. 2013. El laberinto de la exclusión sanitaria: Vulneraciones del derecho a la salud en las Islas Baleares. https://doc.es.amnesty.org/cgi-bin/ai/BRSCGI/sanidad%20espa%C3%B1a?CMD=VEROBJ&MLKOB=32500201246. Accessed 12 July 2016.

Aramayo, Rodríguez R., and Díez T. Ausín (eds.). 2008. *Interdependencia: Del bienestar a la dignidad.* Madrid-México: Plaza y Valdés.

Beltrán, Alejandro, et al. 2009. *Impulsar un cambio posible en el Sistema Sanitario.* Madrid: FEDEA-McKinsey&Co. http://www.cambioposible.es/documentos/sanidad_cambio_posible.pdf. Accessed 12 July 2016.

Butler, Judith. 2006. *Vida precaria.* Barcelona: Paidós.

Calderón-Larrañaga, Amaia, et al. 2011. Primary care utilization patterns among an urban immigrant population in the Spanish National Health System. *BMC Public Health* 11: 1–8.

Committee on Economic, Social and Cultural Rights of United Nations (CESCR). 2012. Concluding observations, Spain (E/C.12/ESP/CO/5).

Consejo General de Colegios Oficiales de Mèdicos de España (CGCOME). 2011. Deontological medical code (Código de Deontología Médica), Madrid. https://www.cgcom.es/sites/default/files/codigo_deontologia_medica.pdf. Accessed 12 July 2016.

Consejo General de Colegios Oficiales de Mèdicos de España (CGCOME). 2012. *La OMC apoya los valores deontológicos de la profesión médica por una asistencia digna para todos en estos momentos de crisis*. https://www.cgcom.es/noticias/2012/07/12_07_13_omc_semfyc. Accessed 12 July 2016.

Council of Europe (COE). 2013. *Report by Nils Muižnieks, Commissioner for Human Rights, Following his visit to Spain from 3 to 7 June 2013*. https://wcd.coe.int/com.instranet.InstraServlet?command=com.instranet.CmdBlobGet&InstranetImage=2389885&SecMode=1&DocId=2077824&Usage=2. Accessed 12 July 2016.

De Benito, Emilio. 2012. Sanidad derivará a los inmigrantes sin papeles a ONG. El País. http://sociedad.elpais.com/sociedad/2012/05/09/actualidad/1336555954_700416.html Accessed 12 July 2016.

Delgado del Rincón, Luis E. 2014. Reflexiones sobre la reforma introducida por el Real Decreto-Ley 16/2012, de 20 de abril. *Revista de Estudios Políticos* 163: 189–231.

Europa Press. 2014. Sanidad dice que los sin papeles tienen en España una de las coberturas más amplias de la UE. *eldiario.es*. http://www.eldiario.es/sociedad/Sanidad-papeles-Espana-coberturas-UE_0_223628011.html. Accessed 12 July 2016.

European Committee of Social Rights (ECSR). 2014. European Social Charter. Conclusions XX-2 (Spain). https://www.coe.int/t/dghl/monitoring/socialchar-ter/conclusions/State/SpainXX2_en.pdf. Accessed 12 July 2016.

Fundamental Rights of Agency (FRA). 2011. *Migrants in an irregular situation: Access to healthcare in 10 European Union Member States*. Luxembourg: Publications Office of the European Union.http://fra.europa.eu/sites/default/files/fra_uploads/1925-FRA-2011-fundamental-rights-forirregular-migrants-healthcare_EN.pdf. Accessed 12 July 2016.

Fundamental Rights of Agency (FRA). 2015. *Cost of exclusion from healthcare. The case of migrants in an irregular situation*. Luxembourg: Publications Office of the European Union. http://fra.europa.eu/sites/default/files/fra_uploads/1771-FRA-2011-fundamental-rights-for-irregular-migrants-healthcare_EN.pdf. Accessed 12 July 2016.

High Commissioner for Human Rights of United Nations (HCHR). 2013. Report on austerity measures and economic social rights. http://www.ohchr.org/Documents/Issues/Development/RightsCrisis/E-2013-82_en.pdf. Accessed 12 July 2016.

García Pedraz, Javier. 2012. Les dejaré la tarjeta a mis amigos para que vayan al médico. *El País*. http://sociedad.elpais.com/sociedad/2012/08/30/actualidad/1346355067_430436.html. Accessed 12 July 2016.

Gimeno-Feliu, Luís A., et al. 2009. Comparative study of paediatric prescription drug utilization between the Spanish and immigrant population. *BMC Health Services Research* 9: 1–9.

González, Carmen, and Miyar, María. 2011. Practical measures for reduce irregular immigration. Spain. http://ec.europa.eu/dgs/home-affairs/what-we-do/networks/european_migration_network/reports/docs/emn-studies/irregularmigration/es_20120329_irregularmigration_final_en_version_en.pdf. Accessed 12 July 2016.

Hanna, Jason. 2015. Enabling harm, doing harm, and undoing one's own behavior. *Ethics* 126(1): 68–90.

Hernando, Lauro A., et al. 2009. Impacto de la inmigración sobre la asistencia hospitalaria: frecuentación, casuística y repercusión económica. *Gaceta Sanitaria* 23: 208–215.

HUMA Network. 2010. Are undocumented migrants and asylum seekers entitled to access healthcare in the EU? A comparative overview in 16 countries. *HUMA Network Report*.http://www.epim.info/wp-content/uploads/2011/02/HUMA-Publication-Comparative-Overview-16--Countries-2010.pdf. Accessed 12 July 2016.

Human Rights Council (HRC). 2013. Report of the Special Rapporteur on contemporary forms of racism, racial discrimination, xenophobia and related intolerance, Mutuma Ruteere. Visit to Spain. United Nations. http://www.ohchr.org/Documents/HRBodies/HRCouncil/RegularSession/Session23/A-HRC-23-56-Add-2_en.pdf. Accessed 12 July 2016.

Jescheck, Hans H. 1993. *Tratado de derecho penal. Parte General*. Granada: Comares.

Lema Tomé, Margarita. 2013. La reforma sanitaria en España: Especial referencia a la población inmigrante en situación administrativa irregular. *Eunomía* 5: 95–115.

Mackenzie, Catriona, and Natalie Stoljar (eds.). 2000. *Relational autonomy: Feminist perspective on autonomy, agency, and the social self*. Oxford: Oxford University Press.

Médicos del Mundo. 2009. El acceso a la sanidad de las personas sin permiso de residencia en once países europeos. https://www.medicosdelmundo.org/index.php/mod.documentos/mem.descargar/fichero.DOC-115%232E%23pdf. Accessed 12 July 2016.

Médicos del Mundo. 2014. Dos años de reforma sanitaria: más vidas en riesgo. https://www.medicosdelmundo.org/index.php/mod.documentos/mem.descargar/fichero.documentos_Impacto-Reforma-Sanitaria-Medicos-del-Mundo_3ec0bdf9%232E%23pdf. Accessed 12 July 2016.

Médicos del Mundo. 2015. *Cambiar algo para no cambiar nada*. http://www.medicosdelmundo.org/index.php/mod.conts/mem.detalle_cn/relmenu.111/id.4272. Accessed 12 July 2016.

Moreno, Miguel. 2013. Déficit democrático y problemas ético jurídicos en el proceso de privatización y gestión de servicios sanitarios en la Comunidad de Madrid. *Dilemata* 12: 95–142. http://www.dilemata.net/revista/in-dex.php/dilemata/article/view/218/253. Accessed 12 July 2016.

Moreno, Francisco J., and Mariá Bruquetas. 2011. *Inmigración y Estado de bienestar en España*. Barcelona: Obra Social. La Caixa.

Muntaner, Carles, et al. 2012. *La sanidad está en venta*. Barcelona: Icària.

Nail, Thomas. 2015. *The figure of the migrant*. Stanford: Stanford University Press.

No a la Exclusión Sanitaria-Cantabria. 2012–2015. *Casos detectados*. ciudadaniacontralaexclusionsanitaria.blogspot.com.es. Accessed 12 July 2016.

Observatorio Del Derecho Universal A La Salud De La Comunitat Valenciana (ODUSALUD). 2012–2015. Informes 1, 2, 3, 4, 5, 6, 7 y 8. odusalud.blogspot. com.es. Accessed 12 July 2016.

Observatorio Del Derecho Universal A La Salud De La Comunitat Valenciana (ODUSALUD). 2015. Informe n° 10. http://www.fadsp.org/documents/2015/Decimo_Informe.pdf. Accessed 12 July 2016.

Organisation for Economic Cooperation and Development (OECD). 2015. Health expenditure in relation to GDP. In *Health at a glance 2015*. Paris: OECD Publishing. http://www.keepeek.com/Digital-Asset-Management/oecd/social-issues-migration-health/health-at-a-glance-2015/healthexpenditure-as-a-share-of-gdp-2013-or-nearest-year_health_glance-2015-graph151-en#page1. Accessed 12 July 2016.

Olías, Laura. 2014. El Gobierno no prueba el ahorro de excluir a miles de personas de la sanidad pública. *eldiario.es*. http://www.eldiario.es/desalambre/exclusion-sanitaria-personas-probar-Gobierno_0_297470798.html. Accessed 12 July 2016.

Prats, Jaime. 2012. El gobierno restringe el acceso a la sanidad a los inmigrantes ilegales. *El País*. http://sociedad.elpais.com/sociedad/2012/04/20/actualidad/1334935039_248897.html. Accessed 12 July 2016.

Puig Junoy, Jaume. 2011. ¿Recortar o desinvertir? *Economía y Salud* 72: 2–5. http://www.aes.es/Publicaciones/boletin72.pdf. Accessed 12 July 2016.

Regidor, Enrique, et al. 2009. La utilización de los servicios sanitarios por la población inmigrante en España. *Gaceta Sanitaria* 23: 4–11. http://www.elsevier.es/en/node/2080453. Accessed 12 July 2016.

Rejón, Paúl. 2015. El gobierno crea un documento especial para que los inmigrantes sin papeles vayan al médico. *eldiario.es*. http://www.eldiario.es/sociedad/Gobierno-volveran-inmigrantes-Atencion-Primaria_0_372362938.html. Accessed 12 July 2016.

Rey del Castillo, Javier. 2011. *Una nueva Ley General de Sanidad para sostener el Sistema Nacional de Salud*. Madrid: Fundación Alternativas.

Rodriguez, Eunice, et al. 1999. The Spanish healthcare system: Lessons for newly industrialized countries. *Health Policy and Planning* 14(2): 164–173.

Sevillano, Elena G. 2014. La ONU ve 'inaceptable' la desatención sanitaria a inmigrantes en España. *El País*. http://sociedad.elpais.com/sociedad/2014/04/29/actualidad/1398797567_706386.html. Accessed 12 July 2016.

Sevillano, Elena G. 2015a. Devolver la primaria a los inmigrantes: un anuncio con muchas lagunas. *El País*. http://politica.elpais.com/politica/2015/03/31/ actualidad/1427803785_615366.html. Accessed 12 July 2016.

Sevillano, Elena G. 2015b. Una 'rectificación a medias' en plena época electoral. *El País*. http://politica.elpais.com/politica/2015/03/31/actualidad/1427 793954_460833.html. Accessed 12 July 2016.

Sevillano, Elena G. 2015c. Sanidad quiere exigir a los sin papeles seis meses de padrón para atenderles. *El País*. http://politica.elpais.com/politica/2015/09/02/actualidad/1441185941_835636.html. Accessed 12 July 2016.

Simón Lorda, Pablo. 2014. Negando la mayor. *Ética y Salud Pública en Tiempos de Crisis. Cuadernos de la Fundación Víctor Grífols i Lucas* 32: 103–125.

Sociedad Española de Medicina de Familia y Comunitaria. (SEMFyC). 2012. Análisis ético ante la retirada de asistencia sanitaria a inmigrantes sin permiso de residencia. https://www.semfyc.es/wp-content/uploads/2016/05/analisis_etico_retirada_asistencia_sanitaria.pdf. Accessed 12 July 2016.

Triviño Caballero, Rosana. 2014a. Segregación sanitaria, derecho a la salud y objeción de conciencia. Reflexiones a propósito del Real Decreto-ley 16/2012. In *Bioética en plural*, ed. María Teresa López de la Vieja. Madrid: Plaza y Valdés.

Triviño Caballero, Rosana. 2014b. *El peso de la conciencia. La objeción en el ejercicio de las profesiones sanitarias*. Madrid: Plaza y Valdés.

Yo Sí Sanidad Universal. 2014. Informe de irregularidades detectadas en la aplicación de las instrucciones sobre la asistencia sanitaria a prestar por el Servicio Madrileño de Salud a todas aquellas personas que no tengan la condición de asegurada o beneficiaria. http://www.vientosur.info/IMG/pdf/INFORME_IRREGULARIDADES_Yo_si_Madrid.pdf. Accessed 12 July 2016.

Part IV
Obligations to Poverty Alleviation

Chapter 12
Poverty, Injustice and Obligations to Take Political Action

Elizabeth Kahn

Abstract Peter Singer has recently reaffirmed his belief that, in response to poverty, individuals have obligations to 'do the most good they can' by donating to those organizations that demonstrate the greatest amount of benefit per dollar donated (Singer, The most good you can do. Yale University Press, Yale, 2015a). Singer's charitable giving based approach to extreme poverty has been criticized for failing to understand poverty as a form of injustice and for not acknowledging that it requires institutional change. This chapter investigates how Singer's response to this criticism has been inadequate by exploring the ways in which Singer's utilitarian understanding of morality and his account of the duties individuals have with regards to poverty can be rejected.

Singer's analysis implies that all those who recognize a common-sense duty to assist others in difficulty must address poverty by donating large amounts of their income to the most effective poverty reducing charities (Singer, The most good you can do. Yale University Press, Yale, 2015a; Philosophy and public affairs, vol. 1, no. 1, pp 229–243, 1972). His work suggests that rationality requires that all those motivated by a genuine concern for others must adopt the action he recommends. Thus his approach suggests that a common-sense approach to moral duties requires agents to donate to the most effective charities. However, Singer's up front appeal to common-sense duties, concern for others and basic rationality hides a commitment to a controversial utilitarian approach to moral obligation. The analysis here will argue that a common-sense approach that identifies multiple duties to others and recognizes the fact that genuine moral action must be rational and grounded in concern for others can in fact make different recommendations from those supported by Singer. In doing so the chapter will articulate an alternative account of the duties individuals have with regards to extreme poverty. It will suggest that, given that poverty is a form of social injustice, individuals have collectivization duties that require that they act responsively with a view to establishing a collective of a particular kind. The collective they work toward forming must be willing and able to establish and maintain procedurally just governing institutions that end poverty by

E. Kahn (✉)
School of Government and International Affairs, University of Durham,
Room 219/Al-Qasimi Building, Durham DH1, UK
e-mail: elizabeth.kahn@durham.ac.uk

H.P. Gaisbauer et al. (eds.), *Ethical Issues in Poverty Alleviation*, Studies in Global Justice 14, DOI 10.1007/978-3-319-41430-0_12

ensuring no agent is placed in a position where they are vulnerable to deprivation or domination. It will be proposed that this duty operates in addition to the duties to assist Singer recognizes.

Keywords Peter Singer • Poverty • Donation • Charities • Common-sense approach • Collectivization duties

12.1 Introduction

Peter Singer has recently reiterated his belief that, in response to poverty, individuals have obligations to 'do the most good they can' by donating to those organizations that demonstrate the greatest amount of benefit per dollar donated (Singer 2015a). Singer's charitable giving based approach to extreme poverty has been criticized for failing to understand poverty as a form of injustice and for not acknowledging that it requires institutional change. This chapter investigates how Singer's response to this criticism has been inadequate by exploring the ways in which Singer's utilitarian understanding of morality can be rationally rejected.

Since 1972, when Singer wrote 'Famine, Affluence and Morality', the question of the moral duties individuals have with regards to extreme poverty has garnered significant attention in the philosophical literature. There have been a wide range of critiques of Singer's position on extreme poverty, yet Singer continues to support an approach that identifies moral duties to donate a substantial part of one's resources to those organizations that one has reason to believe will make the largest quantifiable improvement to the welfare of the global poor (Singer 2015c).

One of the most important recurring critiques of Singer's approach emphasizes the fact that poverty must be understood as a political problem requiring institutional change (Kuper 2002; Deaton 2015; Rubenstein 2015; Acemoglu 2015; Gabriel 2015). This approach criticizes the 'Singer solution' as being apolitical in that it does not recognize that poverty is unjust and thus fails to recognise the duties agents have to alter political institutions in light of this fact. In this paper I discuss why Singer's response to this criticism has been inadequate and argue that Singer is wrong to suggest that all those who wish to rationally respond to poverty must adopt the approach he recommends.

In his original article Singer suggested that when it is in someone's power to prevent something very bad from happening, without sacrificing anything of comparable moral significance, they must do it. He argued that this duty required relatively affluent individuals in western states at the time of the East Bengal famine to donate substantial portions of their income to relief efforts (Singer 1972, 86–112). Since this original article his work has consistently suggested that in a world with so many avoidable deaths resulting from poverty there is no justification for middle and upper class individuals to spend income on luxury goods rather than donating to charities that can relieve extreme poverty (Singer 1972, 2009, 2015a).

Singer's approach to poverty claims to be common sense and rationally required. In his more recent work he implies that all those committed to a rational account of the duties owed to others must adopt the 'effective altruist' approach he promotes (Singer 2015a). He draws a dichotomy between 'effective altruists' and 'warm glow' givers: characterizing those donating to charity as either seeking to maximize the good their donation does or donating on emotional impulse in order to make themselves feel good (Singer 2015a, ix, 5, 18, 90). He suggests that those who give small amounts to many charities (warm-glow givers) are not interested in whether or not they are helping others (Singer 2015a, 5). In contrast he suggests that effective altruists are both rational and motivated by a concern for others. Throughout the book Singer equates rational action based on genuine concern for others with a quantifying approach (Singer 2015a, 18, 82, 90–92). His discussion implies that those who are rational and wish to assist others must adopt the effective altruist strategy of donating to those organisations that can demonstrate that they use that money most effectively. Singer responds to those who criticize quantifying the amount of good done and taking the action with the largest expected benefit as being irrational (Singer 2015c). However Singer's approach is not the only rational way of understanding moral duties with regards to poverty or at least so this chapter will argue.

Singer's original article argued from a duty of aid to the requirement that individuals give substantial amounts of money to charity (Singer 1972). Thus he tried to convince all those who accepted this common-sense moral duty to support his controversial conclusions. Singer's work thus argued that those committed to a common-sense approach to moral duties should support his conclusion. A common sense approach to morality recognizes multiple pro-tanto duties that individuals owe to others. Such an approach is committed to the idea that moral duties require individuals to take rational action out of concern for others.

This chapter will suggest that if we genuinely adopt a plural approach that recognizes multiple pro-tanto moral obligations rather than a single duty to maximize the good we will end up with a different analysis from that which Singer endorses. It will be argued that, since poverty is a form of injustice, a multiple duty approach should recognize additional duties with regards to poverty and not just duties of aid. It will be proposed that these duties include duties to act responsively so as to achieve institutional changes that prevent the continuance of poverty. Thus it will be suggested that individuals have duties to promote and support just (poverty avoiding) institutions. It will be explained that these duties operate in addition to duties to assist others or promote the good. Thus the idea that all rational individuals motivated by concern for others must do is act so as to maximize the good, all things considered, will be rejected. Thus this chapter will argue that, contrary to Singer's implication, there are rational approaches to poverty motivated by genuine concern for others that reject effective altruism.

The chapter begins by recapping Singer's arguments. Next an approach to poverty based on the idea that it is a form of injustice requiring institutional change is outlined. Singer's response to the suggestion that individuals pursue political action is then discussed. In this section an account of how Singer sees the role of political institutions is constructed. In the next section an alternative to this utilitarian account of justice, duties and institutions is sketched. Thus it is argued that there is a plausible, rational and moral alternative to the utilitarian approach. The chapter concludes that, contra Singer's implication, those who accept that individuals should be rational in determining their action, and that they have moral reason to respond to the plight of those in poverty, need not adopt the logic or recommendations of the effective altruist movement. It is argued that they can instead recognize multiple pro-tanto duties, including political duties that require that they act responsively so as to form a collective, willing and able to establish just governing institutions that effectively prevent foreseeable and avoidable poverty.

12.2 Singer's Approach to Poverty and Obligation

Singer's approach to poverty is simple: he suggests that individuals with income beyond what they need for necessities should donate at least large portions of it to poverty relief. He originally argued that they must do so because they have the opportunity to prevent something really bad from happening without sacrificing anything of moral significance (Singer 1972).

The 'effective altruism' movement Singer now supports not only seeks to encourage people to give away a substantial share of their income; it also suggests that they must give it to those charities that will do the most good with the money. This is because the effective altruist movement is committed to a maximizing philosophy. In Singer's latest work he endorses this maximizing philosophy insisting money is spent in a way that efficiently maximizes the good and arguing that, because giving more in absolute terms is better than giving less, agents should seek the career which maximizes their income in order to maximize their giving and thus the good they do (Singer 2015a, 3–13).

In discussing how to give money effectively Singer suggests that we investigate how much good different charities do with the money donated. He recommends organisations like 'Give Well' that seek to measure the amount of good, per dollar, done by various charities (Singer 2015a). What these organisations seek to do is quantify the amount of good done. 'Give Well' rates charities on the basis of the amount of measurable good they do. The methodology they favor is the randomized controlled trial (Holden 2012). Thus those charities that can prove the largest measurable short-medium term improvement are favored (Singer 2015a, 152–154).[1]

[1] Leif Wenar has criticised this approach to judging consequences (Wenar 2011). Wenar argues that the complexities of the situation make the results of any intervention unpredictable. Using randomized trials (the method used by a website Singer recommends – Give Well) to measure effectiveness has been criticized by Emily Clough for taking a short term approach to impact (Clough 2015). Clough notes that NGOs often end up providing services for the 'middle poor'. She notes that this can lead to their abandoning state services. This means state services are only used by the very poorest who are unlikely to monitor these services effectively and demand quality. As a result,

Singer's approach is simple and straightforward. It avoids any controversial debates concerning the causes of poverty and asks individuals to choose the action that is likely to be most effective in addressing poverty. Singer's analysis focuses on what can be done to alleviate poverty and does not explicitly look into what sort of problem poverty is. Singer focuses on working out which actions have the greatest expected benefit in terms of reducing poverty because the approach he adopts is purely focused on identifying ways to improve the situation.

However, if we adopt a 'common sense morality' approach that recognizes multiple duties to others of the kind Singer originally appealed to (Singer 1972), how poverty should be understood will affect what duties we have with regards to it: there are duties with regard to poverty that depend on its nature and causes. In the section below an account that identifies poverty as injustice requiring institutional reform will be briefly outlined. What such an account means, in determining the duties individuals have with regards to it, is discussed.

12.3 Poverty as Injustice Requiring Institutional Change

This section will argue that poverty should be understood as a form of injustice requiring reform to governing institutions. It will begin by identifying poverty as a question of entitlements. It will proceed to consider various grounds under which such a failure of entitlements can be identified as unjust. It will then suggest that governing institutions should not allow such poverty to continue and thus must be reformed. Finally the duties individuals have to ensure governing institutions perform the role of securing social justice will be explored.

Amartya Sen's key insight in his early analysis of famines was to recognize that famine is not always a case of there being a shortage of food but is always a case of a section of the population lacking sufficient *entitlement* to food (Sen 1981, 1, Sen and Drèze 1999). Sen's analysis suggests that in all cases famine occurs when sections of the population lack sufficient funds or rights to goods or income in order to be able to purchase essential food-stuffs at market price. To put it crudely: the problem in a famine is not that there is not enough food but rather that poor individuals have neither rights to sufficient food nor enough income to buy sufficient food at the price at which it is available.

The income individuals have and the property they own are a matter of entitlement. By recognizing a problem of entitlement Sen's analysis forces the reader not to reify poverty (treating it as a natural phenomenon beyond human control) and instead asks us to recognize poverty as the result of a particular legal system. Thus, Sen's work emphasizes the fact that an agent's poverty is social and political rather than natural.

---

she notes, NGO interventions that are effective for those who use them (the middle poor) can make the very poorest worse off. Such effects would not show up in a randomized trial that concentrated on whether an intervention improved the lives of those targeted.

By understanding poverty as concerning *entitlement* we recognize that access to goods, services, positions, political forums and social and cultural events is determined by a socio-political system. Sen's analysis draws attention to the fact that this system (which could be otherwise) is responsible for the distribution of goods. We can build on this analysis to suggest that those features of a situation that make a person poor can be traced back to a system of entitlement. Recognizing poverty as a feature of a system of entitlement leads us to understand poverty as a social and political phenomenon. In this section I will explore why this should lead us to recognize poverty as a form of injustice. How to draw the line between what constitutes injustice rather than merely misfortune is a deeply contested question. Below I will explore how plausible approaches to this distinction should lead to the identification of global poverty as unjust.

Some approaches to social justice identify injustice as occurring when social and political systems place some people in positions of significant disadvantage. Iris Young's approach, for example, suggests that injustice occurs when social processes come together to place a social group in a position where they are vulnerable to deprivation and domination, relative to others. Poverty denotes a condition in which people are extremely vulnerable to deprivation and domination. According to Young the extreme poverty faced by the billion poorest people constitutes injustice because it is the predictable result of social processes (Young 2011).[2]

An alternative approach recognizes injustice when governing institutions can be held morally responsible for a poor social situation. The entitlements that individuals enjoy in the modern world are governed by law, which is backed up by the threat of coercion. Thus poverty is part of a system of rights imposed by governing institutions. Thus, according to this approach, we must recognize poverty as unjust rather than merely unfortunate because it results from entitlements imposed by governing institutions (Blake 2001; Pogge 2008).

A more expansive account of justice recognizes injustice as occurring whenever governing institutions omit to establish a just social scenario. According to such an account governing institutions have a responsibility to establish just social conditions (sometimes called just background conditions) (Rawls 1977; Ronzoni 2009). This requires that we establish governing institutions that effectively prevent the erosion of background justice. The sort of poverty experienced by the poorest billion people on the planet undermines their ability to make fair contracts with others. Any deals they make are in fact likely to be highly unfair. This is because there is no background justice: one party is in a much worse position than the other. Thus, according to an approach that sees the role of governing institutions as securing the conditions in which deals can be fair (maintaining background justice), there is a need for governing institutions to prevent the continuance of extreme poverty. This approach suggests that when there are not governing institutions that effectively prevent poverty there is injustice.

[2] Young identifies systematic vulnerability to deprivation and domination that result from practices and structures, some of which are global in scope. She suggests overcoming them requires coordinated action between individuals in multiple states (Young 2011).

All three of the approaches to injustice discussed above suggest that poverty is a form of injustice. If poverty is a form of injustice then duties with regards to avoiding injustice and promoting justice become relevant to the question of poverty relief. This means that, in response to poverty, we should consider the duties individuals have both to prevent injustice and promote justice. Thus we may have to consider the duty to promote and support just institutions (Rawls 1973, 115) and the duty not to help impose unjust institutional orders (Pogge 2008, 93). Recognizing poverty as a form of injustice should lead individuals to consider whether they are violating duties not to help impose unjust institutional orders that cause poverty or allow it to continue. It should also lead individuals to consider whether they need to initiate or support action aimed at institutional reform that seeks to make governing institutions just. Such an approach is likely to identify duties to take political action aimed at reforming governing institutions or disempowering existing institutions and establishing alternatives.

The discussion above explains why poverty should be identified as unjust and sketches how this insight might affect the obligations individuals have with regards to it. The point of the discussion has been to show that an approach to extreme poverty and obligation that recognizes poverty as a form of injustice and then identifies duties agents have with regards to justice can be articulated. Such an approach rationally seeks to address the plight of the poor rather than give the obligated party a 'warm glow', however it identifies different duties from those identified by Singer and the effective altruist movement. It calls on individuals to work towards institutional reform rather than to maximize their income and make substantial donations to effective charities. This suggests that there are plausible, rational and moral approaches to poverty and obligation that differ from the effective altruist approach.

12.4 Singer on Political Change

In response to the various criticisms he has faced that recommend we solve poverty through institutional change, Singer has suggested that whether or not we should take such action depends on whether or not the action has the greatest expected benefit. Singer has stressed that the 'effective altruism' movement he supports does not rule out taking political action to promote institutional change. Furthermore, he insists that his approach does not, in principle, favor individual aid over political solutions.[3] He explains that, according to the effective altruist approach, whether we

[3] Singer's approach does not rule out the possibility that political action will provide the best expected benefit (Singer 2015c). However the reasoning of the movement Singer supports, coupled with the methodology it employs for comparing the good done by different approaches, makes it more likely to favour donation to charities that provide direct and immediate improvement to welfare over contributing to political movements that seek to fundamentally alter social and political relations through governing institutions.

should donate or join a political movement depends on the expected utility of each option: we should do whichever is likely to maximize the good (Singer 2015c). His book looks into whether advocacy is an efficient route to overcoming poverty and concludes that there is not yet enough evidence to say whether it is or not (Singer 2015a, 162–164).

Thus Singer's effective altruist approach recommends that we take the action with largest expected benefit. Expected benefit is calculated by multiplying the amount of good an action is believed to achieve if successful by the probability of that success. Thus, effective altruism suggests we adopt the strategy that evidence suggests will maximize the good, all things considered. This is consistent with the fact that effective altruism is based around the simple idea that 'we should do the most good we can' (Singer 2015a). The movement is committed to requiring actions that maximize the good and is thus act utilitarian in its logic. Act utilitarianism is the philosophy that morality requires agents to make decisions based on the expected benefit of the available options: it suggests that they should always seek to maximize total utility (usually understood as happiness or preference satisfaction). They work out which action to take by multiplying the amount of good that will be done if a particular possible action is successful by the likelihood of success.

Thus, the effective altruist approach involves embracing individualistic act consequentialism. This is a controversial theory that many moral theorists have identified good reasons to reject. It is right to accept both of Singer's explicit premises: that we have duties to assist others and that we should prefer helping them more to helping them less when the costs are the same. However, this does not mean we need to accept his understanding of what we are required to do, or at least so I will argue.

12.5 Challenging Singer's Approach

What the analysis above reveals is that Singer's approach sees political action as one possible means through which we can do good. He suggests that whether or not we should seek institutional change depends on whether or not the strategy of working towards institutional change is the strategy by which an individual will do the most good. However, this response to the apolitical critique fails to grasp the fact that those who recommend a political solution do not identify working towards institutional change as one means through which individuals can fulfil their duties of aid, instead they see working towards just governing institutions as required by a moral duty to promote and support justice, as compensation for contributions to injustice or as a precaution against making contributions to injustice. If the purpose of working towards institutional change is to fulfil duties that require agents to work towards achieving just governing institutions, whether or not this strategy is the most efficient means to relieve suffering becomes less relevant in determining whether or not to pursue such a strategy.

Those that insist that poverty is a form of injustice requiring institutional change could reject the picture Singer offers of the duties of individuals, role of the state and status of governing institutions. In the remainder of this chapter the assumptions behind Singer's approach will be reconstructed and an alternative that is systematically different from this utilitarian approach will be outlined. The points at which this utilitarian picture can be rejected, whilst still affirming that moral action should be rational and motivated by genuine concern for others, will be identified. Thus it will be shown that there can be a rational approach motivated by genuine concern for others that is not the approach recommended by effective altruism.

Singer's suggestion that effective altruists should take political action if and only if it maximizes expected benefit implies that individuals only have one duty: a duty to maximize the good. His discussion of political action suggests that political institutions are merely one means through which individuals can promote the good. This implies that individuals have duties to take political action to alter governing institutions only as a means to aiding others who are suffering.

Singer is adopting an act utilitarian approach that identifies one moral demand that applies to both individuals and collective agents such as governing institutions. This demand requires they maximize the good all things considered. This utilitarianism understands governing institutions as having a good reason to exist only to the extent that they maximize the good. Below I will identify two stages at which this utilitarian picture of justice, institutions and duties can be rejected.

Firstly it will be suggested that justice is not a matter of maximizing the good. Drawing on work in contemporary political philosophy the ways in which social justice is not a matter of maximizing the good will be identified. The utilitarian understanding of the proper role of political institutions will thus be questioned. It will be suggested that just political institutions are not merely those that maximize the good.

Secondly the duties agents have with regards to justice will be considered. It will be argued that just governing institutions can only be maintained when individuals work together to monitor these institutions and hold them to account. It will be suggested that, given that the maintenance of just governing institutions is morally required, and that this can only be secured through individuals working together, individuals must have collectivization duties. It is explained that the duties that fall on individuals are duties to act responsively with a view to establishing and maintaining a collective capable of ensuring just governing institutions. The features of the proposed duty that differentiate it from a utilitarian duty to maximize the good are noted.

The analysis suggests that we need not see political institutions as one means through which individuals can fulfil their duties to do good. Instead it suggests that justice requires legitimate political institutions that secure just (poverty free) social relations and that individuals have duties that require that they act responsively with a view to ensuing political institutions secure social justice.

12.6 Rejecting a Utilitarian Approach to Justice

Singer's discussion states that individuals must seek to maximize the good, all things considered, and suggest that they should utilize governing institutions as a means to achieve this if and only if this is the most efficient way to do so. This suggests that governing institutions are simply one means through which individuals can maximize the good. Thus Singer's discussion implies that what citizens should aim to achieve through governing institutions is the maximization of the good, all things considered. Thus, Singer can be interpreted as endorsing the proposition that the role of governing institutions is to maximize the good.

Singer loosely defines the good as consisting in 'lives going better' (Singer 2015b). Contemporary political philosophy has identified several ways in which justice differs from the maximizing of the good, all things considered. I will outline some of these ways below and thus show why we can rationally reject the utilitarian account of social justice and thus reject the proposition that governing institutions should promote utility.

Firstly, as Rawls famously noted in his 'separateness of persons argument', distributions of burdens and benefits matter and not just the total sum of interest satisfaction within a society (McKerlie 1988, 22–25, 163; Rawls 1973, 27). Rawls's critique of utilitarianism states that since people are not parts of a single organism it is not right simply to maximize the total good, all things considered. He explains that since people are separate individuals we must ensure a fair system of cooperation. Thus, his work acknowledges that justice requires a fair settlement between competing claims. Rawls's insight suggests that no matter what account we have of what makes an individual's life go well we must adopt an approach to justice that ensures fairness between individuals (in terms of how well their lives go) rather than just seeking to maximize total goodness (understood as lives going well). Thus, from the perspective of social justice, how welfare or the goods needed to achieve welfare are distributed matters as well as the total amount. This point draws attention to the fact that justice is, in part, about fairly adjudicating between competing claims and not just about maximizing some good or measure of goodness.[4]

Secondly, justice is not just about the distribution of burdens and benefits but also concerns the nature of social relationships (Young 1990; Anderson 1999). Whether certain social groups are dominated, oppressed or dependent matters. Thus it is significant whether people have equal access to social, political and economic worlds and that nobody has a secondary status (Anderson 1999). Furthermore, it matters whether one social group is in a systematically superior position to another (Young 1990, 15–39, 2001, 2011; Forst 2007b). Thus justice is not simply about

[4] A utilitarian could respond that we should seek to maximize fairness alongside other social goods in order to make things as good as possible, all things considered. This suggests that fairness is quantifiable and can be maximized alongside other goods. However, translating all concerns of justice in to a quantifiable measure that can be maximized may distort the concepts in order to fit it into the consequentialist framework.

adding together how well each life goes and maximizing the total. Instead we must also examine how the relationships within a society operate and investigate whether certain social groups are systematically disadvantaged.

Finally, as Philip Pettit has famously argued justice requires that agents are not dependent or dominated in a way that makes them vulnerable to the arbitrary will of others (Pettit 1997).[5] Thus governing institutions need to *secure* agents in the status, position and independence justice requires. This in part explains why justice, in most circumstances, requires the coercive imposition of a particular social order. When in a society some are subject to arbitrary powers the society is unjust regardless of the total amount of utility in the society. Thus all powerful parties must be subjected to processes by which those they hold power over can hold them to account.[6]

A just society is one that fairly balances the interests of its members, ensures they live in relations of equality and guarantees that no-one is subjected to arbitrary power. This means that governing institutions should not simply seek to maximize the good, all things considered. Rather they should ensure fairness, prevent problematic relations and be held to account by those they rule. Thus we should reject a utilitarian understanding of social justice that identifies governing institutions as simply one means through which goodness can be maximized.

12.7 Defending Effective Altruism

In his defense of effective altruism Singer has suggested that justice (understood as being not just the maximization of total wellbeing) may be instrumentally valuable (Singer 2015b). He suggests that a just society is desirable because it is conducive to people's lives going better and thus making things better, all things considered. Thus he suggests that values like fairness, justice, the recognition of rights and democracy are important only to the extent that they increase utility.

If social justice does increase the good, all things considered, it is something that utilitarians can support. In fact many utilitarians would agree that having just institutions is essential for maximizing the good long-term because it is conducive to individuals' lives going well. Singer explains that justice, freedom and equality are conducive to maximizing the good (Singer 2015b). Thus perhaps it does not matter so much that utilitarianism does not intrinsically value justice.

---

[5] It is interesting to note that Pettit himself is a consequentialist. How far this is compatible with his political views is a matter of debate.

[6] If those living in poverty are reliant on the charity of the affluent in order to avoid deprivation, despite no longer being deprived, they will still be subject to the arbitrary will of the charitable. In order for the injustice of their situation to be overcome they must not have to rely on the good will of others to avoid poverty. For the situation to be justly resolved they must be freed from poverty without being subject to the arbitrary power of donors or Non Governmental Organizations (NGOs).

Against this position it can be argued that utilitarian approaches support justice and equality for the wrong reasons. To explain why it is important to support justice for its own sake consider why it is that slavery should not be tolerated. The reason we should not permit slavery is not because it is detrimental to the total amount of utility or that a slave-free society is more conducive to lives going well and thus the maximization of utility. Slavery would be wrong even if it maximized welfare, all things considered.

Intuitively, such arrangements would be wrong regardless of their effect on total wellbeing. This is because no matter how happy slavery makes slave-holders it cannot be right because no amount of happiness to slave holders can offset the suffering and disrespect that slavery causes slaves (Rawls 1973, 167). As Rawls recognized, the plight of every individual matters and treating some in a manner that violates their basic rights cannot be offset by producing more satisfaction, all things considered. Thus we must value justice because it ensures every individual is treated fairly and not because it makes lives go better and thus maximizes utility, all things considered. This gives us reason to acknowledge that justice is valuable not just as a means of maximizing utility (Rawls 1958, 187–188).

Singer does note that some effective altruists may also identify justice as intrinsically valuable (Singer 2015b). His merely noting this point suggests that recognizing the intrinsic value of justice should not affect our commitment to maximizing the good we do. Thus it does not affect the fact that we should respond to poverty by seeking to maximize our own income and then donating it to those charities whose effectiveness has been demonstrated using randomized controlled trials.

However, if we adopt an account that recognizes that justice is independently valuable and not just good as a means to maximizing utility we must reject the idea that all that is valuable is utility. If we do so then we must have some account of how to respond to plural values. This means that we will reject the idea that our actions must simply seek to maximize utility all things considered. Thus if we recognize that justice is independently valuable we must recognize additional duties with regards to poverty that will lead us to a different approach from that recommended by effective altruism. Recognizing that justice is not a matter of maximizing utility, and that justice is not just valuable to the extent that it maximizes the good, is important because it allows us to recognize duties to promote justice and not to impose injustice that operate independently of duties to maximize the good. These duties will require something different from us than maximizing income in order to donate to effective charities.

12.8 Collectivization Duties and Injustice

Above it was argued that justice requires governing institutions that secure a just social order. This idea was contrasted with an approach that sees governing institutions as simply one possible means to promoting the good. If we adopt this non-utilitarian understanding of justice, and its value, we can recognize duties to establish and maintain just institutions separate from duties to promote the good. In this section I will discuss what such duties could require.

If justice is morally required then there must be agents with duties to ensure justice: prescribing that societies should be just is pointless if we do not assign duties to secure such a society. Thus we need to pair an understanding of a just society (including just governing institutions) with an account of the duties agents have to secure such a society. However, the question of what duties agents have with regard to justice is a complex one.

Establishing and maintaining just governing institutions that secure a just social order is not something that any particular person can ensure, thus individuals cannot have a duty to ensure justice. However, collectively individuals can effectively ensure justice. By working together a community can establish and maintain governing institutions that are procedurally just and that secure substantive social justice. Achieving such a feat and maintaining it requires collective action. The sorts of duties individuals have with regards to justice must thus be of a complex kind.

Stephanie Collins has developed an account of the duties agents have to act responsively so as to form a collective able to address a pressing moral problem (Collins 2013). Collins' analysis suggests that individuals can have 'collectivization duties' that require this kind of responsive action. In a collaborative piece of work with Holly Lawford-Smith, Collins proposes that individuals have such duties with regards to the state. The pair argue that sometimes individuals facing a moral problem that they cannot themselves solve (at a cost it is reasonable for them to undertake) can take steps towards bringing about a collective that is able to tackle the problem without overly burdening any of its members (Collins and Lawford-Smith 2016, 4). They do this by first signaling their willingness to take part in collective action and, if this signal of willingness is reciprocated, starting to take steps towards reforming institutions collectively. These steps could be organizing a collective, joining an established collective, working to change the capacities or function of an existing collective to which they already belong or investigating whether an existing collective to which they belong is already pursuing reform on their behalf (Collins and Lawford-Smith 2016, 4).

This model of duties could be developed to suggest that, with regards to injustices, individuals have collectivization duties which require them to act responsively so as to form a collective capable of establishing new institutions or reforming existing institutions so that they can adequately address the problem. If we apply this thesis to the case of extreme poverty we will identify collectivization duties that call on all individuals to act responsively so as to form a collective able to establish new governing institutions that can effectively prevent poverty or reform existing governing institutions so they can fulfil this role. Once such a collective is formed it will gain responsibility for ensuring the creation of these institutions or the reform of existing institutions. Once such institutions are established the collective will be responsible for monitoring these institutions to ensure they both remain procedurally just and continue to fulfil their role in preventing poverty.

Although individuals cannot have a duty to prevent injustice and ensure justice, they can have a duty to make reasonable efforts to pursue this goal through collective action. Thus an individual can seek to make existing collective agents take up this task or act responsively so as to form new collective agents who can fulfil this goal.

12.9 Conclusion

In this chapter a thoroughly non-utilitarian approach to poverty and obligation is sketched. The aim of this articulation is to show that a rational person could agree that action with regards to poverty must be based on concern for others rather than giving oneself a 'warm glow' without adopting the effective altruist approach.

The argumentation above shows that if we see poverty as injustice, recognize social justice as about fairness, security and non-vulnerability, and identify governing institutions as not just valuable to the extent that they promote the good this should alter the account of duties we adopt with regards to poverty. It was explained that we could identify collectivization duties that insist that individuals must act responsively so as to establish and maintain governing institutions capable of securing social justice and thus preventing the continuance of poverty. A common sense approach to moral obligations that recognizes multiple duties to others can recognize that individuals have these duties alongside the duty to act effectively to aid others who are suffering that Singer identifies. Recognizing collectivization duties should lead us to recommend that individuals work towards a political solution to extreme poverty even if it is not the most efficient way to relieve suffering. This is because they must take such action in order to fulfil the duties they have to promote and support just governing institutions. Thus this chapter has shown where there is room to disagree with Singer's suggestion that we only take political action if the expected utility of doing so is greater than donating to charities that provide immediate interventions.

Above the utilitarian assumptions behind the effective altruist approach were uncovered and the ways in which we can question these assumptions were outlined. Then the chapter proceeded to outline an alternative to this utilitarian approach to poverty and duty. This alternative approach acknowledges that justice is about fairness and security not simply maximizing the good and recognizes that political institutions are not just instruments for achieving the goal of utility maximization. Why this approach can recognize the moral necessity of collective action was outlined. Thus a radically different approach to poverty and duties was articulated. This approach recognizes that moral action should be rational and motivated by concern for others. However, it denies that individuals must take the action that does the most good.

This chapter has not shown that this non-utilitarian approach must be adopted. However, it has shown that there is no need to adopt Singer's assumptions and conclusions just because we wish to rationally address the problem of extreme poverty.

It has suggested that we can instead argue for political action that aims at ensuring governing institutions that prevent the continuance of poverty. Furthermore, it has been shown that pursuing such a strategy can be justified even when it is not the strategy with the largest expected utility. If we are working within a common sense moral duty framework, as Singer originally did, there is no reason why we cannot recognize duties to promote and support just institutions that reliably avoid poverty in addition to duties of aid that require us to act effectively to rescue those in extreme difficulties.

References

Acemoglu, Daron. 2015. A response to Peter Singer: The logic of effective altruism. *Boston Review* 40(4).

Anderson, Elizabeth. 1999. What's the point of equality. *Ethics* 109(2): 287–337.

Blake, Michael. 2001. Distributive justice, state coercion, and autonomy. *Philosophy and Public Affairs* 30(3): 257–296.

Clough, Emily. 2015. Effective altruisms political blindspot. *Boston Review*. https://bostonreview.net/world/emily-clough-effective-altruism-ngos.

Collins, Stephanie. 2013. Collective duties and collectivization duties. *Australian Journal of Philosophy* 91(2): 231–248.

Collins, Stephanie, and Holly Lawford-Smith. 2016. The transfer of duties: From individuals to states and back again. In *The epistemic life of groups: Essays in the epistemology of collectives*, ed. Michael Brady and Miranda Fricker. Oxford: Oxford University Press.

Deaton, Angus. 2015. A response to Peter Singer: The logic of effective altruism. *The Boston Review* 40(4).

Forst, Rainer. 2007a. First things first redistribution, recognition and justification. *European Journal of Political Theory* 6(3): 291–304.

Forst, Rainer. 2007b. Radical justice: On Iris Marion Young's critique of the "Distributive Paradigm". *Constellations* 14(2): 260–265.

Gabriel, Iason. 2015. A response to Peter Singer: The logic of effective altruism. *Boston Review* 40(4).

Holden. 2012. Title. The GiveWell Blog, 1510/2015. http://blog.givewell.org/2012/08/23/how-we-evaluate-a-study/.

Kuper, Andrew. 2002. More than charity: Cosmopolitan alternatives to the 'Singer solution'. *Ethics and International Affairs* 16(2): 107–128.

McKerlie, Dennis. 1988. Egalitarianism and the separateness of persons. *Canadian Journal of Philosophy* 18(2): 205–225. doi:10.1080/00455091.1988.10717174.

Pettit, Philip. 1997. *Republicanism: A theory of freedom and government: A theory of freedom and government*. Oxford: Oxford University Press.

Pogge, Thomas. 2008. *World poverty and human rights: Cosmopolitan responsibilities and reforms*. Cambridge: Polity Press.

Rawls, John. 1958. Justice as fairness. *Philosophical Review* 67(2): 164–194.

Rawls, John. 1973. *A theory of justice*. Oxford: Oxford University Press.

Rawls, John. 1977. The basic structure as subject. *American Philosophical Quarterly* 14(2): 159–165.

Ronzoni, Miriam. 2009. The global order: A case of background injustice? A practice-dependent account. *Philosophy & Public Affairs* 37(3): 229–256. doi:10.1111/j.1088-4963.2009.01159.x.

Rubenstein, Jennifer. 2015. A response to Peter Singer: The logic of effective altruism. *The Boston Review* 40(4).

Sen, Amartya. 1981. *Poverty and famines: An essay on entitlement and deprivation*. Oxford: Clarendon Press.

Sen, Amartya, and Jean Drèze. 1999. *The Amartya Sen and Jean Drèze Omnibus*. Oxford: Oxford University Press.

Singer, Peter. 1972. Famine, affluence, and morality. *Philosophy and Public Affairs* 1(1): 229–243.

Singer, Peter. 2009. *The life you can save: Acting now to end world poverty*. New York: Random House.

Singer, Peter. 2015a. *The most good you can do*. Yale: Yale University Press.

Singer, Peter. 2015b. Opening the debate. *The Boston Review* 40(4).

Singer, Peter. 2015c. Reply: The logic of effective altruism. *Boston Review* 40(4).

Wenar, Leif. 2011. Poverty is no pond: Challenges for the affluent. In *Giving well: The ethics of philanthropy*, ed. Patricia Illingworth, Thomas Pogge, and Leif Wenar, 104–132. Oxford: Oxford University Press.

Young, Iris. 1990. *Justice and the politics of difference*. Princeton: Princeton University Press.

Young, Iris Marion. 2001. Equality of whom? Social groups and judgments of injustice. *Journal of Political Philosophy* 9(1): 1–18. doi:10.1111/1467-9760.00115.

Young, Iris. 2011. *Responsibility for justice*. Oxford: Oxford University Press.

Chapter 13
Beyond the Redistributive Paradigm: What Philosophers Can Learn from Poor-Led Politics

Monique Deveaux

Abstract Philosophical approaches to alleviating global poverty have overlooked the contributions and insights of poor-led social and political movements. This failure to engage with the strategies and perspectives of poor communities is bound up with global justice theorists' neglect of issues of social and political power in their prescriptions for global poverty reduction. One cause of this neglect is the prominence of the "sufficiency" doctrine, which treats poverty as strictly a matter of material lack and unmet needs. This view gives rise to the belief that poverty can best be redressed through judicious redistributive measures to reduce absolute low-welfare. Yet these assumptions are increasingly at odds with the multidimensional and relational approach to poverty that has emerged in anti-poverty policy and development studies. This approach takes structural inequalities, social exclusion, and relations of subordination and disempowerment to be central to the experience of poverty. Two emerging ethical approaches to deprivation – one emphasizing social exclusion and disempowerment, and one focusing on humiliation and misrecognition – better grasp the relational aspects of poverty. By shifting to a relational understanding of poverty and paying closer attention to the aims and strategies of poor-led organizations and movements, global justice theorists can start to think more expansively about the goals – and agents – of global poverty reduction. I illustrate the significance of looking to poor communities as agents of poverty reduction by discussing the *Slum/Shack Dwellers International* (SDI), a global grassroots network of organizations dedicated to empowering communities of pavement and slum dwellers.

Keywords Poor-led social and political movements • Multidimensional and relational approach to poverty • Slum/Shack Dwellers International (SDI)

M. Deveaux (✉)
Department of Philosophy, University of Guelph,
50 Stone Road, Guelph, Ontario N1G2W1, Canada
e-mail: mdeveaux@uoguelph.ca

H.P. Gaisbauer et al. (eds.), *Ethical Issues in Poverty Alleviation*, Studies in Global Justice 14, DOI 10.1007/978-3-319-41430-0_13

13.1 Introduction

Poverty activists and scholars have long noted the transformative potential of poor-led social initiatives and policies that aim to empower poor communities (Green 2008; Lister 2013). Development theorists and practitioners generally agree that successful development requires *meaningful* participation by the poor in shaping and implementing development practices (Chambers 1997; Hickey and Mohan 2004, 2005), and also aims at their empowerment. Yet, curiously, philosophical approaches to the problems of global poverty and inequality have attributed accorded little if any significance to the priorities, strategies, and initiatives of the poor themselves, as expressed through their social and political organizations and collective movements. Instead, philosophers have asked a trio of questions that take for granted the idea that rich states and their institutions are the proper agents of global justice (Deveaux 2015): do they have obligations to alleviate the poverty of the distant poor? (Miller 2010; Risse 2005; Wenar 2003); if so, what are these duties, and what grounds them? (O'Neill 2000; Pogge 2008, Singer 1972, 2010); and how can states and other responsible agents best be motivated to dispatch them? (Lenard 2012; Lichtenberg 2014).

This familiar philosophical conversation sees acute poverty primarily as a problem of unmet needs, the remedy for which is an urgent global redistribution of resources needed for well-being. The distributive framework within which these Kantian/Rawlsian and Utilitarian scholars generally think thus sets the parameters of poverty-reducing obligations. But while humanitarian crises, such as famine or mass refugee migrations, warrant a focus on the urgent redistribution of resources, the problem of chronic poverty arguably demands that ethicists explore the underlying sources of the poor's powerlessness and engage with proposals and efforts that aim to empower poor communities on their own terms. The present chapter tries to motivate this shift by examining in more detail *why* philosophers have overlooked poor-led social movements in their discussions of global poverty, and by sketching some of the important political insights that poor-led politics holds for normative approaches to poverty alleviation.

Below, in part I, I trace the omission of poor-led movements and perspectives from global justice theorizing to the prominence of "sufficiency thinking" in philosophical writing about poverty and inequality. First advanced by Harry Frankfurt, the sufficiency doctrine asserts that we should care morally about absolute deprivation or low levels of welfare – and about people who fall below the threshold required for a good life – but *not* about relative inequalities (1987). Although his view has been extensively criticized, resulting in more nuanced and sophisticated versions of the sufficiency thesis (Benbaji 2005; Huseby 2010), two intertwined assumptions at the heart of the sufficiency doctrine continue to influence philosophical discussions of poverty: the view that poverty is strictly about material lack and unmet needs; and the belief that such deprivation can best be redressed through judicious redistributive measures to reduce absolute low-welfare. These assumptions are increasingly at odds with the multidimensional and relational approach to poverty (Mosse 2010) that has emerged in policy and development studies, which takes structural inequalities, social exclusion, and relations of subordination and disempowerment to be at the heart of the experience of poverty. It is not a coincidence that, in their activism, poor-led social movements and organizations in the global South target precisely these harms.

In part II, I discuss two normative ethical approaches to deprivation that are broadly in tune with the relational approach to poverty: one that emphasizes social exclusion and disempowerment (Kabeer 2000; Wisor 2012), and one that focuses on humiliation and misrecognition (Dügben 2012; Schweiger 2014; Graf and Schweiger 2013, 2014). In part III, I discuss the *Slum/Shack Dwellers International* (SDI), a grassroots network of organizations in 33 countries dedicated to empowering communities of pavement and slum dwellers. Analyzing the aims, strategies, and successes of groups like SDI, I argue, should lead us to think more expansively about the goals, strategies, and agents of global poverty reduction. Part IV sets out the reasons why the insights and contributions of poor-led social organizations and movements should figure centrally in normative theories of poverty alleviation.

13.2 Poverty as Insufficiency?

The omission of the perspectives and contributions of the organizations and movements of the poor from normative discussions of global poverty reduction has much to do with the over-simplistic picture of poverty at the heart of redistributive approaches to transnational justice. Theorists who emphasize redistribution as a broad solution to chronic and acute poverty disagree on whether the goal should be merely to raise the distant poor up to a level of sufficiency (Blake 2001; Nagel 2005) or instead aim for more egalitarian ends, such as global equality of opportunity, equal respect, or equal capability to achieve a minimum level of functioning (Brock 2009; Caney 2001; Gilabert 2012; Satz 2010). But, as I shall argue, neither sufficiency nor egalitarian approaches to global justice pays much attention to the poor as agents of justice, or to proposals for radical changes to relations and structures that disempower and disenfranchise the poor (Nielsen 1985; Schweickart 2008).

Global redistribution approaches that endorse the sufficiency principle are particularly problematic insofar as they dismiss the significance of inequalities as well as nonmaterial aspects of poverty, such as humiliation and disempowerment. Sufficiency proponents argue that global redistribution should aim not at egalitarian ends but strive instead to meet people's basic unmet needs, the nonfulfillment of which causes them to suffer or prevents them from living a decent life. Michael Blake (2001, 259–260) insists that 'liberalism can concern itself with absolute deprivation abroad, and reserve a concern for relative deprivation in the local arena.…Shared citizenship…gives rise to a concern with relative deprivation that is absent in the international realm.' Similarly, Thomas Nagel argues that duties of justice simply do not apply in the global context, because the coercive (sovereign state) institutions that ground these reciprocal duties are simply lacking; instead, only 'humanitarian duties [arise]...in virtue of the absolute rather than the relative level of need of the people we are in a position to help' (Nagel 2005, 119).

The view that the governments and institutions of rich states have an obligation to address the absolute deprivation of the global poor but not relative inequalities between states (or national populations) echoes the sufficientarian reasoning developed by Frankfurt and others. Although the sufficiency doctrine has been subjected to incisive criticisms from proponents of relational equality and democratic equality (Anderson 1999; Casal 2007), its legacy is evidenced by the tendency within global justice theorizing to treat North-South poverty primary as a problem of unjust distribution rather than caused by global structures of economic and political inequality and domination. It is therefore instructive to see how the sufficiency doctrine – which developed more as a critique of economic egalitarianism than as a fully-fledged normative theory of distribution – conceptualizes poverty more generally. The sufficiency doctrine's core claim is that what matters morally is that everyone has *enough*, and *not* that they have equal shares of resources or assets (Frankfurt 1987). Frankfurt rejects economic equality as an ideal on the grounds that it serves as a kind of moral distraction, diverting our attention away from discovering what is important to each of us as individuals, and from discerning what we need for our own satisfaction and well-being (Frankfurt 1987). His opposition to equality as an intrinsic good pivots on his claim that an egalitarian distribution 'may fail to maximize aggregate utility' and in some cases 'actually minimizes aggregate utility' (Frankfurt 1987, 30). Yet troublingly, Frankfurt generalizes from small-group examples of extreme resource scarcity (where an equal division of resources may fail to maximize survival) to reach the conclusion that economic inequality is essentially unproblematic.

Classic sufficientarians conceive of poverty and inequality in exceedingly narrow terms, mainly in reference to income and wealth (Sen 1999); arguably, this prevents them from recognizing that social and economic inequalities may yield harms not reducible to material deprivation alone. Sharply demarcating poverty from inequality in this way, Frankfurt is able to assert that 'the relationship between low economic status and urgent need is wholly contingent....There is no necessary conceptual connection between a person's relative economic position and whether he has needs of any urgency' (Frankfurt 1987, 35). Yet Frankfurt implausibly generalizes from this (not untrue) abstract claim to actually existing societies. In his critique of Ronald Dworkin's essay, 'Why Liberals Should Care About Equality,' Frankfurt (1987) insists that Dworkin, lamenting the high unemployment and the phenomenon of the working poor in the U.S., simply confuses poverty with inequality. But Frankfurt can only reach this conclusion by bracketing a range of adjacent contributors to (and consequences of) economic inequality, the acknowledgement of which undermines the case for disaggregating deprivation and inequality; inequalities in access to employment, housing, healthcare, and education, as well as in assets like land (particularly important in developing countries), all contribute to absolute low welfare. While we can of course conceptually distinguish poverty from inequality, the sufficiency lens overreaches by claiming that one can have sufficient resources for well-being entirely *irrespective of deep structural inequalities*.

Most versions of the sufficiency doctrine insist that significant inequalities are not in themselves troubling: 'If a person has enough resources to provide for the satisfaction of his needs and his interests, his resources are entirely adequate; their adequacy does not depend in addition upon the magnitude of the resources that other people possess' (Frankfurt 1997, 7). More recently, however, Axelsen and Nielsen, who blend sufficientarianism with a capabilities approach, have acknowledged that there are 'positional aspects' to goods like 'societal status, political influence, and the social bases of self-respect,' (2014, 14) which can make relative inequalities somewhat morally salient. Yet they see this positional inequality as merely one more way in which *insufficiency's harms* can manifest: 'One's absolute position may, thus be determined by one's relative position, in which case a person may become insufficiently free because of a relative deprivation – but it is the insufficiency itself that creates a problem, not the inequality in itself' (15). Axelsen and Nielsen have in mind domestic, not global, problems of insufficiency, and their analysis of sufficiency as 'freedom from duress' in connection with 'a limited set of capabilities or opportunities' (2) is meant to encompass harms that do not reduce to poverty per se. Nevertheless, it is still the case that their sufficiency reasoning leads them to frame even positional social and political inequalities as fundamentally problems of distribution, not domination. Arguably, large inequalities in wealth and resources do not just *indirectly* correlate with insufficiencies, as Axelsen and Nielsen seem to suggest, but rather, correspond to real inequalities of power that in turn prevent people from accessing resources relevant to their absolute well-being (Satz 2010).

Sufficiency thinking in general seems to assume an overly sharp distinction between poverty and inequality. As a consequence, although some revised sufficientarian approaches argue that relative inequalities can prevent individuals from achieving sufficiency in many important area of well-being (Axelsen and Nielsen 2014), they do not recognize that inequalities of power, status, and political voice are *themselves* both a cause and a feature of poverty. Note that this is a different point from the criticism that 'relational egalitarians' make of both classic sufficiency theorists and distributional egalitarians. Relational (or democratic) egalitarians reject the sufficiency claim that relative socio-economic inequalities simply do not matter; inequalities typically *do* matter, say relational egalitarians, insofar as they affect the ability of citizens to interact on terms of equal respect with one another, free from discrimination, oppression, and exploitation (Anderson 1999; Satz 2010). While I concur that inequalities are often instrumental in creating oppressive relations between citizens, my claim here is a different one: namely, that significant socio-economic inequalities are closely intertwined with the political powerlessness that is itself partly *constitutive* poverty, and which locks people into chronic deprivation. If I am right, then ethicists who seek to develop solutions to global poverty need to focus much more on relations and structures of social and political inequality and exclusion than they have hitherto done. Democratic or relational equality points us in the right direction by rejecting the resource-distribution paradigm as over-simple, and by showing that inequalities create unequal social relationships, capabilities, and freedoms (Anderson 1999). They also help us to see that these relative inequalities are relevant in the global context when they contribute to gross transnational power imbalances that undermine equal opportunities and equal respect for many groups, or perpetuate relations of domination and exploitation (Brock 2009; Satz 2010).

A more thorough and in-depth analysis of poverty as consisting of pervasive relations and structures of inequality will require that we look beyond the notion of relational or democratic equality. Specifically, it demands that we look to the arguments of scholars, policy analysts, and activists who define poverty relationally, in terms of processes of social exclusion, subordination, and powerlessness. In the next section, I turn to this emerging, alternative approach to poverty, which better reflects the realities of poverty as understood by poor communities and their organizations.

13.3 Reframing Poverty: Social Exclusion, Vulnerability, and Misrecognition

In contrast to philosophical views which sharply distinguish between poverty and inequality, poverty is increasingly defined by both development economists and those who study market economies as, in effect, a consequence of structural inequalities across multiple levels (Salverda et al. 2009). This emphasis on unequal social and economic relations and structures as constitutive of poverty helps explain why economists often refer to poverty as a condition of 'social exclusion,' and why the study of poverty is increasingly called the study of 'poverty dynamics' (Addison et al. 2009). So important are these relative and relational dimensions that poverty in developed countries is usually measured using the metric of relative income: specifically, according to the OECD, those living on less than 50 % of the median income of their society are said to be poor (or 60 % for Europe). The reason for this is that, in developed societies, *relative* household income (after tax and transfers) gives a much clearer picture than does absolute income of what individuals have access to, in terms of material resources, opportunities, and activities. Or as poverty researchers explain, 'the underlying rationale [for the focus on relative income] is that those falling more than a certain 'distance' below the average or normal income in their society are unlikely to participate fully in it' (Nolan and Marx 2009, 318).

While the emphasis on relative deprivation and social exclusion has mainly been used to understand poverty in advanced industrialized societies, some researchers use it to explain poverty in developing countries as a dynamic social process involving multiple inequalities and relations of structural disadvantage (Kabeer 2000; Wisor 2012). The social exclusion analysis of poverty needs, of course, to be adapted to developing societies; for example, it needs to be acknowledge that the informal sector is often the primary workforce in poor countries, thereby changing what it means to be excluded from the formal workforce (Wisor 2012). Nonetheless, a social exclusion analysis can help us to see the multidimensional nature (and causes) of deprivation in poor countries, as well as draw our attention to the issues of power and inequality that are so important to poor-led politics. Exclusion from needed social services is very often a central component of poverty in low-income countries (Wisor 2012), and not coincidentally, is the focus point of much pro-poor activism.

Wisor gives four reasons why the social exclusion approach makes an essential contribution to a multidimensional analysis of global poverty, even though it is not synonymous (as some argue in the case of poverty in high income countries) with poverty itself. First, it frames poverty as a 'dynamic process rather than a static state of affairs,' in which the poor suffer from 'active exclusion from public services and private markets [and] passive exclusion from social and public participation' (Wisor 2012, 117). Or, as Kabeer puts it, 'a focus on processes of exclusion is a useful way to think about social policy because it draws attention to the production of disadvantage through the active dynamics of social interaction, rather than through anonymous processes of impoverishment and marginalisation' (Kabeer 2000, 84). Second, the social exclusion lens grasps the importance of misrecognition and group-based discrimination and disadvantages and affirms 'the significance of 'representation' for individuals and groups...through cultural activities, social and political participation, and community respect' (Wisor 2012, 118). As such, this may help us to understand the centrality of political demands for recognition, respect, and inclusion by pro-poor organizations and movements. Third, 'the social exclusion necessarily focuses on the *contexts* in which deprivation occur. Individuals are thus not understood as unembedded units of production...[or]consumption, but as highly embedded in social and political environments that are deeply interrelated with the deprivations they face' (119). Poor-led social movements and groups in low and middle-income countries usually aim to transform the specific social and political context in which their poverty arises by targeting national social policies and structures of injustice, as I shall argue shortly. Finally, Wisor notes that 'the social exclusion approach is explicitly political,' allowing us to see 'the political processes by which people become and are kept poor' (119). In their struggles and organizations, poor communities have understood this connection between social-political processes of exclusion and material poverty much better than have philosophers writing about global poverty.

To better understand why relative deprivations can and do translate not only into poverty but also powerlessness, it is also helpful to look to Iris Young's discussion of social-structural inequalities and injustices (Young 2011). These inequalities, and the vulnerabilities to which they give rise, are not readily grasped from within a distributive justice framework, in part because the latter overemphasizes resources and reduces poverty to a matter of material scarcity. Sufficiency thinking, as we saw, dismisses the significance of inequalities that shape people's access to the opportunities and goods they need for well-being, and also fails to see that such inequalities are in a very real sense constitutive of the experience of poverty. Young's account of one woman's (Sandy's) structural vulnerability to homelessness highlights the ways in which multiple institutions and social rules prevent her from finding decent housing, without any one factor being dispositive in her homelessness (Young 2011). The structural vulnerability to poverty and homelessness that Young describes is bound up with institutions and rules that accord greater power and opportunities to some rather than others. Her account of social-structural injustice helps to explain why poor-led social movements and organizations focus so much on empowering poor communities, and on challenging the corruption and lack of transparency and accountability that contribute to their powerlessness. The remedy for this vulnerability is not simply more resources (although these of course help); rather, it is collective action (Young 2011; Chandhoke 2013).

'Recognition theorists' propose an understanding of poverty that complements Young's emphasis on vulnerability and structural injustice, as well as the social exclusion approach to poverty. Recognition theory similarly emphasizes aspects routinely overlooked by resource-focused approaches – specifically, those of disrespect, humiliation, shame, and lack of recognition (Schweiger 2014). These experiences, recognition theorists argue, are typically part of the processes of social exclusion that many social scientists and anti-poverty advocates now say best capture the reality of poverty. The recognition approach to poverty is therefore able to capture a number of the subjectively-felt aspects of poverty that are not well captured by standard poverty measures – much like Young's analysis of the structural injustices that many people *experience as* entrenched barriers to their ability to live a life of self-respect:

> Misrecognition, as well as recognition, is an umbrella term, and neither focuses on a single feature of human life in the way that much poverty research does in its focus on money and material assets. Recognition theory, rather, argues that injustices such as poverty have to be understood in their multidimensionality….It focuses on the increased vulnerability of poor people to forms of misrecognition and on how poverty disrupts families, communities, and other relations of care and love, and how it affects the self and identity of the poor (Schweiger 2014, 269).

While recognition theorists aim to bring the (often overlooked) subjective and relational experiences of poverty to our attention, they by no means ignore the more standard measures of deprivation. Rather, they see these experiences as inextricably bound up with – and shaped by – material and social disadvantages along many dimensions (Graf and Schweiger 2013, 2014).

As with both Young's analysis of structural injustice and vulnerability and the social exclusion view, then, the recognition view of poverty is deeply concerned with the stigmatizing, exclusionary, and disempowering effects of deprivation and inequality. As a first step towards reversing these harms, all three approaches ask us to notice and hear what poor individuals *themselves* say about their experience of poverty. The subjectively felt and relational aspects of disadvantage and scarcity simply cannot be well understood in the absence of this first-hand knowledge; while some conventional poverty measurements can gauge the extent of a person's (or group's) social exclusion, they cannot readily convey the interior experience of disrespect, shame, or humiliation to which conditions of social and material deprivation give rise. Moreover, many of the material and social-relational aspects of poverty are deeply contextual – that is, sensitive to the particular structures, norms, and expectations of particular societies; as a result, we cannot know fully or precisely what set of factors or conditions makes a person (or a group) vulnerable to disrespect, shame, or to a sense of powerlessness without hearing their perspectives (Graf and Schweiger 2013). Poverty activists in advanced industrialized states have long protested governments' failure to recognize and include the poor in planning and implementing anti-poverty initiatives, arguing that it signals a lack of respect for the poor and their first-hand knowledge (Lister 2013). In the context of developing countries, development aid programs that fail to include the perspectives of the poor, or to include them as active participants in poverty solutions, have been the subject of extensive criticism and backlash. Non-inclusive development interventions may in some sense reinforce the exclusion and status-subordination of the poor in developing states because it 'often fails in treating its target population as equivalent partners and valid agents of knowledge production. The rhetoric of partnership is undermined by the practices of strongly asymmetric power relations' (Dügben 2012, 74–75).

In addition to encouraging us to include the perspectives and insights of the poor themselves, the alternative, relational approaches to poverty discussed here also show us why collective action by poor communities must become a critical component of poverty alleviation. Disrespect, lack of recognition, shame, and humiliation, are not readily redressed by top-down solutions to deprivation that treat the poor as passive recipients. To truly reverse the social exclusion and sense of powerlessness that both chronic and acute poverty engender, the poor must come to feel that they have a say in demanding and directing the changes that they need. This is true not only for symbolic reasons of the sort that Frantz Fanon (1968) wrote about – that is, the need to throw off the colonial legacy of cultural domination and disrespect in order to clear the way for an emancipated consciousness and identity to emerge. Rather, it is also because recognizing and validating the political agency of poor individuals is critical to acknowledging their equal status as fellow citizens (in the national context) and treating them as persons with human rights (in the global context), including rights of democratic participation. As Lister notes, the view that participation by the poor is important 'acknowledges the agency of rights-bearers and their potential to play a role in the development of rights and services. In strengthening that agency it enables people with experience of poverty to act more effectively as democratic citizens and bearers of human rights' (2013, 118).

It is no coincidence that poor-led organizations and movements of the poor (in both the global South as well as the North) increasingly frame their struggles in the language of human rights, particularly social and economic human rights. This framing certainly intersects well with domestic social policy, which poor activists are most often seeking to change. But more importantly, by demanding that their human rights be respected, poor activists are in a sense interpellated as political agents. As Neera Chandhoke explains, in reaching for human rights, 'the global poor are not seen as victims who have to be given cash transfers because the West is guilty but instead are treated as rights-bearers and thus people who possess irreducible moral status' (Chandhoke 2010, 80). The very act of claiming rights and articulating social policy draws attention to the interests of the poor as a concrete political entity within a society; these entities can have a surprisingly strong degree of influence when they form regional or national coalitions and/or transnational networks (Sandbrook 2002). Poverty alleviation strategies or initiatives that recognize and validate the collective actions of poor organizations (or movements) can also arguably bolster disadvantaged communities' sense of political inclusion: 'political mobilization…makes people conscious of what is due to them, and what they have been denied…this is what these networks of solidarity accomplish' (Chandhoke 2010, 80). While there is of course a risk that the language of poor empowerment, citizenship, and social rights can be co-opted by the neoliberal agenda of 'inclusive liberalism,' there is no shortage of examples of genuinely radical poor-based social movements that use these framings, particularly in Latin America and South Africa (Hickey 2010).

Poor-led social movements and organizations are inherently political insofar as they seek to mobilize poor communities in order to exert pressure on local and/or national governments to introduce social policies or other reforms that will make the lives of the poor better. At the local level especially, it is instructive that many such poor-led groups specifically target structures of bureaucratic control and corruption that hamper the poor in their efforts to survive, and therefore seek explicitly to empower them. Policy-oriented poor social movements in particular are thus best seen as 'forms of political action that attack the social relationships underlying chronic poverty' (Bebbington 2007, 798) whose aim is to make relevant agents reform the policies (or policy vacuums) that reinforce their poverty. Nor is this connection between collective action and empowerment limited to developing countries, as there is by now a wealth of research on participatory anti-poverty initiatives that supports the connection between participation and empowerment among the poor in industrialized states. The transformative possibilities of poor-led organizations and social movements in the developing world is however my focus here, as their omission from normative discussions of global poverty has been accompanied by a general disregard for the poor as actual or potential agents of social change (Deveaux 2015). In the next section, I discuss the SDI in order to illuminate some of the surprising foci, strategies, and accomplishments of this global network, and to show why the insights and contributions of this and similar poor-led movements (and organizations) to poverty alleviation is distinctive and critical to the theory and practice of global justice.

13.4 What Theorists Can Learn from Poverty Activists: Slum Dwellers International

SDI is an international network of grassroots, community-based organizations of the urban poor, chiefly homeless and landless residents. Launched in 1996 and founded by Mumbai grassroots leader Jockin Arputham, it evolved from the work and alliance of three groups in India: the Mumbai-based SPARC (focused on pavement dwellers) and *Mahila Milan* ('Women Together,' empowering women residents of slums and pavements); and the National Slum Dwellers Federation (NSDF), founded in 1974. With chapters and partners in 33 countries, the SDI is by far the largest network of urban poor residents and their advocates in the world. In a nutshell, 'SDI groups seek to identify a political space and then use this space to secure developmental benefits, generally around secure tenure, infrastructure, services and housing, that address immediate needs and build the capacity of the poor to innovate, strategise and negotiate for further benefits' (d'Cruz and Mitlin 2007, 235). My purpose here is to sketch out some of the key aims and organizing strategies of SDI and its affiliates, in order to make the case that pro-poor politics holds important insights for normative theorizing about poverty.

From its inception, the SDI has been committed to community-directed change: 'SDI affiliates support people-centred development, with organized communities leading and implementing activities to secure a pro-poor urban transformation recognized and resourced by the state' (Mitlin 2013, 484). The participatory and grassroots orientation of SDI is an extension of the beliefs and organizing style of the three Indian groups whose alliance paved the way for the transnational network. As Arjun Appadurai (2002, 28) explains,

> The Alliance has evolved a style of pro-poor activism that consciously departs from earlier models of social work, welfarism, and community organization....Instead of relying on the model of an outside organizer who teaches local communities how to hold the state to its normative obligations to the poor, the Alliance is committed to the methods of organization, mobilization, teaching, and learning that build on what poor persons already know and understand. The first principle of this approach is that no one knows more about how to survive poverty than the poor themselves.

As this description suggests, SDI and its national affiliates are at the vanguard of what has come to be known as 'pro-poor' political organizing and change; indeed, the organization's mission statement says that 'SDI believes that the only way to manage urban growth and to create inclusive cities is for the urban poor to be at the center of strategies for urban development' (SDI website, 2015). What does this mean, in practice? First, SDI and the national federations that it comprises are actually led by urban poor representatives who are activists in slums or among pavement dwellers. As one observer notes, 'the NGOs that support each federation...have redefined the role of professionals away from being the talkers, managers and solution generators to being listeners and supporters of community-generated solutions' (Satterthwaite 2001, 136).

Second and relatedly, SDI focuses on facilitating knowledge exchanges between the different national federations of slum dwellers, aimed at building up the organizing capabilities and political strategies of urban poor groups and their social movements. From its inception, it has sponsored face-to-face meetings of delegations of national slum dweller federations who travel to meet their counterparts in other countries. Typically the visits 'involve immediate immersion in the ongoing projects of the host community' (Appadurai 2002, 41). Beyond sharing experiences and tactics for supporting and protecting slum communities, these exchanges have made possible the 'building of deep democracies locally' (Appadurai 2002, 42). This is not only because of the examples of grassroots organizing that SDI activists are exposed to, but because of the network's commitment to democratic internal criticism and debate: 'When members of the SDI meet in one another's localities (as well as on other occasions, such as meetings in London, New York, or the Hague), they have the occasion to raise hard questions about inclusion, power, hierarchy, and political risk or naïveté in their host's local and regional organizations' (Appadurai 2002, 43). At the same time, these visits between the national federations have garnered considerable media attention and even funding from important bodies (both governmental and non-governmental), thereby increasing the political clout of the national federations and their affiliates (Appadurai 2002, 42). In addition to improving the federations' bargaining power with local and national governments, the heightened profile of the global SDI exchanges has made it possible for the organization to move into 'more long-term strategic plans for funding, capacity building, and what they call scaling up' (Appadurai 2002, 42).

The political knowledge and strategies that the representatives and members of the member federations of SDI share with one another is intended to build up the political capacities of these federations and their member groups through tactical information and solidarity. But what, concretely, are these political capacities in turn directed at achieving for slum-dwellers? Many of the national slum and pavement dweller federations (and their member groups) provide concrete support to communities of urban poor who are fighting evictions from informal settlements, including legal and tactical support against shack demolition – or in some cases, to minimize the destruction of personal possessions through voluntary dismantling. Saving and credit schemes to assist slum and pavement dwellers have also quickly emerged as a central part of the work of member groups of the national federations. In India, *Mahila Milan* was founded to link together hundreds of women's collectives which help women pavement and slum dwellers to create income and savings so as to better weather the various crises that punctuate their precarious living situations (Patel and Mitlin 2004, 219). The Indian Alliance has helped to extend this group's success, and by 2011, the savings network consisted over 750,000 savers in 65 cities in the country (Satterthwaite and Mitlin 2014, 140). *Mahila Milan*, like many other members of the national federations within SDI, is active in other areas of empowerment, teaching slum dwellers how to do community-based enumerations as well as to construct housing (Patel and Mitlin 2004). Indeed, enumeration of slum and pavement dwellers has been a longstanding cornerstone of the work of SDI members, because it throws light on the paucity of services and infrastructure for these dwellers as well as providing proof of the (undercounted) vast number of residents of informal settlements:

> Enumeration is a simple but powerful tool designed by the residents of informal settlements, who own and use the information that they gather themselves. Through enumerations they survey and map themselves, and build the skills and knowledge to represent themselves and their needs to government…They develop a critical collective identity that helps form the political basis for their engagement with government. For these reasons, the motto within SDI is 'When in doubt, count!' (Patel et al. 2012, 14)

SDI's federations and their member groups also advocate for the provision of badly needed social services to slums, such as sanitation facilities. Drawing attention to the political obstacles to these municipal services has also been an important part of the strategy of some of the federations and their member groups. The Indian Alliance publicized the fact that the budget allocated to the construction of public toilets by the Mumbai Municipality went unused, revealing that the problem lay in the 'city's patronage-based politics...[and the ad-hoc] way in which the city dealt with the sanitation needs of the vast majority of the city's residents' (Menon 2013, 164). The Alliance's revelation of this fact and its outspoken criticism of the few (poorly designed and maintained) public toilets that were supplied was soon followed up with their own grassroots initiative to design, construct, and maintain what they called a 'community toilet' – with the support of the local municipality. Within the Alliance, the women's group *Mahila Milan* took the lead in assessing the different needs of children, men and women in slum communities, designing neighborhood toilet blocks that were subsequently replicated across Mumbai (Satterthwaite and Mitlin 2014). Drawing on her ethnographic research on Mumbai's informal settlements, Gayatri Menon explains the significance of this project in empowering its residents and altering the state's engagement with them:

> Less an architectural model and more an ethico-political innovation that seeks to transform the way in which the state invests in and engages with the urban poor, the community toilet seeks to expand the decision-making power of the subjects of social policy. The public toilet as conceived by the Municipality relegates the poor to the position of welfare recipients.... The community toilet on the other hand, calls forth a substantive, and insurgent understanding of citizenship that empowers impoverished communities by creating the conditions for them to exercise a degree of local, democratic control over the conditions of their living, that is, to recover agency. (Menon 2013, 165)

While my discussion has focused on the Indian organizations within SDI, the goals and strategies of other national federations and their members very much echo those discussed here. In Namibia, South Africa, Zimbabwe, Kenya, Malawi, Uganda, Brazil, Cambodia, and the Philippines, for example, the SDI and its affiliates have secured housing plots and subsidies, spearheaded community-led slum upgrading projects, helped to build up the resources of slums through community-managed savings practices, and developed (and delivered) innovative, alternative public sanitation facilities. They have earned the support of local and national governments with their large, low-income community housing construction projects, housing subsidy plans, and savings schemes (Bolnick 2008; d'Cruz and Mitlin 2007). Sometimes SDI's national federations work with select NGOs and draw on their professional expertise, but importantly, these are genuine (as well as strategic and often temporary) partnerships, and not driven by the interests or agendas of NGO professionals. Importantly, however, the latter are kept at arm's length from the core policy-setting process within SDI organizations, and are 'held to account through a community-led governance process' that 'treats professionals as an executive, there to enact the wishes of democratic representatives of the community' (Mitlin 2013, 494). Despite its successes with government in some places and its endorsement (at times) by powerful entities like the World Bank, the SDI has not wavered in its commitment to poor-directed change, as is evidenced in its ongoing efforts to train local leaders (particularly women), create community knowledge, and expand the capabilities of its ever-growing membership base (d'Cruz and Mitlin 2007; Satterthwaite and Mitlin 2014).

As this analysis suggests, the success of SDI and its affiliates must be measured not only by the housing that it has managed to supply or generate for slum and pavement dwellers, which is certainly considerable – between 15,000 and 30,000 housing units annually in the last several years (Bolnick 2008). Rather, it must also be measured in terms of the political shifts that it has effected, or at least begun to effect. One of these shifts has to do with the consciousness and capabilities of slum and pavement dwellers themselves, in places where SDI and its members have been active. By becoming directly involved in the multi-tiered process of bringing housing and services to their communities – from enumerating neighbors and assessing communal needs to designing facilities and working with local and national government officials for this infrastructure – the disempowered urban poor become political agents. Where it has worked well, the SDI's model of grassroots organizing has thus not only challenged the marginality of pavement dwellers, but created a new 'subject of public policy' modeled on a kind of insurgent citizenship (Menon 2013, 158). These political subjects do not work in isolation; rather, SDI aims to create 'poor communities able to engage in partnerships with more powerful agencies… [in such a way as to increase] the capability of these communities to perform more powerfully as instruments of deep democracy in the local context' (Appadurai 2002, 46). Building the knowledge and capacities of poor communities not only gives members a sense of agency, but it makes it possible for them to press their demands for needed reforms much more effectively; after all, 'the main focus of the members of Shack/Slum Dwellers International is not on donor-funded projects but on changing government institutions and policies within each locality and nationally so that they respond to the needs and priorities of urban poor groups' (Satterthwaite 2001, 138). Through their SDI activism, the urban poor demand the accountability of government agencies, to be sure, but on terms very different from those of traditional welfarism or even development: 'SDI groups are involved in developing new relationships between the urban poor and the city authorities and politicians' (d'Cruz and Mitlin 2007, 234). These relationships, and indeed a new kind of politics, are made possible by the interventions and openings that SDI and member organizations create through their community activism, institutional and political capacity-building, and pro-poor solidarity work.

13.5 What Poor-Led Political Struggles Can Teach Us About Poverty

SDI's efforts to transform the powerlessness of poor communities by fostering slum dwellers' 'agency as a fundamental aspect of their demand for a fairer distribution of public goods and claims to a right to the city' (Menon 2013, 157) pushes against a *merely* redistributive understanding of global justice. SDI and its federations have arguably developed a political model for poverty alleviation that supports the 'agency and collective capacity' of the urban poor (Satterthwaite and Mitlin 2014,

133) far better than state-sponsored or even I/NGO-led anti-poverty initiatives do. Yet the priorities and strategies of this and other poor-led organizations are conspicuously absent from mainstream poverty-reduction approaches in philosophy, notably those of Peter Singer (2010) and Thomas Pogge (2008). This serious omission has had the ironic effect of marginalizing poor communities within global justice discourse—in effect, obscuring the poor's own analyses and insights regarding poverty, as well as their concrete efforts to transform the structures that perpetuate it. Relational accounts of chronic poverty, such as those emphasizing social exclusion and misrecognition, are better able to acknowledge the significance of poor communities' contributions to poverty analysis and alleviation.

The work of poor-led social movements and political organizations contains valuable normative insights for ethical and political approaches to reducing poverty and inequality – insights that philosophers would do well to heed. Importantly, the priorities and strategies of poor communities sometimes depart from normative theorist's usual assumptions about what those living in poverty most want and need, thus leading us to reconsider these assumptions. For example, it is striking that the redistribution of goods and resources is rarely the sole (or even primary) goal of poor-led organizations' and movements' politics. Instead, pro-poor political struggles aim first and foremost to transform the social and political structures that systematically disempower poor citizens. In Young's terms, they take aim at the structural injustices to which they are subjected, and which produce what Charles Tilly refers to as 'durable inequalities' – persistent inequalities often transmitted across generations. These structural injustices cannot be undone by shifting resources alone – if indeed such a thing were possible without a seismic shift in power. Neither the redistributive paradigm in general, nor 'sufficiency' thinking in particular, then, grasp the importance of politically transforming processes and structures of social inequality. By contrast, a relational account of poverty sees the transformation of unjust structures and relations of power inequality as critical to reducing deprivation.

Poor-led political movements and organizing also reveal important sources of discrimination, disadvantage, and exclusion that perpetuate poverty – and which blind-side many resourcist poverty reduction initiatives. The existence of these structures – which deepen the poverty of certain subgroups of the poor, like women and ethnic/racial/religious minorities – helps explain why poor organizations target oppressive social and political structures and relations in their struggles to reduce poverty. Concurrently, pro-poor groups often target the empowerment of these doubly disadvantaged groups in their organizations. Early on, the NSDF identified women's particular disadvantages as key to understanding the entrenched vulnerability of slum and pavement dwellers, and women's leadership as a crucial part of any struggle to reduce urban poverty. These were the reasons for establishing *Mahila Milan*:

> With most savers and savings-groups managers being women, these savings groups help address the multiple forms of disadvantage, oppression and exploitation that they face.... This challenges and helps overturn discrimination and limited social expectations as women engage with each other as activists (rather than remaining subservient to male and/or older household members), public agents (rather than enclosed in the household) and strategic thinkers (rather than passive)....As women take up new leadership roles in providing essential goods and services centred on the home and neighbourhood, an engagement with the state begins. (Satterthwaite and Mitlin 2014, 162)

Understanding the vulnerability to poverty of certain groups (like women) arguably requires a fine-grained analysis of social relations, family dynamics, norms, and local political institutions and structures – as capability approach proponents have argued (Sen 1999). But equally, reducing this vulnerability requires that those suffering disadvantage, discrimination and exclusion be at the center of processes that seek to dismantle structures of inequality.

Pro-poor organizations and movements thus care very much about enhancing the capabilities and political voice of poor communities – a priority overlooked by broadly redistributive approaches to poverty reduction. This is partly so that they can be more effective at holding relevant agents (usually government) accountable for failing to deliver social goods to which they, as citizens, are entitled. But equally, the capacity-building focus of poor-led groups also has to do with transforming deprived individuals' powerlessness and sense of exclusion into one of empowerment and inclusion. As Green (2008, 20) writes, 'such an assertion of power is both an end in itself – a crucial kind of freedom – and a means to ensure that the different institutions of society (the state, the market, the community, and the family) respect people's rights and meet their needs, via laws, rules, policies, and day-to-day-practices'. In seeking to develop the social and political capabilities of the poor, activists often hold out a new model of citizenship, like the insurgent, activist citizenship of the urban poor in the case of SDI, or 'agrarian citizenship' in the case of the Brazil's agrarian land movement, MST (*Movimento dos Trabalhadores Rurais Sem Terra*) (Wittman 2010). Human rights claims (especially social and economic rights) are increasingly part of these alternative, radical models of citizenship.

Whether they appeal to their social rights as citizens or invoke the language of human rights (or both), poor communities aim through their activism and organizing to challenge and transform their powerlessness in the face of local, national, and global institutions. This may strike us as wishful thinking or a fantastical, modern-day David and Goliath fable. But if we view poverty in relational terms (Mosse 2010), as was suggested earlier, it becomes clear that some of its central harms – humiliation, shame, disrespect, voicelessness, lack of recognition – require remedies that specifically target the social exclusion and disempowerment of the poor. Pro-poor social movements and organizations understand this, and are motivated by the belief that freedom from poverty (like exploitation and domination) is not something that can be achieved passively in the sense of being granted to the poor. Rather, they proceed on the assumption that a lasting reduction of poverty and the achievement of 'durable empowerment' (Drydyk 2008) demands a process of social and political struggle in which unjust power structures and relationships are identified, challenged, and transformed by citizens. Not only do these groups and movements demand accountability, transparency, and reform, then, but they assert their own nascent agency by developing alternative visions and proposals for development and poverty alleviation, as the example of SDI showed. These two aspects – transforming unjust structures that disempower poor and marginalized citizens, and enhancing the creative political capabilities of citizens – are essential, and closely linked (Drydyk 2013). Importantly, such empowerment efforts must be attentive to relational inequalities that produce vulnerability to poverty, particularly to 'group subjection and intra-group dominance' (Drydyk 2013, 260).

The scope and aims of poor social movements and organizations differ from redistribution-focused approaches to poverty in an another respect: while the former very often focus on activism at the local, regional and national levels, the latter target the transnational level (with the exception of capability theorists like Martha Nussbaum). There are of course many good reasons why philosophers concerned with acute poverty and inequality would choose to focus their attention on global processes and institutions – not least, their sheer power and scope. But given the importance of local and national institutions, structures, and social policies for the daily lives and capabilities of the poor, it is critical that normative theorizing does not ignore these entities, or activism directed at them. Although global coalitions can and do enhance the solidarity of the disenfranchised, arguably 'the main agent that can realize rights and thus justice remains the national, democratic state upon which demands can be made, and from which accountability can be demanded' (Chandhoke 2013, 312). The injustices that poor communities care most about are often sedimented by processes and structures at these sub-global levels; as a result, poor politics often target lack of accountability, lack of transparency, and the corruption of government and NGOs (McGee and Gaventa 2010). While some theorists have drawn attention to the lack of accountability of global financial institutions, they have paid little attention to issues of transparency, accountability, and corruption at more proximate levels. And yet, as Gillian Brock has noted,

> Corruption plays a huge role in sustaining high levels of poverty, undermining beneficial development and undermining many countries' ability to enjoy reasonable opportunities for development….There is an underappreciated connection between corruption and people being unable to meet their basic needs (2014, 256).

Equally important, pro-poor activists target local, regional, and national level processes and policies because it is at these levels that they can most readily transform their own sense of disempowerment. The urban poor mobilized through SDI's federations and their member groups are actively involved not only in protesting unjust policies and practices at these sub-global levels, but in developing and implementing alterative solutions to their lack of housing and social services. As we saw, this often takes place through partnerships with (or support from) local and sometimes regional and national governments. In Brazil, for example, SDI partnered with both private sector entities and a support NGO (*Interaçao*) to secure legal land tenure for 7000 families in the space of 3 years (Bolnick 2008). Contributing in these ways, and building social and political capabilities more generally, is not as easy in activism that targets global structures, as significant as these are to poverty. Rather, 'everyday struggles for livelihood take place in particular localities or 'communities' whose vitality is a function of the density and depth of their civil associations, especially among the poor' (Friedmann 1996, 170). If poverty is a relational process in which multiple, cross-cutting structural inequalities are sustained, then empowerment initiatives must make it possible for people to take aim at these relational structures at close range (Cornwall and Rivas 2015).

Finally, by paying closer attention to the social movements and organizations of the urban and rural poor, philosophers will acknowledge their status as moral and political agents of justice. Too often the poor have been overlooked as possible agents in poverty reduction; arguably, our 'analyses need to consider the full range of different agents who might be able to play a part in reducing global injustice' (Brock 2014, 258). Skeptics who are unconvinced that poor activism can amount to much may not be persuaded by descriptions of poor-led politics; they might, however, be moved by appeals to democratic justice. Justice conceived according to principles of democratic legitimacy demands that those directly affected both by poverty and by attempts to alleviate it have a central role (should they wish to take it up) in articulating and developing responses to poverty. Nancy Fraser's idea of the 'all-subjected' principle — an expanded and amended version of the all-affected principle — is helpful here in explaining why 'parity of participation' (Fraser 2008; Fraser 2010) should be understood as a core requirement of global justice by democratic theorists. To the extent that normative theorizing about poverty ignores or fails to include poor citizens, it reinforces their exclusion from political power. While philosophers cannot transform the poor's lack of power and voice, by incorporating their communities' and social movements' insights into our normative theories of poverty reduction (and of global justice generally), we can help to recognize and validate their voices. Beyond demonstrating solidarity, such a move would make ethical approaches to poverty more relevant to the relational realities of poverty that poor activists have long understood – and more consistent with the radical democratic principles that theorists of global justice usually espouse.

I have argued that political philosophers writing on global poverty need to take seriously the social and political organizations and movements of the poor. This does not mean that they should not also engage the question of what duties rich states owe to the poor; nor have I denied that that global redistribution on a massive scale is required in order to eradicate poverty or achieve global justice. Rather, my aim has been to show that the value of theorists' usual conversations about global poverty is greatly reduced if it ignores the priorities and perspectives of existing poor organizations and struggles. We need our normative discussions of poverty alleviation to intersect and resonate much more closely with poor-led politics if such theorizing is to be of use in framing and challenging the vast power inequalities and injustices that make acute poverty possible.

References

Addison, Tony, David Hulme, and Ravi Kanbur (eds.). 2009. *Poverty dynamics: Interdisciplinary perspectives*. Oxford: Oxford University Press.

Anderson, Elizabeth. 1999. What is the point of equality? *Ethics* 109: 287–337.

Appadurai, Arjun. 2002. Deep democracy: Urban governmentality and the horizon of politics. *Public Culture* 14: 21–47.

Axelsen, David, and Lasse Nielsen. 2014. Sufficiency as freedom from duress. *The Journal of Political Philosophy*. doi:10.1111/jopp.120-48.

Bebbington, Anthony. 2007. Social movements and the politicization of chronic poverty. *Development and Change* 38: 793–818.
Benbaji, Yitzhak. 2005. The doctrine of sufficiency: A defense. *Utilitas* 17: 310–332.
Blake, Michael. 2001. Distributive justice, state coercion, and autonomy. *Philosophy and Public Affairs* 30: 257–296.
Bolnick, Joel. 2008. Development as reform and counter-reform: Paths travelled by Slum/Shack Dwellers International. In *Can NGOs make a difference?: The challenge of development alternatives*, ed. Anthony Bebbington. London/New York: Zed Books.
Brock, Gillian. 2009. *Global justice: A cosmopolitan account*. Oxford: Oxford University Press.
Brock, Gillian. 2014. Some future directions for global justice. *Journal of Global Ethics* 10: 254–260.
Caney, Simon. 2001. Cosmopolitan justice and equalizing opportunities. *Metaphilosophy* 32: 113–134.
Casal, Paula. 2007. Why sufficiency is not enough. *Ethics* 117: 296–326.
Chambers, Robert. 1997. *Whose reality counts?* Sterling: Stylus Publishing.
Chambers, Robert. 1999. *Whose reality counts?: Putting the last first*. London: Intermediate Technology Publications.
Chandhoke, Neera. 2010. How much is enough, Mr. Thomas? How much will ever be enough? In *Thomas Pogge and his critics*, ed. Alison Jaggar, 66–83. Cambridge: Polity Press.
Chandhoke, Neera. 2013. Realising justice. *Third World Quarterly* 34: 305–320.
Cornwall, Andrea, and Althea-Maria Rivas. 2015. From 'gender equality' and 'women's empowerment' to global justice: Reclaiming a transformative agenda for gender and development. *Third World Quarterly* 36: 396–415.
D'Cruz, Celine, and Diana Mitlin. 2007. Shack/slum dwellers international. In *Membership-based organizations of the poor*, ed. Martha Chen. London/New York: Routledge.
Deveaux, Monique. 2015. The global poor as agents of justice. *Journal of Moral Philosophy* 12: 1–25.
Drydyk, Jay. 2008. Durable empowerment. *Journal of Global Ethics* 4: 231–245.
Drydyk, Jay. 2013. Empowerment, agency, and power. *Journal of Global Ethics* 9: 249–262.
Dügben, Franziska. 2012. Africa humiliated? Misrecognition in development aid. *Res Publica* 18: 65–77.
Fanon, Frantz. 1968. *The wretched of the earth*. New York: Grove Press.
Frankfurt, Harry. 1987. Equality as a moral ideal. *Ethics* 98: 21–43.
Frankfurt, Harry. 1997. Equality and respect. *Social Research* 64: 3–15.
Fraser, Nancy. 2008. *Scales of justice*. New York: Columbia University Press.
Fraser, Nancy. 2010. Injustice at intersecting scales: On 'social exclusion' and the 'global poor'. *European Journal of Social Theory* 13: 363–371.
Friedmann, John. 1996. Rethinking poverty: Empowerment and citizen rights. *International Social Science Journal* 49: 161–172.
Gilabert, Pablo. 2012. *From global poverty to global equality*. Oxford: Oxford University Press.
Graf, Gunter, and Gottfried Schweiger. 2013. Capabilities, recognition and the philosophical evaluation of poverty: A discussion of issues of justification and the role of subjective experiences. *International Critical Thought* 3: 282–296.
Graf, Gunter, and Gottfried Schweiger. 2014. Poverty and freedom. *Human Affairs* 24: 258–268.
Green, Duncan. 2008. *From poverty to power: How active citizens and effective states can change the world*. Warwickshire: Oxfam International and Practical Action Publishing.
Hickey, Sam. 2010. The government of chronic poverty: From exclusion to citizenship? *Journal of Development Studies* 46: 1139–1155.
Hickey, Sam, and Giles Mohan (eds.). 2004. *Participation: From tyranny to transformation? Exploring new approaches to participation*. London: Zed Books.
Hickey, Sam, and Giles Mohan. 2005. Relocating participation within a radical politics of development. *Development and Change* 36: 237–262.

Huseby, Robert. 2010. Sufficiency: Restated and defended. *Journal of Political Philosophy* 18: 178–197.

Kabeer, Naila. 2000. Social exclusion, poverty, and discrimination: Towards an analytical framework. *Institute of Development Studies Bulletin* 31: 91–114.

Lenard, Patti Tamara. 2012. Motivating cosmopolitanism? A skeptical view. In *Global justice and international affairs*, ed. Thom Brooks, 93–119. Leiden: Brill Academic Publishers.

Lichtenberg, Judith. 2014. *Distant strangers: Ethics, psychology, and global poverty*. Cambridge: Cambridge University Press.

Lister, Ruth. 2013. Power, not pity: Poverty and human rights. *Ethics and Social Welfare* 7: 109–123.

McGee, Rosemary, and John Gaventa. 2010. *Review of impact and effectiveness of transparency and accountability initiatives: Synthesis report*. Brighton: Institute of Development Studies.

Menon, Gayatri. 2013. Citizens and 'squatters': The contested subject of public policy in neoliberal Mumbai. *Ethics and Social Welfare* 7: 155–169.

Miller, Richard. 2010. *Globalizing justice: The ethics of poverty and power*. Oxford: Oxford University Press.

Mitlin, Diana. 2013. A class act: Professional support to people's organizations in towns and cities of the global south. *Environment and Urbanization* 25: 483–499.

Mosse, David. 2010. A relational approach to durable poverty, inequality and power. *Journal of Development Studies* 46: 1156–1178.

Nagel, Thomas. 2005. The problem of global justice. *Philosophy and Public Affairs* 33: 113–147.

Nielsen, Kai. 1985. Ideal and nonideal theory: How should we approach questions of global justice? *The International Journal of Applied Philosophy* 2: 33–41.

Nolan, Brian, and Ive Marx. 2009. Economic inequality, poverty, and social exclusion. In *The Oxford handbook of inequality*, ed. W. Salverda et al. Oxford: Oxford University Press.

O'Neill, Onora. 2000. *The bounds of justice*. Cambridge: Cambridge University Press.

Patel, Sheela, and Diana Mitlin. 2004. Grassroots-driven development: The alliance of SPARC, the National Slum Dwellers Federation and *Mahila Milan*. In *Empowering squatter citizens*, ed. Diana Mitlin and David Satterthwaite, 216–225. London: Earthscan.

Patel, Sheela, Carrie Baptist, and Celine d'Cruz. 2012. Knowledge is power: Informal communities assert their right to the city through SDI and community-led enumerations. *Environment and Urbanization* 24: 13–26.

Pogge, Thomas. 2008. *World poverty and human rights*. Cambridge: Polity Press.

Risse, Mathias. 2005. Do we owe the poor assistance or rectification? *Ethics & International Affairs* 19: 9–18.

Salverda, Wiemer, Brian Nolan, and Timothy Smeeding (eds.). 2009. *The Oxford handbook of economic inequality*. Oxford: Oxford University Press.

Sandbrook, Richard. 2002. Deepening democracy to fight poverty: What role for human internationalists? *The International Journal* 57: 175–192.

Satterthwaite, David. 2001. From professionally driven to people-driven poverty reduction: Reflections on the role of Shack/Slum Dwellers International. *Environment & Urbanization* 13: 135–138.

Satterthwaite, David, and Diana Mitlin. 2014. *Reducing urban poverty in the global south*. Abingdon/New York: Routledge.

Satz, Debra. 2010. Ideals of egalitarianism and sufficiency in global justice. *Canadian Journal of Philosophy* 40(Supp. 1): 53–71.

Schweickart, David. 2008. Global poverty: Alternative perspectives on what we should do — And why. *Journal of Social Philosophy* 39: 471–491.

Schweiger, Gottfried. 2014. Recognition theory and global poverty. *Journal of Global Ethics* 10: 267–273.

Sen, Amartya. 1999. *Development as freedom*. Oxford: Oxford University Press.

Singer, Peter. 1972. Famine, affluence, and morality. *Philosophy and Public Affairs* 1: 229-243.

Singer, Peter. 2010. *The life that you can save: How to do your part to end world poverty*. New York: Random House.

Slum/Shack Dwellers International (SDI). http://sdinet.org/about-us/what-we-do/. Accessed 21 Aug 2015.

Wenar, Leif. 2003. What we owe to distant others. *Politics, Philosophy & Economics* 2: 283–304.

Wisor, Scott. 2012. *Measuring global poverty: Toward a pro-poor approach*. New York: Palgrave Macmillan.

Wittman, Hannah. 2010. Mobilizing agrarian citizenship: A new rural paradigm for Brazil. In *Contesting development: Critical struggles for social change*, ed. Philip McMichael, 164–181. New York: Routledge.

Young, Iris. 2011. *Responsibility for justice*. Oxford: Oxford University Press.

Chapter 14
Migration in a World of Citizens, Nonsensical Morality and Academia's Role in Addressing Hidden Poverty

Tendayi Bloom

Abstract In a world that is built upon the logic of citizenship, the fact of an unrecognized noncitizen relationship between an individual and a State gives rise to some problematic outcomes. This chapter presents two main ones, using some extreme real-world cases, and explores the particular role of academics in resolving these difficulties. First, the chapter shows how a nonsensical morality towards noncitizens within their State of noncitizenship can develop. This is demonstrated through the example of some irregular immigrants who may find facts of life nonsensically illegalized, a problem even more basic than human rights concerns. Second, the chapter presents how the non-recognition of some persons who do not have any form of citizenship or citizen-like relationship with the State where they live gives rise to a form of intractable hidden poverty impairing access even to basic rights. This chapter then goes on to explore how academia can play a special role in addressing this, emphasizing four main aspects. First, academia itself is dependent upon the possibility of alternative forms of individual-State relationships. Second, academics have the space and time to research topics that may otherwise go unexplored. Third, academics, if they draw a conclusion that something that they have found is unjust, have an obligation to try to correct it. Fourth, the status of the academic, as interlocutor, and as legitimizer of interlocutors, gives rise to a special role in enabling often silenced voices to be heard.

Keywords Citizenship • Noncitizenship • Hidden poverty • Human rights • Academics

T. Bloom (✉)
Global Justice Program, MacMillan Center, Yale University,
230 Prospect Street, New Haven, CT 06511, USA
e-mail: tendayi.bloom@yale.edu

H.P. Gaisbauer et al. (eds.), *Ethical Issues in Poverty Alleviation*, Studies in Global Justice 14, DOI 10.1007/978-3-319-41430-0_14

14.1 Introduction

We live in a world built for citizens, in which lacking citizenship is seen as an anomaly, the absence of the proper (or even only) form of political relationship with a particular State. This means that many people find themselves unrecognized in the State where they live. This chapter shows how this lack of recognition can give rise to nonsensical privations and hidden, and so unaddressed, poverty and human rights violations. Noncitizens *in situ* (i.e. within a State of which they are not citizens) do not always fare badly. There is a range of recognized statuses that provide territory-based access to citizen-like relationships with States.[1] In many existing States, non-citizens may become 'residents', gaining access to labor markets, welfare systems and even political entitlements so long as they retain their status of 'resident'. Other statuses like 'worker', 'refugee' or 'student' provide access to different dimensions of citizen-like relationships within States and explicitly offer approximations to citizen-like access to rights, including human rights, but these are always contingent on certain conditions being met and the continued goodwill of the State in question. The situation is quite different for *irregular* immigrants who have no such status (though they may have had status in the past). Often forbidden from working and unable to access welfare systems, such persons, even within wealthy States, may find life or core aspects of life effectively legally forbidden and human rights out of reach. Their relationship with the State where they live is often denied and the fact of their poverty rendered invisible. This can give rise to a hidden poverty among noncitizens, as poverty measurements and initiatives may often focus on citizens. This chapter proceeds on the liberal egalitarian premise that humans are individual and equal. It assumes that human lives are of equal moral importance and that a political structure that assigns different values to different human lives is morally troubling. Having shown that there are persons who can both find their lives nonsensically illegalized and their poverty difficult to voice, this chapter then goes on to indicate a unique role that academics could play in efforts to alleviate this situation.

14.2 People Fall Through the Cracks: Rejected Asylum Claimants

When the only recognized form of relationship with a State is citizenship, or some other citizen-approximating status, bestowed by that State, an individual's relationship with the State where he or she is can go unrecognized. To see this at its extreme, consider rejected asylum claimants: (persons who have made an unsuccessful claim for protective refugee status), who remain in the State where they claimed asylum. In the UK, for example, they are considered to be irregular immigrants, since the State in which they are located has not consented to their entry and has not granted

[1] E.g. see interesting analysis in Soysal (1994 ch 7).

them any license to remain. Members of this group, now find themselves without access to any useful citizen-like status. Some may be considered to be *de facto* or even *de jure* stateless (e.g. see useful discussions in Blitz 2009; Batchelor 1998; Blitz and Otero-Iglesias 2011; UNHCR 2012), but to avoid entanglement in legal definitions, these persons and others are here considered to fall into the category of being 'functionally stateless'.

The notion of 'asylum seeker' is not a legal one. It refers informally to someone seeking to become recognized as a refugee[2] (e.g. see discussion in Weissbrodt 2008). This lack of a recognized status means that persons seeking asylum in several States in particular, and especially those whose asylum claim has been rejected, do not have access to labor markets, to welfare systems, or to other means of sustaining themselves. The fact of this gap before refugee status is obtained demonstrates a problem with building a citizen-assuming structure with a logic of status of this sort – it lets some people fall through the cracks.[3] A proliferation of statuses is not the way forward (Weissbrodt and Divine 2015), since each new status, so long as it must be proven, leaves room for those who fall outside it. Moreover, eligibility for any such status must be approved by the same State that thereby becomes obligated to offer citizen-like protections. As such, there is reason to expect that there will be some persons excluded.

Moreover, proliferating statuses in order to ensure everyone is protected by a useable citizen-like status seems inefficient compared to acknowledging a more-encompassing individual-State relationship to begin with – one that does not require any proof and will not assume exclusion. This could potentially merely be the category of those eligible for human rights, though I think experience until now shows that this is insufficient and, furthermore, there is in fact a special relationship with a State that thereby goes unacknowledged (developed in Tonkiss and Bloom 2015, and in more detail in Bloom forthcoming). For the purposes of this chapter, however, it is sufficient to show that building a system only on citizen-like relationships allows there to be gaps between statuses into which persons can fall.

There are various reasons given for why persons whose asylum claims have been denied remain in the country where they applied for that status. Some main explanations are (e.g. Crawley et al. 2011, 17): removal is not possible (the country

[2] To claim asylum, an individual must currently prove to an official (usually of a State, sometimes of UNHCR) that he or she is someone that, because of a rational fear of persecution 'for reasons of race, religion, nationality, membership of a particular social group or political opinion', cannot return to his or her country of citizenship, or of 'habitual residence' if that person is stateless (Refugee Convention 1951 with the 1967 Protocol). That official then decides if the story the person tells is accurate and, if accurate, if it is the sort of story that allows that person to be called a refugee and so be given the selection of citizen-like protections and benefits attached to that status. Some of those who do not gain refugee status may receive other humanitarian statuses. Some may not.

[3] Some versions of the Islamic concept of *aman* could be useful here, offering protection on the basis of mere presence (i.e. not necessarily certified residence) for a period of a year (Shoukri 2010). Indeed, in theory this protection is offered on the basis of the person being a foreigner and in a relationship with the receiving State. This could be seen as a form of recognition of noncitizenship, or at least noncitizenship *in situ*.

they would return to is considered too dangerous or refuses to allow return); they are afraid of return; and/or they are appealing the decision on their status. Still others may remain because they cannot find a route home (e.g. Wari 2016), or because they would be unable to earn enough money at home to satisfy their basic needs and those of their families. For some persons, who have made extraordinary sacrifices in order to travel, return may also be problematic for other, social and personal, reasons (see discussions in Gebrewold and Bloom 2016). Such individuals' lack of a functional citizenship excludes them from legal personality, except perhaps by being on lists of illegal entrants.[4] This is not because they do not have any such relationship with a State. Indeed, their engagement in the asylum system is itself an instantiation of such a relationship, but it is a lack of an acknowledged relationship.

The theoretical gaps can also be exacerbated because, like any social policy, the asylum system is flawed, run by humans within a context that is intensely political. While non-deportation under these circumstances could be seen as positive (Mark Edwards' 'muddling through', Edwards 2015), and does mean that persons are not sent to places where they would be in urgent danger, in effect this leaves people trapped, forced to be in opposition to the State where they live in virtue of unavoidable activities. Such individuals are manifestly present and sometimes even at the acquiescence of the host State – either because the State recognizes that the person cannot be returned to the place from which they have come (e.g. Bloom 2015) or for other reasons (e.g. discussed in Joppke 1998). As I will now argue, if people *are* 'here', they must also be allowed to *live* 'here' even if one allows the claim that they should not be allowed to *remain*. While the reasons for a person's presence and how long he or she has been present are important, here I focus only on the bare minimum: the implications of merely *being* within a State.

14.3 Nonsensical Morality: 'Failed Asylum-Seekers Ought Not to Be Here'

The quoted comment in the title of this subsection comes from a 2009 Judicial Decision in the UK.[5] It is constructed like a moral claim and this, and statements like it, have the effect of wielding some sort of moral justification for action (or non-action) that would not be considered acceptable if the claims of those persons on the

[4] Note that the Sustainable Development Goal to give everyone a legal identity allows for problematic cases like, for example, providing a legal identity that is some not-citizenship approximation to citizenship, situating someone as perhaps illegal or lesser and making it difficult for that person to move beyond this status.

[5] Lord Justice Ward in R(on the application of YA) v Secretary of State for Health [2009] EWCA Civ 225 UK – (quoted and discussed further in Bloom 2015).

State in question were recognized. The logic of the statement '[f]ailed asylum-seekers ought not to be here' alongside the fact that such individuals are in fact 'here' seems somehow to legitimize the denial of their right to 'be'. Considering real-world practice regarding persons in this group makes this particularly clear.[6]

To show this, I develop an analogue of one of the arguments presented in Jeremy Waldron's discussion of homelessness.[7] This is not because the situations for homeless persons and functionally stateless persons discussed here are the same, but because the argument structure Waldron sets up is useful. Distilled from his papers on this topic, and with slightly different wording and ordering, his argument can be summarized as follows (Waldron 1991, 2000, 2009):

1. Persons with homes can perform activities either in their homes or in public.
2. Persons without homes can only perform activities in public.
3. There are some activities that city authorities would like to ban in public (urinating, defecating, cooking, having sex) in order to make public spaces more pleasant.
4. If persons without homes can only perform activities in public and these activities are made illegal in public, this effectively makes urinating, defecating, cooking and having sex illegal for persons without homes.

Waldron argues that rules banning such activities in public without providing alternative provision work on the incorrect assumption that everyone has a home. In the real-life situation in which there are people without homes, however, this becomes, for Waldron, an unacceptable constriction of their freedom (Waldron 1991) and homeless persons end up bearing the burden for property-ownership, losing access to human rights, without enjoying its benefits (Waldron 2009). But the situation that Waldron sets up can be seen as more than a constriction of freedom, and about something more basic than human rights. The power of his argument is that it is simply nonsensical to make it illegal for a human to urinate, for example. As such, the regulations he describes fail adequately to acknowledge human life as it really is.

That this should be seen as *illogical* rather than only a privation or a violation of rights, or constriction of freedom, is that there are some things that a human just cannot avoid doing (i.e. not only that they have a basic interest or need for, e.g. Shue 1980). Killing a person acknowledges that person's life, albeit assigning it less value. Forbidding a person from standing in any place, or from performing certain bodily functions that he or she cannot control is a non-acknowledgement of life.

---

[6] E.g. this interpretation seems to be the logic behind the UK Home Office aim, stated in 2007, to deny failed asylum seekers and other irregular immigrants 'the benefits of life in the UK' (Home Office 2007).

[7] Note that I am not sure what Waldron would make of my using his argument in this way. In the three presentations that I have seen of his position on homelessness (Waldron 1991, 2000, 2009), he explicitly discusses American citizens in American cities. However, interestingly, in one of these papers, he does mention statelessness as a potential parallel (Waldron 2009, 189), but not only does he not develop this, he in fact in the same paper seems to remove 'undocumented aliens' from the sphere of those who can count among the homeless persons under discussion (Waldron 2009 185).

Some things are not rights, they are more basic than that. They are just facts – albeit facts that we would rather not admit – about being human. That is, acknowledging a human life means acknowledging that person will urinate and defecate, will need to stand, sit or lie down in some place. It also means that even those people with whom a State would rather not have a relationship are human and if they are already 'here' then that State already *has* such a relationship in the moments that they are 'here' (indeed it may well have a relationship even if they are not 'here'). This chapter argues that building institutions upon the logic of citizenship alone allows that such things may be outlawed for some people who are unable to demonstrate any citizen-like relationship with the State where they live. This goes deeper than the homelessness case described by Waldron.

Joseph Carens asserted something similar in 2010: '…we should be wary of efforts to criminalize actions that irregular migrants take simply to live ordinary lives'. Carens explains, for example, that if a person needs documents to work and needs to work to eat, it becomes nonsensical to impose even what seem to be 'sensible laws intended to prevent fraud' against someone using false documents (Carens 2010, 46).[8] Although related, this goes deeper than what he has argued elsewhere about a 'firewall'. It is one thing to say that someone is entitled to some basic human rights and protections (Carens 2008, 166) and it is another to say it just does not make sense to require someone to act in a certain way.

This, then, takes the argument a little further. In some situations, denial of the means to eat can be seen purely as a rights violation – and unacceptable as such.[9] It is physically possible for a person not to eat – though this will make his or her life very unpleasant and will eventually bring about his or her death. However, in the case of the functionally stateless persons described, it looks like the thinking (or lack of thinking) behind the denial is not so much a denial of access to food, but a denial of that person's need for food and, as such, can be seen as a rights violation arising from a similarly nonsensical logic to that discussed above.

The comparison between homelessness as conceived by Waldron and functional statelessness as discussed here also becomes useful for the disanalogy. That is, while homeless persons do have access to public space in the city (even if activities there are restricted), in the world as a whole, there *is* no public space. That is, there is no Stateless land. The most analogous regions are probably the High Seas, though no one can stand there without a boat, or Antarctica, though life there is hard to sustain. All land on earth is divided somehow into States. As such, leaving it to territorial States to decide whether or not to relate to noncitizens (in the way that a home-owner can decide whether or not to allow some homeless person into his or her home) makes it theoretically possible and in fact the case that some persons can be denied the right even to stand lawfully anywhere on the earth within a system that does not, by the same logic, offer them the opportunity to consent.

---

[8] Recently in the UK, a magistrate was forced to resign for giving someone 40 GBP. The law had required him to impose a fine on that person for non-payment of a previous fine, even though the person is not legally allowed to work. The magistrate said that the law made no sense.

[9] E.g. see analysis of hunger and famine and rights in classic text: (Drèze and Sen 1989).

The citizen-based State system assumes that everyone has a citizenship or, at least, some approximation to a citizenship, and on this basis, a specific State within which to live. However, restriction over what a person can do 'here', irrespective of what he or she could do in some other country, is a restriction over what that person can do *tout court*, because that person is in fact 'here'. It is worth mentioning, though not necessary for the current discussion, that even in a much more ideal world than this one, persons may not have access to a protective State of citizenship. As a result, banning some people from earning money or joining welfare systems, or indeed from standing legally anywhere on a State's territory, on the basis of that person's lack of citizenship allows the logical next step that a stateless person is banned from sustaining life anywhere, from standing on any piece of land. As in Waldron's homelessness cases, this just does not make sense. And, again, as in the case of homelessness described by Waldron, it is, the illegalized persons who are forced to bear the burden of the system that benefits citizens, but excludes noncitizens by definition.

14.4 Hidden Poverty

This chapter has so far provided two main reasons to look beyond citizenship. First, the assumed logic of citizenship allows that some people may fall through the cracks between citizen-like statuses. Second, this gives rise to the possibility of nonsensical moralities relating to the lives of those who fall through the cracks, codified into legal and political structures. Now note a third aspect. The way things are currently set up means that noncitizens can find themselves not only forced into poverty, but into a poverty that can itself somehow be defined away. Most pertinent to this chapter, the poverty of noncitizens *in situ* may not register as poverty within the State where they live. Even those with citizen-like statuses may be excluded from calculations made about the population of a State.

For irregular immigrants and functionally stateless persons, this is particularly problematic. Irregular migrants often live in the shadows. Fear of arrest and/or deportation may deter individuals from reporting crimes, seeking medical and other help, or putting children in school (e.g. Carens 2008). Irregular immigrants may fall outside States' recorded population figures and many States struggle to estimate how many irregular immigrants they host, let alone how those persons live. Stateless persons, similarly, live largely unrecorded lives. They may lack the facility to register births, deaths and marriages, let alone access medical and other welfare services (e.g. ISI 2015). Like irregular immigrants, stateless persons may well work outside formal labor markets. Indeed, as Kristy Belton has commented, the situation for stateless persons remains a 'blind spot on the international community's agenda' (Belton 2013, 223).

That these forms of poverty are allowed to persist, even in the wealthiest States, is problematic. It further dehumanizes those who sit beyond citizenship or citizen-like statuses and perpetuates the logic of citizenship. If a State is defined only by its citizenry, perhaps it does not matter that some of those who happen to live among the citizens experience such nonsensical or impoverished existences. However, it is a problem for a theory that proceeds on the liberal egalitarian assumption that every human life and every human's well-being is of equal moral value. Willful ignorance of the difficulties described in this chapter (e.g. through lack of data or research) is another case of non-acknowledgement to be addressed.

Indeed, the situations described here are facilitated by two related aspects of a citizen-assuming political system. First, without a recognized political voice, many of the most vulnerable and impoverished noncitizens *in situ* are easy to pass over, their poverty to ignore. This is for a number of reasons. Most obviously, in the construction of a democratic context, the interests of those not considered part of the *demos* are less worrying to those leaders depending on votes. However, more deeply, seeing citizens as the primary interlocutors with citizens, and noncitizens not as interlocutors, means noncitizen perspectives can continue to be ignored and reproduces their disempowerment. This becomes apparent from looking at noncitizen political movements which challenge exactly this, forcing themselves as interlocutors, to be seen as persons with a credible political voice (e.g. Johnson 2015).

Second, even global moves to reduce poverty and engage in more inclusive development may fail to take these noncitizens into account because the indicators and measures used often fail to count the poverty of noncitizens, or some noncitizens in particular. In this way, a State might look like its society is doing well in terms of levels of poverty or extreme poverty and inequality when in fact, this is because some groups are not captured by usual measures. While noncitizen poverty is as worrying as citizen poverty for a liberal egalitarian, it is often not captured. This gives an inaccurate picture of how things really are and makes change both difficult and unlikely.

Through cases and contexts like those touched upon in this chapter and elsewhere, States protecting the sole logic of citizenship confront, and are challenged by, the fact of noncitizenship. The logic of non-citizenship (note the hyphen) as merely a lack of citizenship has allowed the dehumanization and illegalization of life in some of the darkest moments of modern human history (Bloom forthcoming) and the indifference to the suffering of some 'featherless bipeds' outside the range of moral concern (Rorty 1998, 124; see also Glover 1999). Moreover, the featherless bipeds mentioned in this chapter are not far away, but in fact on the territory of the State in question. Conversely, where noncitizens are seen living a life illegalized within a State, they also draw attention to the millions, perhaps billions, of noncitizens elsewhere whose stake in that State is also not acknowledged (addressed in other chapters in this book). The discussion in this chapter indicates the importance and urgency of a general mental/cultural shift to acknowledge the political being, the stake, the just claim, and the humanity of persons living in a State where no citizen-like relation is currently available to them.

14.5 Academia and Noncitizenship

In 2000, Phillip Cole wrote that if theorists are committed to national borders that exclude, 'political philosophy understood as normative discourse ... comes to an end at the national border' (Cole 2000, 13) and his work is directed towards explaining an egalitarian solution to immigration justice which may have to move beyond liberal understandings (e.g. Cole 2014). For James Hampshire, who had a similar worry to that of Cole, and wrote in 2013 that '...the intractable nature of immigrant policy is ... a reflection of the contradictory imperatives of the liberal state', the answer is instead to muddle through, pursuing contradictory policies (Hampshire 2013, 2). While it may well be necessary in the interim to 'muddle' through, finding ways to ensure basic human protections and access to rights for those currently without them, in the longer term, more substantial changes are needed as suggested by Cole. This includes a crucial role for academics, partially because of the particular relevance of noncitizenship to academic communities, and partly because of the more general task and privilege of academics.

Academia can sometimes be described as functioning as a global community. Academics often act beyond the confines of citizenship and rely on being able to travel, to conduct research and fieldwork, attend conferences, workshops and meetings, to take up positions and give lectures.[10] Beyond this, academics also have a special role. They are generally paid to try to understand the world, to develop theories and ways of thinking that help us to see the reality we live in more clearly, diagnose its problems and look for solutions. They then examine such theories as rigorously as possible and defend, teach and disseminate their findings. If a theory shows that x is the case and that x is unjust, then this implies an imperative for action.

Michael Dummett (1925–2011) was a celebrated logician. Working with his wife, Ann Dummett, a respected scholar on UK immigration policy, Dummett was part of the creation of the UK's Joint Council for the Welfare of Immigrants and of other now large national organizations against racial discrimination. In an interview in the early 2000s, Dummett is quoted as saying: 'I've always thought that intellectuals, if they see a possibility – which usually there isn't – of making a practical difference, they have the duty to try to do so' (Fara and Salles 2005, 10). In another context, Dummett argued that 'the duty of the philosopher is simply to follow where the argument leads'[11] (Fara and Salles 2005, 13). Migration control and the failure to recognize noncitizenship have continued to create illogical exclusions of persons from human recognition, basic rights and participation in political systems in many

[10] Frank Brennan, for example, opens a 2010 paper by expressing his frustration at arriving to a conference and being told that some key advertised speakers had been unable to attend because of migration restrictions (Brennan 2010).

[11] Dummett explicitly says in his book on migration that it has not been philosophy that has driven him (Dummett 2001 xii). However, he also widely uses moral arguments in explaining the need for action, suggesting he perhaps means in particular that it is not his professional work in the philosophy of truth and logic that grounds his migration work.

countries. For theories based on an equal moral value of persons this is problematic. Having seen this, those who have recognized the illogicality and injustice, and have a means to try to rectify it, should do so, or at least to try to stop as much as possible of the suffering that arises as a result.

In the final chapter of this book, Thomas Pogge and Luis Cabrera offer three types of activities that academics can and should engage in to alleviate poverty: (1) outreach; (2) direct impact; (3) creating inclusion (Pogge and Cabrera 2012, 171; reprinted in this volume). Dummett did all three of these in the area of immigration in the UK to a certain extent. He wrote and spoke publicly about the areas that he saw as most unjust. He created forums for discussion and debate, and for collective organizing around these areas. He sought direct impact on the ground, travelling to airports to interrupt deportations, for example. However, there is a sense in which he did not challenge the system itself, but addressed symptoms of it. It is possible that a more radical approach to creating inclusion is also necessary.

Academics are in a privileged position with regard to dissemination and giving legitimacy to points of view. Someone holding a particular academic title or a position in a university speaks with that title or position behind him or her. Such a person can also use this to give credibility to the words of others. Persons without the same means to express their political understandings and their needs, or even to have their bare humanity recognized, can offer a unique analysis of the legitimacy of States and what it is to have a relationship with a State. As well as learning from such persons themselves, academics are in a special position to lead wider engagement. Such engagement can both: demonstrate even the most excluded noncitizens as interlocutors (in Lyotard's sense; 1993, 140); and it may well also find that such perspectives can inform and strengthen theorizations of society and political being within it, to provide more accurate understandings of how people can live within States and how institutional structures can better represent this.

Academics are also in a position to conduct original and independent research into the poverty and exclusion of groups that often go unstudied. By developing new measurement tools and providing comparable data they can make the extent of *in situ* noncitizen poverty knowable and provide means of tracking whether it is increasing or decreasing. Academics can use analyses of law, society, culture and politics to uncover reasons for the failure to recognize noncitizenship and what can be done about it. Dummett has been mentioned here, not only for the work he did in the area of migration, but also to demonstrate that it did not require a great sacrifice. While in an interview he admitted that he and his wife thought he was potentially scuppering his career as a philosopher through his activism, in fact this turned out not to be the case. He is now considered to have been one of the pre-eminent scholars in truth and logic of his generation and is also recognized for the convictions he showed in his activism work. For most of his life he held a comfortable and prestigious position at Oxford University and in his later years was awarded a Knighthood. Not only is there a duty to act when the argument shows that such action is needed, this is in fact part of what it is to be a public scholar.

14.6 Concluding Remarks

In the area of noncitizenship discussed here, then, there are two levels upon which to proceed. First, it is crucial to ensure that those who currently lack access to human rights and basic needs are given such access, whether through citizenship or citizenship-like statuses. Second, it is necessary to work towards the developing acknowledgement and understanding of noncitizenship. Both of these need academics to engage in original research, ensuring the findings are disseminated broadly and analyzed; to pursue specific policy goals; and crucially to use their position to ensure a wider range of voices and perspectives are heard and that noncitizens are acknowledged as interlocutors.

Acknowledgements The author thanks the book editors, Helmut P. Gaisbauer, Gottfried Schweiger and Clemens Sedmak, for inviting her to contribute and for their editorial comments on this chapter. She also extends particular thanks to participants at the Yale Global Justice Workshop for reading and providing helpful comments on an earlier draft of the chapter, and in particular, thanks Shmulik Nili for putting the workshop together and inviting her to present, and Yao Lin whose last-minute flexibility helped her meet the publication deadline. She also thanks the Springer editors for their editorial support. While many people have helped to improve the chapter, remaining errors and weaknesses are the fault of the author alone.

References

Batchelor, Carol. 1998. Statelessness and the problem of resolving nationality claims. *International Journal of Refugee Law* 10: 156–183.

Belton, Kristy. 2013. Statelessness and economic and social rights. In *The state of economics and social human rights: A global overview*, ed. Lanse Minkler, 221–248. Cambridge: Cambridge University Press.

Blitz, Brad. 2009. *Statelessness, protection and equality*, Forced migration policy briefing 3. Oxford: Refugee Studies Centre, University of Oxford.

Blitz, Brad, and Miguel Otero-Iglesias. 2011. Statelessness by any other name: Refused asylum-seekers in the United Kingdom. *Journal of Ethnic and Migration Studies* 37(4): 1–17.

Bloom, Tendayi. 2015. London's 'ghosts: The capital and the UK policy of Destitution of Refused Asylum-Seekers. In *London the promised land revisited: The changing face of the London migrant landscape in the early 21st century*, ed. Ann Kershen, 77–96. Abingdon: Ashgate.

Bloom, Tendayi. forthcoming.

Brennan, Frank. 2010. Human rights as a challenge to national policies that exclude refugees. In *Driven from home: Protecting the rights of forced migrants*, ed. David Hollenbach, 97–114. Washington, DC: Georgetown University Press.

Carens, Joseph. 2008. The rights of irregular migrants. *Ethics and International Affairs* 22: 163–186.

Carens, Joseph. 2010. *Immigrants and the right to stay*. Cambridge, MA: MIT Press.

Cole, Phillip. 2000. *Philosophies of exclusion*. Edinburgh: Edinburgh University Press.

Cole, Phillip. 2014. Beyond reason: The philosophy and politics of immigration. *Critical Review of International Social and Political Philosophy* 17(5): 503–520.

Crawley, Heaven, Hemmings Joanne, and Price Neil. 2011. *Coping with destitution*. Oxfam Research Report.

Drèze, Jean, and Amartya Sen. 1989. *Hunger and public action*. Oxford: Clarendon.
Dummett, Michael. 2001. *On immigration and refugees*. Abingdon: Routledge.
Edwards, Mark. 2015. *The limits of political belonging: An adaptionist perspective on citizenship and society*. New York: Palgrave Macmillan.
Fara, Rudolf, and Maurice Salles. 2005. Interview with Michael Dummett: From analytical philosophy to voting analysis and beyond', *LSE Research Projects*.
Gebrewold, Belachew, and Tendayi Boom. ed. 2016. *Understanding migration decisions*. Abingdon: Ashgate.
Glover, Jonathan. 1999. *Humanity: A moral history of the twentieth century*. London: Jonathan Cape
Hampshire, James. 2013. *The politics of immigration*. Cambridge: Polity.
Home Office (UK). 2007. *Enforcing the rules*. London: Her Majesty's Stationary Office.
ISI. 2015. *The world's stateless*. Tilburg: Institute for Statelessness and Inclusion.
Johnson, Heather. 2015. These fine lines: Locating noncitizenship in political protest in Europe. *Citizenship Studies* 19(8): 951–965.
Joppke, Christian. 1998. Why liberal states accept unwanted immigration. *World Politics* 50(2): 266–293.
Pogge, Thomas, and Luis Cabrera. 2012. Outreach, impact, collaboration: Why academics should join to stand against povert. *Ethics and International Affairs* 26(2): 163–182.
Rorty, Richard. 1998. Human rights, rationality, and sentimentality. In *Truth and progress: Philosophical papers, volume 3*, ed. Richard Rorty, 167–185. Cambridge: Cambridge University Press.
Shoukri, Arafat Madi. 2010. *Refugee status in Islam: Concepts of protection in Islamic tradition and international law*. London: I.B. Tauris.
Shue, Henry. 1980. *Basic rights: Subsistence, affluence, and U.S. foreign policy*. Princeton: Princeton University Press.
Soysal, Yasemin. 1994. *Limits of citizenship; Migrants and post-national membership in Europe*. Chicago: University of Chicago Press.
Tonkiss, Katherine, and Tendayi Bloom. 2015. Theorising noncitizenship: Concepts, debates and challenges. *Citizenship Studies* 19(8): 837–852.
UNHCR. 2012. *Guidelines on statelessness no.1: The definition of 'Stateless Person' in Article 1(1) of the 1954 Convention Relating to the Status of Stateless Persons*, (HCR/GS/12/01) 20th Feb 2012.
Waldron, Jeremy. 1991. Homelessness and the issue of freedom. *UCLA Law Review* 39(1991–1992): 295–324.
Waldron, Jeremy. 2000. Homelessness and community. *University of Toronto Law Journal* 50: 371–406.
Waldron, Jeremy. 2009. Community and property – For those who have neither. *Theoretical Inquiries into Law* 10: 161–192.
Wari, Iddrissu. 2016. You make a decision and you start your journey: Reflections of a Ghanaian economic migrant and founder of the NGO, CEHDA'. In *Understanding migrant decisions*, eds. Belachew Gebrewold and Tendayi Bloom, 195–218. Abingdon: Ashgate.
Weissbrodt, David. 2008. *The human rights of non-citizens*. Oxford: Oxford University Press.
Weissbrodt, David, and Michael Divine. 2015. Unequal access to human rights: The categories of noncitizenship. *Citizenship Studies* 19(8): 870–891.

Chapter 15
Poverty Alleviation: An Opportunity for Universities

Clemens Sedmak

Abstract How can universities promote a preferential "option of the poor"? In my chapter I will articulate three dimensions and show how they are connected with issues of identity: education, positioning, transformation.

(i) Education is the central idea of a university. Education can strengthen the abilities to deal with difficult situations, like poverty. In fact, the university has the opportunity and the responsibility to cultivate such resources. According to Martha Nussbaum a university should promote the ability to lead an "examined life". It should promote the ability to think in terms of common humanity and the ability to narrative imagination, such as the use of myths, symbols, narratives and poetry. In this way education helps to cultivate a sense of belonging that is not contingent of social groups (humanity), a sense of detachment from external circumstances ("examined life") and a sense of interiority and orientation beyond material values (narrative imagination).

(ii) Universities can contribute to an "option for the poor" by taking up positions. There are at least four important dimensions: First, the university recognizes academic freedom. Universities are free to address the situation of people experiencing poverty and poverty alleviation, e.g. in lectures. Second, the university knows freedom of research. Hence also research can contribute to a deeper understanding of poverty and the development of social innovation and poverty reduction efforts. Third, universities build communities of teachers and students, networks within the scientific community. Granting access to such networks for socially disadvantaged students or teachers or collaboration between the University and poverty stricken persons can express an "option for the poor". Fourth, the University has political weight and can take up positions in the sense of Ignacio Ellacurías considerations on the political role of universities.

(iii) Finally, such a positioning and consequent involvement offers opportunities for transformation. Transformation is in fact the basic idea behind the Christian understanding of an "option for the poor". It is about to be touched by the

C. Sedmak (✉)
Centre for Ethics and Poverty Research, University of Salzburg, Mönchsberg 2a, 5020 Salzburg, Austria
e-mail: clemens.sedmak@sbg.ac.at

H.P. Gaisbauer et al. (eds.), *Ethical Issues in Poverty Alleviation*, Studies in Global Justice 14, DOI 10.1007/978-3-319-41430-0_15

mystery of poverty. It is about to develop real friendships with people experiencing poverty. Such encounter opens the scope for a transformation that converts people's interiority. This may just be possible within a university.

Keywords University • Options for the poor • Identity • Education • Positioning • Transformation

15.1 Introduction

A university is a place where a great deal of time and effort is spent pondering systematically and methodically upon those issues deemed worthy of the time and the effort invested. The process of considering and reflecting on fundamental questions via the human faculty of intellect is, as John Henry Newman stated, "a clear conscious view of his [her] own opinions and judgments, a truth in developing them, an eloquence in expressing them, and a force in urging them" (Newman 1887, 178). A university is in a certain sense a community of learners and learned; a community built on knowledge which attempts to probe and find out more about the cosmos, literally and metaphorically speaking. With this in mind then, what can a university do to alleviate poverty? I would like to address this "question" by looking at two real life experiences, examining three views of what poverty is or might be and investigating existing realistic options for the poor, and how they might be implemented on the basis of three universal indicators.

15.2 Two Stories: Adverse Circumstances

A German student by the name of Thomas Mahler completed his degree in Philosophy and, unable to find immediate employment, had to live 1 year on jobseeker's allowance, *Hartz IV*, a strict reform agenda of cutbacks in unemployment benefits introduced in Germany in January 2005. Thomas Mahler found himself queuing up – standing in line – for his government handout. Not a nice situation; his self-confidence plummeted, and phrases such as *at the top*, *at the bottom*, *failure*, *mediocre* made him nervous, made him feel queasy (Mahler 2011, 14). He soon realized that any notion of confidence one might entertain was very much part and parcel of, determined by even, where one happened to be at any one time, and that sense of "self" varied according to the demands of those particular circumstances. As an unemployed person he felt like a product that *no one* wanted to buy. He described his sense of self as "the leftovers", "idle inventory", those "dead articles on the shelf" (Mahler 2011, 127). Strange. He had just graduated from a prestigious university. He had just been working flat out to finish his Master's dissertation on some profound philosophical debate. A fellow student had once told him about his dissertation topic which was on "hunger as aesthetic category". Thomas had asked his colleague if he was investigating or considering real-life hunger issues in the world in general. His colleague had been rather amused by this perspective and was eager to reject any such ludicrous thinking. He seemed repulsed by the very idea and even surprised that anyone might consider such a question. Of course not, was the clear imperative; such notions were superfluous to the needs of academic research (Mahler 2011, 37).

This world of wise words, intellectual debate and mulling over of abstract ideas, a world of pompous braggarts and know-it-alls with their comfortable salaries and one which had become Mahler's own way of life was suddenly a thing of the past: overnight it seemed he had slid down some slippery slope from that ivory tower power-house into an unknown world of living hand-to-mouth, a world in which a living wage was an enigma. At the same time he finds himself overcome with fear, a real fear that grows stronger, digs deeper into his being. He is afraid of being asked what he is doing now he has finished his degree; he is afraid of going to visit his aunt on her birthday for fear of being asked how his new job is going. He begins making a point of deliberately avoiding "successful" people on their way up the career ladder in order not be forced to think about his own dilemma of joblessness. He begins wondering about what he had actually learned at university and now feels a sense of doubt creeping into his mind. Standing in line, he finds himself pulling the wool over his own eyes to fool himself that he is *not* standing in a dole queue – what a bizarre idea (Mahler 2011, 6).

The university Thomas Mahler had attended provided – or at least created the impression of providing – a cozy, sheltered atmosphere, where it was possible to think about "hunger as an aesthetic factor". The university had not cultivated much of a sense of orientation in the student Mahler, but had taught him how to doubt. In this idea of hunger and poverty, the university had failed by creating both the enticement and trap of a closed environment lacking sound, tenable foundations. The snares and temptations of a closed world is that it relies on a self-contained construct of protection and security, running according to its own red-tape principles and based on its own laws – "Parkinson's Laws"; a world built on its own hierarchies of officialdom (Northcote, Gough 2011, ch. 6, 8, 24). This inward looking, self-referential universe regards its own sense of purpose and procedures to achieve this end as an end in itself. This is a picture we know from poverty statistics and the poverty alleviation industry (Schicho 2007). On entering such a closed cocoon-like world patterns of perception and sense of priorities change, imperceptibly but palpably; everyday, routine circumstances become insurmountable problems creating their own sense of agency and meaning which in turn endorses and "approves of" time and effort invested to combat them. The untenability factor comes into play when an intellectual culture such as this conveys the idea that everything – no matter what – is "dodgy" and therefore to be doubted. Landmarks, hallmarks and benchmarks can be *ad-libbed* at will: in short there are no fixed signposts of orientation. In his "This is Water" lecture, David Foster Wallace highlighted academia's penchant for over-interpretation. The knock-on effect of this approach is that a vast ocean of ad infinitum possibilities is opened up to willing candidates and any existing proneness to abstraction is intensified: "Probably the most dangerous thing about college education, at least in my own case, is that it enables my tendency to over-intellectualize stuff, to get lost in abstract arguments inside my head instead of simply paying attention to what's going on right in front of me" (Wallace 2009).

Seen thus, university had failed Thomas Mahler twofold, but it opened up the way for him to a life dependent on *Hartz IV*. His academically honed skills in style and expression together with his well-refined powers of observation means that there are possibilities; he is invited to write a book on his life and experiences as an Hartz IV citizen. This opportunity not only enables him to voice his personal perspective but opens a door out of the poverty in which he finds himself. The university did at least equip him with skills of expression and train his cognitive powers.

A second story is penned from the other side of the "desk". Don Snyder, a successful university professor, describes his personal fall from grace – suddenly losing his well-paid prestigious job and, like Thomas Mahler, being forced to live on the dole (Snyder 1997). At 41, Snyder was envisaging a further step up the university career ladder but instead is handed his notice, unexpectedly, out of the blue. He is allowed to teach three more terms at the university in order to prepare himself for a job change. He analyses his own situation from a critical point of view: he is unwilling to face up to reality and prefers instead to believe that he can continue "this" life "somewhere else". The institution is to blame he would like to think and he loses himself in a wave of self-induced fears and fantasies about his wife leaving him, and living beneath the breadline. His self-confidence, like that of Mahler, plummets to a record low; he feels humiliated and is enraged. This angry middle-aged man is offered a job as a maintenance hand and gradually Snyder becomes aware of the unpleasant reality and truth that somewhere along the line something is missing; he lacks a real inner strength of body and mind, he discovers too that he lacks confidence. In the cold light of reality however, he is unable to do what needs to be done; with only $7000 left in the bank, he still clings to the illusion that there must be another solution: he has to learn the hard way. He is forced to admit that he has misjudged the demands of the job market and is forced to admit that he has been living in a bubble, a balloon world of "make-believe" and all the implications the word suggests. He suddenly realizes that life as he has hitherto experienced it in the confined comfort zone of academia is perhaps not life at all. He remembers a situation at university in which a hot water pipe had burst in the wall of a conference room; the water ran out into the corridor and through the ceiling down into the floor underneath. For safety purposes, the electricity supply had to be cut off at the mains. This meant that the room was in utter darkness and the plumbers and maintenance men were working away feverishly to sort out the mess (literally) and get things up and running again as quickly as possible. A Classics professor with a bundle of essays and student papers stuffed under his arm appeared in the doorway and said into the darkness: "Excuse me, but it is awfully cold in my study and I was wondering if the heating is going to be turned back on by midday so I can get back to work?" Snyder describes the dumbfounded look on the workers' faces on hearing this utterance: these "laborers" working hard to repair the damage were as lost for words in attempting to understand this man from another planet as he was for these beings intent on the thing they classed as physical work. Their look of utter incredulity said it all: "Who is this guy? He can't be for real."

Snyder had "lived" and made his way up the academic career ladder in this cocoon world. He was only acquainted with upwards and onwards. When this world falls apart, Snyder is unable to cope with the loss. He withdraws into a room on the top floor of his house and gets through the day with a steady supply of sleeping tablets: he spends an entire year doing this, coming out only at night to lead a nocturnal existence of foraging for food in the fridge and checking the post. He spends 11 whole months like this until bit by bit he begins to take stock of current reality – as it really is. He looks back to his childhood and teenage years in which he had learnt rudiments of carpentry and it is with these skills that he is now able to make a living as carpenter and handy-man.

The university had in some ways been like a sort of private club for Snyder with its members-only, closed-shop nature; he had felt confident and at home in this temperate zone, free to move around and do as he chose. It had never really occurred to him that university was an artificial, man-made vacuum existing alongside (indeed, outside of) a non-university world. Gradually, he has to acknowledge that there is an outside reality which has little to do with the academic cocoon in which (he now realizes) he had been ensnared. He had been caught in the trap of thinking he was preparing and being prepared for life; this was not the case he discovers, university had not prepared him for life beyond the confines of academic ivory tower. He gets on fine and even succeeds in the comfort zone of university, the place where he teaches and where he is admired and held in high esteem. But those intellectual ivory towers had not taught him how to stand on his own two feet, something he was now being expected to do. This too was the harsh reality of life outside university and which he now had to learn – quickly – to survive; the harsh realization that an academic degree did not provide him with the resources he required to conquer life's tricky traps, to overcome life's vicissitudes, such as poverty.

One might hesitantly conclude from these stories that a university is perhaps not the best place in the world to acquire resources needed to live a real life in a real world. Its closed-shop environment is not conducive to strengthening life-skills. Once caught in the trap of a closed system there was no way of being prepared for a life of possible poverty beyond the walls of academic life.

15.3 First Point of Reference: Education

Of course, it doesn't have to be like that, universities should be able and capable of preparing students for "life after" academia, those adverse circumstances outside of the secure confines of university. In fact universities should be paragon institutions which convey to and equip their students with all the necessary skills required to master difficult times. On 23rd January 1944, Dietrich Bonhoeffer wrote to Renate and Eberhard Bethge to inform them that he had been in prison since 5th April 1943; he notes: "it is quite clear to me that an education which falls apart when confronted with danger is not education. Education must be able to withstand peril and death"[1] (Bonhoeffer 2011, 292). Education of the kind only a university can provide should be able to prepare its wards for life's most difficult situations, for crises even. How and why? Because it is the deception of a concrete abstract enclosure and the ruse of a volatile environment engendering instability which could be recognized and avoided, and it was this approach to education of which Dietrich Bonhoeffer had first-hand experience. Whilst in prison he kept himself busy and his mind alert by studying literature, politics, ethics and history. Education proves to be a means of gaining access to knowledge about that inner world of self and being; the process of learning, even in prison, is a chance to cultivate inner strengths. The acquisition of knowledge can perhaps be best described as learning about and finding out about self – a lesson in self-awareness. The Swiss Philosopher and writer Peter Bieri sees the capacity to express self, the ability to implement language as the key to understanding self (Bieri 2011, 46ff and 62ff). Education in its most basic sense is learning about expression of some kind or another; learning to learn heightens one's sense of perception of the world around, and over time and experience learning provides its own points of reference – not for its own sake but as coordinates with which one can then read any map, orientate oneself and decode new experiences. Education such as this is a firm foundation stone on which to build and expand. In learning about the world outside, we learn about ourselves and the way we perceive A and B and why it is that we perceive it in the way we do (and perhaps go about making alterations if and when the need arises). Learning cannot take place in isolation, learning requires a sparring partner; after all, books do not write themselves, words of wisdom we make our own have been penned by someone, somewhere, going through a quasi, similar experience to ourselves: this is all part of the process. Only with a counterpart can there be dialogue, only with a conversation partner can I genuinely converse and gain access to a world of ideas beyond the limits of my own. With this "*gegenüber*" I practise reading other maps with the cartography skills I have acquired; I am equipped to recognize and link up familiar landmarks, general topography know-how means I can work out specific features relevant to particular sites and situations. This enables me to make judgements and ascertain necessary facts. In the same way as map-reading enables me to find my way in unknown territory, education should equip and enable me to find my way in unknown everyday situations: I should be empowered, inwardly mobile and proficient to survive and progress. This inner strength and ongoing process of strengthening can be fortified by learning, learning which requires regular exercise and self-discipline. Only through regular exercise, only through habitually going over things learnt can I move on in confidence to the unknown. Cultivating good habits will affect the way I perceive my surroundings. Bonhoeffer described this focus of perception as the *polyphony of life*, brought about by learning and looking, repeatedly, habitually; looking at the multifaceted kaleidoscope of life. A man of learning, a woman of letters believes in the polyphony of life and through it can hear those

[1] Translated from the German original: "Klar ist mir … nur, daß eine 'Bildung', die in der Gefahr versagt, keine ist. Bildung muß der Gefahr und dem Tod gegenübertreten können".

deeper chords resounding through and underlying life. Education provides the ways and means to see a spiritual reality reflected in the material goods of the world.

University as a center of education can cultivate this sense of polyphony and appreciation of an inner heritage. This is not some idle pipe-dream but hard-fact reality which has passed the litmus test of practical implementation: the "barbed-wire university" which POW allies built during WWII (Gillies 2012, chapters 20, 21, 29). In prisoner of war camps, improvised universities were set up, becoming vital life support systems in conveying – or maintaining – a genuine concept of real life beyond the barbed-wire fence of the prison-camp. Examples such as these show that education has to do with sensing possibility and recognizing the contingency of the status quo which doesn't have to be as it is, but could be otherwise. Learning teaches me to see a range of alternatives in the situation before me and to both sense and know that it could be different. In a more recent POW-like context, Shin Dong-hyuk, born to two prisoners in a North Korean gulag (Camp 14), in 1982 managed to escape the camp when he was 23 years old (Harden 2013). His means of and reason for escape had to do with finding out about learning: education. Born in this camp, growing up in this camp, he knew nothing other than this camp, its guards and its inmates. He had no idea, no knowledge of an – the – outside world. He had no way of making a comparison, of assessing his situation. Yes, there was some sort of schooling in the camp but never any mention of where it was on the world map, no information about neighboring countries or the world in general. It was impossible for Shin to get his bearings, impossible for him to develop some holistic *weltanschauung* until he met Park – an educated prisoner. He hears for the first time that there is something else beyond the fence, for the first time in his life Shin learns things he had no idea of; he can tap into information and experiences with which he can develop his own co-ordinates, get his own bearings; he is able to see and set his life – the camp – in the context of something other, something bigger. He finds out about things like television sets and computers, the way the earth is formed, that the prison camp is in a "country" and that south, east and west there are other countries such as South Korea and China. Park gives Shin the cognitive tools to think, think about possibilities, think about life outside of the confined world of the camp. An idea of escape is awakened in Shin and he begins to plan ways and means of "getting out", a concept which had formerly not existed at all in his range of thinking. New ways of thinking, new ideas provide him with possibilities to form his own ideas, create his own ways of thinking. This case study, academically speaking, illustrates not only the possibilities but also the huge responsibility a university has; it is an institution of authority which has a duty, an obligation to question the *status quo*. In the thirteenth century, the Franciscan monk, Francis Bacon thought long and hard about the role and responsibility of the university and how it could be reformed to equip its students better. He realized that there were basically four major hurdles on the road to knowledge which universities could help students overcome; the first was, ingrained, "institutionalized" habits, a multitude of (in part, conflicting) opinions and principles, lack of authority and self-conceit: attitudes and approaches which could and can only hinder, paralyze and impede any attempt to educate in the best possible meaning of the word.

If we consider these hurdles, we will find key reference points which might help us in our current enquiry: a university as an influential institution has both a responsibility and the chance to access and cultivate resources which can be deployed in tackling life's untoward circumstances. This can only be achieved by creating and constructing a culture of mindful interiority through making core reference points available and enabling access to them; providing ways and means of classifying and codifying necessary information and encouraging "learners" to develop good habits in the way they learn and in what they do and do not (should not) learn which can only work if the key skill is conveyed of learning *how* to think and the range of possible ways of perception. Equipped with these tools, together with a sensitive understanding of how to express such ideas, a sense of Bonhoeffer's polyphony of life will be awakened together with the will to pursue it. University as an educational establishment can prepare "people" to face and tackle poverty in their own lives and in the lives of others.

15.4 Three Stories: Poverty

Which all sounds very nice, but doesn't bring us any nearer to finding an option for the poor, or does it? So far we have observed that "poverty" is a condition which can, to a certain extent, be prepared for with the right education. There are all sorts of stories about poverty of one kind or another and I would like to look at three stories describing three types of poverty to gain a deeper understanding of this condition. The first one has to do with income poverty; in this instance the level of poverty can be measured, weighed up and worked out; it can be managed in one way or another. The second one is poverty as social exclusion which makes it hard to classify due to its multifaceted character and nature. The third one characterizes poverty as the "deprivation of capabilities" and the "absence or marked lack of opportunities" which suggests that poverty as a definition has to do with a lack or loss of opportunities to acquire skills and abilities (Sen 1999, ch. 4). The common denominator of all three types of poverty description is human identity.

(i) Money universally represents ways and means of acquiring goods and services, particularly in a product orientated society and a world in which "having" and "getting" things is vital. There have been a number of investigations into this phenomenon of possessions affecting and/or determining identity; the British anthropologist, Daniel Miller, looked at the subjective "worth" of "things" in people's homes in one road in south London (Miller 2008). The things a home "has" are rarely there by chance and often have a "story" attached to them – they mean something to the owner, are there for a reason and as such are alive in a certain sense of the word for the owner. These are not temporary stage props, but their impact has affected the life and soul of one or more persons in one particular household. Things are not mere things; they are perceived as part of a person's life, contributing to a person's identity. Postcards are kept for years – a lifetime – as are lover letters, souvenirs of holidays, mementoes and photographs of special occasions. Some people collect football trophies others are mad about stamp-collecting: a home is a portrait of its owners. Trinkets and ornaments may be "externalized memories" which may strengthen the recollection of having had *this* or *that* experience – the experience the object stands for and embodies. Things *carry* weight, they *attach* value for someone else; they may serve as a "prop" to trigger habits, actions, memories. Russell Belk has shown that belongings also have the power to express the self they are part of, in other words they constitute an "extended self" (Belk 1988). Souvenirs tell stories about trips and travels and enable their owners to relive the experience in the mind's eye of memory and emotion. Seen thus, the things we own carve out a part of our identity, go towards constructing that identity, at the same time, this identity affects the way these things are then seen and perceived, lending them additional weight and depth which in turn will impact identity anew – ad infinitum.

(ii) Even when poverty is characterized by social exclusion, one can still see elements of and connections to identity resources since being part of something, belonging to a defined group of people, is one of the highest goods a community can offer someone. Being accepted into this group, "getting" and "having" some sort of membership card opens up whole new possibilities to "do" and "be". The dynamics of social exclusion mean that basic social affiliations and attachments are withheld and vital social connections are missing. Universally held standards are, like prices, constantly rising (we can see this in *must have* designer labels and mobile phones, to name but two instances, which it seems are now vital even in lower school), at the same time, the job market is making greater demands and putting increased pressure on employees to perform better, longer, quicker; it does therefore logically follow that many cannot keep pace with the spiraling demands on their skills and capacities, resulting in what Alain Ehrenberg describes as the "weary self" syndrome (Ehrenberg 2009). Kathrin Hartmann traced the dynamics of this phenomenon in Germany and found that poverty had arrived in middle-class society, and that job security and social benefits were a scarce resource in more and more segments of society (Hartmann 2012). It is in such circumstances that identity becomes fragile and brittle – one day you are on a roll, and the next day you have lost everything.

(iii) Poverty, as having been deprived of capacities, is an unpleasant experience that individuals often undergo; they are unable to realize their potential, in many cases are not even aware that they do indeed have potential since their circumstances cannot provide the space or wherewithal to find out and experiment; there is no one to spot any hidden talents, no way of knowing what they might be capable of because they have never had an opportunity or lack the necessary resources. Capabilities are "invaluable" assets with which a future can be built, assets which enable us to turn a world we would like to be into reality. Capabilities are a cornucopia of possibilities; being capable of doing something can be like a key to open doors of opportunities, cross thresholds into new realities and realize dreamt-of intentions. A capability is thus a force to be implemented, to coordinate, and reshuffle the dynamics of the present condition. Aristotle's *dynamis* is the power of possibility according to which a change can be brought about or take place (Aristotle, Metaphysics V 12, 1020a1ff; IX 1, 1046a11). It may provide or be a source of change. Depending on the type of change to take place it may also be regarded as an attribute, an asset to get something moving or to bring something finally to a standstill. We may deduce from this that capacity to do and scope to maneuver the human playing field can be expanded upon and that a sense of agency is vital to empower, enable and embolden the cultivation of capacities and capabilities. People hit by poverty have a restricted scope of possibilities and rarely have options to choose from. Thus, self-expression and self-awareness as agent are severely limited. Poverty stunts the growth of agency – a vital source of identity.

Poverty is being deprived of identity-giving resources. In his research into poverty, William Vollmann pinpointed its main characteristics, namely, feelings of "invisibility", "deformity", "unwantedness", "dependence", "accident-prone-ness", "pain", "numbness" and "estrangement" (Vollmann 2007). These qualifiers all suggest stumbling blocks in finding and anchoring identity. Poverty erodes essential resources for identity, as we have seen above in the case of Don Snyder. The South African Literary Nobel Prize winner gives a splendid description of the dynamics at work in the erosion process of identity resources. In his autobiographical novel *Boyhood – scenes from provincial life* – J.M. Coetzee (re)traces the life of his father after he is forced to shut his law firm (Coetzee 1997). He continues to leave the house at 7 am on the dot as he has always done and heads off to town. The difference now is that he returns home 2 h later – and that is the big secret – knowing that everyone will have left the house leaving it empty till late afternoon. He puts his pajamas back on and crawls into bed with a hip flask of brandy and the Cape Times newspaper crossword puzzle. Several hours later at 2 in the afternoon, he gets back up again, puts his clothes back on and leaves the house for his club before anyone else comes home and finds out that he has been there. The son discovers the father's secret by chance when, feeling unwell, he comes home early from school one day. Not only does the father no longer leave the house but he becomes an alcoholic; he hides any bills that arrive by post and the whole situation spirals out of control with the family losing just about all they have. The son loses all respect for his father and tells his mother that she should let "this man" be sent to prison and have done with it. If we look at the situation being described here, we see a father who withdraws from public and even private life; his life revolves around guarding this secret. Similar to Don Snyder, the father is unable to cope with this new reality and flees into a world of his own imagination; he no longer has the resources at his disposal which would allow him to come to terms in some realistic way with this drastic change in circumstances. The father forfeits all family affiliation and his son denies him all the benefits reserved for family members; he is so bogged down in his own apathy and languid indifference to self; he lacks the capabilities and tools he once had to narrate his own life simply because he has had to flee into a world founded on and constructed out of lies. All his resources of identity have been eroded away and he is no longer able to develop, or capable of developing, or even living in and with his own real identity. His abstract world of lies brings only shame and humiliation.

Identity needs resources to grow, to flourish. Resources can include a real sense of belonging or recognition, coherent narration or structures of care and concern. A *sense of belonging* means being part of an identifiable group which provides group and individual identity. *Recognition* happens when self and things of self are acknowledged and identified as stemming from this self by third party "others". *Coherent narration* is the ability to tell one's – my – own unique and single life story with all it implies with none of the bits being left out or needing to be left out. *Structures of care and concern* result from the interested involvement of B or C in the life of A, with their serious appreciation and acceptance of the things that really, really matter to A and need looking after with genuine TLC. People in poverty have a hard time on all of the above: in being socially excluded by whatever mechanisms dictate, people lose all sense of belonging, they receive no recognition and gaining access to a group which provides identity is well-nigh impossible. Having to suffer the sudden shipwreck of one's life and feeling one's very being has been smashed on the rocks in the process, any notion of possible rescue and/or survival by coherent narration or caring for another person (when caring for self no longer seems to be a viable option) is beyond what is physically and mentally possible. To live in poverty is to be deprived of all those resources "I" need to be "me" with all the bits and pieces which make up "my" identity.

So where does the university come in to all this? If we think back to our first point of reference – education as providing map-reading skills – in other words providing core points of orientation, then identity can be built in the sense and meaning outlined above, a "robust identity" that will weather the storms and vicissitudes of life. Such "inner" resources, which can survive independently of external factors, can be part of the curriculum of an educational establishment. Martha Nussbaum earmarked the three main challenges for schools and universities as follows: firstly any center of learning, particularly a university, must be able to foster an examined life, secondly, it must be able to think in terms of "general" human kind and thirdly it must be able to engage with a narrative of the imagination which thinks and expresses itself in myths, symbols, narration and poetic metaphor (Nussbaum 1997). Such universal guidelines in thinking and narrating will provide a sense of belonging which is not contingent on one specific group e.g., humanity as the overriding family. Such guidelines will afford a safe distance from external realities ("examined life") and cultivate a sense of inner orientation beyond the confines of material values and belongings (narrative imagination). A university as an institution can be an active agent in combating poverty specifically because it is well able to furnish those essential resources required to build identity. In his classic study, Children of the Great Depression, Glen Elder examined the role and effect of higher education on the resilience of those caught up in the Great Depression of the 1930s exactly because colleges and universities are a source of identity resources (Elder 1999).

15.5 Three Stories: Three Options for the Poor

If we characterize poverty as the state of being deprived of identity resources, one option must be to develop a real first-hand awareness of the reality of those living in poverty and not focus on third hand reports. This option includes paying particular attention to being able to recognize the weakest members of a community. Here too, we might understand what options for the poor involve in the light of three stories. (a) One option can be interpreted and applied as "robust concern"; (b) one option must be anchored in keen awareness; (c) and a third option must be to experience transformation. If we look at that first option of robust concern, then any decision to work in poverty alleviation must be a free-will decision, chosen, and not a work-related obligation. Free choice is an essential component in this option because the work demands one to accept and assume responsibility for others and to care about and for those others. Harry Frankfurt characterizes love as "robust concern", as that volitional aspect which has to be willingly and freely chosen (Frankfurt 1998, 159–176, 2004, 10–17). (a) Robust concern, as an option for the poor, means investing in possibilities, endowing others with structures and building blocks which will enable them to take effective action in their own lives. This option for the poor is a decision to assume responsibility for those others in the true sense of the word. (b) Awareness as an option relates to the way we see the world, the way we see those around us. It is a known fact that we can go through our entire lives never coming into contact with – not even being aware of the existence of – certain sectors or groups of the society in which we live. This option goes one step further than conscious decision to act; it demands an aspect of perception we are perhaps unfamiliar with since the poor are "invisible": poverty engenders blindness as we saw with William Vollmann mentioned above. Poverty makes people invisible. This was the experience of an office cleaner, a cashier working at the checkout of a supermarket and someone taking money at a motorway toll booth: they were simply "not there" for the people they "served". This is hardly a new phenomenon, since Colonial Literature is chiefly based on stories and incidents, events in which local inhabitants, the indigenous population, play no part because they are not there in the eyes of those recounting the events. It does of course make a huge difference whether human beings are perceived as human beings or as stage props, part of the scenery backdrop. This "blindness to the human aspect", was a phenomenon Avishai Margalit investigated in depth. He describes this condition of blindness as the result of a "lop-sided" relationship, i.e., a relationship which favors one partner more than the other. An "Option for the Poor" cannot allow this to happen and must prevent such blindness to the human aspect creeping in and taking hold. People who are poor are people – individuals – regardless and must be seen primarily as human beings and only then as people who are poor, not the other way round. This perspective is very much what Martha Nussbaum describes in her objectives of education. (c) An Option for the Poor can be an experience of transformation such as Jean Vanier underwent. He was a member of the teaching staff at a university in Toronto and chose to transform his life via an option for the poor which led him out of the safe vacuum of the university. In 1964 Vanier made a major, life-changing decision to set up a community and live together with a group of people with intellectual disabilities. Originally he had embarked on a "promising" career first in the British Royal Navy and then in the Canadian Navy, but after the War in 1950, he realized this type of life was not for him – there had to be more, and so his spiritual quest (similar to Henri Nouwen's) began – he searched for real meaning in life, a journey on which he would encounter human beings labelled by their disabilities and the transformative power of such encounters. He realized that people commonly known only as "retards" were at the bottom of the social scale of hierarchies. When he made the acquaintance of Raphael and Philippe at the psychiatric hospital south of Paris, it was their "cry for friendship which touched him" and made Jean Vanier see – and feel – how vulnerable each and every human being is. This chance meeting transformed his inner state of mind and he decided to serve those more vulnerable than himself by being there for them and being their friend; this was a new journey, setting out for an unknown land, for all three of them. Jean Vanier's new life was not merely a framework within which he could work and actively "help", it was an – the – opportunity to see not only others but also himself in a new way – a transformation of which most of us only dream. Again, we see here an option for the poor lying not only in being concerned and aware of the plight of others, but as a transformative power to change human lives.

All these three stories share a common denominator, too: they are all about options for the poor which contribute towards identity. This notion of changing – impacting – identity positively works on two levels: it transforms the identity of the person stricken by poverty (Jean Vanier describes how he witnesses the sense of dignity and of self-respect blossoming again and again in "L'Arche") but it also transforms the identity of those who have embraced the task and made it their own mission in life. Any genuine "Option for the Poor" will transform identity on both sides and in many ways: it will transform our consciousness of being, of being a particular individual, a special person who "has a life" in the deepest and widest sense. An option of such force and power will empower encounters with people suffering from poverty but more importantly than their plight is the fact that they are human beings, each as unique as the other, each as special as only they can be: irreplaceable. Such an option helps us perceive that each individual *poor* person has his own life story, her own background with its unmistakable profile and contours. Such an option helps us see, too, that those hit by poverty are not passive items sitting on a shelf but active agents with needs, dreams and desires, who, live life in their own individual way, in a way that only they as themselves can do. However, such options will also impact those who avail themselves of these options and they will experience "self" and "being" anew.

An option for the poor is a decision to create identity, an option which will impact the perception of life as much as it will the way of life and this in turn will affect, transform and construct human lives. University as space and place, molding and shaping identities, is a place for such an option and with this in mind, let us now look at three further points of reference.

15.6 Second Point of Reference: Research, Knowledge, Wisdom

A university knows the value of freedom e.g., in research, and in this it can contribute towards an option for the poor in its own unique way. Subject matter and topic areas can be tackled which go towards shedding light on the plight of the poor and developing social innovative ideas, such as street newspaper projects for example *Street News* in the US and *The Big Issue* in the UK which was founded to help homeless people combat their own poverty and get back into the social order. Moreover, a university can address certain pertinent questions by systematically reflecting and carrying out research in relevant areas to gain insight and hopefully answers to the *whys* and *hows* in alleviating poverty. The actual questions themselves play a decisive role in determining both measures of poverty and methods for alleviating poverty; question areas to be considered include (i) clarifying and simplifying the terminology applied, (ii) investigating the real costs of opportunities, (iii) outlining the methods of evaluation to employ, (iv) minimizing measures-induced damage.

(i) When we discuss possible solutions to poverty, the language we use to put across a point of view plays a huge role. It makes a difference purely what words we choose to employ (or not). Language and its hidden meanings is important; it is relevant too because political decisions about measures to be taken depend on individual nuances of meaning. It makes a difference if we refer to poverty as "being deprived of essential identity-building resources" or if we refer to it as a state of "destitution" or "the lack of any control over assets" (Harriss-White 2002). There is an enormous difference as to whether we talk about: "poverty alleviation", "poverty reduction", "combating poverty", "poverty eradication" or "poverty relief". The notion underlying "alleviation" is a metaphor most commonly associated with reducing or taking away intense pain being suffered, which is symbolic of poverty in that negative aspects of poverty are painful and one aim is to both reduce "painful" effects and provide some kind of *consolatio*, solace, comfort, relief but not so far as to eradicate it. *Poverty reduction* suggests that poverty is a quantifiable entity comparable e.g., to the amount of water in a bucket or the water-holding capacity of the bucket. The "water" level can be measured and by adding or siphoning off amounts, the level can be adjusted to a "satisfactory" level, which, applied to poverty, would mean that a degree and type of intervention can be employed to reduce the "pressure" and achieve an acceptable or "satisfying" level (mode) of living. *Combating poverty* is rooted in battle terminology, the idea of fighting and subduing an enemy, something evil. It has over time become a favorite medical term with which most of us can associate a positive result e.g., combating lung cancer, or child-polio in developing countries or malaria in areas of Africa. Poverty is an evil disease which needs to be destroyed in the same way as a life-threatening disease like an enemy in battle.

Once destroyed, measures must be implemented to ensure the enemy is sufficiently disarmed to no longer pose a threat. *Poverty eradication* has to do with getting to the roots, the rock bottom of an issue and sorting it out from the bottom. Unwanted weeds getting in the way of wanted cultivars need to be pulled up by the roots: pest control must be applied seriously if it is to be effective and eradicate the pest completely; it must be prevented from establishing itself again. Mohammad Yunus accused our pervasive modern-day culture of not having enough imaginative power and of lacking the trust to believe in the possibility of a poverty-free world (Yunus 2007a, 263ff, b). We tend too easily and too "habitually" to perceive poverty as a social fact of life because it has always been like that, backed by a blinkered interpretation of Jesus' statement, "For you always have the poor with you" (Matthew 26:11). The core meaning of poverty *relief* lies in being able to breathe *freely* with no obstacles or hindrance; relief aid is an emergency measure enabling people to *breathe again*, have *a breather*; providing *breathing space* (literally and metaphorically) after a natural disaster or catastrophe such as a Tsunami, earthquake or volcanic eruption does not mean the damage can be undone, the ruins put back to what they were before and it is the same with poverty as a catastrophe, the damage cannot be undone, the clock not turned back, what can be provided is aid and assistance to get things up and running again. These metaphors are apt, they are not there merely for decorative purposes, useful illustrative descriptors, they pinpoint basic universal human understanding and perception – objective assumptions of suffering in adverse circumstances and conditions; at the same time, they encapsulate the steps commonly taken in emergency situations, and outline too what an emergency is – what sets it apart from hardship and being hard-up (which we all experience from time to time); it directs our line of thinking with regard to first-step poverty *relief*, *combating* the ill-effects and spread of poverty – *containing* it and *eradicating* cause and effect via thought-through measures.

(ii) There are costs involved in fighting anything, and poverty is no exception. It would be ludicrous and naive to suggest that it can be achieved at no cost at all to anyone. This point is often overlooked and not systematically considered as part of a long-term plan. Basically, we need to ask: "What happens if we invest in such and such a measure to combat poverty?" The French economist, Bruno Crépon, analyzed so-called "randomized trials" to see how successful school-leavers' advisory services were in integrating youngsters into the job market. What Crépon found was that a particular group of young people stood a higher chance of getting employment, but the opposite could also be the case with some experiencing a higher chance of never getting a foothold on the employment ladder. This is a classic example of opportunity costs such as we find in poverty alleviation and in what is known as "displacement effects", the "pricing out of markets" among those hit by poverty (Crépon et al. 2013a, b). Owen Barder, to mention another example to underpin the point we are addressing, has put forward the idea of "trade-offs" of alleviation measures which can be broadly split into three categories: *deep* versus *broad*, *today* versus *tomorrow*, *symptoms* versus *causes* (Barder 2009). Should an in-depth approach be taken (i.e., less broad), or a broad approach (i.e., less in-depth)? Should poverty prevention or poverty alleviation be invested in? Should the symptoms, or structural root causes be combated? These are core questions which need to be looked at long and hard before embarking on any poverty-reduction research project.

(iii) A third relevant question has to do with the type of research and the method(s) adopted in evaluating measures employed in combating poverty; should "randomized trials" (RT) act as major source? Martin Prowse examined RTs in 2007 because they are based on scientific methodology and human beings as fragile social beings cannot be neatly ticked off in the appropriate boxes in the chain of cause and effect (Prowse 2007). Moreover, there are moral questions which have to be asked, such as: if there is sufficient evidence to warrant intervention envisaged to have X effect, why is such intervention reserved for some and denied to others? Then there is the question of transfer and reception with regards to "data base line", in other words, if intervention Y worked well in a village in Indonesia, say, would it work with the same effectiveness in a city in Burkina Faso?

(iv) A fourth and (perhaps not) final area, regarding research requirements – the whole *whens* and *ifs* of research – concerns the damage, loss or injury caused by intervention measures and how – if – they can be minimized. Why do poverty alleviation measures so often do more harm than good? I can think of four reasons as to why this is so: (a) there is a *second agenda*, since poverty alleviation measures involve a wide range of stake-holders with hidden – secondary – agendas, e.g., they are working with the main aim of getting more contracts, making a name for themselves in increasing their *reputational capital*; (b) *pressure*, as most projects for poverty alleviation are under enormous pressure either due to deadlines and time, fulfilling quotas, monetary demands, too-high expectations: a lot of people do not work well or even vaguely efficiently under such pressure. An unrealistic workload can give rise to feelings of anxiety and humiliation, one hurdle in the "clearing" process or selection procedure is picking a chosen few while the rest are "rejected" (and not surprisingly feel the same). Such procedures invariably mean that some suitable candidates are never even considered for selection even though they may fulfil criteria; in other words, measures and projects tend to reach those who do not necessarily need it the most (and those who do, go empty handed). This is an odd way of doing things you may say, but the logic is that if measures are successful then the organization that implemented the measures will be successful, too, and to clinch success it makes sense to select projects which are more likely to work – those *not* with the greatest need – rather than those deemed tricky because the chances of success are greater where the need is lower and thus less demanding; (c) "*social and epistemic discontinuity of care*", meaning a constant shift and change in those in charge and those involved on the ground in project measures, in other words a lack of continuity in measures and those who put them into practice. Projects have to be performed within a limited time frame and are additionally under constraints of innovation, meaning that as soon as a measure is up and running it is left to its own devices in favor of new measures being initiated which have nothing whatever to do with the former project. Then there is the age-old corruption factor which has to be avoided and the necessary preventive measures taken: often corruption is a knock-on effect of change in organizational head: in other words, organization A introduces measures X; 3 years later organization B implements measures Y with the same client. The result is an overall loss of knowledge and expertise, and of course, a loss of trust on the part of the receivers because they constantly have to adjust to new supervisory powers with a different style and approach and those measures which had been introduced 3 years previously and are now beginning to bear fruit are then simply ditched. (d) "*meticulously planned frustration*": a word of warning – promises with regard to measures should be made only after keen consideration; if, for example, attempts are made to get youngsters on the employment ladder how are promising measures interpreted by youngsters themselves? Realistically speaking, any promise in this regard is: we can raise your chances of getting a job, but it won't be anything remarkable, it will be badly paid, a low-income job with hard, grinding work, day in day out, with little likelihood of promotion. When such things are fact, the real truth, the type of measures taken need to be considered – particularly what should they include or not include so as not to promise people jobs in somewhere with a dead-end perspective which is enough to demoralize anyone and everyone? It is here that a university could make realistic, objective evaluations of possible measures, to keep damage to a minimum and make future broken promises no longer possible (or worthwhile).

A university has the skills and an obligation to address these issues. The fate of many lies in their hands; universities have the capacity and research facilities to do something about it. At the same time they are – should be – in a position to convey a real understanding and appreciation of wisdom, the knowledge that the essential things in life cannot always be solved or constructed in a way we would like, but we can learn to live with them.

15.7 Third Reference Point: A Question of Attitude

Apart from being a center of research and furthering the acquisition of knowledge, universities must be able to develop strategies – useable strategies – which reflect and underpin a certain attitude to any option for the poor. This does of course include research and providing framework conditions for research projects to be carried out properly and responsibly which in itself relies on at least three factors: a university is a place of *Lehrfreiheit* (academic freedom) which is a perfect place and opportunity for life as it really is for the poor to be confronted within the structure of the syllabus. Secondly, a university relies as an institution on its unique structure and relationship between teacher and learner – there cannot be the one without the other – this special relationship is a special community which needs its own networks to survive *and* prosper. Networks can be expanded to reach a wider "audience" or "target group", an option for the poor might include facilitating access to university resources for the socially deprived (both teachers and learners) or cross-over projects outside of the usual domain of the university precinct to encompass the socially disadvantaged as was mentioned above in Muhammad Yunus' project with the poor. Thirdly, the university has political clout and can make its political power felt as, for example, Ignacio Ellacuría outlined in his idea of universities being involved more centrally as key figures in social and political life. Ellacuría was President of the University of Central America and very much aware of the special role and responsibility the university was obliged to shoulder (Burke 2000). In his well-known opening address to the Santa Clara University in June 1982, he emphasized the importance of the university being involved in real life social issues and recognizing that social reality was an unjust reality – the university was under an obligation to take a clear stand (Ellacuría 1991). It is this overriding attitude and academic approach which a university can integrate into its teaching program; this is a political attitude and social frame of mind which can transform the lives of both those studying about and those living in poverty.

This attitude and approach could be summed up as social positioning. It goes without saying that any positioning can only work effectively if the university as an institution has not had its own values and freedoms eroded away by commercial dependency and excessive competition which would mean it would first have to free itself from its own epistemic trap. At the beginning of our enquiry we talked about the trap and temptations of a university being a self-referential, parallel universe world, a confined inward-looking comfort zone and this now needs to be supplemented by the third trap of one-way vision – the danger of examining the phenomenon of poverty through the microscope of research and dissecting it in the science lab for the sole purpose of one's own academic career and future life.

We are concerned with a moral trap and an epistemic trap. We might for example ask on what do experts base their understanding and knowledge of poverty in their management and administration of poverty issues and how does politics impact poverty in its policy-making decisions? The privileged perspective of poverty within the comfort zone of a university is the third-person perspective, in other words it is a factual rationalized perspective which analyses poverty within the clinical conditions of the seminar room. This clinical perspective objectifies the circumstances of poverty since it takes an *outside(r's)* view with a researcher's eye, and herein lies the danger of a hegemonic perspective. Michal Krumer-Nevo emphasizes the importance of "counter narratives", as we know from the works of Spivak (Krumer-Nevo 2010). Robert Chambers repeatedly mentioned the selective distortion which often goes hand in hand with this perspective (Chambers 2013). By exploiting case studies as they are so often referred to for research purposes, with their typical third-party point of view, "the" poor suddenly become epistemic objects which can be twisted to neatly fit into the necessary pigeon hole of theory.

Any honest, well-meaning option for the poor will and can only work if the university bypasses the soft trap of exploitation and manages to adopt a real second person perspective, in other words a perspective from the person *in* the situation and not merely the view of the observer and a second person perspective is imperative since no dialogue can take place without it; effective dialogue needs both the me *and* the you point of view. The first person perspective is, in the words of Thomas Nagel, the perspective of the "victim", or in epistemic terms, the irreducible perspective (Nagel 1986). Indigenous and local knowledge is now universally acknowledged as playing a key role in attaining an objective perspective and plays a key factor in poverty discourse. Perspectives of this kind are revealed in utterances such as: "I know poverty is …". In a major study undertaken by the World Bank on the first-person experience of poverty, this was a personal assessment based on personal experience from someone living in poverty in Lithuania: "Poverty is humiliation, the sense of being dependent on them, and of being forced to accept rudeness, insults, and indifference when we seek help" (Narayan et al. 2000, 26). This first-hand perspective of experiencing and being exposed to certain conditions on a day-to-day basis expresses an important perspective, namely, the sense of ownership. It is only this first-person perspective with that experienced sense of ownership which can endow any serious dialogue with authenticity – something a third person utterance can neither claim nor convey. It is blindingly obvious that the university as an establishment enjoys the scope and space to combine both perspectives. Both sides of the "issue" are vital, as we have already said, because any point of view can only find its own weight when set against a counter balance. In the South African Truth and Reconciliation Committee, a "social truth" was sought by means of men and women putting across and expressing what they as individuals had gone through; they did this in dialogue with each other (TRC 1998, 39–42). Genuine dialogue engenders corrective procedures and enables "my" counterpart to make the next move, have his or her say, too. This dialogue setting is one we are well acquainted with from Gadamer's and Levinas' studies and writings; it is a perspective which requires participation and it is this participatory methodology which has advanced poverty research (cf. Brock 1999). The second-person perspective is also ethically relevant because it allows claims and counter claims to be raised and justified. Stephen Darwall has researched the ethical role and meaning of second-person accounts in depth (Darwall 2006). If we were to imagine discussing poverty with those who are on the front line and experience poverty day in, day out, how would that change our perspective and attitude? In other words, what would be the difference between what we say when we look these people in the face, and what we say when they are not present? Gerald Cohen saw questions linked with the source of normative needs and rights as the "interpersonal test", a litmus test for justifying ways and means of communication and approach: "The test asks whether the argument could serve as a justification of a mooted policy when uttered by any member of society to any other member" (Cohen 2008, 42). Cohen wants to dismantle the distortion which arises between subject, object and content – "who says what to whom"? If we put it another way, how would statements made by third persons in an isolated context differ from those made within a one to one dialogue context?

Which would be the same and which would be left out (or added)? This is basically asking, do we say the same things about the poor to their face as we do when we are talking *about* them? We need to look at the style and manner in which we "research"; it makes a huge difference if research is dialogue-based, meaning working with those concerned as source and resource rather than reading about them as statistical items for the sole purposes of research.

If the university as a universal institution can advance a multi-perspective approach, it will be able to genuinely and authentically pursue an option for the poor in the three core subject areas of research, community building and political education. Most of all, a clear line in attitude and approach depends on a culture of dialogue for its authenticity: these are the preconditions for the successful amalgamation of perspectives.

15.8 Concluding Comments

In his book, *Injustice*: *Why Social Inequality Still Persists*, Daniel Dorling tackles the question of why there is such dogged injustice in society (Dorling 2011). Social inequality is not caused by having too few resources for everyone, instead it is driven by beliefs that perpetuate the inequality. The evidence shows that these beliefs are unfounded but they provide (false) justification for those who benefit most from inequality. The natural result of such thinking is thus: "Elitism is efficient; exclusion is necessary; prejudice is natural; greed is good and despair is inevitable!" There is a marked numbness of imagination and a pronounced lack of inner mobility. A university as institution is in a position to expand the human imagination and ensure that the intellectual cogs of mobility do not freeze up. A university should, as John Henry Newman envisaged, be and remain articulate regardless of circumstances, conditions and context; in doing so it will pass the Gerald Cohen "interpersonal test" when faced with victims of poverty. Universities are in the enviable privileged position of being able to promote communication competences when faced with poverty; they can develop universal models for community-based learning with all the challenges this would entail (cf. Hammersley 2013). The high road to the wise tackling of poverty is facing up to one's own vulnerabilities and sense of helplessness. Only a culture of encounter and *congress* in a new university framework, rejecting elitist thinking and vulnerability induced by over-competitiveness, would be able to rise to this challenge. A daring prospect but not impossible.

References

Barder, Owen. 2009. *What is poverty reduction?* Working paper 170. Washington, DC: Center for Global Development.

Belk, Russell W. 1988. Possessions and the extended self. *Journal of Consumer Research* 15: 139–168.

Bieri, Peter. 2011. *Wie wollen wir leben?* Salzburg: Residenz.

Bonhoeffer, Dietrich. 2011. *Widerstand und Ergebung. Briefe und Aufzeichnungen aus der Haft.* Vollständige Ausgabe, versehen mit Einleitung, Anmerkungen und Kommentaren. Ed. Chr. Gremmels, E. Bethge, R. Bethge in collaboration with I. Tödt. Bonhoeffer Werke. Volume 8. Gütersloh: Bertelsmann.

Brock, Karen. 1999. It's not only wealth that matters – it's peace of mind too: A review of participatory work on poverty and illbeing. IDS study report, Brighton.

Burke, Kevin F. 2000. *The ground beneath the cross. The theology of Ignacio Ellacuría.* Washington, DC: Georgetown University Press.

Chambers, Robert. 2013. *Rural development. Putting the last first.* Abingdon: Routledge.

Coetzee, John M. 1997. *Boyhood.* London: Penguin.

Cohen, Gerald A. 2008. *Rescuing justice and equality.* Cambridge, MA: Harvard University Press.

Crépon, Bruno, et al. 2013a. Do labor market policies have displacement effects? *Quarterly Journal of Economics* 128: 2.

Crépon, Bruno, et al. 2013b. *Job placement and displacement.* J-PAL Policy Briefcase. Cambridge, MA: Abdul Latif Jameel Poverty Action Lab.

Darwall, Stephen. 2006. *The second-person standpoint.* Cambridge, MA: Harvard University Press.

Dorling, Danny. 2011. *Injustice. Why social inequality persists.* Bristol: Policy Press.

Ehrenberg, Alan. 2009. *The weariness of self.* Quebec: McGill Queen's University Press.

Elder, Glen. 1999. *Children of the great depression. Social change in life experience. Reprint.* Boulder: Westview.

Ellacuría, Ignacio. 1991. Is a different kind of university possible? In *Towards a society that serves its people*, ed. Hassett John and Lacey Hugh. Washington, DC: Georgetown University Press.

Frankfurt, Harry G. 1998. *The importance of what we care about.* Cambridge: Cambridge University Press.

Frankfurt, Harry G. 2004. *The reasons of love.* Princeton: Princeton University Press.

Gillies, Midge. 2012. *The Barbed-Wire University. The real lives of allied prisoners of war in the Second World War.* London: Aurum.

Gough, Leo. 2011. *C. Northcote Parkinson's Parkinson's Law. A modern interpretation of a management classic.* Oxford: Infinite Ideas.

Hammersley, Laura. 2013. Community-based service-learning: Partnerships of reciprocal exchange? *Asia-Pacific Journal of Cooperative Education* 14(3): 171–184.

Harden, Blaine. 2013. *Escape from camp*, 14th ed. London: Penguin.

Harriss-White, Barbara. 2002. *A note on destitution*, Queen Elizabeth House working paper 86. Oxford: University of Oxford.

Hartmann, Katharina. 2012. *Wir müssen leider draußen bleiben. Die neue Armut in der Konsumgesellschaft.* Munich: Blessing.

Krumer-Nevo, Michal. 2010. Critical poverty knowledge: Contesting othering and social distancing. *Current Sociology* 58(5): 693–714.

Mahler, Thomas. 2011. *In der Schlange.Mein Jahr auf Hartz IV.* Munich: Goldmann.

Miller, Daniel. 2008. *The comfort of things.* Cambridge: Polity Press.

Nagel, Thomas. 1986. *The view from nowhere.* Oxford: Oxford University Press.

Narayan, Deepa, et al. 2000. *Voices of the poor. Can anyone hear us?* Oxford: Oxford University Press.

Newman, John H. 1887. *The idea of a university.* London: Longmans, Green and Co.

Nussbaum, Martha. 1997. *Cultivating humanity.* Cambridge, MA: Harvard University Press.

Prowse, Martin. 2007. *Aid effectiveness: The role of qualitative research in impact evaluation. Background note.* London: Overseas Development Institute.

Schicho, Walter. 2007. What did Mr. Wolfensohn mean (intend), when he spoke of (about) poverty? In *Perspectives in poverty alleviation*, ed. Thomas Böhler and Clemens Sedmak, 265–280. Münster: LIT.

Sen, Amartya. 1999. *Development as freedom.* New York: Basic Books.

Snyder, Don J. 1997. *The cliff walk.* New York: Little, Brown and Company.

Truth and Reconciliation Commission, Report, Vol 1. Johannesburg 1998.
Vollmann, William T. 2007. *Poor people*. San Francisco: Harper.
Wallace, David F. 2009. *This is water*. New York: Little, Brown and Company.
Yunus, Muhammad. 2007a. *Banker to the poor*. Philadelphia: Perseus.
Yunus, Muhammad. 2007b. *Creating a world without poverty*. Philadelphia: Perseus.

MIX
Papier aus verantwortungsvollen Quellen
Paper from responsible sources
FSC® C105338

If you have any concerns about our products,
you can contact us on
ProductSafety@springernature.com

In case Publisher is established outside the EU,
the EU authorized representative is:
Springer Nature Customer Service Center GmbH
Europaplatz 3, 69115 Heidelberg, Germany

Printed by Libri Plureos GmbH
in Hamburg, Germany